Being Amoral

Philosophical Psychopathology

Jennifer Radden and Jeff Poland, editors

Being Amoral: Psychopathy and Moral Incapacity, Thomas Schramme, editor (2014)

A Metaphysics of Psychopathology, Peter Zachar (2014)

Classifying Psychopathology: Mental Kinds and Natural Kinds, Harold Kincaid and Jacqueline Sullivan, editors (2014)

The Ethical Treatment of Depression: Autonomy through Psychotherapy, Paul Biegler (2011)

Addiction and Responsibility, Jeffrey S. Poland and George Graham, editors (2010)

Psychiatry in the Scientific Image, Dominic Murphy (2005)

Brain Fiction: Self-Deception and the Riddle of Confabulation, William Hirstein (2004)

Imagination and Its Pathologies, James Phillips and James Morley, editors (2003)

Imagination and the Meaningful Brain, Arnold H. Modell (2003)

When Self-Consciousness Breaks: Alien Voices and Inserted Thoughts, G. Lynn Stephens and George Graham (2000)

The Myth of Pain, Valerie Gray Hardcastle (1999)

Divided Minds and Successive Selves: Ethical Issues in Disorders of Identity and Personality, Jennifer Radden (1996)

Being Amoral

Psychopathy and Moral Incapacity

Thomas Schramme, editor

The MIT Press
Cambridge, Massachusetts
London, England

MIT Press books may be purchased at special quantity discounts for business or sales promotional use. For information, please email special_sales@mitpress.mit.

This book was set in Stone Sans and Stone Serif by the MIT Press. Printed and bound in the United States of America.

Being amoral : psychopathy and moral incapacity / edited by Thomas Schramme.
    pages cm. — (Philosophical psychopathology)
Includes bibliographical references and index.
ISBN 978-0-262-02791-5 (hardcover : alk. paper) 1. Psychopaths—Ethics. 2. Antisocial personality disorders—Moral and ethical aspects. I. Schramme, Thomas, editor of compilation.
RC555.B36 2014
174.2′9689—dc23
2014003876

10 9 8 7 6 5 4 3 2 1

Contents

Acknowledgments

I have accumulated many debts in preparing this volume. Some of the papers were presented at a conference in 2010 in Swansea, UK, which was funded by a generous grant of the Wellcome Trust. I would like to thank the participants at this event for their valuable input and suggestions, and my former colleagues at Swansea University, who helped me enormously. The series editors, Jennifer Radden and Jeffrey Poland, as well as Philip Laughlin of the MIT Press, showed just the right amount of lenience and encouragement. Finally, I am most grateful to the authors of this book. When the project started I didn't foresee all the circumstances that delayed publication. Thank you for your patience and support!

1 Introduction

Thomas Schramme

To research and write about psychopathy from an interdisciplinary perspective involves trying to pin down quickly moving targets. Almost nothing in relation to this phenomenon can be taken for granted. Psychopathy has been described in various ways in the psychiatric, legal, and philosophical literature; indeed, the terminological landscape has changed in the last few decades. It is also yet to be determined exactly how *psychopathy* relates to similar, but different, constructs, such as *sociopathy* or *antisocial personality disorder*.[1] Hence, it is certainly fair to say that psychopathy is a contested concept, and that it is hard to identify clear-cut cases of psychopathy in practice.

In philosophy, psychopathy has been used as a test case for several theoretical assumptions, most notably in metaethics (Prinz 2006, 32, 38; Haidt 2001, 824; cf. Greene 2005, 344). Here, we also experience shifting conceptual foundations. For instance, a lot of philosophers were impressed by the psychiatric description of psychopathy as an affective deficit, often seen in relation to a lack of empathy. Since psychopathy is also fairly often interpreted as a condition that goes along with a lack of morality, it seems that here we have a real-life test case of a traditional metaethical dispute—namely, whether human morality is due to reason or to affect. This description of the philosophical dispute itself is hardly satisfactory since it would need to be clarified as to exactly what "morality" means. But be that as it may, it is also obvious from the empirical literature on psychopathy that the criterion of lack of empathy hardly provides the unambiguous test case that philosophers like to find. "Empathy" is far too multifaceted a concept in order to serve as a foundation for settling philosophical disputes. As will become clear in this introduction, the very fact that the discussion on psychopathy calls for both empirical input as well as conceptual clarification makes it a suitable target for multi- and interdisciplinary research. This anthology is an attempt to add a systematic and focused contribution to this burgeoning literature. It pursues the question of what psychopaths lack, of what their incapacities are. This could then possibly illuminate which capacities are needed to be a moral person or for moral agency.

However, to scrutinize the idea of moral agency through this negative approach requires an elucidation of the concept of psychopathy as well, and there are at least two serious obstacles to this endeavor I would like to mention: First, "psychopathy," or "antisocial personality disorder" for that matter, not only are used to describe psychiatric conditions, but carry heavy normative connotations (Reimer 2008). They are seen in close relation to violent, offensive, and criminal behavior and indeed have been based on very unusual—some would say, unscientific—criteria, such as "superficial charm," "impulsiveness," or "callous unconcern for the feelings of others." It is no wonder psychopaths are usually seen as people who are in opposition to the interests of society. Hence the way the construct is defined is in fact at least partly determined by societal or legal interests and poses not merely a scientific category. Whether this is an acceptable practice is not my main concern here, but we need to be wary of such influences when discussing psychopathy.

Second, most lay people believe they know what psychopathy is; indeed, many would be able to name at least one or two psychopaths. Hannibal Lecter, Myra Hindley, Jeffrey Dahmer, or Norman Bates immediately come to mind. The fact that we all are allegedly experts when it comes to psychopathy makes it harder to discuss the construct in an unbiased way. The very concept has become a folk concept, occasionally referred to in a colloquial way to describe rather familiar people we deem strange, somewhat antisocial, or regard as violent characters (Kantor 2006; Stout 2005). Since folk differ in how they use the word, it will be very hard to define it in a way that will be universally authoritative.

It should also be added that our interpretations of the condition are heavily influenced by cultural products, most importantly novels and films, as can be seen from the list of names provided earlier, where two are drawn from fiction (Hamilton 2008). Psychopaths, for many, are the personification of evil (Haybron 1999, 2002; Russell 2010; cf. Adshead 2006)—yet another shaky notion that carries unscientific connotations, especially religious ones (Levine 2006). This strong condemnation, which includes a possible excommunication of humans from mankind, might be a way to cope with what often makes psychopathic forms of violence and cruelty unintelligible and "outlandish" (Russell 2012)—namely, the fact that psychopaths are apparently not at all troubled by any moral concerns but still perform their actions in a nonimpulsive, planned, and seemingly purposeful way.

Quite possibly the very unintelligibility of extreme forms of psychopathic behavior might be responsible for the conflicting intuitions regarding the culpability of psychopaths (Feinberg 2003). On the one hand they seem clearly insane; on the other hand such a verdict would undermine seeing them as "evil."

All these problems might lead one to simply give up the concept of psychopathy when discussing it from a scientific point of view. Indeed, this drastic step might even help in reducing yet another severe common misconception, namely, the mistaken identification of psychopathology and psychopathy. It seems that people occasionally confuse any person who suffers from a psychopathology with psychopaths and hence deem, say, persons with schizophrenia more dangerous or violent than healthy people. However, it is doubtful whether such an elimination of the word "psychopathy" would change much in relation to the ideas linked with it. It might seem that we need some category to refer to a condition that makes people unable to be moral, or that makes them amoral. At least this is what is supposed to be established in this introduction and in the anthology as a whole. Whether or not we call these cases instances of "psychopathy," there are indeed certain psychiatric phenomena that seem to prevent people from taking the moral point of view.

The latter formulation is a typical philosophical expression that summarizes in one phrase a very complicated fact about ourselves, namely, that we are normally able to see the world from a particular perspective, the perspective of morality, which carries certain weight in making decisions—something that is often referred to as the normativity of morality. It seems obvious that philosophers will be better equipped to exactly determine what they mean when they talk about the moral point of view if they link this debate in moral philosophy to the psychiatric notion of psychopathy, since here we have some, if contested, ground for explaining what human beings need in order to be able to feel the normative pull of morality. Conversely, psychiatrists and those researchers who investigate the phenomenon of psychopathy scientifically can benefit from the conceptual work being done in philosophy. As has been pointed out, many of the diagnostic criteria are only inadequately defined and indeed contested, so no tangible progress is to be expected in empirical research before these conceptual issues are addressed. Altogether, this seems to strengthen the case for interdisciplinarity regarding this particular topic. It might even, in the end, help us to actually pin down the quickly moving targets mentioned earlier.

Having set the stage for the importance of thinking about psychopathy in a more concerted fashion, we will move on to introduce the main points of discussion and findings in relation to the concept of psychopathy within several disciplinary perspectives. First, the various conceptual problems we encounter when discussing psychopathy as a psychiatric notion will be investigated in a little more detail. In this part some of the scientific findings will also be addressed. Then we will move on to the philosophical debate, which revolves around the notions of amorality and moral agency. Finally, the individual chapters of this anthology will be briefly introduced.

1.1 Conceptual Problems

"Psychopathy" is not part of the official psychiatric nomenclature. The diagnostic term cannot be found in either the *Diagnostic and Statistical Manual of Mental Disorders* (DSM) or the *International Classification of Diseases* (ICD). These nosological systems contain entries for "antisocial personality disorder" (301.7, DSM-5) or "dissocial personality disorder" (F60.2, ICD-10), respectively. The latter two disorders are fairly similar to each other in terms of the diagnostic criteria but should not be identified with psychopathy although, to be sure, the ICD-10 contains "psychopathic disorder" as a subtype, and there were some signs DSM–5 (released in 2013) would include an entry on antisocial/psychopathic personality disorder (Skodol 2012, 329), yet this did not materialize.[2] Occasionally, the term "sociopathy" is also in use in the scientific literature (Mealey 1995; Jacobs 2012) though this term apparently has fallen out of favor, at least in psychiatry. It seems, though, that the latter term would have the benefit of emphasizing the social aspects of the putative disorder. Finally, there is the construct of "dangerous and severe personality disorder," of which more will be said later, especially in Susie Scott's contribution to this anthology.

The conception of psychopathy in its most recent and common version is mainly due to the work of the criminal psychologist Robert D. Hare, who based his Psychopathy Checklist—released in a revised edition in 1991—on the research of Hervey M. Cleckley, who published the first edition of his influential book *The Mask of Sanity* in 1941 (Cleckley 1982).[3] Another influence on Hare's conceptualization was Joan and William McCords's (1964) book *The Psychopath: An Essay on the Criminal Mind.* Hare's own (revised) Psychopathy Checklist (PCL–R) (Hare 2003) has come into increasingly frequent use, especially in the United States, mostly in forensic and research settings. Hare's conceptualization of psychopathy is narrower than the related entities in DSM and ICD, that is, it has a smaller extension. Somewhat oversimplifying, one could say that "psychopathy" covers the most severe cases of the mentioned personality disorders (Widiger 2006, 157; Hare 1998, 193).[4]

According to the PCL–R, psychopathy is identified operationally by using a test, the mentioned checklist, which determines a particular score for each person undergoing a semi-structured interview, that is, an examination allowing some degree of flexibility for the interviewer, in combination with an anamnestic review that focuses on the case history—for instance, regarding past behavior. Therefore, in a strict sense, the test does not define what psychopathy is, but it offers a means to determine who can be deemed a psychopath; it is a diagnostic tool (Skeem et al. 2011, 95). There are two "factors" and some "other items" to be checked, altogether 20 items, where the first factor focuses on personality traits, such as "glibness/superficial charm," "grandiose sense of self-worth," "lack of remorse or guilt," or "shallow affect," the second factor concerns the "socially deviant lifestyle," including "parasitic lifestyle" and "irresponsibility," and the other items contain "traits not correlated with either factor," for instance "promiscuous sexual behavior," or "criminal versatility." Each person undergoing the test gets scores for the individual items, 0 if it is absent, 1 if it is possibly or partially present, and 2 if it is definitely present. Everyone who scores more than 30 points is supposed to be a psychopath although there is some scope for discussing cultural variety in the determination of scores and cutoff points (Cooke et al. 2005).

From a philosophical perspective, there are obviously serious issues with this interpretation of psychopathy, most notably the vague description of the items that, again, carry heavy normative connotations. It would probably take philosophers a lifetime to work out the notion of "grandiose sense of self-worth" alone. However, there are also methodological issues that need mentioning. First, one of the criteria of psychopathy is a manipulative and conning personality. If true, this might prove a considerable problem for the authenticity and truthfulness of the interviewee. Whether this problem can be sorted out by adequate training and experience on the side of the interviewer remains to be proven. One might also argue, for instance, that the interviews are not intended to establish facts about a person, but about his or her personality, which will be released by any statement of self-presentation, be it veridical or not (Blackburn 2009, 125; Lilienfeld and Fowler, 111f.).

Second, the methodology of the PCL seems unusual since the individual scores are mainly determined by practitioners. Although the latter need to be persons trained for the specific purpose, there seems nevertheless to be some scope for variation in scores, based on different interpretations of the interview results by the respective practitioners. In short, psychopathy, in terms of this operational understanding, appears to be at least partly "in the eye of the beholder." Note that this is different from many contested normal and abnormal values in somatic medicine, such as pathologically high blood pressure. Here the thresholds, that is, where pathology begins, might themselves be contested, but the individual results are usually objective and reliable. When using the PCL–R, however, the individual scores are based on subjective interpretations of subjective reports.

To be sure, this is not unusual in psychiatry more generally, as there are several diagnoses that are based on interpretable data. However, in this case the context is arguably more critical, as a particularly vulnerable group is being considered. Persons undergoing the test usually have committed serious crimes and are often imprisoned. They are not only under a threat to be deemed dangerous to society and potentially "hopeless cases,"[5] which alone carries a stigma—including a common cultural interpretation as being almost nonhuman—but might also find themselves in a situation where significant individual, economic, political, and legal interests are attached to the result of the test. To simplify this complicated situation by way of example, an offender might have an interest in being deemed a psychopath in order to avoid the death penalty or other heavy sentences whereas society might have conflicting interests because of a desire to severely punish the person.[6] There are therefore numerous serious repercussions of handing out PCL–R scores, and these seem to differ in impact from other psychiatric diagnoses although the latter are quite significant for the lives of people, too. This should make us wary of the many methodological and conceptual pitfalls surrounding the construct of psychopathy.

There are other models of psychopathy than Hare's approach (Blackburn 2006; Patrick 2010) although his is probably the most influential. For instance, there has been a considerable debate regarding the utility of dimensional versus categorical approaches in psychiatric diagnoses (Millon 2010, 162ff.; Skodol 2010). It seems sensible to assume that every person can be seen as being on a continuum with respect to personality traits. Someone might, for instance, be extremely modest but also quite self-confident. The same applies to diagnostic criteria of psychopathy. As said before, it might seem rather arbitrary to set the cutoff score at 30, and it could well be that a person scores unusually high on one factor but low on the other and hence does not meet the threshold of psychopathy. A couple of dimensional approaches have accordingly been introduced, most notably a conceptualization based on the so-called five-factor model, which defines five broad domains of personality (Widiger and Lynam 1998; Lynam and Widiger 2007), and the Psychopathic Personality Inventory, which draws from self-reports in nonclinical samples, resulting in 154 items in the revised version (Lilienfeld and Fowler 2006), organized into eight subscales, including, for instance "Machiavellian Egocentricity" and "Coldhearted-ness" (cf. Skeem et al. 2011, 102f.).[7]

Several models also allow categorization of different subtypes, or variants, of psychopathy, which might be more adequate to the variability of the phenomena (Poythress and Skeem 2006; Blackburn 2009; Millon and Davis 1998). Most importantly, a distinction is often drawn, though not always in the same way, between primary and secondary psychopathy. Sometimes this distinction had been introduced with respect to etiology, that is, based on the assumption that some people have a congenital, genetic defect and others an acquired deficit, usually through "bad parenting." However, this seems to be based on an outdated model of the nature–nurture relationship. More recently, the distinction is marked by emotional differences (Skeem et al. 2011, 115). Primary psychopaths are, for instance, supposed to be less anxious in commonly stressful situations than secondary psychopaths (Blackburn 2009, 117ff.). However, it is still contested, perhaps not surprisingly, whether secondary psychopaths are to be considered genuinely psychopathic at all (Skeem et al. 2011, 119)—a problem that obviously involves, yet again, conceptual considerations.

There might also be a need for alternatives to, or amendments of, the PCL–R because it might seem useful to be able to include nonviolent and noncriminal persons in a definition of psychopathy. If psychopaths lack certain capacities, such as empathy, volitional control, or rational advance planning, it seems that these do not necessarily lead to deviant behavior. After all, psychopathy—and mental disorders more generally—supposedly is a disorder of the mind, not of behavior itself, though deviant behavior might of course be deemed a symptom of a mental disorder.[8] To put it differently and more colloquially, we would like to be able to distinguish between "mad" and "bad," but if we identify the two from the outset, it seems difficult not to see psychopathy as a moralized notion. In contrast, Cleckley included noncriminal psychopaths in his study, and it is now common in lay terms to see manipulative and uncaring, though socially inconspicuous, persons as psychopaths, sometimes called "successful psychopaths" (Hall and Benning 2006; Gao and Raine 2010), "corporate psychopaths" (Babiak et al. 2010), or indeed "white collar psychopaths" (Hare 1993, 102ff.). The PCL–R, however, arguably identifies mainly criminals as psychopaths (Skeem and Cooke 2010; cf. Hare and Neumann 2010b), and the antisocial-behavior-disorder category contains references to physical fights and assaults as evidence of aggressiveness, which raises troubling issues of circularity regarding deviant behavior as a component of psychopathy (Howells 2009, 199). This might also lead to problematic methodological biases in research since almost all research subjects are recruited in forensic clinics and prisons.

Considering all these different ways to conceptualize psychopathy, it might not come as a surprise that the scientific community is divided about its definition. Indeed, a recent survey of the psychopathy literature concludes that "there is a lack of consensus about what psychopathy really is" (Skeem et al. 2011, 136). Another study finishes off by stating that "despite the large volume of accumulated research, theoretical understanding of psychopaths continues to be limited, and the answer to the question 'What is psychopathy?' remains elusive" (Blackburn 2009, 128). More constructively, a recent textbook entry attempted to distill three main features of psychopathy from the diverging conceptualizations (Patrick 2010): disinhibition, boldness, and meanness, which together, but not individually, are supposed to adequately explain the phenomenon of psychopathy.

From a philosophical point of view, the diversity and elusiveness of the psychopathy construct might be an expectable result because—as has been pointed out—the conceptual landscape to define the phenomenon is heavily laden with contested and vague notions. Still, the lack of consensus might be mainly a problem of a lack of scientific validity and rigor in the research being performed so far. Lots of attempts have been undertaken more recently to base the definition and diagnosis of psychopathy on a more stringent and scientifically valid foundation (Patrick and Bernat 2010). As with other areas of psychiatric studies, the "gold standard" is now defined by neuroscientific approaches, as this area of research has a more objective ring to most experts and laypeople alike than the study of less tangible mental or personality traits. Today, to be scientific therefore usually implies a biological approach, especially in psychiatry, and accordingly much of the recent research findings regarding psychopathy can be found in neuroscience (Blair et al. 2005; Craig et al. 2009; de Oliveira-Souza et al. 2008; Weber et al. 2008; Müller 2010; Kiehl 2008; Decety et al. 2013; cf. Douard and Schultz 2013, 113ff.). This raises interesting general issues about the significance of and need for biological approaches to the conceptualization of mental disorder (Garnar and Hardcastle 2007). It appears also that there are many misconceptions regarding the theoretical conclusiveness and practical consequences of such neuroscientific findings. Indeed, it seems unlikely that even validated correlations between mental and brain phenomena will solve the theoretical riddles of psychopathy that we have identified so far. What is more, it is worrying to find a rather naive attitude toward these findings even in nonscientific experts—for instance, regarding the consequences of alleged brain lesions for applying criminal responsibility (Aspinwall et al. 2012).[9] This is obviously not to say that neuroscientific research is useless, but it should be done in collaboration with disciplines that work closer to the psychological phenomena. It requires an exchange between hypothesized conceptualizations, that is, theoretical approaches, and empirical validation, where the latter does not only need to proceed on the level of neurobiology.

Before moving on to the philosophical discussions surrounding psychopathy, it might be worth considering yet another contested issue in referring to psychopaths, or people with antisocial personality disorder for that matter. This final problem actually links up with similar debates in philosophy, so it might serve as a bridge to the next part of the introduction. In order to talk of psychopaths or psychopathic personalities, we need to assume that there are such things as personalities, characters, or at least somewhat stable mental traits of persons. The adequacy of referring to personalities, however, is a contested matter, and its justification has, again, complex conceptual foundations that cannot be settled scientifically. Neither can they be completely clarified here, but they should at least be mentioned.

Note that this is not meant as an issue regarding the ontology of minds or selves, which also needs some acknowledgment. Psychologists and psychiatrists, or indeed anyone who refers to "personality" or a "self," need not assume that these exist as material entities, like a "ghost in the machine," to use Gilbert Ryle's memorable phrase (Ryle 1949, chapter 1). It has become custom, at least in philosophy, to talk about the mental realm from the perspective of nonreductive materialism, that is, an approach that allows the mind not to be seen as an entity separated from its material basis but, at the same time, to be seen as not fully explainable on this physiological, that is, brain-related, level. The issue at hand is not the ontology of personality, however, but whether there are grounds for assuming any stable mental traits of people at all (Blackburn 1988, 506). Many researchers and laypeople alike would probably claim that although personalities do not exist in the same way as hearts or other organs, we can still use this construct in order to refer to features of persons. For instance, in a recent psychiatric handbook entry "personality" is defined as "an individual's characteristic patterns of thinking, feeling, and acting" (Lynam and Derefinko 2006, 133). In line with this definition we call people, say, friendly, honest, or reliable. We do this, apparently, by way of induction from experiences with the behavior of these people, including their verbal behavior. To be sure, we do not call a person friendly unless we have experienced the person performing some friendly acts. However, once we see a certain level of consistency in this behavior, we are prone to impute more steady traits to individual people. In fact, we tend to also attribute more generally certain characteristics to all people—not just a particular individual—in certain contexts, for instance, when they are in dangerous situations. These ascriptions of personalities make prediction of behavior far easier than it would be if we had to always work out, on the basis of experiences alone, how others might behave. Several languages allow for expressions referring to these features of people, especially concerning incongruencies of assumed personality and behavior, for instance "to not be oneself" or "to act out of character." Thus, it seems fairly natural to most people to make the assumption that we can ascribe to people somewhat stable and consistent dispositions to think, feel, and behave in a particular way, traits we summarize as "personalities."

However, it has also already been mentioned that some characteristics might only show in specific contexts. A particular person might be a polite person but maybe would not act politely when under a lot of stress or when treated in an impolite manner herself and hence would not show a "global" trait. This might be generalized: Since every situation in which people may find themselves could be deemed of an individual kind—hence not really sufficiently comparable to any other situation—it might simply happen that people show apparently consistent behavior, but that it would be a mistake to impute any more permanent psychological characteristics to them. This is, in a nutshell, the basic assumption of *situationism*, a fairly recent philosophical theory that is based on some empirical findings, mostly drawing from social psychology, where it has been shown that persons are regularly influenced by circumstantial aspects, often quite trivial, of certain situations (Harman 2009; Doris 2002; cf. Kristjánsson 2010; Upton 2009). Situationism regularly targets virtue theory, a philosophical approach dating back to the times of Plato and Aristotle, which assumes that there are certain behavioral dispositions of people that can be morally assessed, called virtues and vices. If the critique of situationism is on target, then it might also undermine the basis of the notion of personality disorder. This conflict cannot be settled here, but it seems to be obvious that it is based on conceptual questions, mainly to do with how to understand the notion of a character (Flanagan 2009). Similar remarks would apply to the concept of personality. It seems that there are hardly any conceptual undertakings to clarify this core notion from a psychiatric point of view (but see, e.g., Sass 1987; Glas 2006) whereas the philosophical debate has been going on for millennia. Once again, a more concerted approach would therefore be of help.[10]

1.2 Psychopathy in the Philosophical Debate

In this section I will present four basic disputes in moral philosophy that have been discussed in relation to psychopathy. These are closely related but need some differentiation. The first issue is the problem of justifying morality, the second the problem of moral motivation, the third is the problem of the origin and nature of moral judgments, and the fourth concerns moral responsibility.

Before I discuss the relevant philosophical issues, though, I would like to add a more external observation regarding the recent history of the philosophical debate. Psychopathy has been mostly discussed in the subfields of moral philosophy and moral psychology. These areas have undergone significant change within the last twenty years or so, especially the latter. Today it has become common for moral philosophers to acknowledge empirical research, occasionally even to contribute to it. This is especially pertinent for the topic at hand, that is, psychopathy. Before, and still today, philosophers dealt with the aforementioned topics by using thought experiments, fictitious examples, for instance as found in novels or films (McGinn 1997; Raatzsch 2009; Carr 2010). Philosophical arguments have proceeded mostly by making claims that were tested for their intuitive plausibility (Deigh 1995; Milo 1984; Benn 1985). Today, some philosophers and scientists alike seem to believe that they can solve the questions of moral philosophy and moral psychology by referring to empirical findings. Admittedly, this might be a too simple and extreme description of quite complex theories.[11] However, I believe it helps to make clear something that has been stressed in this introduction. I believe neither stance—to ignore empirical research or, in contrast, to see it as being able to provide solutions to philosophical questions—is justified. There needs to be a genuine interchange between philosophical and empirical approaches, and there are now indeed many examples of such collaborative work (Flanagan 1991; Decety and Ickes 2009; Sinnott-Armstrong 2008; Narvaez and Lapsley 2009; Adshead et al. 2008).

Many philosophers are interested in psychopathy because it seems to provide a real-life case of amorality. Moral philosophers have always grappled with the problem of how to justify morality. "Why should I be moral at all?" is a sensible question to ask (Nielsen 1989, 167ff.). After all, moral requirements pose serious restrictions on our options, often especially on those we would like to pursue. If philosophers could come up with a plausible account as to why we either are necessarily moral, for example, because of our nature, or because we have an independent reason—preferably one

that is based on our self-interest[12]—why we should take moral considerations into account, then we would have achieved a justification of morality. Within the philosophical debate, this problem of basic justification is
occasionally described as regarding an amoral person or "the amoralist"
(Williams 1976, 17ff.; Jacobs, this volume). If we could provide a sufficient
reason for the amoralist to be moral, then we will have apparently justified
morality. Now psychopaths seem to be such amoralists since they do not
seem to care about morality, and it is therefore no wonder that they have
been of interest in moral philosophy.

Note that an amoralist is not the same as an immoralist. Someone who,
perhaps even regularly, acts in an immoral fashion—a person we might
want to call an immoral person—could generally take moral considerations
into account but could regard other motives to be more important in particular situations or might simply be too weak-willed to actually act according to his or her moral motives. An amoral person, in contrast, does not
care about moral standards at all. Yet an amoral person might never act
immorally, simply because he or she might not happen to violate any moral
requirements (see also the discussion on "successful psychopaths" above).
There is a notable ambiguity, however, concerning the idea of an amoralist
since it could either mean a person *rejecting* moral considerations as significant for his or her decision making or a person who *lacks the capacity* to take
moral requirements into account (Schramme, this volume). This difference
seems to be especially pertinent when assessing moral responsibility, an
issue to which we will return shortly. A psychopath seems to be a person
who does indeed not care about moral requirements; he or she does not
take "the moral point of view." It would therefore be helpful to study the
basis of the psychopath's lack of care to make progress in the philosophical debate concerning the "Why be moral?" question. Maybe it turns out
to be a misconceived question insofar as it might emerge that the putative
real-life exemplars of amoralists, that is, psychopaths, are not rejecting any
possible justification of morality's demands but simply are morally incapacitated (Benn 2000, 39f.). They might not reject the moral point of view
but might be incapable of entering it. To decide between those alternatives,
we need a better grasp of the phenomenon of psychopathy, a goal that cannot be achieved merely by philosophical armchair reflection.

A second issue that has been widely discussed in moral philosophy is
whether moral requirements are intrinsically motivating. This would make
them special in that often "oughts"—for instance, legal requirements—are
not necessarily motivating. A perhaps natural assumption is that if people
judge that something is the morally right thing to do, they will be motivated

to act accordingly. The thesis therefore states that moral judgments are "practical" (Smith 1994, 6f.)—though, of course, people might fail to actually act correspondingly for other reasons, such as weakness of will. According to this assumption, there is an internal connection between moral motivation and judgments regarding moral obligation, a position usually called (motivational) *internalism* (Falk 1947; Frankena 1958; Svavarsdottir 1999, 165). The contrasting position, called *externalism*, does not see this implication and allows for people to accept something as morally required without being at all motivated to act accordingly. Now, it seems obvious that, again, psychopaths might be an interesting test case to solve this issue (Prinz 2007, 42ff.) since they seem to know what is morally required but lack the disposition to do it. This appears to speak in favor of externalism (Roskies 2003). However, it is not straightforward to assume that psychopaths actually do have an understanding of what is morally required; indeed, they might even lack an understanding of what it at all means that something is morally required (Smith 1994, 66ff.). In fact, the very notion that people who are not at all motivated to do what is morally required, that is, possible psychopaths, actually could lack a real understanding of the moral "ought" might be turned in favor of internalism since it would then be implied that making moral judgments and being motivated to act accordingly are closely linked. Thus, the case for externalism or internalism is still open (Bedke 2009, 191), and it might have become obvious that it again calls for some conceptual settlement since whether moral understanding is something a psychopath has or lacks depends on what we mean by "moral understanding" or "moral judgement" (Kennett and Fine 2008, 218; Kennett 2010, 245; Sinnott-Armstrong, this volume).

So part of the question regarding moral motivation is whether the idea of amoralism—to return to the notion discussed in the earlier section—is supposed to be a conceptual or an empirical matter. One might wonder if an amoralist can coherently be assumed to exist. Could there at all be a person who acknowledges moral requirements and still does not care a whit about them? For philosophers who believe that the recognition of moral requirements intrinsically motivates one to act, an amoralist might be conceptually impossible, which again seems implausible since we know of psychopaths (Brink 1986, 29f.; Brink 1989, 45ff.). Now it turns out that a presupposition in this debate between internalists and externalists seems to be—at least partly—an empirical issue, namely, whether a psychopath understands that it is wrong, say, to violate basic moral rules but still does not care. We would have to find out what judgments putative amoralists, that is, psychopaths, actually make and also what kinds of judgments they are able to make (Elliott 1996, 71ff.). Since this, again, depends partly on conceptual assumptions, we would need the collaboration of empirical sciences and philosophy to make progress on the issue of the practicality of morality. However, in what way exactly this cooperation is supposed to be pursued—for instance, what precisely can be established from empirical findings for conceptual issues—has not been settled yet (Joyce 2008; Jones 2006).

A lot of researchers and philosophers alike believe that there actually is an empirical test for moral understanding (Blair 1995; Blair et al. 2005; Levy 2007). There seems to be an important distinction between conventional and moral rules, in that the former depend on authority, that is, their demands can be overridden, whereas moral demands seem to obligate categorically. Children, from a very early age, are able to grasp the difference between conventional and moral rules, and it can therefore be assumed that they have an understanding of morality. Interestingly, many findings establish that psychopaths, in contrast, indeed lack a proper understanding of the relevant difference. Psychopaths therefore seem to lack moral understanding, a finding that seems to underline internalism and might also have important implications for moral responsibility. However, others claim that there are serious flaws in the relevant research, partly concerning its methodology (Kelly et al. 2007), but most notably in respect to its conceptual presumptions (see Shoemaker, this volume.)

Yet another related, third issue in moral philosophy is to do with the question of whether moral distinctions, or moral judgments, are due to sentiments, such as sympathy or fellow feeling, or to reason. Here we are presented with the debate between Moral Sentimentalism and Moral Rationalism. David Hume and Immanuel Kant, two of the most important moral philosophers in the history of philosophy, were involved in this debate, but other well-known philosophers were as well, such as Francis Hutcheson and Adam Smith on the sentimentalist and Ralph Cudworth on the rationalist side. From the perspective of this quarrel it seems interesting to find out whether psychopaths, who apparently lack morality, have a rational or an affective deficit (Maibom 2005, 2010; Nichols 2002; Kennett 2006; Herpertz and Sass 2000; Prinz 2011, 137ff.; see also the essays by Maibom and Matthews in this volume). Either could be a necessary element of morality, and it would appear to be of significant value to be able to solve this issue by empirical studies of psychopaths. As will become abundantly clear in this volume, however, such a solution of a basic philosophical dispute does not seem to be forthcoming, if only because of the already mentioned conceptual issues surrounding the notion of psychopathy. In addition it seems that the best explanation of the deficits of psychopaths includes both affective and cognitive, or rational, elements (McGeer 2008; Kennett 2010; Craigie 2011).

A pertinent example of the multifaceted and complex nature of psychopathy is the lack of empathy, which is often described as one of its features—for instance, in the PCL–R. The notion of empathy has been used for many different phenomena, ranging from emotional contagion—that is, unconsciously resonating with others' affective states—and perspective-taking—that is, mirroring someone else's state of mind, either by vicarious feeling or by cognitive simulation—to fellow feeling—that is, having empathic concern for others (see also Maibom, this volume). As Daniel Batson, a renowned psychologist specializing in empathy research, succinctly puts it: "Application of the term *empathy* to so many distinct phenomena is, in part, a result of researchers invoking empathy to provide an answer to two quite different questions: How can one know what another person is thinking and feeling? What leads one person to respond with sensitivity and care to the suffering of another?" (Batson 2009, 3). Indeed, these aspects of empathy are certainly different, and there can and should be a debate as to whether we should call all of them "empathy" (Coplan 2011). For instance, the aspect of empathic concern (Batson 2011, 11ff.), which is perhaps most relevant for the issue of psychopathy, might perhaps better be called "sympathy" (Benn, this volume). More importantly for our purposes, though, it needs to be assessed in what way exactly, if at all, psychopaths lack empathy. In relation to this question the recent progress in conceptual precision has helped enormously (Debes 2011; Coplan and Goldie 2011; Decety 2012; Engelen and Röttger-Rössler 2012). It seems fairly obvious that psychopaths lack empathic concern; this is the reason why many would deem them amoral. Not caring for others seems to be going hand in hand with not caring for morality. But now it can be studied what the bases for this lack of concern or fellow feeling are, especially whether they might be related to any deficit in the perspective-taking aspect of empathy. Here, again, recent research has improved our thinking about these issues, as it has become possible to distinguish, conceptually and empirically, between cognitive and affective empathy (Eisenberg and Strayer 1987; Eisenberg and Eggum 2009, 73; Shamay-Tsoory 2009; Smith 2006). What's more, an interesting parallel case to psychopathy can be found in autism (McGeer 2008; Baron-Cohen 2012). It has long been discussed that people who suffer from severe forms of autism lack the capacity to "read" other people's minds; they lack what is called a *Theory of Mind* and hence cannot really take the perspective of someone else. On the face of it, autists therefore lack empathy and one might expect that they would also be unable to take the moral point of view, similar to psychopaths. However, it seems more likely to speculate, first, that autists have difficulties especially with the cognitive aspects of empathy but are able to have vicarious feeling (de Vignemont and Frith 2008), and, second, that empathy might not be a necessary requirement of moral agency, but merely one road to taking the moral point of view. Yet another speculation is that autists indeed are inhibited in their capacity for morality, though in a peculiar way that does not need to result in any deviant behavior, since it might be due to a lack of interest in other people quite generally. An important research question regarding this thesis is whether autists show genuine helping behavior (Best 2012).

Psychopaths, on the other hand, seem to have no problem with the cognitive aspects of empathy (understood as perspective taking; Blair et al. 1996; Schaich Borg 2008, 161); in fact, they can exploit their mind-reading ability for deceitful and often cruel behavior. They seem to lack the affective elements of empathy though, and maybe that is the reason, or one of the reasons, why they also lack empathic concern. They might not be able to understand what it feels like for others to be treated in a derogative or mean manner and therefore cannot identify with others, which arguably is a necessary condition for being able to take the moral point of view.

In summary, it is unlikely that morality is due to either sentiment or rationality alone. Psychopaths have deficits in showing empathic concern for others, but this alone would not necessarily lead to immoral behavior, as might be speculated when considering the case of severe autism. Certainly many psychopaths do grasp that their behavior is considered morally wrong by others, and they might therefore have at least some motivation not to act immorally, if only for instrumental reasons, such as avoiding a penalty (Glannon 2008). To be sure, these reasons would not be regarded as the right kind of normative reasons for observing moral rules by some moral philosophers, but be that as it may, even if people lack empathic concern for others, they are usually able to control and steer their behavior. This seems harder for psychopaths, so in addition to deficits in relation to empathy they seem to have deficits that have to do with action control. For instance, it is often mentioned that they have difficulties in planning ahead and lack foresight. Now this again seems more like a cognitive deficit (Flor 2007).

I will return to these issues in the concluding chapter when I introduce the notion of moral agency as a generic term which might provide a common framework for the different philosophical and scientific features of psychopathy in relation to morality. The perspective of agency combines aspects of individual capacities and skills, motivation, control, and actual behavior, but also of social circumstances and norms. As indicated earlier, in the psychiatric literature there are mainly three general characteristics of psychopathy that are mentioned—namely, disinhibition (i.e., lack of control, lack of planning and foresight), boldness (i.e., lack of stress and fearlessness in emotionally taxing circumstances), and meanness (lack of concern, callousness, or coldheartedness). Now it seems obvious that these three characteristics point at different aspects of moral agency.

I will finish this section on philosophical discussions in relation to psychopathy by introducing a fourth topic—namely, the problem of moral responsibility. It has close connections to the legal notion of culpability. There is, of course, a long tradition regarding the connection between moral and legal responsibility and mental illness more generally (Feinberg 1970; Deigh 2008; Reznek 1997). However, psychopathy seems to be special since it potentially affects the very basis of moral agency, in that it does not simply weaken the actual use of required capacities at a particular time but undermines the very abilities. If psychopaths lack moral understanding or other capacities necessary to be able to act morally, they seem to also generally lack responsibility for their behavior (Haksar 1965; Duff 1977; Haji 1998; cf. Smith 1984). This could be seen as a reason why they should not be deemed on a par with "normal criminals" and hence treated differently as regards legal measures. Some people accordingly argue that psychopaths should not be kept in prisons (and eventually released) but that they are mentally deranged individuals—"morally insane," as used to be the preferred expression (cf. Morse 2008)—and therefore are potentially to be treated by medical means. Nevertheless, it might be sensible to keep them in custody to safeguard the public as long as they have not been treated adequately; after all, psychopaths are supposed to have an amoral disposition, which might, of course, easily result in immoral behavior. As described, this is more or less the actual situation of people who are considered to suffer from a pseudo-medical disorder called dangerous and severe personality disorder. It is a term in use specifically in the United Kingdom, and although it sounds like a psychiatric diagnosis, it is a purely legal construct that serves certain societal interests (see Scott, this volume; Beck 2010; Bartlett 2010). Since the outlook for actual cures for psychopaths is currently bleak, the potential length of commitment of affected people is indefinite, which obviously raises severe ethical and, again, legal issues, as it might be a practice that undermines human rights.

Moral responsibility seems to be closely related to the perennial problem of free will. However, in the early 1960s, a new idea concerning the notion of responsibility was introduced that has allowed for a discussion without the need to address the metaphysical issues of the debate on free will, which after all seems to lead us nowhere in terms of any sensible practical consequences. Peter Strawson pointed out that we cannot but react toward other people's deeds with moral feelings or sentiments, such as indignation or resentment (Strawson 1962). If we realize that people did not intend to do what they did, we might suspend those particular "reactive attitudes," but we still see the respective agents as members of the moral community and will react accordingly next time. However, if we assume that a person is somehow so disturbed or abnormal that we would not see him or her as a moral agent at all—as someone who lacks moral sense (ibid., 18)—we might take an "objective attitude" toward the person and exclude the person from the moral community. For Strawson, the main purpose of his essay was to show that the truth-value of determinism is inconsequential regarding this practice of having reactive attitudes. Even if we would believe determinism to be true, this belief would not lead us to a permanent suspension of moral feelings toward others.

Now, in relation to psychopaths, Strawson's account seems to imply that they might be the kind of persons we would not hold accountable at all because they seem to lack the capacities necessary to be a member of the moral community and cannot be reached by moral feelings or judgments. At least that is an idea that can be found in the philosophical literature (Murphy 1972) although the community is divided as to whether psychopaths really lack responsibility as a result of their deficits (Watson 1987, 2011; Wallace 1994, 25ff.; Scanlon 2008; Greenspan 2003; Talbert 2008, 2012; Shoemaker 2007; Deigh 2011; McKenna 2008). We might hold them accountable, and indeed justifiably show moral feelings, such as resentment and blame, toward them, even though they might not be regarded as full moral agents. The main question here is what kind of deficits would actually lead to a suspension of reactive attitudes, and conversely what capacities psychopaths might still have that would deem them apt targets of such feelings (see Deigh, this volume; Talbert, this volume).

1.3   The Essays

Henning Sass and Alan Felthous examine the history of the concept of psychopathy and its continuities with more recent perspectives. "Psychopathy," as understood today, has many predecessors in different countries, which also had influences on each other, and Sass and Felthous accordingly scrutinize the different developments and alterations in several intellectual

and national traditions. It is important to be aware of the manifold connotations that different conceptual traditions imply since they show that the
way we categorize phenomena of our lifeworld does not have a conceptual
necessity. In other words, we need to find reasons as to why we establish a
concept like psychopathy in the first place and why it is conceptualized in
a particular way. Surely, merely by establishing differences and variations of
historical constructs we cannot undermine the validity of any such viewpoints, but it can stress the fact that it is our making. For example, there has
regularly been established a link between mental development and moral
capacities, so that phenomena we are used to calling psychopathy today
could be seen as a kind of degeneration, which easily led to the label of
"moral insanity." This link has been strong throughout history, and in fact
the connection between morality and mental maturity is not only due to
psychiatric perspectives, but has a strand that is visible still today in the
tradition of virtue ethics (see, for instance, Foot 2001). In line with this, Sass
and Felthous show from a historical point of view that the notions of character and personality have been central for the categorization of psychopathy and related constructs. They also point out the potential problems of
linking psychopathy to nonmedical types of deviation. This can lead to a
fusion of social value judgments and medical terminology—arguably most
clearly visible today in the construct of dangerous severe personality disorder, which has been mentioned before and is discussed by Susie Scott in
this volume. Another important point of their discussion is the methodology of classification, especially categorical versus dimensional models, an
aspect that also has important philosophical features and that has been
a significant topic for the debate surrounding the DSM. As Sass and Felthous put it, classifications tend to reflect theoretical assumptions, and it is
hence important to acknowledge different ways to categorize psychopathy
in order to make theoretical progress.

The next five essays are grouped under the heading of moral capacities and incapacities. Although the idea of moral incapacity is the overarching theme of the whole volume, these essays address specific deficits
that can be linked to psychopathy. They range from impairments in rationality (Matthews), fellow feeling (Maibom), language (Adshead), volition
and evaluation (Jacobs), and sympathy (Benn). Together, they can show
that it is rather unlikely to identify *the* deficit of psychopaths. As has been
mentioned before in this introduction, moral philosophy has traditionally
attempted to analyze morality as being either due to reason or due to feelings. Eric Matthews and Heidi Maibom discuss this issue in relation to psychopathy. Matthews begins by introducing phenomena—as philosophers

would put it—that is, with describing cases of people who are apparently incapable of moral considerations: We might want to call these persons amoral, in contrasts to immoral people, who have the capacity to recognize these considerations but simply do not use their capacity. Only the former, Matthews argues, can be linked to psychopathy. In his analysis, he then first puts into doubt the close link that is often established between lack of empathy and psychopathic amorality. This critique is then developed into the claim that feeling alone cannot be the basis of moral action. This speaks against Hume's account of moral motivation, as Matthews stresses. The main aspect of psychopathic amorality according to Matthews's analysis is the lack of intelligibility of psychopaths' explanations for their behavior. These imply failures of reason-giving capacities, or, briefly, a defect in an aspect of practical rationality. However, since psychopaths do not lack rationality *tout court*—for instance, they can still be capable of instrumental reasoning—one might wonder whether these other rational capacities might be sufficient to be moral after all. Matthews stresses that the prototypical moral rationalist, Immanuel Kant, cannot help us in answering this question because he does not have the theoretical resources to account for moral motivation. Matthews therefore reverts to Aristotle, especially his focus on action and his idea of linking human practical rationality to an account of what it means to be human. Intelligibility and good reasons for action hence become a social phenomenon. Moral reasons need to be specified to the moral domain in order to be intelligible. For Matthews, this implies that an action under consideration would need to be unselfish in order to be deemed moral. This, in turn, leads us back to the notion of empathy, though now empathy, in the sense of a concern for others, is seen as a precondition for possessing moral rationality. Matthews finally relates these insights to recent developments in virtue ethics, most notably to Philippa Foot's account of "natural goodness."

Heidi Maibom builds on her earlier work that has been focused on the link between psychopathy and the debate between moral sentimentalism and rationalism, and in which she casts doubt on the sentimentalists' story that psychopathy undermines moral rationalism. In this respect she is in line with Matthews's point of view. In her essay for this volume, Maibom specifically challenges the influential idea that psychopaths lack empathy. Her approach combines conceptual analysis with perspectives on empirical data. Starting from a common account of the psychological mechanisms of empathy and its empirical backing, especially as regards aggression inhibition, she then distinguishes between different aspects of empathy that are often lumped under this term, and also between sympathy and empathy.

In the end, she is rather skeptical about the role of empathy as regards relevant psychological mechanisms that are seen in relation to psychopathy, and also about the supposed empirical measures of empathy. But she also stresses differences in constructing the notion of empathy in relation to different research focuses, which shows the need to reconceptualize empathy for the purposes of debating, and empirically researching, psychopathy. In conclusion Maibom suggests a more inclusive approach to explaining empathy, which allows a wider scope of psychological structures to be relevant. Maibom speculates, in the end, that psychopaths' problems in feeling for others might be due to a related lack of ability to feel for themselves in imagined scenarios. So this would call for a perspective on psychopathy that focuses less on intersubjective, and more on self-concerned, psychological faculties.

Gwen Adshead is concerned with a connection between emotional deficits of psychopaths and their inability to linguistically express and communicate emotions. This idea goes back to Cleckley's account of "semantic dementia." In pursuing her thesis that psychopaths "know the words but not the music," Adshead draws on her previous qualitative empirical research concerning forensic psychiatric patients which she performed with philosopher Jonathan Glover. She endorses the view that certain negative emotions, such as guilt, shame, and disgust, are relevant for moral understanding, and she also discusses the role of empathy, here understood as involving both cognitive and affective elements. In order to understand and to cause emotions, Adshead goes on to argue, we can make use of language since words can represent feelings. The specific deficit of alexithymia, that is, the incapacity to put feelings into words, seems pertinent in this regard, but Adshead stresses that respective research is inconclusive. She therefore uses a different approach that does not focus on linguistic parts, but on meaning-conferring narratives. In conclusion, Adshead aims to identify traits of narrative incoherence in psychopathy, using examples from her own interviews. Again, this links her results to the philosophical notions of moral reasoning and moral identity.

Kerrin Jacobs expands on her previous extensive philosophical work on psychopathy, where she had distinguished between different deficits of sociopaths along the lines of rational, emotional, and volitional capacities. Like Adshead and Maibom, she addresses an issue of a mainly intrasubjective failure in psychopathy, here described as a lack in moral self-realization. Jacobs takes a phenomenological approach, drawing especially on Martin Heidegger's related notion of comportment (*Verhaltung*). Phenomenological perspectives usually address the subjective dimension of psychiatric conditions, or its "lived experience"—for instance, "how it feels" to suffer from a mental affliction. Jacobs aligns her findings to the notion of a scope of possibilities and aims to show how there is both a restriction in the case of psychopathy—as psychopaths cannot act morally—and a pathological widening of such a scope, in that psychopaths transgress moral and social rules. According to her analysis, psychopathy involves an impairment of a general evaluative sense of oneself and the world. In her analysis of psychopaths' identity-related deficit, Jacobs then makes use of Harry Frankfurt's notion of caring. This implies that psychopaths might suffer from defects not only in respect to specific moral capacities, but more generally in terms of general mental human faculties, which might show in the realm of morality—a result she shares with other contributors in this collection.

Piers Benn begins with the obvious experience of people regarding their usual reaction toward suffering: They want it to end. He addresses empathic concern as the basis for altruistic concern. Although every one of us may sometimes be indifferent to the suffering of others—for instance, because of compassion fatigue—psychopathic indifference seems to be unusual, or abnormal. In addition, lack of actual concern does not count as an excuse—we see the suffering of a person as a reason for others to alleviate it. Again, psychopaths seem to fail to appreciate such a reason. Benn carefully delineates, but also links, the notions of sympathy and empathy and considers the thesis that psychopaths' lack of sympathy might be due to a lack of empathy. Interestingly, if we believe that normal or healthy people are able to empathize with other people, that is, to see the world from their point of view, then it should be possible to empathize with a psychopath, that is, the person who apparently cannot empathize. We also know from our own experience that we might occasionally fail in empathizing with other people. This might help us to understand otherwise incomprehensible behavior and, indeed, to go at least a little bit along the lines of gaining knowledge of "what it is like" to be a psychopath. Still, Benn also entertains the thought that there is something more deeply different about psychopaths. He considers the idea that they lack free will and the alternative assumption that they cannot really participate in moral life because we are bound to see them from an objective point of view—an idea of Peter Strawson's that has been mentioned earlier in this introduction. In conclusion, Benn also addresses our related shaky grounds for assuming, or not assuming, moral responsibility of psychopaths.

The next three essays address issues in moral psychology, more specifically moral motivation (Sinnott-Armstrong), moral emotions (Deigh), and moral character (Schramme). Walter Sinnott-Armstrong focuses on the philosophical debate between moral internalism and externalism that has been explained above. He meticulously analyzes and thereby challenges the conceptual problems underlying this quarrel in relation to the apparent empirical findings on psychopathy. As mentioned before, the phenomenon of psychopathy has been used in philosophy as evidence for both internalism and externalism. According to Sinnott-Armstrong, major obstacles in making progress in this debate are conceptual and methodological problems. First, there is not a clear-cut and undisputed definition of moral internalism. Second, empirical results about a lack of moral judgment are not forthcoming, since it is not certain how to test such an impairment, and also who is to count as psychopaths in the first place. In conclusion Sinnott-Armstrong believes both externalists and internalists to be wrong in some respect: internalists in that they see an internal connection between moral judgments and motivation, externalists in their rejection of internalism on grounds of findings about psychopathy. This seems to be a negative result, and in a certain way it is. However, it also shows how philosophy may help in making progress in important theoretical debates, which have practical implications, by pointing out unsuccessful contributions.

John Deigh connects his contribution to the already mentioned philosophical debate regarding reactive attitudes such as resentment, indignation, and guilt. In discussing psychopathy, many philosophers assume or imply that psychopaths lack the capacity for these emotions since they do not seem to be able to make proper moral judgments, that is, seeing oneself as a member of a moral community. After all, how can someone feel mistreated or victimized by an injustice if he or she does not accept or recognize these claims in others? One might think that the egocentricity of psychopaths is a plausible basis for assuming an incapacity regarding reactive attitudes. Yet, in exploring the plausibility of such a claim regarding the lack of specific moral emotions in psychopaths, Deigh refers to psychopathic characters drawn from films by Alfred Hitchcock, *Shadow of a Doubt* and *Strangers on a Train*, who clearly seem to experience resentment. This poses first a conceptual question, as some philosophers, most notably Stephen Darwall, who is a target of Deigh's chapter, identify "moral judgement" with seeing oneself as an addressee of moral reasons. This would make resentment and related reactive attitudes wholly "moralized" emotions, which, in turn, would prevent us from using these emotions to explain moral agency. Hence, to sever the strong link between resentment and the capacity for moral judgment seems to be a better basis for explaining psychopathic resentment. For Deigh, it might be possible to establish the phenomenon of resentment without the capacity for moral judgment—although he agrees that other reactive attitudes, such as indignation and guilt, indeed do require such a capacity. Resentment does not require a moral point of view, but merely intentions toward others, a kind of mutual goodwill. Deigh concludes that psychopaths—in being unable to experience vicarious and self-reactive moral attitudes but being able to show resentment despite a lack of moral judgment—are thoroughly egocentric.

Thomas Schramme starts from a specific interpretation of what it means to know the difference between right and wrong—yet another way to describe the capacity to make moral judgments. This account is due to a less known essay by Gilbert Ryle, in which he develops an idea that has strong links to virtue ethics, namely, that to know the difference between right and wrong implies caring about morality. Ryle puts forward his argument by pointing out the inconceivability of forgetting the difference between right and wrong. For Ryle, this seems impossible since knowing such a difference implies caring about it, and although it might seem possible to stop caring about it, it seems impossible to forget the difference between right and wrong. Schramme links Ryle's ideas to the notion of being a moral person. He delineates two different ideas found in moral philosophy, namely, the amoral person, that is, someone who rejects the demands of morality, and the morally incapacitated person, that is, someone who cannot take those demands into account. He argues in favor of seeing psychopaths not as amoral in the philosophers' sense of the word, but as being incapable of, or seriously deficient in, taking the moral point of view.

In the final section, social aspects in responding to psychopathic behavior are addressed, namely, the basis of ascriptions of moral responsibility (Shoemaker), the justification of moral blame (Talbert), and the social response toward perceived dangerousness of people (Scott). The issue of moral and legal responsibility is maybe the most discussed problem in relation to psychopathy. David Shoemaker addresses an underlying assumption of ascriptions of moral responsibility, especially when it comes to diagnostic testing: a capacity, or lack thereof, to distinguish between moral and conventional rules. On the one hand, he shows the fractured nature of the distinction between the moral and the conventional; on the other hand, he uses one aspect of this difference for establishing a thesis about criminal responsibility. Altogether he proposes a hybrid theory of responsibility, where criminal responsibility is possible without full moral responsibility. In pursuing this thesis, Shoemaker points out empirical findings which undermine a straightforward distinction between the moral and the conventional. He then focuses specifically on the issue of authority dependence or independence as a potential criterion for drawing the distinction.

In this respect, we seem to find the most significant differences between psychopaths and controls. Still, not all moral rules seem to be authority independent; hence there is a need of moral agents to be able to appreciate practical reasons. Now, psychopaths seem insensitive to authority-based reasons, but this would still allow for criminal responsibility as it only seems to demand being able to act like a moral agent, not necessarily being a moral agent. Again, Shoemaker's chapter is another example of a plea—if only implicitly—for empirical research to be conceptually valid.

Matthew Talbert also addresses the issue of responsibility, but his focus is more on the possible reactions of people who are the targets of wrongdoing, that is, resentment, which is the characteristic feature of moral blame. As we have already seen, there has been an intensive debate within philosophy on this issue, starting from Peter Strawson's pioneering work on reactive attitudes. Talbert draws on this debate, specifically on Gary Watson's influential interpretation. Are we really justified in attributing to a psychopathic wrongdoer the necessary characteristics that would justify moral appraisal? Talbert believes that this is indeed so because such behavior can have morally significant expressive content, which is based on the way a psychopath guides his or her behavior in relation to judgments about reasons. Psychopaths' actions might be based on disregard, contempt, or ill will, hence on capacities of guidance that are at least sufficient for justifying reactive attitudes. Psychopaths are not simply driven by internal forces but can weigh reasons and understand consequences of their actions; at least this seems to be a sensible, if contested, assumption. Talbert accordingly concludes that blame toward psychopaths can be justified. Yet again, the problem of what it means to understand moral reasons is at the forefront of philosophical considerations regarding the responsibility of psychopaths.

Susie Scott challenges the legal notion of dangerous and severe personality disorder from a sociological point of view. This is a pertinent example to illuminate the possible influence of social interests in shaping psychiatric, or pseudo-psychiatric, categories, and hence, more generally, in determining our way of seeing the world. To see these influences can help in acknowledging the fact that phenomena such as psychopathy are not clear-cut or necessarily conceptualized in a particular way. Scott also argues for appreciating evaluative aspects of conceptual issues in psychiatry, in addition to the scientific perspective. Here she draws on collaborative research she has done with colleagues from the perspective of Values-Based Medicine, a framework that has been developed by Bill Fulford. In the proposed definition of dangerous and severe personality disorder, there is a reference to a risk of serious offense in some people with severe personality

disorder. This potential risk then becomes the main rationale for demanding detainment in forensic psychiatric clinics for such persons. Scott presents data from a study in which she conducted semi-structured interviews
with mental health professionals who work in forensic settings. Different
values held by the respondents are grouped into six different models of
sociopathy or psychopathic disorder. In conclusion, Scott shows how different values underlie different views on perceived dangerousness and psychopathy. These values are determined by subjective perspectives but also
by pragmatic considerations regarding treatability and fear of being held
accountable for errors in assessment.

The final chapter by Thomas Schramme is an attempt to wrap up the
discussion put forward in this book, but also to point out future directions
of interdisciplinary research on psychopathy. Most notably, it presents the
notion of moral agency as a potential integrative focus.

Notes

1. I follow common practice in the psychiatric literature of referring to the "construct" of psychopathy though I also occasionally use "concept." The latter is the
more common phrase in philosophy, but it seems adequate to emphasize the fact
that psychopathy is a term of our making. There does not seem to be a (so-called)
real definition of the disorder, which would identify its essence or nature.

2. There is a confusing line in the narrative section of the DSM–5, where it is said
that the pattern associated with antisocial personality disorder "has also been
referred to as psychopathy, sociopathy, or dyssocial personality disorder" (American
Psychiatric Association 2013, 659). This might be correct as a description of the
actual usage, but the statement may also be misread as an endorsing identification
of the DSM taxonomy with the other mentioned terms, which was almost certainly
not intended. Finally, DSM-5 contains an "Alternative DSM-5 Model for Personality
Disorders" that explicitly refers to psychopathy as a "distinct variant" of antisocial
personality disorder (ibid., 765).

3. Before Cleckley, the most influential conceptualizations of "psychopathic personality" were due to Kurt Schneider (1923) and George E. Partridge (1928, 1930).
For historical accounts of the conceptual changes, see Sass and Felthous, this
volume, 2007; Blackburn 1988; Millon et al. 1998; Ward 2010; and Busfield 2004,
for a perspective from social history.

4. Hare himself gives an account as to why his PCL–R had no more significant
impact on DSM–IV (Hare and Neumann 2010a, 103; cf. Widiger 2006). He implies
that it was mostly due to DSM's continuation of former editions and "institutional
inertia." There is an even more surprising explanation of the lack of reference to the

notion of psychopathy in DSM–IV in journalist Jon Ronson's book *The Psychopath Test*. Here he reports that it was due to a "backstage schism—between Bob Hare and a sociologist named Lee Robins" (whose research had some influence on the DSM–III classification), where the DSM committee sided with the latter and, as a result, "Psychopathy was abandoned for Antisocial Personality Disorder" (Ronson 2011, 252).

5. Psychopathy is regarded, by most laypersons and many experts as well, as a non-treatable condition though there is an ongoing debate about this important issue (Harris and Rice 2006; Salekin et al. 2010; Ogloff and Wood 2010).

6. A well-known real example, which somewhat fits this description, is the case of the mass murderer Anders Breivik in Norway.

7. Obviously, a major problem, at least to my mind, of the dimensional account—which is sometimes underrated—is that all people are then "up to a certain degree" psychopathic.

8. It should be noted that there is also a debate in psychiatry as to whether personality disorders are properly called mental disorders at all (Charland 2004; Kendell 2002; Bendelow 2010). This is a problem that cannot be dealt with here adequately, as it would require an analysis of the concept of mental disorder, or mental illness for that matter (but see, e.g., Wakefield 1992; Schramme 2000).

9. In a BBC documentary "Are You Good or Evil?" we can learn about a neuroscientist specializing in researching the brain pathology of psychopathy, who realizes that his own brain is similar to the brain of psychopaths. Instead of calling into doubt the supposed causal connections between brain pathology and particular mental traits, he instead starts hunting for psychopathic personality traits in himself (http://www.bbc.co.uk/programmes/b014kj65).

10. As far as I can see, there is indeed fairly little conceptual work in psychology or psychiatry regarding the basic concept of personality though there are many theories about particular factors or dimensions of personality. Arguably one of the most elaborate psychological models of personality is the five-factor model, which has been mentioned before. It lists "neuroticism," "extraversion," "openness to experience," "agreeableness," and "conscientiousness" as dimensions (or factors) of personality. The model has been applied to psychiatric purposes and more specifically to elaborate the notion of personality disorder by Paul T. Costa and Thomas A. Widiger (1994). Again, the approach does not seem to be based on a general theory of personality but reflects generalizations from research findings. This might have to do with the fact that to develop personality theories merely by conceptual ("armchair") reflection, or "grand theory," has fallen out of favor, and more statistically driven methods have come into the foreground (Digman 1994, 14). But still, empirical research into personality relies, first, on an assumption that there are stable mental traits at all and, secondly, on certain conceptual assumptions, for instance,

about the proper delineation of psychological traits. The way we map personality cannot be simply imposed on us by empirical data alone.

11. Here are just a few examples: The philosopher Neil Levy published a book called *What Makes Us Moral?* (Levy 2004) that seems to be asking a genuine philosophical question but then discusses almost exclusively evolutionary explanations of morality. More recently, the philosopher Patricia Churchland gave a neuroscientific explanation of morality (Churchland 2011). Neuroscientists, on the other hand, publish books with titles such as *The Moral Brain* (Verplaetse et al. 2009; see also Tancredi 2005) or *The Ethical Brain* (Gazzaniga 2006), which, for philosophers, sound like a textbook example of a category mistake. Now, obviously one has to take some of these apparently grandiose titles with a pinch of salt, and I definitely do not want to deny the importance of these works—quite the contrary. However, some perspectives, which after all put forward just a perspective of many possible ones, set agendas within the research community, and one should be wary of possible reductionist misconceptions of quite complicated phenomena (see also Schleim 2012).

12. Although, again, some philosophers would claim that these kinds of reasons cannot be of the right kind (Prichard 1912), as they believe morality to be commanding independent of our interests, that is, categorically, or, to put it differently, that morality requires doing something "because it is right" (Schmidtz 2007).

References

Adshead, G. 2006. Capacities and Dispositions: What Psychiatry and Psychology Have to Say about Evil. In *Forensic Psychiatry: Influences of Evil*, ed. T. Mason, 259–271. Totowa, N.J.: Humana Press.

Adshead, G., C. Brown, E. Skoe, J. Glover, and S. Nicholson. 2008. Studying Moral Reasoning in Forensic Psychiatric Patients. In *Empirical Ethics in Psychiatry*, ed. G. Widdershoven, 211–230. Oxford: Oxford University Press.

American Psychiatric Association. 2013. *Diagnostic and Statistical Manual of Mental Disorders: DSM-5*. 5th ed. Washington, D.C.: American Psychiatric Publishing.

Aspinwall, L. G., T. R. Brown, and J. Tabery. 2012. The Double-Edged Sword: Does Biomechanism Increase or Decrease Judges' Sentencing of Psychopaths? *Science* 337:846–849.

Babiak, P., C. S. Neumann, and R. D. Hare. 2010. Corporate Psychopathy: Talking the Walk. *Behavioral Sciences & the Law* 28:174–193.

Baron-Cohen, S. 2012. *Zero Degrees of Empathy: A New Theory of Human Cruelty*. London: Penguin.

Bartlett, P. 2010. Stabbing in the Dark: English Law Relating to Psychopathy. In *Responsibility and Psychopathy: Interfacing Law, Psychiatry, and Philosophy*, ed. L. Malatesti and J. McMillan, 25–40. Oxford: Oxford University Press.

Batson, C. D. 2009. These Things Called Empathy: Eight Related but Distinct Phenomena. In *The Social Neuroscience of Empathy*, ed. J. Decety and W. J. Ickes, 3–15. Cambridge, Mass.: MIT Press.

Batson, C. D. 2011. *Altruism in Humans*. Oxford: Oxford University Press.

Beck, J. C. 2010. Dangerous Severe Personality Disorder: The Controversy Continues. *Behavioral Sciences & the Law* 28:277–288.

Bedke, M. S. 2009. Moral Judgment Purposivism: Saving Internalism from Amoralism. *Philosophical Studies* 144:189–209.

Bendelow, G. 2010. Ethical Aspects of Personality Disorders. *Current Opinion in Psychiatry* 23:546–549.

Benn, P. 2000. Freedom, Resentment and the Psychopath. In *Philosophy, Psychiatry and Psychopathy: Personal Identity in Mental Disorder*, ed. C. Heginbotham, 29–45. Aldershot: Ashgate.

Benn, S. I. 1985. Wickedness. *Ethics* 95:795–810.

Best, L. J. 2012. Early Social Behaviour in Young Children with Autism Spectrum Disorders. Thesis submitted to the Department of Psychology, Queen's University, Ontario, Canada, http://qspace.library.queensu.ca/handle/1974/7544.

Blackburn, R. 1988. On Moral Judgements and Personality Disorders: The Myth of Psychopathic Personality Revisited. *British Journal of Psychiatry* 153:505–512.

Blackburn, R. 2006. Other Theoretical Models of Psychopathy. In *Handbook of Psychopathy*, ed. C. J. Patrick, 35–57. New York: Guilford.

Blackburn, R. 2009. Subtypes of Psychopath. In *Personality, Personality Disorder and Violence*, ed. M. McMurran and R. Howard, 113–132. Chichester: Wiley.

Blair, J. R., D. R. Mitchell, and K. Blair. 2005. *The Psychopath: Emotion and the Brain*. Malden, Mass.: Blackwell.

Blair, J. R., C. Sellars, I. Strickland, F. Clark, A. Williams, M. Smith, and L. Jones. 1996. Theory of Mind in the Psychopath. *Journal of Forensic Psychiatry* 7:15–25.

Blair, R. J. R. 1995. A Cognitive Developmental Approach to Morality: Investigating the Psychopath. *Cognition* 57:1–29.

Borg, J. S. 2008. Impaired Moral Reasoning in Psychopaths? Response to Kent Kiehl. In *Moral Psychology, Volume 3: The Neuroscience of Morality*, ed. W. Sinnott-Armstrong, 159–163. Cambridge, Mass.: MIT Press.

Brink, D. O. 1986. Externalist Moral Realism. *Southern Journal of Philosophy* 24 (S1):23–41.

Brink, D. O. 1989. *Moral Realism and the Foundations of Ethics*. Cambridge: Cambridge University Press.

Busfield, J. 2004. Class and Gender in Twentieth-Century British Psychiatry: Shell-Shock and Psychopathic Disorder. In *Sex and Seclusion, Class and Custody: Perspectives on Gender and Class in the History of British and Irish Psychiatry*, ed. J. Andrews and A. Digby, 295–322. Amsterdam: Rodopi.

Carr, D. 2010. Moral Madness. *Philosophical Investigations* 33:103–125.

Charland, L. C. 2004. Character: Moral Treatment and the Personality Disorders. In *The Philosophy of Psychiatry: A Companion*, ed. J. Radden, 64–77. New York: Oxford University Press.

Churchland, P. S. 2011. *Braintrust: What Neuroscience Tells Us about Morality*. Princeton, N.J.: Princeton University Press.

Cleckley, H. M. 1982. *The Mask of Sanity*. New York: New American Library.(Originally published in 1941)

Cooke, D. J., C. Michie, S. D. Hart, and D. Clark. 2005. Assessing Psychopathy in the UK: Concerns about Cross-Cultural Generalisability. *British Journal of Psychiatry* 186:335–341.

Coplan, A. 2011. Will the Real Empathy Please Stand Up? A Case for a Narrow Conceptualization. *Southern Journal of Philosophy* 49:40–65.

Coplan, A., and P. Goldie. 2011. Introduction. In *Empathy: Philosophical and Psychological Perspectives*, ed. A. Coplan and P. Goldie, ix–xlvii. Oxford: Oxford University Press.

Costa, P. T., and T. A. Widiger (eds.). 1994. *Personality Disorders and the Five-Factor Model of Personality*. Washington, D.C.: American Psychological Association.

Craig, M. C., M. Catani, Q. Deeley, R. Latham, E. Daly, R. Kanaan, M. Picchioni, et al. 2009. Altered Connections on the Road to Psychopathy. *Molecular Psychiatry* 14:946–953.

Craigie, J. 2011. Thinking and Feeling: Moral Deliberation in a Dual-Process Framework. *Philosophical Psychology* 24:53–71.

Debes, R. 2011. Editor's Introduction. *Southern Journal of Philosophy* 49:1–3.

Decety, J. 2012. *Empathy: From Bench to Bedside*. Cambridge, Mass.: MIT Press.

Decety, J., and W. J. Ickes. 2009. *The Social Neuroscience of Empathy*. Cambridge, Mass.: MIT Press.

Decety, J., L. R. Skelly, and K. A. Kiehl. 2013. Brain Response to Empathy-Eliciting Scenarios Involving Pain in Incarcerated Individuals with Psychopathy. *JAMA Psychiatry* 70:638–645.

Deigh, J. 1995. Empathy and Universalizability. *Ethics* 105:743–763.

Deigh, J. 2008. Moral Agency and Criminal Insanity. In *Emotions, Values, and the Law*, ed. J. Deigh, 196–219. Oxford: Oxford University Press.

Deigh, J. 2011. Reactive Attitudes Revisited. In *Morality and the Emotions*, ed. C. Bagnoli, 197–216. Oxford: Oxford University Press.

de Oliveira-Souza, R., R. D. Hare, I. E. Bramati, G. J. Garrido, F. Azevedo Ignácio, F. Tovar-Moll, and J. Moll 2008. Psychopathy as a Disorder of the Moral Brain: Fronto–Temporo–Limbic Grey Matter Reductions Demonstrated by Voxel-Based Morphometry. *NeuroImage* 40:1202–1213.

de Vignemont, F., and U. Frith. 2008. Autism, Morality, and Empathy. In *Moral Psychology, Volume 3: The Neuroscience of Morality*, ed. W. Sinnott-Armstrong, 273–280. Cambridge, Mass.: MIT Press.

Digman, J. M. 1994. Historical Antecedents of the Five-Factor Model. In *Personality Disorders and the Five-Factor Model of Personality*, ed. P. T. Costa and T. A. Widiger, 13–18. Washington, D.C.: American Psychological Association.

Doris, J. M. 2002. *Lack of Character: Personality and Moral Behavior*. Cambridge: Cambridge University Press.

Douard, J., and P. D. Schultz. 2013. *Monstrous Crimes and the Failure of Forensic Psychiatry*. Dordrecht: Springer.

Duff, A. 1977. Psychopathy and Moral Understanding. *American Philosophical Quarterly* 14:189–200.

Eisenberg, N., and N. D. Eggum. 2009. Empathic Responding: Sympathy and Personal Distress. In *The Social Neuroscience of Empathy*, ed. J. Decety and W. J. Ickes, 71–83. Cambridge, Mass.: MIT Press.

Eisenberg, N., and J. Strayer. 1987. Critical Issues in the Study of Empathy. In *Empathy and Its Development*, ed. N. Eisenberg and J. Strayer, 3–13. Cambridge: Cambridge University Press.

Elliott, C. 1996. *The Rules of Insanity: Moral Responsibility and the Mentally Ill Offender*. Albany: State University of New York Press.

Engelen, E.-M., and B. Röttger-Rössler. 2012. Current Disciplinary and Interdisciplinary Debates on Empathy. *Emotion Review* 4:3–8.

Falk, W. D. 1947. "Ought" and Motivation. *Proceedings of the Aristotelian Society* 48.

Feinberg, J. 1970. *Doing and Deserving: Essays in Theory of Responsibility*. Princeton, N.J.: Princeton University Press.

Feinberg, J. 2003. Evil. In *Problems at the Roots of Law: Essays in Legal and Political Theory*, 125–192. Oxford: Oxford University Press.

Flanagan, O. 2009. Moral Science? Still Metaphysical after All These Years. In *Personality, Identity, and Character: Explorations in Moral Psychology*, ed. D. Narvaez and D. K. Lapsley, 52–78. New York: Cambridge University Press.

Flanagan, O. J. 1991. *Varieties of Moral Personality: Ethics and Psychological Realism.* Cambridge, Mass.: Harvard University Press.

Flor, H. 2007. Cognitive Correlates. In *International Handbook on Psychopathic Disorders and the Law*, ed. A. Felthous and H. Sass, 103–116. Chichester: Wiley.

Foot, P. 2001. *Natural Goodness.* Oxford: Clarendon Press.

Frankena, W. K. 1958. Obligation and Motivation in Recent Moral Philosophy. In *Essays in Moral Philosophy*, ed. A. I. Melden, 40–81. University of Washington Press.

Gao, Y., and A. Raine. 2010. Successful and Unsuccessful Psychopaths: A Neurobiological Model. *Behavioral Sciences & the Law* 28:194–210.

Garnar, A., and V. G. Hardcastle. 2007. Neurobiologcal Models: An Unnecessary Divide—Neural Models in Psychiatry. In *The Philosophy of Psychiatry: A Companion*, ed. J. Radden, 364–380. New York: Oxford University Press.

Gazzaniga, M. S. 2006. *The Ethical Brain.* New York: Harper Perennial.

Glannon, W. 2008. Moral Responsibility and the Psychopath. *Neuroethics* 1:158–166.

Glas, G. 2006. Person, Personality, Self, and Identity: A Philosophically Informed Conceptual Analysis. *Journal of Personality Disorders* 20:126–138.

Greene, J. D. 2005. Cognitive Neuroscience and the Structure of the Moral Mind. In *The Innate Mind: Structure and Contents*, ed. S. Laurence, P. Carruthers, and S. Stich. New York: Oxford University Press.

Greenspan, P. S. 2003. Responsible Psychopaths. *Philosophical Psychology* 16:417–429.

Haidt, J. 2001. The Emotional Dog and Its Rational Tail: A Social Intuitionist Approach to Moral Judgment. *Psychological Review* 108:814–834.

Haji, I. 1998. On Psychopaths and Culpability. *Law and Philosophy* 17:117–140.

Haksar, V. 1965. The Responsibility of Psychopaths. *Philosophical Quarterly* 15:135–145.

Hall, J. R., and S. D. Benning. 2006. The Successful Psychopath: Adaptive and Subclinical Manifestations of Psychopathy in the General Population. In *Handbook of Psychopathy*, ed. C. J. Patrick, 459–478. New York: Guilford.

Hamilton, G. 2008. Mythos and Mental Illness: Psychopathy, Fantasy, and Contemporary Moral Life. *Journal of Medical Humanities* 29:231–242.

Hare, R. D. 1993. *Without Conscience: The Disturbing World of the Psychopaths among Us*. New York: Guilford.

Hare, R. D. 1998. Psychopaths and Their Nature: Implications for the Mental Health and Criminal Justice Systems. In *Psychopathy: Antisocial, Criminal and Violent Behavior*, ed. T. Millon, E. Simonsen, M. Birket-Smith, and R. D. Davis, 188–212. New York: Guilford.

Hare, R. D. 2003. *The Hare Psychopathy Checklist—Revised*. North Tonawanda, N.Y.: Multi-Health Systems.

Hare, R. D., and C. S. Neumann. 2010a. Psychopathy: Assessment and Forensic Implications. In *Responsibility and Psychopathy: Interfacing Law, Psychiatry, and Philosophy*, ed. L. Malatesti and J. McMillan, 93–123. Oxford: Oxford University Press.

Hare, R. D., and C. S. Neumann. 2010b. The Role of Antisociality in the Psychopathy Construct: Comment on Skeem and Cooke (2010). *Psychological Assessment* 22:446–454.

Harman, G. 2009. Skepticism about Character Traits. *Journal of Ethics* 13:235–242.

Harris, G. T., and M. E. Rice. 2006. Treatment of Psychopathy: A Review of Empirical Findings. In *Handbook of Psychopathy*, ed. C. J. Patrick, 555–572. New York: Guilford.

Haybron, D. M. 1999. Evil Characters. *American Philosophical Quarterly* 36:131–148.

Haybron, D. M. 2002. Moral Monsters and Saints. *Monist* 85:260–284.

Herpertz, S. C., and H. Sass. 2000. Emotional Deficiency and Psychopathy. *Behavioral Sciences & the Law* 18:567–580.

Howells, K. 2009. Angry Affect, Aggression and Personality Disorder. In *Personality, Personality Disorder and Violence*, ed. M. McMurran and R. Howard, 191–211. Chichester: Wiley.

Jacobs, K. A. 2012. *Soziopathie: Eine Untersuchung moralischer Unfähigkeit* [Sociopathy: An examination of moral incapacity]. Uelvesbüll: Der Andere Verlag.

Jones, K. 2006. Metaethics and Emotions Research: A Response to Prinz. *Philosophical Explorations* 9:45–53.

Joyce, R. 2008. What Neuroscience Can (and Cannot) Contribute to Metaethics. In *Moral Psychology, Volume 3: The Neuroscience of Morality*, ed. W. Sinnott-Armstrong, 371–394. Cambridge, Mass.: MIT Press.

Kantor, M. 2006. *The Psychopathy of Everyday Life: How Antisocial Personality Disorder Affects All of Us*. Westport, Conn.: Praeger.

Kelly, D., S. Stich, K. J. Haley, S. J. Eng, and D. M. T. Fessler. 2007. Harm, Affect, and the Moral/Conventional Distinction. *Mind & Language* 22:117–131.

Kendell, R. E. 2002. The Distinction between Personality Disorder and Mental Illness. *British Journal of Psychiatry* 180:110–115.

Kennett, J. 2006. Do Psychopaths Really Threaten Moral Rationalism? *Philosophical Explorations* 9:69–82.

Kennett, J. 2010. Reasons, Emotion, and Moral Judgement in the Psychopath. In *Responsibility and Psychopathy: Interfacing Law, Psychiatry, and Philosophy*, ed. L. Malatesti and J. McMillan, 243–259. Oxford: Oxford University Press.

Kennett, J., and C. Fine. 2008. Could There Be an Empirical Test for Internalism? In *Moral Psychology, Volume 3: The Neuroscience of Morality*, ed. W. Sinnott-Armstrong, 217–225. Cambridge, Mass.: MIT Press.

Kiehl, K. A. 2008. Without Morals: The Cognitive Neuroscience of Criminal Psychopaths. In *Moral Psychology, Volume 3: The Neuroscience of Morality*, ed. W. Sinnott-Armstrong, 119–149. Cambridge, Mass.: MIT Press.

Kristjánsson, K. 2010. *The Self and Its Emotions*. Cambridge: Cambridge University Press.

Levine, M. 2006. Mad, Bad, and Evil: Psychiatry, Psychoanalysis, and Evil. In *Forensic Psychiatry: Influences of Evil*, ed. T. Mason, 295–312. Totowa, N.J.: Humana Press.

Levy, N. 2004. *What Makes Us Moral? Crossing the Boundaries of Biology*. Oxford: Oneworld.

Levy, N. 2007. The Responsibility of the Psychopath Revisited. *Philosophy, Psychiatry, & Psychology* 14:129–138.

Lilienfeld, S. O., and K. A. Fowler. 2006. The Self-Report Assessment of Psychopathy: Problems, Pitfalls, and Promises. In *Handbook of Psychopathy*, ed. C. J. Patrick, 107–132. New York: Guilford.

Lynam, D. R., and K. J. Derefinko. 2006. Psychopathy and Personality. In *Handbook of Psychopathy*, ed. C. J. Patrick, 133–155. New York: Guilford.

Lynam, D. R., and T. A. Widiger. 2007. Using a General Model of Personality to Identify the Basic Elements of Psychopathy. *Journal of Personality Disorders* 21:160–178.

Maibom, H. 2005. Moral Unreason: The Case of Psychopathy. *Mind & Language* 20:237–257.

Maibom, H. 2010. Rationalism, Emotivism, and the Psychopath. In *Responsibility and Psychopathy: Interfacing Law, Psychiatry, and Philosophy*, ed. L. Malatesti and J. McMillan, 227–241. Oxford: Oxford University Press.

McCord, W. M., and J. McCord. 1964. *The Psychopath: An Essay on the Criminal Mind*. Princeton, N.J.: Van Nostrand.

McGeer, V. 2008. Varieties of Moral Agency: Lessons from Autism and Psychopathy. In *Moral Psychology, Volume 3: The Neuroscience of Morality*, ed. W. Sinnott-Armstrong, 227–257. Cambridge, Mass.: MIT Press.

McGinn, C. 1997. *Ethics, Evil, and Fiction.* Oxford: Clarendon Press.

McKenna, M. 2008. The Limits of Evil and the Role of Moral Address: A Defense of Strawsonian Compatibilism. In *Free Will and Reactive Attitutes: Perspectives on P. F. Strawson's "Freedom and Resentment,"* ed. M. McKenna and P. Russell, 201–218. Farnham: Ashgate.

Mealey, L. 1995. The Sociobiology of Sociopathy: An Integrated Evolutionary Model. *Behavioral and Brain Sciences* 18:523–541.

Millon, T. 2010. Classification Considerations in Psychopathology and Personology. In *Contemporary Directions in Psychopathology: Scientific Foundations of the DSM–V and ICD–11*, ed. T. Millon, R. F. Krueger, and E. Simonsen, 149–173. New York: Guilford.

Millon, T., and R. D. Davis. 1998. Ten Subtypes of Psychopathy. In *Psychopathy: Antisocial, Criminal and Violent Behavior*, ed. T. Millon, E. Simonsen, M. Birket-Smith, and R. D. Davis, 161–170. New York: Guilford.

Millon, T., E. Simonsen, and M. Birket-Smith. 1998. Historical Conceptions of Psychopathy in the United States and Europe. In *Psychopathy: Antisocial, Criminal and Violent Behavior*, ed. T. Millon, E. Simonsen, M. Birket-Smith, and R. D. Davis, 3–31. New York: Guilford.

Milo, R. D. 1984. *Immorality.* Princeton, N.J.: Princeton University Press.

Morse, S. J. 2008. Psychopathy and Criminal Responsibility. *Neuroethics* 1:205–212.

Müller, J. L. 2010. Psychopathy—An Approach to Neuroscientific Research in Forensic Psychiatry. *Behavioral Sciences & the Law* 28:129–147.

Murphy, J. G. 1972. Moral Death: A Kantian Essay on Psychopathy. *Ethics* 82:284–298.

Narvaez, D., and D. K. Lapsley (eds.). 2009. *Personality, Identity, and Character: Explorations in Moral Psychology.* New York: Cambridge University Press.

Nichols, S. 2002. How Psychopaths Threaten Moral Rationalism. *Monist* 85:285–303.

Nielsen, K. 1989. *Why Be Moral?* Buffalo, N.Y.: Prometheus Books.

Ogloff, J. R. P., and M. Wood. 2010. The Treatment of Psychopathy: Clinical Nihilism or Step in the Right Direction? In *Responsibility and Psychopathy: Interfacing Law, Psychiatry, and Philosophy*, ed. L. Malatesti and J. McMillan, 155–181. Oxford: Oxford University Press.

Partridge, G. E. 1928. A Study of 50 Cases of Psychopathic Personality. *American Journal of Psychiatry* 7:953–973.

Partridge, G. E. 1930. Current Conceptions of Psychopathic Personality. *American Journal of Psychiatry* 10:53–99.

Patrick, C. J. 2010. Conceptualizing the Psychopathic Personality: Disinhibited, Bold, or Just Plain Mean? In *Handbook of Child and Adolescent Psychopathy*, ed. R. T. Salekin and D. R. Lynam, 15–48. New York: Guilford.

Patrick, C. J., and E. M. Bernat. 2010. Neuroscientific Foundations of Psychopathology. In *Contemporary Directions in Psychopathology: Scientific Foundations of the DSM–V and ICD–11*, ed. T. Millon, R. F. Krueger, and E. Simonsen, 419–452. New York: Guilford.

Poythress, N. G., and J. L. Skeem. 2006. Disaggregating Psychopathy: Where and How to Look for Subtypes. In *Handbook of Psychopathy*, ed. C. J. Patrick, 172–192. New York: Guilford.

Prichard, H. A. 1912. Does Moral Philosophy Rest on a Mistake? *Mind* 21:21–37.

Prinz, J. 2006. The Emotional Basis of Moral Judgments. *Philosophical Explorations* 9:29–43.

Prinz, J. 2007. *The Emotional Construction of Morals*. Oxford: Oxford University Press.

Prinz, J. 2011. Sentimentalism and Self-Directed Emotions. In *Self-Evaluation: Affective and Social Grounds of Intentionality*, ed. A. Konzelmann Ziv, K. Lehrer, and H. B. Schmid, 135–153. Dordrecht: Springer.

Raatzsch, R. 2009. *The Apologetics of Evil: The Case of Iago*. Princeton, N.J.: Princeton University Press.

Reimer, M. 2008. Psychopathy without the Language of Disorder. *Neuroethics* 1:185–198.

Reznek, L. 1997. *Evil or Ill? Justifying the Insanity Defence*. London: Routledge.

Ronson, J. 2011. *The Psychopath Test: A Journey through the Madness Industry*. New York: Riverhead Books.

Roskies, A. 2003. Are Ethical Judgments Intrinsically Motivational? Lessons from "Acquired Sociopathy." *Philosophical Psychology* 16:51–66.

Russell, L. 2010. Evil, Monsters and Dualism. *Ethical Theory and Moral Practice* 13:45–58.

Russell, L. 2012. Evil and Incomprehensibility. *Midwest Studies in Philosophy* 36 (1):62–73.

Ryle, G. 1949. *The Concept of Mind*. London: Hutchinson.

Salekin, R. T., C. Worley, and R. D. Grimes. 2010. Treatment of Psychopathy: A Review and Brief Introduction to the Mental Model Approach for Psychopathy. *Behavioral Sciences & the Law* 28:235–266.

Sass, H. 1987. *Psychopathie, Soziopathie, Dissozialität: Zur Differentialtypologie der Persönlichkeitsstörungen* [Psychopathy, sociopathy, dissociality: Towards a differential typology of personality disorders]. Berlin: Springer.

Sass, H., and A. Felthous. 2007. History and Conceptual Development of Psychopathic Disorders. In *The International Handbook of Psychopathic Disorders and the Law, Volume 1: Diagnosis and Treatment*, ed. H. Sass and A. Felthous, 9–30. Chichester: Wiley.

Scanlon, T. 2008. *Moral Dimensions: Permissibility, Meaning, Blame*. Cambridge, Mass.: Belknap Press of Harvard University Press.

Schleim, S. 2012. Brains in Context in the Neurolaw Debate: The Examples of Free Will and "Dangerous" Brains. *International Journal of Law and Psychiatry* 35:104–111.

Schmidtz, D. 2007. Because It's Right. *Canadian Journal of Philosophy* 37, Supplement 33:63–95.

Schneider, K. 1923. *Die psychopathischen Persönlichkeiten: Handbuch der Psychiatrie* [The psychopathic personality handbook of psychiatry], Volume 7, Part 1. Leipzig: Deuticke.

Schramme, T. 2000. *Patienten und Personen: Zum Begriff der psychischen Krankheit* [Patients and persons: On the concept of mental illness]. Frankfurt am Main: Fischer.

Shamay-Tsoory, S. G. 2009. Empathic Processing: Its Cognitive and Affective Dimensions and Neuroanatomical Basis. In *The Social Neuroscience of Empathy*, ed. J. Decety and W. J. Ickes, 215–232. Cambridge, Mass.: MIT Press.

Shoemaker, D. 2007. Moral Address, Moral Responsibility, and the Boundaries of the Moral Community. *Ethics* 118:70–108.

Sinnott-Armstrong, W. 2008. *Moral Psychology*. 3 vols. Cambridge, Mass.: MIT Press.

Skeem, J. L., and D. J. Cooke. 2010. Is Criminal Behavior a Central Component of Psychopathy? Conceptual Directions for Resolving the Debate. *Psychological Assessment* 22:433–445.

Skeem, J. L., D. L. L. Polaschek, C. J. Patrick, and S. O. Lilienfeld. 2011. Psychopathic Personality: Bridging the Gap between Scientific Evidence and Public Policy. *Psychological Science in the Public Interest* 12:95–162.

Skodol, A. E. 2010. Dimensionalizing Existing Personality Disorder Categories. In *Contemporary Directions in Psychopathology: Scientific Foundations of the DSM–V and ICD–11*, ed. T. Millon, R. F. Krueger, and E. Simonsen, 362–373. New York: Guilford.

Skodol, A. E. 2012. Personality Disorders in DSM–5. *Annual Review of Clinical Psychology* 8:317–344.

Smith, A. 2006. Cognitive Empathy and Emotional Empathy in Human Behavior and Evolution. *Psychological Record* 56:3–21.

Smith, M. A. 1994. *The Moral Problem*. Oxford: Blackwell.

Smith, R. J. 1984. The Psychopath as Moral Agent. *Philosophy and Phenomenological Research* 45:177–193.

Stout, M. 2005. *The Sociopath Next Door: The Ruthless versus the Rest of Us*. New York: Broadway Books.

Strawson, P. F. 1962. Freedom and Resentment. *Proceedings of the British Academy* 48:1–25.

Svavarsdottir, S. 1999. Moral Cognitivism and Motivation. *Philosophical Review* 108:161–219.

Talbert, M. 2008. Blame and Responsiveness to Moral Reasons: Are Psychopaths Blameworthy? *Pacific Philosophical Quarterly* 89:516–535.

Talbert, M. 2012. Moral Competence, Moral Blame, and Protest. *Journal of Ethics* 16:89–109.

Tancredi, L. R. 2005. *Hardwired Behavior: What Neuroscience Reveals about Morality*. New York: Cambridge University Press.

Upton, C. L. 2009. *Situational Traits of Character: Dispositional Foundations and Implications for Moral Psychology and Friendship*. Lanham: Lexington Books.

Verplaetse, J., J. Schrijver, S. Vanneste, and J. Braeckman. 2009. *The Moral Brain: Essays on the Evolutionary and Neuroscientific Aspects of Morality*. Dordrecht: Springer.

Wakefield, J. C. 1992. The Concept of Mental Disorder: On the Boundary between Biological Facts and Social Values. *American Psychologist* 47:373–388.

Wallace, R. J. 1994. *Responsibility and the Moral Sentiments*. Cambridge, Mass.: Harvard University Press.

Ward, T. 2010. Psychopathy and Criminal Responsibility in Historical Perspective. In *Responsibility and Psychopathy: Interfacing Law, Psychiatry, and Philosophy*, ed. L. Malatesti and J. McMillan, 7–24. Oxford: Oxford University Press.

Watson, G. 1987. Responsibility and the Limits of Evil: Variations on a Strawsonian Theme. In *Responsibility, Character, and the Emotions*, ed. F. Schoeman, 256–286. Cambridge: Cambridge University Press.

Watson, G. 2011. The Trouble with Psychopaths. In *Reasons and Recognition: Essays on the Philosophy of T. M. Scanlon*, ed. R. J. Wallace, R. Kamar, and S. Freeman, 307–331. Oxford: Oxford University Press.

Weber, S., U. Habel, K. Amunts, and F. Schneider. 2008. Structural Brain Abnormalities in Psychopaths—A Review. *Behavioral Sciences & the Law* 26:7–28.

Widiger, T. A. 2006. Psychopathy and DSM–IV Psychopathology. In *Handbook of Psychopathy*, ed. C. J. Patrick, 156–171. New York: Guilford.

Widiger, T. A., and D. R. Lynam. 1998. Psychopathy and the Five-Factor Model of Personality. In *Psychopathy: Antisocial, Criminal and Violent Behavior*, ed. T. Millon, E. Simonsen, M. Birket-Smith, and R. D. Davis, 171–187. New York: Guilford.

Williams, B. A. O. 1976. *Morality: An Introduction to Ethics*. Cambridge: Cambridge University Press.

2   The Heterogeneous Construct of Psychopathy

Henning Sass and Alan R. Felthous

The concept of "psychopathy," which is at the beginning of our notion of "personality disorders," has important roots in the French, German, and Anglo-American psychiatric traditions. Well into the twentieth century, sociocultural factors caused these conceptions of psychopathy to develop more or less independently. This chapter deals with all three traditions and the development of standard nomenclatures. A brief overview of the main conceptual milestones is given in table 2.1. Earlier descriptions of this complex development can be found in Sass (1987), Sass and Herpertz (1995), and Sass and Felthous (2008).

2.1   French Conceptualizations of Psychopathy

2.1.1   Mania without Delirium and Monomania
Pinel's concept of a *manie sans délire* (mania without delirium) can be looked upon as the beginning of the scientific study of personality disorders (Pinel 1809). For the first time in contemporary psychiatry the field of deranged personality was conceptualized as a nosological entity.

According to its rationalistic way of thinking, the eighteenth century regarded mental diseases exclusively as disturbances of the intellect. Pinel was one of the first to stress that in some disorders it was the emotions that are primarily involved while the intellectual functions are essentially undisturbed. In his well-known dissertation *Traité médico-philosophique sur l'aliénation mentale* (Medico-Philosophical Treatise on Mental Derangement) he distinguished between five nosological categories: melancholia, mania without delirium, mania with delirium, dementia, and idiocy. Pinel gave some examples of what he regarded as mania without delirium, only one description of which stands out for extreme emotional instability and dissocial tendency and would probably fit our present diagnostic view whereas today the other disorders would be considered to be cases

Table 2.1

Milestones in the history of the concepts of personality disorders and psychopathy
(cf. Sass 1987)

Concepts of personality disorders and psychopathy	Reference
French concepts	
Manie sans délire (mania without delirium)	Pinel (1809)
Les monomanies (mononmania)	Esquirol (1839)
Dégénérés (degenerates)	Morel (1876)
Delinquente nato (the born criminal)	Lombroso (1876)
Déséquilibration mentale (mental instability)	Dupré (1925)
Anglo-American concepts	
Moral alienation of the mind	Rush (1812/1962)
Moral insanity	Prichard (1835)
Sociopathy	Partridge (1930)
Psychopathic states	Henderson (1939)
Anethopathy	Karpman (1941)
Semantic dementia	Cleckley (1941)
German concepts	
Pschopathische Minderwertigkeiten (psychopathic inferiorities)	Koch (1891/1893)
Der geborene Verbrecher (the born criminal)	Bleuler (1896)
Konstitutionelle Degeneration (constitutional degenerations)	Ziehen (1905–1912)
Psychopathische Persönlichkeiten (psychopathic personalities)	Kraepelin (1909–1915)
Körperbau und Charakter (body type and character)	Kretschmer (1921)
Psychopathische Persönlichkeiten (psychopathic personalities)	Schneider (1923/1950)
Psychopathische Verbrecher (psychopathic criminals)	Birnbaum (1926)

of epilepsy and paranoid schizophrenia. What was path breaking was not Pinel's diagnostic concept but his empirical observation of a syndrome that shows disturbance of emotion and behavior without intellectual deficits.

With respect to etiology, Pinel thought of an inadequate education or a perverse, unrestrained constitution and therefore alluded to the still valid discussion of whether psychopathy is the result of a psychosocial development or is primarily endogenous and hereditary based.

Despite the efforts of nineteenth-century psychiatrists such as Pinel, the definition of madness remained in the main cognitive in nature (Berrios 1985). Indeed, to this day, disorders of affect have been rather neglected in psychiatric phenomenology, at least in comparison to the intensive concern with cognition and perception.

Esquirol, the most prominent of Pinel's students, developed the idea of monomania, a diagnostic category which in succession of his teacher also referred to disorders of the noncognitive side of personality. Esquirol (1839) presented his concept in his main work *Des Maladies Mentales* (Mental Diseases) wherein he proposed a division of mind into understanding, will, and feeling. Defects of understanding were named "intellectual monomanias." "Instinctive monomanias" meant changes of will, so that the subjects are forced to act and behave in a way that does not correspond to their wishes. The group of illnesses called "affective monomanias" subsumed changes of emotions that cannot be controlled.

The problem is that Esquirol extended his theory of monomania to a certain point of circularity. He worked out conceptions of circumscribed monomanias so that a single behavioral disturbance became the only criterion needed to diagnose the condition. Well-known examples are pyromania, kleptomania, erotomania, and even homicidal monomania. His concept of monomanias has survived in present classification systems with their diagnostic categories of disorders of impulse control, kleptomania, and pathological gambling, for example. The idea of monomania also had great influence on the further scientific work on psychopathy at the turn of the century: The instinctive monomanias transitioned easily into *"Impulsives Irresein,"* that is, the impulsive insanity of German psychiatry, and the affective monomanias were one of the roots of the British concept of moral insanity.

Nevertheless, Esquirol's concept of monomania also met with severe criticism from a psychopathological view as well as from medicolegal reasoning. One of the most significant critics was the great German psychiatrist Griesinger (1845), who can be regarded as the founder of the biological epoch of psychiatric research. He emphasized that every single *"idée fixe"* is the expression of a deeply deranged psychic individuality and probably an indicator of an incipient form of mania. In regard to criminal law, he proposed that the correct procedure was first to look for evidence of a mental disease before and after the time of the criminal act and not to consider the act itself already as a significant criterion of a presumably abnormal state of mind.

2.1.2   Degeneration Theory

A work that proved to be of great significance for further concepts of abnormal personalities was Morel's (1857) *Traité des dégénéréscences physiques, intellectuelles et morales de l'espèce humaine* (Treatise on the Physical, Intellectual and Moral Degeneration of the Human Species). Morel's idea of degeneration was not primarily a scientific one but traced back to philosophical thinking and to a religious worldview. In close connection with Genesis, degeneration was looked upon as the true nature and destiny of humankind after the Fall. Morel worked out a theory of degeneration that included three characteristics: (1) Degenerative alterations are pathological deviations from normality; (2) mental diseases are mostly hereditary—originally caused by harmful external influences, the disorders are inscribed into the biology of the subject and are passed on from generation to generation, with ever increasing pathological deviation and even progressive deterioration within one's own life time (hence, the idea of progressive degeneration); and (3) degeneration occurs not only quantitatively, with the same symptoms becoming worse, but also qualitatively, resulting in completely new disorders. According to Morel's model, all variants of mental and even neurological syndromes can be traced back to one common hereditary origin (the idea of polymorphic heredity).

Consequently, his nosology of mental diseases was no longer symptom based but was grounded in his hypothetical etiology of disorders. Morel divided the hereditary madnesses (*les folies héréditaires*) into different categories corresponding to the increasing degree of degeneration. He started with groups of individuals who presented no severe defects of cognitive function but rather stood out for eccentricity, emotional instability, disregard for rules, unreliability, and absence of sense of duty. They suffered from "*folie morale*," a notion that was similar to the British concept of "moral insanity."

In the middle of the nineteenth century, Morel's conception of progressive and polymorphic degeneration was generally accepted as the source of most mental illnesses. Second only to Morel, the psychiatrist Magnan (see Magnan and Legrain 1895) was the most famous representative of the theory of degeneration in France. Magnan dissociated himself, however, from Morel's religious point of view and regarded himself as a disciple of Darwin. It was Magnan who formulated the concept of predisposition as a result of hereditary transformations, which could be either latent (not yet expressing themselves in any symptoms) or manifest since birth. Mental disorder was thus an expression of degenerative changes of cerebrospinal centers as its neurophysiological substrate. It induced a fateful lifelong fragility that made the individual vulnerable to fail through difficult environmental influences. In his opinion, the progressive evolution of humankind was constantly endangered by destructive influences that caused degeneration by ruining humans' mental equilibrium. Magnan as well distinguished different degrees of degeneration, the least degenerated class being the higher degenerates (*dégénérés supérieurs*), who appeared to have significant affective disturbance but no intellectual deficits.

Ideas of degeneration theory were also expressed by the well-known Italian psychiatrist Lombroso (1876), who developed the central idea of the born criminal (*delinquente nato*). Inspired by Darwin's evolutionism, he regarded a criminal individual as a form of human atavism, a step back in the phylogenesis of mankind. According to his opinion, criminal acts were rooted in biology and the criminal could be recognized by specific anatomical stigmata of degeneration. He was considered to lack higher nervous centers that represent moral faculties. Social prognosis was very poor. Although Lombroso's "social Darwinist" concept was heavily criticized, his thoughts have obviously maintained some subliminal significance and have supported prejudice against mental illness and psychopathy.

After the First World War, Dupré (1925) was the true founder of the concept of mental imbalance (*déséquilibration mentale*). However, within the beginning of the twentieth century the idea of degeneration was abandoned. Instead the doctrine of constitution, which is connected with German views of a hereditary-based psychopathic constitution, gained in importance.

In sum, the French psychiatry of the nineteenth and early twentieth centuries, with its synthesis of doctrines of Pinel, Esquirol, Morel, and Magnan, gave momentum to the development of additional concepts of psychopathy. An important concept following that of mania without delirium was Prichard's (1835) "moral insanity," which as well was influenced by the French School, as it responded to the research on mental diseases in France. After other modifications by German psychiatry, the process of development went on from the concept of "higher degenerates" (*dégénérés supérieurs*) to "unbalanced degenerates" (*déséquilibrés dégénérés*) and eventually to the constitutionally imbalanced (*déséquilibrés*). In regard to the classification of syndromes, the main element of the French concept is that psychopathy represents disorders of emotion and social behavior while intellectual functions remain undisturbed. From the pathogenetic point of view, the idea of an inborn constitution combined with psychic disequilibrium and fragility was favored.

2.2   Anglo-American Theories of Psychopathy

2.2.1   The Concept of Moral Insanity
Benjamin Rush (1812/1962), known as the Father of American Psychiatry, was the first Anglo-American psychiatrist who studied individuals whose disturbances were primarily characterized by irresponsibility, unscrupulousness, and aggressiveness. Rush spoke of "perversion of the moral faculties" and of "moral alienation of the mind." He believed that reprehensible acts were manifestations of mental diseases that were committed without motive and were driven "by a kind of involuntary power" (Rush 1827, 261). As with historical British concepts, we find the main accent on dissocial and amoral aspects in early American ideas about psychopathy.

Prichard's (1835) definition of "moral insanity" was based in part on the earlier thoughts of French psychiatry. He gave the following definition of moral insanity:

…madness, consisting in a morbid perversion of the natural feelings, affections, inclinations, temper, habits, moral dispositions, and natural impulses, without any remarkable disorder or defect of the interest or knowing and reasoning faculties, and particularly without any insane illusion or hallucinations. (ibid., 6)

Lest "moral insanity" be interpreted in purely moralistic terms, the reader must bear in mind that the word "moral" has various meanings in different languages. These various possible meanings have given rise to confusion and misunderstandings. One can distinguish between the following meanings: (1) "Moral" can describe a method of treatment that made use of psychological methods and environmental influences; (2) in a nonbiased sense "moral" was used for the affective and volitional, in contrast to the intellectual, side of human nature; (3) in its limited context "moral" was a synonym for "ethical," which is also the contemporary meaning of the word.

Prichard's "moral insanity" essentially denoted the second broad meaning of the word and can therefore be translated with terms such as "emotional" and "affective." Similar to Pinel, he relinquished the view that mental disorders were only disturbances of the intellect, but he considered other dysfunctions beyond just the cognitive (cf. Berrios 1993). One might speculate that today's shift in meaning favored an early tendency to restrict the concept of abnormal personality to a type of habitual social deviation and criminality. Etiologically, Prichard considered different causes of moral insanity, ranging from cases in which the defect is constitutional to those with "a well-marked change of character" resulting from "moral shock" or from "fever" (Tuke 1884, 80). Epilepsy was associated with moral insanity as well. Therefore, it seems to have been a broad heterogeneous group of mental diseases under which Prichard subsumed this nosological entity.

The well-known English psychiatrist Maudsley (1874) strove for clarification between evil as an expression of mental derangement in the sense of moral insanity on the one hand and as that of an eccentric and dissolute personality on the other hand. In his prominent medicolegal work *Responsibility in Mental Disease*, he resisted many lawyers of his day who considered moral insanity to be just a "groundless medical invention" (ibid., 68) and argued for the acceptance of the concept of diminished criminal responsibility in English law. In contrast to his contemporaries, Maudsley believed that emotions and impulses alone, without disturbed reason, could drive one to commit criminal acts.

By the turn of the century in America, Ray's idea of "moral mania" came closest to contemporary European notions of psychopathy (Ray 1838). Based on his familiarity with phrenology, he believed in well-defined cerebral localizations for both intellectual and emotional faculties. This facilitated his acceptance of the idea of "moral insanity." However, a lively dispute took place around him that involved not only scientific assessments but also religious and philosophical ideals.

For a long while in the twentieth century, the British concept of psychopathy was shaped by Henderson (1939), a Scottish disciple of the American psychiatrist Alfred Meyer (1903). Henderson considered "psychopathic states" to be constitutional abnormalities. In contrast to others, especially German psychiatrists, he conceived of constitution as resulting from both heredity and environment. He defined three psychopathic conditions: those that were (1) predominantly aggressive, (2) predominantly inadequate, and (3) predominantly creative. While the third type was not commonly applied, the inadequate and aggressive types of psychopathy entered into the Anglo-Saxon concepts of personality disorders that were mainly characterized by dissocial traits. The British Mental Health Act still uses the term "psychopathic disorder" exclusively in the sense of abnormally aggressive and irresponsible behavior. The term "psychopathic disorder" is also used in psychiatric literature to refer to aspects of personality that have relevance in forensic psychiatry (Sass and Herpertz 1994).

Even today, the ambiguous meaning of the term "psychopathy" has persisted. On the one hand, it serves as a general term for different abnormalities of personality—both neurotic and psychopathic. On the other hand, it is used as a specific term for the aggressive, dissocial type of offender who is prone to recidivism.

Besides its legal significance, Henderson assumed that psychopathic conditions hold special importance with regard to the prognosis of mental diseases in general: "It is the underlying psychopathic state which constitutes the rock on which our prognosis and treatment in relation to many psychoneurotic and psychotic states becomes shattered" (Henderson 1939, 37).

2.2.2 Psychoanalytic Views on Psychopathy
Alfred Meyer (1903) contributed to the subsequent distinction between psychopathy and neurosis. He designated neurasthenia, psychasthenia, and hysteria as forms of neurosis which he distinguished from constitutional inferiority. Here he included a large group of various inferiorities that were not sufficiently differentiated to be regarded as definite mental diseases. As views shifted away from the concept of definitely inherited conditions, the term constitution was conceived in the broad meaning of early and permanently fixed characteristics of the mind. Toward the end of the 1920s "constitutional inferiority" was replaced by "psychopathic personality" in the Anglo-American nomenclature. Partridge (1930) was one of the main advocates of the new concept of psychopathy. He described personalities whose abnormality was mainly expressed in impulsiveness and in moral deficiency.

From 1908 until 1923 Freud had worked out his conception of infantile psychological development, which he described as a succession of organization–forms of libido under the priority of erogenous (oral, anal, genital) areas. During recent decades psychoanalytic interest has shifted from the dominance of sexual drive to the leading role of object relations and their influence on emotional development. Common to all psychoanalytic schools is the thought that the roots of all psychiatric disorders lie in disturbances during the early formative years. That means specifically that distortions and arrests during these early developmental stages cause conflicts that arise over unresolved infantile sexual drives and especially relationships, leading to neurotic or psychotic symptoms in adult life. In this special sense of a "concept of continuum," psychoanalysts have established a continuous sequence of psychiatric disorders extending over neurosis, psychopathy, and psychosis, the severity of the disorder depending on the time when significant traumas were experienced.

After Freud's (1908) work on character and anal eroticism (*Charakter und Analerotik*), Alexander (1928) and Reich (1933) proposed the concept of "character neurosis." They argued that neurosis manifests itself not only in circumscribed symptoms but also in the character as a whole. Alexander limited his definition of "neurotic character" to those cases wherein individuals act out their deviance in impulsive behavior. According to him, most criminals suffer from an unconscious conflict between parts of the ego, and they surely possess a superego. However, instead of suffering from symptoms, they disturb other people (actions instead of symptoms). Later the difference between the ego-syntonic psychopath and the ego-dystonic neurotic became established.

Reich (1933), in turn, regarded character primarily as a defensive structure against inner impulses and external stress. In contrast to Alexander, he rejected a principal difference between symptomatic neurosis and character neurosis and assumed that the neurotic character is the basis for every neurotic symptom. Based on this hypothesis, he developed a special form of character analysis. Reich was of the opinion that character neurosis stands for the integrated product of symptoms that can no longer be averted. Character neurosis can therefore be looked upon as the progressive effort at adjustment in contrast to the regressive symptom neurosis.

2.2.3 From Psychopathy and Sociopathy to Dissocial Personality Disorder

At least in North America's common and technical language usage, the problematic term "dissocial behavior" has all but disappeared. To English readers, the term is ambiguous, meaning neither "dissocial reaction" of the earlier *Diagnostic and Statistical Manual of Mental Disorders* (DSM) nor "dissocial personality disorder" of the current version of the *International Classification of Diseases* (ICD–10). In fact our use of "dissocial behavior" is not intended to suggest any disorder whatsoever. It is a behavior that may be criminal when produced by adults, delinquent when done by youths, but not necessarily in violation of the law. Basically, it is behavior that is offensive to others and violates social norms. It may but does not have to be the result of a disorder. The behavior itself, not its cause, is indicated by the term. However, because the prefix "anti" means "against" and in keeping with earlier writings of Sass's formulation of concepts of psychopathic disorders (see Felthous et al. 2001, 297), the seemingly less pejorative descriptor "dissocial" is retained.

As explained above, the conception of psychopathic personality was in Anglo-Saxon literature increasingly narrowed until it basically meant dissocial behavior. Therefore it seems to be consequent that Partridge (1930) proposed the notion "sociopathy" for this main psychopathic group. "Sociopathy" was defined as a persistent maladjustment that cannot be corrected and brought into normal social patterns by ordinary methods of education or by punishment. Although the sociological perspective, with its focus on behavioral disturbances, had existed since the beginning of the development of psychopathy concepts, it had by the 1930s gained more and more importance. Partridge writes, "[we] might say that pragmatically the psychopath is mainly reduced to types which are of importance from the standpoint of society and the effect of personalities adversely upon the social life seems to be recognized as a justification for a category within the field of the psychopathological in its more individual and subjective aspects" (75).

From the time of Partridge, the emphasis has been on descriptions, and etiological speculation has taken the backseat (e.g., concepts regarding degeneration, constitution psychodynamic background).

By providing inclusion and exclusion criteria, Craft (1966) formulated the first operational view of psychopathy in the sense of a dissocial disorder. As "primary" features, he identified lack of feeling toward other human beings and a tendency to act on impulse. As secondary features, he listed aggressiveness, absence of shame and remorse, an inability to profit from experience, and a deficit of drive or motivation. The presence of psychosis, a significant mental disability, or normal criminal motivation excluded the diagnosis of psychopathy (Craft 1966, 5).

Karpman (1941) suggested a distinction between idiopathic and symptomatic forms of psychopathy. Under "symptomatic psychopathy," he grouped all those reactions that were basically neurotic and therefore could be traced back to intrapsychic conflicts. According to Karpman, there was another smaller group of true psychopaths whose behavior could not be explained by any psychodynamic formulations. He considered these "anethopaths" to lack a conscience.

The restriction of "psychopathy" to the dissocial "sociopathy" continues to dominate the Anglo-Saxon sphere, so that both expressions and also the new term "dissocial personality disorder," of DSM–III (American Psychiatric Association 1980), and later on in DSM–III-R/DSM–IV (American Psychiatric Association 1987, 1994, 2000), are used virtually as synonyms. The current DSM–5, however, provides more opportunity to base the diagnosis on functional psychological deficits (see section 2.A.A).

Cleckley (1976) had remarkable influence on American conceptualizations of psychopathy. His famous treatise, *The Mask of Sanity*, in which he proposed the idea of psychopathy as a form of "semantic dementia," went through five editions beginning in 1941, the last in 1976. It contained a number of case reports that reflected the clinical–intuitive procedure of the author and became the basis of empirical research on psychopathy in North America. Cleckley's "psychopath" was characterized by dissocial behavior that could not be deduced from any adequate motivation and that was caused by neither psychosis, nor neurosis, nor mental handicap. He listed sixteen criteria which he thought to be typical and distinctive for psychopathy, including superficial charm and undisturbed intelligence, unreliability and insincerity, inability to accept blame or shame, failure to learn from experience, pathological egocentricity and incapacity for love, lack of emotions in general, impersonal and poorly integrated sexual relationships, and inability to follow one's aim in life. Indeed, the DSM–5 concept of antisocial personality disorder (American Psychiatric Association 2013) includes most of these criteria. Cleckley was convinced that "psychopathy" should be accepted as a "severe disease" having the quality of a psychosis that had not manifested itself. Cleckley coined the speculative notion of "semantic dementia." It described the incapacity of the psychopath to have central human experiences with any degree of emotional depth, even though intellectual understanding is undisturbed.

A similar picture of the psychopath was offered by the sociologists McCord and McCord (1964), who researched the long-term association between psychopathy and criminality. Influential in modern clinical work within the realm of psychopathology is the work of Hare (1970). From the descriptions of Cleckley he developed a standardized instrument, the Psychopathy Checklist, later in a revised form (PCL–R), which is widely used for diagnosis and research (Hare 1990).

In her well-known monograph *Deviant Children Grown Up*, Robins (1966) described a population of more than 500 males who were observed over a period of 30 years. These data gave the most important empirical basis for the current concept of dissocial personality disorder in the United States. The conclusion of a synopsis of twenty-nine great inquiries about course and prognosis of dissocial personality disorder was as follows: The degree of dissocial and especially aggressive behavior in childhood and youth can be looked upon as the best early predictor for developing a sociopathic disorder. This finding also supported the widespread supposition that disordered personality traits are stable and enduring.

In sum, the development of conceptions of "psychopathy" proceeded quite homogeneously in the Anglo-American area. Significant was the early restriction of the wide concept of personality disorders to a type of habitual social deviation and criminality. This tendency had already emerged in the narrow usage of the term "moral insanity" and later in the concept of "psychopathy" and finally "sociopathy." Early on, American psychiatrists absorbed psychoanalytic views that were based on the idea that most abnormal personalities and even criminals suffer from a neurotic unconscious conflict. Therefore the differentiation between an idiopathic and a neurotic symptomatic form was accomplished. The basically neurotic psychopath was thought to act out his or her impulses in deviance. Besides psychoanalytic ideas, etiological speculations such as the concept of "anethopathy" or "semantic dementia" refer to the assumption of a basic mental and spiritual defect that cannot be explained by any psychodynamic formulation and that is regarded as responsible for the individual's inability to have central human experiences.

2.3   Conceptual History of Psychopathy in Germany

2.3.1   Psychopathic Inferiorities and Constitutions
In Germany the term and concept of "psychopathy" came to embrace most forms of abnormal personalities. Up to the 1840s "psychopathy" meant what the etymologist would expect: For von Feuchtersleben (1845) "psychopathy" meant a psychological defect, psychosis, or illness of personality. In the 1840s, Griesinger defined "nervous constitution," the "sensitive weakness" as that individual predisposition that can lead to mental suffering and to loss of mental stability. Griesinger and Koch's concepts corresponded somewhat with the French ideas of mental instability ("*déséquilibration mentale*") and to the idea of asthenia, which gained considerable importance later in German psychiatry.

The current German meaning is traceable to Koch. Through his monograph *Die Psychopathischen Minderwertigkeiten* (The Psychopathic Inferiorities, Koch 1891–1893), he gained recognition for his conceptualization of abnormal personalities, similar to his predecessors Pinel in France, Rush in the United States, and Prichard in Great Britain. The German ideas of psychopathy also influenced French and Anglo-American views. This was more noticeable after the 1930s when many German-speaking psychiatrists and psychoanalysts emigrated to these countries.

In his group of "psychopathic inferiorities" Koch included a wide range of conditions that mostly stood out because of minor mental defects. It is remarkable that he already described some definite forms of psychopathic inferiority in the sense of our present concepts of psychopathy. Therefore, it was Koch who not only established our present notion of psychopathy as an integral part of today's use of language in psychiatry but also contributed to the currently still valid concept of psychopathy in the manner of a typology.

Koch divided the "psychopathic inferiorities" into congenital and acquired, and each of these categories into psychopathic predisposition, psychopathic defect, and psychopathic degeneration. In his expositions many of the psychopathic types of later concepts were already identified. For example he referred to those individuals who are distinguished by psychic fragility (*"psychische Zartheit"*), by a weak, vulnerable constitution.

Ziehen (1905–1912) developed Koch's views one step further but preferred to speak of "psychopathic constitutions," which were also considered to be genetic in nature. In his writing *Geisteskrankheiten des Kindesalters* (Mental Diseases of Childhood) Ziehen presented twelve forms of psychopathic constitutions, among them the hysterical, the neurasthenic, the depressive, the hyperthymic, the paranoid, and the obsessive types.

2.3.2 Psychopathic Personalities

In contrast to the Anglo-American sphere, the German concept of personality disorders was broader than the Anglo-American sphere and included far more than dissocial criteria. Nevertheless, Koch's term "inferiority" also led to negative connotations and even moral condemnation. Although one does not encounter explicitly pejorative intentions in the writings of Koch, it was probably also he who provided the unfortunate amalgamation of aspects of amorality, inferiority, and socially harmful behavior.

Kraepelin's concept of psychopathy was influenced by the French theory of degeneration (Kraepelin 1896) and in turn formed the basis of Kurt Schneider's typology, and through the latter, of today's well-established German view of psychopathy. In successive editions of his textbook, Kraeplin continued to develop his concept of "psychopathic conditions" in the meaning of our current view on abnormal personalities. The expression *"die psychopathischen Zustände"* appeared for the first time in the fifth edition (1896) and consisted of compulsive conditions, impulsive insanity, homosexuality, and disturbances of the mood, the so-called *"konstitutionellen Verstimmungen."* In the seventh edition (Volume 2, 1904), under the heading "Insanity of Degeneration" (*Entartungsirresein*), he treated the anomalies of personality considerably in the tradition of the theory of degeneration. After that, an innovation was introduced: Henceforth Kraepelin distinguished between "original disease conditions" (*Originäre Krankheitszustände*)—the group he had earlier called psychopathic states—and "psychopathic personalities" (*Psychopathische Persönlichkeiten*). The latter were regarded as stable psychopathic conditions corresponding to personality defects.

Kraepelin employed the term "psychopathic personalities" in a predominantly socially judgmental sense. In the seventh edition, he subsumed under this well-known designation the inborn delinquents, the unstable individuals, the liars, the swindlers, and the pseudo-querulants. In the eighth edition (1909–1915), he named the following types of psychopathic personalities besides those who were dissocial *"Gesellschaftsfeinde"* (enemies of society): the excitable, the unstable, the *"Triebmenschen"* ("driven persons," relating to impulsive insanity), the eccentric, the liars and swindlers, and the quarrelsome. It is remarkable that Kraepelin now considered the states of disturbed mood—today's subaffective disorders—not to be psychopathic conditions but preliminary attenuated phases of manic–depressive diseases. This change corresponds with current classification systems of mental diseases (cf. Akiskal 1981).

Birnbaum (1926) also researched the social aspects of psychopathy, and in his monograph, *Die psychopathischen Verbrecher* (The Psychopathic Criminals), he concerned himself with the forensic significance of abnormal personality. Birnbaum assumed that psychopathic personalities show constitutionally conditioned deviations in personality of a moderate degree. Following the French theory of degeneration, the criterion of an abnormal, inherited predisposition was of decisive importance for Birnbaum and the psychiatric schools in Germany that followed. Moreover, in accordance with Dupré's concept of mental instability (*déséquilibration mentale*), he also paid attention to disharmony of personality traits and abnormal liability of mental stability.

Kretschmer suggested that there was a specific correlation between body type and personality, and he divided all people into one of three body types: the pyknic, the leptosomic, and the athletic type. The pyknic body type was associated with the cyclothymic character. In Kretschmer's opinion the boundaries between the normal cyclothymic character, the abnormal cycloid variant, and manic–depressive psychosis were fluid so that mental health and illness were regarded as a continuous phenomenon. Correspondingly, the leptosomic and athletic body type were related to a schizothymic temperament and therefore to the schizoid form of psychopathy and, finally, to schizophrenia.

During this period there also appeared various forms of systematic typologies. This means that the different psychopathic modes of appearance were inferred from prototypic ideas about the structure of personality. Foremost among these is Kretschmer's (1921) *"konstitutionstypologisches*

Modell." However, there were many others. Gruhle (1956) deduced his types from fundamental characteristics of the human mind such as activity, basic mood, affective responsiveness, will power, and so on. Other psychiatrists such as Kahn (1928), Schultz (1928), Homburger (1929), and Rothacker (1947) proposed a hierarchical model of personality (*"Schichttypologien"*). Others such as Kretschmer and Ewald (1924) also introduced the notion of "typologies of reaction" (*Reaktionstypologien*), which referred to different ways of digesting experiences. After K. Schneider's monograph (1923/1950) was published, the systematic typologies lost most of their significance.

2.3.3 K. Schneider's Concept of Psychopathy

Kurt Schneider's famous monograph *Die psychopathischen Persönlichkeiten* (The Psychopathic Personalities), first published in 1923, takes root in his earlier *Persönlichkeit und Schicksal eingeschriebener Prostituierter* (Studies on the Personality and Fate of Registered Prostitutes; 1921), wherein he already recognized twelve characterological types. K. Schneider, like Kraepelin (1909–1915), used a typology approach. However, in contrast to Kraepelin's predominantly socially judgmental concept with its sociological forms of psychopathic states, K. Schneider intended to maintain a value-free concept. Therefore, he took some nondissocial forms into his typology.

K. Schneider did not consider psychopathy to be a mental illness because, according to his idea, illnesses were necessarily associated with somatic injury or disease process. In this, he opposed Kretschmer and Bleuler, who believed psychosis and psychopathy were just different degrees on a continuous scale of derangement.

Approaching the problem of psychopathy from the perspective of the normal personality, K. Schneider regarded abnormal personalities as statistical deviations from an estimated average norm although this norm was only vaguely conceptualized. For K. Schneider (1923/1950)—who also regarded eminently creative or intelligent individuals as abnormal—not all abnormal personalities were of psychiatric significance: "Psychopathic personalities are those abnormal personalities that suffer from their abnormality or whose abnormality causes society to suffer" (unless otherwise noted, all translations are our own).

K. Schneider's typology differentiated in detail ten forms of psychopathic personalities, which were based on clinical views and were not intended to be of systematic quality: the hyperthymic and depressive psychopaths with their stable deviations of mood and activity, the insecure psychopaths with their subgroups of the sensitive and anankastic psychopaths, the fanatics, the self-assertive psychopaths, the emotionally unstable psychopaths, the explosive, the callous, the weak-willed, and the asthenic psychopaths. In particular, the subtle descriptions of Petrilowitsch (1966) deepened K. Schneider's typology portrayals from the perspective of character pathology. K. Schneider's doctrine influenced all future descriptive typologies. The current classification systems DSM–5 and ICD–10 have also integrated many essential parts of Schneider's conception of psychopathic personalities.

In sum, current connotations of the term "psychopathy" in the German tradition trace back to Koch's "psychopathic inferiorities," which represented a first attempt at a descriptive typology. It is remarkable that already Koch had addressed precursor concepts of psychasthenia. Early German writings on psychopathy were highly influenced by the French theory of degeneration. Later French concepts were replaced by German concepts in many respects. Kraepelin's and Birnbaum's writings focused on the social aspects of psychopathy, and especially Kraepelin's dissocial psychopath—"*der Gesellschaftsfeind*"—gained special importance. K. Schneider intended to maintain a value-free concept of psychopathy; however, he did not completely succeed in erasing immoral and pejorative connotations. To this day, K. Schneider's unsystematic typology has received great interest and has caused earlier systematic typologies to fade away. In contrast to Kretschmer and Bleuler, K. Schneider did not regard psychopathy as a mental disease but as a deviation from the norm. Thus, he relinquished the idea of a continuous scale between psychopathy and psychosis. Up to the present day, the German traditional views of psychopathy—especially in the form of K. Schneider's concept—have continued to influence psychopathological research on abnormal personalities.

2.4   Some Selected Historical and Conceptual Issues with Significance for Today's Research on Personality Disorders

2.4.1   Sociological Aspects of Personality Disorder

As we have argued in detail, concepts of personality disorders have tended toward an unfavorable amalgamation of psychopathological disturbances and social deviation through the nineteenth and twentieth centuries. Even though the sociological perspective especially dominated the Anglo-American sphere, this historical line of development was to be found in the French view of degeneration and in the German tradition as well. The strong emphasis placed on the sociological aspects of personality disorder are demonstrated impressively by the concept of "moral insanity."

The disturbance of man's affective side, in contrast to his intellectual side, was originally regarded as the characteristic of moral insanity. This idea evolved into a predominantly ethical insanity in the sense of a socially reprehensible propensity toward criminality. In spite of contrary intentions, which often remained only as lip service, the emphasis on the harmful social aspects also crept into the German view of psychopathy. Kraepelin explicitly relinquished the differentiation between the sociological and psychopathological aspects. The different editions of his textbook present an increasing limitation on his own originally broader concept of socially harmful forms of psychopathy. In the course of time, some primarily psychopathic types, especially those with disturbed mood, were no longer subsumed under disorders of personality but were regarded upon as preliminary stages of endogenous psychoses. In contrast to Kraepelin's later writings, Kurt Schneider favored a value-free psychological and characterological point of view that was comprised of subaffective disturbances. Distinguishing two forms of psychopaths—those who suffer from their psychic abnormality and those from whom society suffers—K. Schneider achieved a conceptual clarification and in this way also combined psychopathological and sociological aspects (cf. Sass 1987).

Nevertheless, the German tradition was constructed more broadly from the very beginning, by introducing a second significant type beside the dissocial forms. This type was the asthenic, feeble psychopath to whom the group of subaffective abnormalities of personality was added later on. One could suppose that this completion contributed to the greater significance the concept of psychopathy in the broader sense of personality disorders achieved in German-speaking countries.

Probably in the Anglo-American sphere the early distinction between the suffering, ego-dystonic neurotic and the disturbing, ego-syntonic psychopath (cf. Karpman 1941) supported the restriction of the concept of psychopathy to forms of persistent maladjustment to society. Contrary to American development, K. Schneider's concept contains the two manifestations of psychopathy mentioned above, which partly overlap with the Anglo-Saxon differentiation between neurosis and psychopathy. Thus many of the ego-dystonic neurotics correspond with K. Schneider's criteria of psychopathy.

2.4.2   The Differentiation between Personality Disorder and Psychosis

Personality disorders present conditions that belong to a border zone between mental health and current phenomena of everyday life on the one hand and specific mental diseases on the other hand. While fluid transitions between normal and slightly abnormal personalities are generally accepted, the borderland at the other end of the continuum of psychiatric disturbances—including most severe pathology of character and endogenous psychoses—causes greater difficulties (cf. Sass and Koehler 1983).

The different facets of an "idea of continuum" especially concerned the German tradition of psychiatry beginning with the unitarian concepts of Zeller (1840) and Griesinger (1845) (cf. Sass 1990). The French theory of degeneration and its idea of polymorphic heredity considered all varieties of mental and neurological syndromes to trace back to one unitary hereditary origin. The French notion of *manie sans délire* as the forerunner of the later term "psychopathy" stood for the broad field of mental derangement that was not yet definitely conceptualized but represented a low level on a continuous scale of increasing degeneration.

In the development of the German concept of psychopathy, two lines can be distinguished from one another. The first one, above all linked to Kretschmer, claimed gradual transitions between normal personality traits, psychopathies, and endogenous psychoses. The other one, represented by Schneider but also by Birnbaum, Jaspers (1959), and Gruhle, rejected any possibility of a continuous development of endogenous psychosis through intensifying psychopathic traits but insisted on a categorical difference. Conceding only a few cases of diagnostic doubt, Schneider challenged psychiatrists to reach a decision as to whether a patient has an abnormal personality or an endogenous psychosis.

Empirical research in recent decades has not found a significant accumulation of specific personality disorders preceding the onset of schizophrenia, for instance, in the sense of Kretschmer's schizoid dimension. Nevertheless, characteristics of increased psychic vulnerability have been found. Also in the field of affective psychoses, typical premorbid traits of personality have been described. Already Kraepelin referred to subaffective states of disturbed mood as personality features in his early writings.

In the discussion of the concept of unitary psychosis and the "idea of continuum," the structural–dynamic concept, worked out by Janzarik (1988), is worth mentioning. This structural–dynamic approach differentiates the mental whole into two aspects, the dynamic and the structural. Simplistically, "dynamics" means the vital, mostly constitutionally based affective side of human beings whereas "structure" refers to the intentions, attitudes, and values that are determined to a large extent by life history. Premorbid traits of personality are characterized by dynamic and structural peculiarities. Considering the dynamic side, the vulnerability to developing an endogenous psychosis seems to be determined by a basic instability and proneness to psychic derailment. Which consequences dynamic deficits however have, whether they lead to a mental disease or not, depends on the situational and biographical circumstances and on the qualities of the "structure." It is also "structure" that determines the kind of psychotic disorder (schizophrenic or affective) the individual displays (cf. Sass 1992).

The completion of purely criteria-based diagnostics of personality through fundamental and *"ganzheitliche"* (holistic) models of personality could usher in a new access to the understanding of mental diseases. Faced with today's level of knowledge, however, it seems to be useful to base diagnostic classification systems on a multiaxial assessment that registers "states" and "traits" independently and therefore enables further research on possible associations.

2.4.3 Categories and Dimensions: Two Different Models of Personality

Historical concepts of personality disorders predominantly present classical typology descriptions of special types of personality. These categorical systems have developed naturalistically without a systematic and comprehensive scheme. In particular, academic psychology promotes dimensional models of personality that conceptualize personality disorders in relation to normally occurring traits, and the dimensions therefore are better suited for empirical verification and broader generalizability.

One of the best-known dimensional models of personality is that of Eysenck (1952), who, using factor analysis, reduced the variety of possible traits to the dimensions of extraversion, neuroticism, and psychoticism. During the last decades some other dimensional models of personality have been developed, which can be related to some extent to one another. Millon (1981) proposed the following three dimensions: "self–other orientation," "activity–passivity" and "pleasure–pain." Widiger et al. (1987) presents a differentiated, methodologically demanding attempt to dimensionalize personality disorders. He refers to the dimensions of "high social involvement vs. low social involvement," "high assertion or dominance versus low assertion or dominance," and "anxious rumination versus behavioral acting out." Cloninger (1987) correlates three dimensions of personality with the neurotransmitter systems and neurogenic mechanisms of learning: "novelty seeking" (dopaminergic system), "harm avoidance" (noradrenergic system), and "reward dependence" (serotonergic system). The five-factor model (McCrae and Costa 1989) derives from Eysenck's three dimensions and the two dimensions of the interpersonal circumplex model (Wiggins 1982) and consists of neuroticism, extraversion, openness, agreeableness, and conscientiousness.

Because of their high level of abstraction, dimensional models still seem removed from clinical realities and remain of secondary importance in clinical usage in comparison with categorical models. New developments in personality research have attempted to combine categorical and dimensional elements. Widiger (1991), for example, has proposed retaining the categorical format of today's international classification systems but adding weighting diagnostic criteria including a measure of "prototypicality." In this way dimensional elements could improve present categorical prototypic models that are characterized by a clear set of definitional features that "are not considered to be singly necessary or jointly sufficient" (Widiger and Frances 1985, 616). This polythetic rather than monothetic method permits multiple personality diagnoses. From the historical perspective, it is remarkable that the first conceptual roots of prototypic models can be found in writings of Max Weber and in Jaspers (1959) on "ideal" personality types.

2.4.4   Standardization of Nomenclature in the DSM System

Until the middle of the twentieth century, no single standard nomenclature of mental disorders prevailed. In the United States, at least three separate nomenclatures were in use: a standard nomenclature of disease, a project initiated by the New York Academy of Medicine in 1927; a nomenclature developed for use in the armed forces; and the Veterans Administration nomenclature (American Psychiatric Association 1952). Clinicians tended to use diagnostic terms and concepts taught at their medical schools and residency programs, and the terminology of various educational centers was far from uniform. This frustrated attempts to learn and advance knowledge by sharing information through publications and seminars. It also impeded research because the resulting babel did not allow accurate comparisons of investigative results from different centers. Eventually the American Psychiatric Association developed its nomenclature in the form of its first edition of the DSM (1952).

A challenge in gaining general acceptance of any new nomenclature was the disharmony in theoretical orientation of mental health professionals. Names and criteria of mental disorders can reflect etiological assumptions. Adolf Meyer's psychobiological approach was thought to be more unifying than a strictly biological or psychodynamic model, for example, would have been. Thus, disorders were termed "reactions." Symptoms and aberrant behaviors were considered to contribute to total adaptive reactions to internal (biological) or external (psychological) stresses.

In the first DSM, personality disorders were considered to be pathological conditions, usually lifelong, with little stress or distress, characterized more by behavioral features than subjective symptoms. Among the three main groups within the category of personality disorders were the sociopathic personality disturbances characterized by failure to conform to social norms. Four disturbances within the sociopathic personality disturbances were antisocial reaction, dissocial reaction (DSM term), sexual deviation, and addiction. Dissocial reaction was described by Clecklian features, such as chronic dissocial behavior, failure to learn from adverse experience, and callousness. The condition previously designated as "constitutional psychopathic state" would henceforth be known as dissocial reaction (American Psychiatric Association 1952).

Less familiar to North Americans, because the term has long been discarded, was the above-mentioned "dissocial reaction," a condition wherein a person disregards norms of the prevailing culture because he or she was brought up in a contrary moral environment. A Mafia family member, for example, would be considered a product of social learning from a deviant subculture rather than mentally disordered in a pathological sense.

By 1968 the concept of dissocial reaction was dropped from the DSM, then in its second edition. The salient pathological antisocial condition, no longer a reaction, was now one of several personality disorders. The diagnostic criteria for the DSM–II's antisocial personality were essentially the same as those for the DSM–I's antisocial reaction. The condition "group delinquent reaction of childhood," which retained the etiological implication of a "reaction," had to be ruled out before settling on the diagnosis of dissocial personality (DSM–II, American Psychiatric Association 1968).

The most significant change in diagnostic criteria and method occurred in the third edition, in which all pathological personality disturbances, indeed most mental conditions, became known as disorders. Reflecting the seminal research of Robins (1966) described above, the criteria for the DSM–III's antisocial personality disorder (American Psychiatric Association 1980) included childhood behaviors that establish the lifelong course of the disorder. Out of concern that the diagnosis could be falsely made based on subjective impressions and unclear inferences about psychological functions, DSM–III criteria were essentially behavioral. Methodological consistency in diagnosis and objective signs were thought to result in more accurate diagnoses and improved interrater reliability. Subsequent editions of the DSM up to DSM–IV–TR have continued this basic methodological and conceptual approach to antisocial personality disorder.

At present there are heavy discussions about the conceptualization of personality disorders in DSM–5. The current edition actually has two systems for diagnosing personality disorders: The system in section II of the manual is an update of the behavioral criteria of the DSM–IV–TR, whereas that of section III presents an "Alternative Model for Personality Disorders," which is based on specific impairments in personality functioning and pathological personality traits. A diagnostic evaluation following this second system should include an assessment of the level of personality functioning using the "Level of personality functioning Scale" (LPPS). Future research including clinical studies must clarify the utility of this rather sophisticated "Multidimensional Personality Functioning and Trait Model."

Antisocial personality disorder is not to be found in the current ICD Classification of Mental Disorders (ICD–10; World Health Organization 1989). The closest diagnostic condition is dissocial personality disorder, the criteria of which are much more like those of the earlier DSM's antisocial personality disorder than those of dissocial reaction in the first DSM. Included within the ICD–10's concept of dissocial personality disorder are the sociopathic, asocial, dissocial, and psychopathic disorders, respectively. Incidentally, the diagnostic method is much more like that in the pre-1980 versions of the DSM and, therefore, relatively flexible. Important to note, however, are the altogether different meanings of the earlier dissocial reaction of the DSM and the current dissocial personality disorder of the ICD.

2.5 Summary

The meshing of the concepts of abnormal personality and social deviance was treated in detail in this chapter (especially in discussing the Anglo-American theories of psychopathy). The socially deviant personalities are now described by different diagnostic criteria, that is, antisocial personality disorder (DSM–5), dissocial personality disorder (ICD–10), and the core group "psychopathy" in the sense of Hare (1970, 1990). The differentiation of personality disorders from mere dissocial behavior without additional psychopathological peculiarities is of importance, especially in forensic psychiatry. This requires a differentiation into more pathological and more dissocial variants of abnormal personality (Sass 1987), thus yielding the following differentiations:

1. Personality disorders occur in individuals who suffer from their psychopathological peculiarities and/or whose social life is impaired by these

peculiarities. Their symptoms resemble those of psychiatric patients in the strict sense.

2. Moreover, some of these individuals show a potential for social conflict as their behavior is marked by deviance and criminality in a way that is evidently related to their psychopathological abnormalities. Due to the close correlation between social deviance and psychopathological abnormalities, the term antisocial personality disorder would seem justified.

3. Some individuals show a clear and persistent disposition toward deviant and delinquent behavior without psychopathologically relevant abnormalities throughout their lives. This criminologically important core group corresponds to the "psychopathy" described by Hare (1971, 1990) in the strict sense: It usually shows a "dissocial character structure" and is now also defined quite well biologically (Herpertz and Sass 2000). They may be regarded as persons with antisocial personality or as "psychopaths" in the American sense, but only some of them would qualify for a diagnosis of personality disorder according to the traditional psychiatric understanding of that term.

Only by means of a differentiation such as this can forensic questions of legal responsibility, prognosis, and therapy be settled. On no account should we speak of a personality disorder when dealing with only recurring

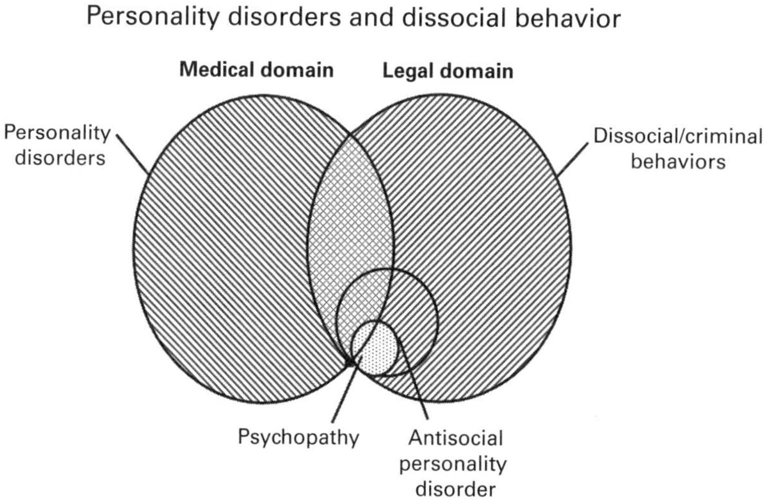

Personality disorders and dissocial behavior

Figure 2.1
Personality disorders, psychopathy, and the law (cf. Sass 1987).

social deviance and criminality, as shown by chronic repeat offenders or professional criminals, since this diagnostic term can lead to erroneous connotations of an illness-like disorder. A scheme for this differentiation is shown in figure 2.1 (cf. Sass 1987).

References

Akiskal, H. S. 1981. Subaffective Disorders: Dysthymic, Cyclothymic and Bipolar II Disorders in the Borderline Realm. *Psychiatric Clinics of North America* 4:25–46.

Alexander, F. 1928. Der neurotische Charakter [The neurotic character]. Seine Stellung in der Psychopathologie und in der Literatur. *International Journal of Psycho-Analysis* 14:26–44.

American Psychiatric Association. 1952. *Diagnostic and Statistical Manual: Mental Disorders.* Washington, D.C.: American Psychiatric Association.

American Psychiatric Association. 1968. *Diagnostic and Statistical Manual of Mental Disorders.* 2nd ed. Washington, D.C.: American Psychiatric Association.

American Psychiatric Association. 1980. *Diagnostic and Statistical Manual of Mental Disorders.* 3rd ed. Washington, D.C.: American Psychiatric Association.

American Psychiatric Association. 1987. *Diagnostic and Statistical Manual of Mental Disorders.* 3rd ed., revised. Washington, D.C.: American Psychiatric Association.

American Psychiatric Association. 1994. *Diagnostic and Statistical Manual of Mental Disorders.* 4th ed. Washington, D.C.: American Psychiatric Association.

American Psychiatric Association. 2000. *Diagnostic and Statistical Manual of Mental Disorders.* 4th ed., text revision. Washington, D.C.: American Psychiatric Association.

American Psychiatric Association. 2013. *Diagnostic and Statistical Manual of Mental Disorders.* 5th ed. Washington, D.C.: American Psychiatric Association.

Berrios, G. E. 1985. The Psychopathology of Affectivity: Conceptual and Historical Aspects. *Psychological Medicine* 15:745–758.

Berrios, G. E. 1993. European Views on Personality Disorders: A Conceptual History. *Comprehensive Psychiatry* 34:14–30.

Birnbaum, K. 1926. *Die psychopathischen Verbrecher* [The psychopathic criminals]. 2nd ed. Leipzig: Thieme.

Bleuler, E. 1896. *Der geborene Verbrecher: Eine kritische Studie* [The inborn delinquent: A critical study]. München: Lehmann.

Cleckley, H. 1976. *The Mask of Sanity: An Attempt to Clarify Some Issues about the So-Called Psychopathic Personality.* 5th ed. St. Louis: Mosby.

Cleckley, H. 1941. *The Mask of Sanity: An Attempt to Clarify Some Issues about the So-Called Psychopathic Personality.* St. Louis: Mosby.

Cloninger, C. R. 1987. A Systematic Method for Clinical Description and Classification of Personality Variants. *Archives of General Psychiatry* 44:573–588.

Craft, M. 1966. *Psychopathic Disorders and Their Assessment.* Oxford: Permagon Press.

Dupré, E. 1925. La doctrine des constitution. In *Pathologie de l'imagination es de l'émotivité.* Göttingen: Ruprecht.

Esquirol, E. 1839. *Des maladies mentales considérées sous les rapports médical, hygiénique et médico-legal* [Mental diseases under medical, hygienic and medico-legal aspects]. Paris: Bailliè.

Ewald, G. 1924. *Temperament und Character* [Temperament and character]. Berlin: Springer.

Eysenck, H. J. 1952. *The Scientific Study of Personality.* London: Routledge & Kegan Paul.

Felthous, A. R., H. L. Kröber, and H. Sass. 2001. Forensic Evaluations for Civil and Criminal Competencies and Criminal Responsibility in German and Anglo-American Legal Systems. In *Contemporary Psychiatry, Volume 1: Foundations in Psychiatry,* ed. F. Henn, N. Sartorius, H. Helmchen, and H. Lauter, 287–302. Berlin: Springer.

Feuchtersleben, E. von. 1845. *Lehrbuch der ärztlichen Seelenkunde.* [Textbook of medical mental science] Wien: Gerold.

Freud, S. 1908. *Charakter und Analerotik* [Character and anal eroticism], GW VII. Frankfurt: Fischer.

Griesinger, W. 1845. *Die Pathologie und Therapie der psychischen Krankheiten* [On neuropathy and mental illness]. Stuttgart: Krabbe.

Gruhle, H. W. 1956. Psychopathie [Psychopathy]. In *Lehrbuch der Nerven- und Geisteskrankheiten.* 2nd ed., ed. W. Weygandt, 664–686. Halle: Marhold.

Hare, R. D. 1970. *Psychopathy: Theory and Research.* New York: Wiley.

Hare, R. D. 1990. *The Psychopathy Checklist Revisited Manual.* Toronto, ON: Multi-Health-Systems.

Henderson, D. 1939. *Psychopathic States.* New York: Norton.

Herpertz, S., and H. Sass. 2000. Emotional Deficiency and Psychopathy. *Behavioral Sciences & the Law* 18:567–580.

Homburger, A. 1929. Versuch einer Typologie der psychopathischen Konstitution [Attempt of a typology of psychopathic constitution]. *Der Nervenarzt* 2:134–136.

Janzarik, W. 1988. *Strukturdynamische Grundlagen der Psychiatrie* [Structural–dynamic foundations of psychiatry]. Stuttgart: Enke.

Jaspers, K. 1959. *Allgemeine Psychopathologie* [General psychopathology]. 7th ed. Berlin: Springer.

Kahn, E. 1928. Die psychopathischen Persönlichkeiten [The psychopathic personalities]. In *Handbuch der Geisteskrankheiten*, vol. 5., ed. O. Bumke, 227–487. Berlin: Springer.

Karpman, B. 1941. On the Need of Separating Psychopathy into Two Distinct Clinical Types: The Symptomatic and the Idiopathic. *Journal of Criminal Psychopathology* 2:112–137.

Koch, J. L. A. 1891–1893. *Die psychopathischen Minderwertigkeiten* [The psychopathic inferiorities]. Ravensburg: Maier.

Kraepelin, E. 1896. *Psychiatrie: Ein Lehrbuch für Studirende und Ärzte* [Psychiatry: A textbook for students and doctors]. 5th ed. Leipzig: Barth.

Kraepelin, E. 1909–1915. *Psychiatrie: Ein Lehrbuch für Studirende und Ärzte* [Psychiatry: A textbook for students and doctors]. 8th ed. Leipzig: Barth.

Kretschmer, E. 1921. *Körperbau und Charakter* [Physique and character]. Berlin: Springer.

Lombroso, C. 1876. *L'uomo delinquente*. Milan: Hoepli.

Magnan, M., and M. Legrain. 1895. *Les dégénérés (état mental et syndromes épisodiques)* [The degenerates (state of mind and episodical syndromes)]. Paris: Rueff.

Maudsley, H. 1874. *Responsibility in Mental Disease*. London: King.

McCord, W., and J. McCord. 1964. *The Psychopath: An Essay on the Criminal Mind*. 2nd ed. New York: Van Norstrand.

McCrae, R., and P. Costa. 1989. The Structure of Interpersonal Traits: Wiggins's Circumplex and the Five-Factor Model. *Journal of Personality and Social Psychology* 56:586–595.

Meyer, A. 1903. An Attempt at Analysis of the Neurotic Constitution. *American Journal of Psychiatry* 14:354–367.

Millon, T. 1981. *Disorders of Personality: DSM–III: Axis II*. New York: Wiley.

Morel, B. A. 1876. *Traité des dégénérescences physiques, intellectuelles et morales de l'espèce humaine et des causes qui produisent ces variétés maladives* [Treatise on the physical, intellectual and moral degeneration of the human species]. Paris: Baillière.

Partridge, G. E. 1930. Current Conceptions of Psychopathic Personality. *American Journal of Psychiatry* 10:53–99.

Petrilowitsch, N. 1966. *Abnorme Persönlichkeiten* [Abnormal personalities]. 3rd ed. Basel: Karger.

Pinel, P. 1809. *Traité médico-philosophique sur l'aliénation mentale* [Medico-philosophical treatise on mental derangement]. 2nd ed. Paris: Brosson.

Prichard, J. C. 1835. *A Treatise on Insanity and Other Disorders Affecting the Mind.* London: Sherwood, Gilbert & Piper.

Ray, I. 1838. *A Treatise on the Medical Jurisprudence of Insanity.* Boston: Little, Brown.

Reich, W. 1933. *Charakteranalyse: Technik und Grundlagen* [Analysis of character: Techniques and basic principles]. Berlin: Selbstverlag.

Robins, L. N. 1966. *Deviant Children Grown Up: A Sociological and Psychiatric Study of Sociopathic Personality.* Baltimore: Williams & Wilkins.

Rothacker, E. 1947. *Die Schichten der Persönlichkeit* [Layers of personality]. 3rd ed. Leipzig: Barth.

Rush, B. 1827. *Medical Inquiries and Observations upon the Diseases of the Mind.* 3rd ed. Philadelphia: Kimber & Richardson.

Rush, B. 1962. *Medical Inquiries and Observation upon the Diseases of the Mind.* Philadelphia: Kimber & Richardson (Facsim. of the 1812 edition). New York: Hafner Press.

Sass, H. 1987. *Psychopathie—Soziopathie—Dissozialität: zur Differentialtypologie der Persönlichkeitsstörungen* [Psychopathy—sociopathy—dissociality: The differential typology of personality disorders]. Berlin: Springer.

Sass, H. 1990. Einheitspsychose [Unitary psychosis]. In *Psychiatry: A World Perspective: Proceedings of the 8th World Congress of Psychiatry*, ed. C. N. Stephanis, C. R. Soldatos, and A. D. Rabavilas. Athens: Congress Series 900.

Sass, H. 1992. Strukturelle und dynamische Persönlichkeitsvarianten im Vorfeld idiopathischer Psychosyndrome [Structural and dynamic variants of personality in the run-up to idiopathical brain syndromes]. In *Für und Wider die Einheitspsychose*, ed. Ch. Mundt and H. Sass, 37-48. Stuttgart: Thieme.

Sass, H., and A. R. Felthous. 2008. History and Conceptual Development of Psychopathic Disorders. In *International Handbook of Psychopathic Disorders and the Law, Volume 1: Diagnosis and Treatment*, ed. A. R. Felthous and H. Sass, 9–30. Chichester: Wiley.

Sass, H., and S. Herpertz. 1994. Psychopathic Disorder. In *Forensic Psychiatry*, ed. A. R. Felthous and P. Bowden. *Current Opinion in Psychiatry* 7: 437–441.

Sass, H., and S. Herpertz. 1995. Personality Disorders. In *A History of Clinical Psychiatry: The Origin and History of Psychiatric Disorders*, ed. G. E. Berrios and R. Porter, 633–64C. New York: New York University Press.

Sass, H., and K. Koehler. 1983. Borderline-Syndrome: Grenzgebiet oder Niemandsland? Zur klinisch-psychiatrischen Relevanz von Borderline-Diagnosen [Borderline syndromes: True borderland or no-man's-land?]. *Der Nervenarzt* 54:221–230.

Schneider, K. 1921. *Persönlichkeit und Schicksal eingeschriebener Prostituierter* [Studies on the personality and fate of registered prostitutes]. Berlin: Julius Springer.

Schneider, K. 1950. *Die psychopathischen Persönlichkeiten* [The psychopathic personalities]. 9th ed. Wien: Deuticke. (1st ed. 1923, Leipzig: Thieme).

Schultz, J. H. 1928. Die konstitutionelle Nervosität [The constitutional nervosity]. In *Handbuch der Geisteskrankheiten*, vol. 5, ed. O. Bumke, 28–111. Berlin: Springer.

Tuke, D. H. 1884. *Prichard and Symonds in Especial Relation to Mental Science with Chapters on Moral Insanity*. London: J. & A. Churchill.

Widiger, T. A. 1991. Personality Disorder Dimensional Models Proposed for DSM–IV. *Journal of Personality Disorders* 5:386–398.

Widiger, T. A., and A. Frances. 1985. The DSM–III Personality Disorders: Perspectives from Psychology. *Archives of General Psychiatry* 42:615–623.

Widiger, T. A., T. Trull, S. Hurt, J. Clarkin, and A. Frances. 1987. A Multidimensional Scaling of the DSM–III Personality Disorders. *Archives of General Psychiatry* 44:557–563.

Wiggins, J. S. 1982. Circumplex Models of Interpersonal Behavior in Clinical Psychology. In *Handbook of Research Methods in Clinical Psychology*, ed. P. C. Kendell and J. N. Butcher, 183–221. New York: Wiley.

World Health Organization. 1989. *ICD–10*. Geneva: WHO Division of Mental Health.

Zeller, A. 1840. Bericht über die Heilanstalt Winnenthal. *Medizinische Korrespondenzblaetter des Württembergischen Medizinvereins* 10:17.

Ziehen, T. H. 1905–1912. Zur Lehre von den psychopathischen Konstitutionen [The doctrine of the psychopathic constitutions]. *Charité-Annalen* 29, 31, 32, 36.

I Moral Capacities and Incapacities

3 Psychopathy and Moral Rationality

Eric Matthews

3.1 Introduction

The word "psychopathy" is used in the *Diagnostic and Statistical Manual of Mental Disorders* (fourth edition; DSM–IV; American Psychiatric Association 1994) only as a possible synonym for that work's preferred term "antisocial personality disorder" (which I shall henceforth normally abbreviate to "APD"). The essential feature of APD is said to be "a pervasive pattern of disregard for, and violation of, the rights of others" (American Psychiatric Association 1994, 645): In short, it is defined in terms of the *behavior* of the person. However, other diagnostic criteria are said to include what we might rather call *attitudes*: impulsivity, aggressiveness, callousness, cynicism, "an inflated and arrogant self-appraisal," "glib, superficial charm," irresponsibility, and so on (see American Psychiatric Association 1994, 646–647). From this description, taken at face value at least, it is hard to see how APD/psychopathy differs from simple criminality or immorality, or why it should be medicalized as a psychiatric disorder rather than treated as a simple deviation from morally desirable human behavior and attitudes. Louis Charland, for example, argues that "several core personality disorders are actually really moral, and not medical, disorders" (Charland 2004, 64), and George Agich finds one of the basic conceptual problems in APD to be "its apparent insensitivity to ... the evaluative commitments that underlie its very meaning" (Agich 1994, 244).

Other writers and researchers, however, want to differentiate between APD and psychopathy. For instance, Blair et al. (2005), in a major study of psychopathy, insist that this disorder is not simply synonymous with the DSM diagnosis of APD. They support this claim by first distinguishing between "reactive" and "instrumental" aggressiveness. "Reactive" aggression is the kind which responds to frustration or threat. APD, as defined in DSM–IV, refers, they then argue, to the behavioral pathologies associated with heightened levels of such reactive aggression. On the other hand, "instrumental" aggression is the kind which is goal-directed, a way of achieving one's ends by force or the threat of force. As such, they claim, it implies a certain kind of *emotional* dysfunction, so that heightened levels of it constitute an *emotional* rather than simply a *behavioral* disorder. The claimed difference between APD and psychopathy can then be expressed in these terms. "In short," they conclude, "psychopathy is an emotional disorder, which, if it develops into its full form, puts the individual at risk of extreme antisocial behavior" (Blair et al. 2005, 17). Nevertheless, "psychopathy," as so defined, does not seem to be *essentially* different from APD, but to be simply an extreme form of the condition. The associated emotions seem to be "disordered" only in the sense that they generate antisocial behavior, so that behavior remains the core of the definition.

Even when we include such characteristics as lack of guilt or remorse for their actions, or lack of insight into the suffering of their victims, which contribute so much to the popular image of the psychopath as a moral monster, we do not seem to have a picture which is all that different from that of an extreme type of "normal" criminal or wicked person. Any honest examination of human behavior in general, indeed, would show that callousness, or lack of concern about the feelings of others, or even lack of remorse about actions which infringe the rights of others, are not all that uncommon. It is a fairly widespread characteristic of human beings of all cultures, manifested every day in the way people treat others, especially those who are perceived as being ethnically different or socially inferior, and in more extreme forms in such phenomena as the Holocaust, the gulag, outbreaks of violence fueled by fanaticism, or behavior in times of war. This fact raises a fundamental philosophical question: What, if anything, is the difference between this kind of "normal" disregard for the rights of others and what is diagnosed as psychopathy or APD?

There only seem to be three possible answers to this question. Either we say that all behavior and attitudes which disregard other people's rights are psychopathic, the product of mental disorder; or we say that the term "psychopathy" is simply a misguided attempt to medicalize normal human disregard for moral considerations (differing, if at all, only in degree); or we find a convincing account of the difference between psychopathy and "normal" behavior. Each of the first two alternatives has its supporters, but each seems to me to be problematic. If we adopt the first, then the implications for morality and law would seem to most people unacceptable. If we take the second line, however, then we are committed to accepting that there is never any excuse for such behavior on grounds of mental illness. While not so obviously objectionable as the implications of the first alternative, this would still seem to many people to be inhumane and, as such, morally unacceptable. That leaves only the third possibility, and it is this one that I should like to explore in this chapter. I shall argue that we can distinguish between normal "*im*morality," in which people have the capacity to recognize moral considerations (they are "morally rational") but fail to use that capacity, and psychopathic "*a*morality," in which even the capacity to recognize such considerations does not exist (the psychopath lacks "moral rationality"). Clearly, such an argument requires for its support a philosophical exploration of the notion of rationality in general, and of moral rationality in particular.

3.2   Psychopathic Amorality

If it is possible to distinguish the kind of amorality which we call "psychopathic" from "normal" immorality, it must be possible to show what it is about psychopaths which grounds this distinction. In order to have some concrete basis for analysis, I need to begin with some brief descriptions, taken from the literature, of typical behavior and attitudes of real people who might be described as psychopathic. First, two examples cited by Heidi Maibom. The first, taken from Robert Hare (1993), is of a man who knocked a gas-station attendant unconscious "just to steal a case of beer that he wanted to bring to a party. He had forgotten his wallet at home and did not want to go back for it." The second is of a man released from prison on bail who, shortly after release, "murdered a waiter who asked him to leave a restaurant for rowdy behaviour" (both examples taken from Maibom 2010, 234). We may also consider an example given by the neuropsychiatrist Simon Baron-Cohen. This concerns a young man detained in a secure prison after being found guilty of murder. He, however, denies guilt, on the grounds that he was provoked by something his victim had said in reply to him when he (the killer) had asked him why he (the victim) was staring at him. "The man had replied … 'I wasn't staring at you. I was simply looking around the bar.'" The killer had regarded this reply as disrespectful, and concluded that the victim needed to be taught a lesson: so he smashed a handy beer bottle and pushed the jagged end into the victim's face, causing his victim's death (Baron-Cohen 2011, 44).

By any standards, there is clearly something pathological about all three men. One obviously abnormal characteristic is that they appear to lack any concern with the rights, interests, or feelings of their victims. This is, presumably, what lies behind the popular view among empirical researchers in the field that psychopaths suffer from a deficit in "empathy." For example,

DSM–IV says that, "Individuals with Antisocial Personality Disorder frequently lack empathy..." (American Psychiatric Association 1994, 647).
Baron-Cohen defines empathy as "our ability to identify what someone else
is thinking or feeling, and to respond to their thoughts and feelings with
an appropriate emotion" (Baron-Cohen 2011, 11). Psychopaths are then
said to be characterized by having no capacity for empathy, which means
"you have no awareness of how you come across to others, how to interact
with others, or how to anticipate their feelings or reactions" (Baron-Cohen
2011, 29). For their part, Blair et al. suggest that psychopathy is caused by
an impairment in emotional learning. This impairment is in turn caused, in
their opinion, by a deficit in systems which enable us to respond empathically to the distress of victims (Blair et al. 2005, 53): that is, in the capacity
to be so affected by the distress of others that we are inhibited from aggressive behavior toward them. So, for them too, lack of empathy, albeit in a
slightly more roundabout way, is a central feature of psychopaths.

But there is a problem about this concept of empathy which is relevant to our present concerns. Baron-Cohen's definition lumps together
two rather different elements, and thereby glosses over the difference. The
"ability to identify what someone else is thinking or feeling" is a *cognitive*
ability, which could be present regardless of the way the person responded
to the thoughts and feelings thus identified, and the lack of which might
well be explicable in terms of defective brain systems (like any other cognitive deficiency). However, to talk about "respond[ing] ... with an *appropriate*
emotion [my italics]" is to invoke, not neuroscientific facts, but socially
rooted value judgments. Blair and his colleagues show some recognition of
this: In their account, the lack of empathy is used to explain the inability to
learn what is regarded in society as an appropriate response to the distress
of others. But their account, too, is open to objection, on grounds that will
be explained a little later on.

Why is this criticism of Baron-Cohen relevant? First of all, because his
definition of empathy, with its failure to distinguish these different elements, and his claim that psychopaths lack it, implies that anyone who is
capable of empathy will necessarily feel "appropriate" emotions, such as
distress at the suffering of others. However, his explanatory theory holds
that nonpsychopaths have levels of empathy above zero. The difficulty
then is the fact, already mentioned, that many nonpsychopaths are capable
of sadistic violence toward others, for which they appear to feel no remorse.
Indeed, they logically could not engage in sadism *unless* they were capable
of identifying what their victims are thinking or feeling. To intentionally
cause pain to someone else, it is logically necessary that one should know

that the other person is feeling pain—I could not be sadistic toward a stone, say, or a block of wood (unless I deludedly thought these objects were in fact persons, with feelings such as pain). Indeed, what shows that psychopaths *do* have, at least in some degree, the capacity to identify what someone else is thinking or feeling (the *cognitive* element of the concept of "empathy") is precisely that they are often manipulative and disdainful of others' feelings, as Grant Gillett points out (Gillett 2010, 285f.). Equally, someone who entirely lacked this cognitive capacity to identify other people's feelings would not only be incapable of being taught to feel distress at their suffering, but also of learning to manipulate others' feelings or be disdainful of them. The notion of empathy thus seems inadequate as the basis for a distinction between psychopathic amoralism and "normal" immorality.

The other objection to the "zero degrees of empathy" theorists is more directly relevant to moral philosophy. It is that they assume that, essentially, moral action is the expression of a certain human *feeling*, of concern for the distress of others, and that this feeling is a nonrational "given" of human psychology. In this, they are following in the tradition of the "sentimentalist" account of the nature of morality, espoused, for instance, by Hume, and a critique of such philosophical sentimentalism will therefore be a further objection to the explanation of the difference between psychopaths and others in terms of degrees of empathy. To develop such a critique, we need to begin by reminding ourselves of some salient features of Hume's account of the relation between sentiment and reason in morality. Reason is allowed some role in deciding "the pernicious or useful tendency of qualities and actions," but what is essential to morality, according to Hume, is a certain *sentiment*. Sometimes, he refers to this as the sentiment of "humanity," consisting in a "feeling for the happiness of mankind, and a resentment of their misery" (Hume 1975, 286). However, elsewhere, for instance in the *Treatise of Human Nature*, Hume speaks rather of a sentiment of "sympathy," our capacity to "enter into the sentiments of others" (Hume 1978, 318), as the basis for morality. In Book III, Part III, Section VI of the *Treatise*, Hume says, "the happiness of strangers affects us by sympathy alone. To that principle, therefore, we are to ascribe the sentiment of approbation, which arises from the survey of all those virtues, that are useful to society, or to the person possess'd of them. These form the most considerable part of morality" (Hume 1978, 619). Hume's "sympathy" thus seems very like Baron-Cohen's "empathy," but it is worth saying that Hume also acknowledges that sympathy is "the soul or animating principle" also of other, not so morally admirable, passions, such as "pride, ambition, avarice, curiosity, revenge or lust" (Hume 1978, 363).

Moral behavior at its core, on this view, is nonrational. For Hume, the "sentiments" which motivate our actions, and which are expressed in our moral judgments, are contingent facts of (some people's) nature, and reason's role is only to find the most effective way to achieve the ends implicit in these sentiments. This view depends in its turn on a particularly narrow conception of reason, as no more than the human capacity for establishing truth by inference. "All reasonings may be divided into two kinds, namely, demonstrative reasoning, or that concerning relations of ideas, and moral reasoning, or that concerning matter of fact and existence" (Hume 1975, 35). (Hume's eighteenth-century use of the term "moral" here may be a little confusing in the present context: he is not using it to refer to reasoning about morality, but, as he says, "that concerning matter of fact and existence"—what we might call "inductive" reasoning). But establishing truth, whether, as we would say, analytic or synthetic, cannot of itself, he argues, achieve more than "the cool assent of the understanding," and this does not have "any tendency to regulate our lives and actions" (Hume 1975, 172). If ethics is to be practical, therefore, that is, to be able to influence what we do, it must appeal to sentiment, rather than reason. Blair and Baron-Cohen seem to assume the conclusion for which Hume argues (though translated into the idiom of modern neuroscience). What makes most of us who are not psychopaths refrain from excessive instrumental aggressiveness against others, they imply, is not, or not primarily, a rational apprehension of the moral wrongness of such behavior, but simply our possession of a brain mechanism which gives rise to inhibiting feelings, or which allows us to learn to inhibit aggression by making use of our feelings of empathy.

However, whether expressed in terms of "sentiments" or in terms of "interconnected brain regions," such assumptions are at least questionable. To see this, we need only to examine again the three examples of psychopathic behavior described earlier. Nonpsychopathic people could have committed equally violent actions, with an equal lack of remorse or guilt. They might even consistently behave in this violent fashion. The lack of empathy, in itself, cannot therefore be what defines "psychopathic" amoralism. The difference seems to lie rather in the ways in which the person thinks it appropriate to *explain* his behavior. The first psychopath says he knocked the gas station attendant unconscious *because he did not want the inconvenience of going home to get his wallet* to pay for the case of beer. The second says he murdered the waiter *because he objected to the latter's request to leave the restaurant*. The third man felt no remorse for his action and pleaded not guilty to a particularly brutal murder *because the man he had killed had answered him "disrespectfully."* What is strange about these explanations is that they betray a complete failure to understand their inappropriateness. Above all, no one could intelligibly offer them if they understood that these actions were contrary to moral standards, so that no normal person would find these three explanations even intelligible in the relevant context. In this sense, psychopaths are human beings who do not recognize moral considerations as applying to certain kinds of actions and the reasons for performing them, or, more often, for refraining from them. This could be expressed by saying that they are defective in a certain aspect of practical rationality, which might be called "moral rationality." To use a term which was sometimes used before the invention of the concept of psychopathy, they suffer from "moral insanity."

Psychopaths may *appear* to accept conventional moral rules and standards. But empirical research in this field suggests that this is merely appearance. They fail to recognize the distinction which most people— even children from the age of about three years—can make between "moral" and "conventional" transgressions. A "conventional" transgression is one which infringes some more or less arbitrary rule: for example, a rule which might exist in a school requiring boys to wear a particular style of cap on school days whenever out of doors. Such a rule ought to be obeyed only because, and for as long as, the school authorities insist on it. It has no rational justification but is purely "contingent." Thus, someone who breaches such a rule does not need to offer any such justification in explanation of his or her action: The psychopath is thus in no different a position from anyone else in such cases. A "moral" transgression, on the other hand, is one which infringes a rule which can be justified in terms of moral standards: for example, doing something harmful to another person (such as knocking them unconscious) offends against the moral rule that we must not harm others. Psychopaths do not appear, as we have seen, to be aware of the need to justify actions which infringe moral rules. If, for example, their actions cause harm to their victims, their explanations of those actions tend to make no reference to this harm, but only to their own wishes, interests, purposes, and so forth. If they acknowledge their action as transgressing a rule at all, therefore, they do not distinguish between a moral and a conventional rule (see Blair et al. 2005, 58f.). In this sense, they do not really understand the concept of morality and so are incapable of moral rationality.

Saying all this is quite compatible with saying that psychopaths do not lack rationality in other recognized senses. For instance, they may have as much capacity as nonpsychopaths for Hume's two types of reasoning, concerning relations of ideas and concerning matters of fact and existence. Having the capacity for the latter type would make it possible, as it does with other people, to engage in "instrumental reasoning," or reasoning concerning efficient means to achieve one's ends. Assaulting someone in order to acquire possession of a case of beer is one *effective* way to achieve this end, though it is also a *morally unacceptable* means. Psychopaths are not, as the popular description has it, "animals," incapable of any kind of rational thought, and to describe them as such seems morally undesirable.

Being "morally insane" is nevertheless different from being straight-forwardly immoral. Immoral people are those who are capable of understanding that certain actions, including some of their own, are normally considered to be morally wrong, with all that that implies about intelligible explanations, but are not sufficiently constrained by this knowledge to avoid acting in morally wrong ways. However, practical rationality includes more than moral rationality: That is, the intelligible reasons for acting or not acting are not all moral. To be morally rational is not necessarily to act only and always for moral reasons in appropriate cases (otherwise, none of us would be morally rational!); rather, it is to be capable of recognizing what count as "moral reasons" and "appropriate cases."

Equally, moral insanity is different from what Philippa Foot calls "ideological immoralism": that is, the attitude of those, like Thrasymachus in Plato's *Republic*, Nietzsche, or André Gide, who "queried whether human goodness and badness are what they are supposed to be" and brought "arguments in favour of some different standard of human goodness" (Foot 2001, 20). Such an immoralist might, for instance, argue that the truly admirable human being was one who engaged in ruthless violence in pursuit of his ends: for example, by killing someone who did not show him what he regarded as proper respect. They understand the concept of moral standards, and of the need to morally justify one's actions, but do not have the same idea of what those moral standards are as most people. In this sense, the ideological immoralist, too, is morally rational.

The psychopath, by contrast, offers an argument in *explanation* of his or her behavior, but does not see that what is required is a moral *justification*, or at least an *excuse*, for what he or she has done. It is for this reason that psychopathic amoralism is distinctive. Psychopaths do not merely behave contrary to moral standards, or advocate alternative moral standards to those generally accepted, but seem in some sense not even to *understand* the notion of a moral standard in any "serious" sense, that is, as meaning anything more than a conventionally accepted rule. If we are to say that this means that psychopaths, while capable of being rational in Hume's two senses, and of being practically rational in other respects, are not "morally rational," then we must explicate further what that term means, including how it differs from other forms of rationality. The other forms of rationality mentioned require only certain cognitive capacities—the ability to see what does or does not follow logically from the truth of a proposition, or to see what is, as a matter of fact, in one's own self-interest. There is no reason for thinking that these capacities are not as widespread among psychopaths as among the general population (certainly nothing in the definition of a "psychopath"). The question thus becomes this: Are such capacities sufficient for moral rationality, too?

3.3   Kant and Moral Rationality

Kant is generally regarded as a paradigm case—perhaps even the clearest case—of a moral rationalist. However, I shall argue that Kant's account of practical rationality fails to explain how a psychopath can be perfectly capable of logical thought—of recognizing logical inconsistency—and of instrumental, or "means–end," rationality, and yet be incapable of *moral* reasoning. First, however, we must explore the sense in which Kant is a moral rationalist. The core of ethics, for Kant, is the "pure," rational or metaphysical, part. Because of this, we cannot, Kant argues, base ethics on any *empirical* investigation—for example, of human psychology or sociology. Rather, it must be based on pure practical reason. Kant goes on to explain what he means by this:

for example, the command "thou shalt not lie" does not hold only for human beings, as if other rational beings did not have to heed it, and so with all other moral laws properly so called; ... therefore, the ground of obligation here must not be sought in the nature of the human being or in the circumstances of the world in which he is placed, but a priori simply in concepts of pure reason... (Kant 1998, 2)

A *rational* argument for saying that something is morally obligatory (or forbidden) is thus, for Kant, one based on concepts whose understanding does not depend on any specific features of human beings as such—for instance, their particular psychological constitution. If moral action were thought of as rooted in certain specifically human characteristics, then, the argument seems to be, the question of whether or not something was morally required would depend on *contingent* facts about human psychology, which may, of course, vary from individual to individual. Kant therefore concludes that only an action which is done only in order to conform to a law which must apply to any rational being of any species can count as having true moral worth. A being could therefore be morally rational without sharing any psychological features with us.

It seems to be Kant's view, then, that "rationality" is an attribute which can meaningfully be predicated of beings of very different psychological constitutions—of beings who have emotions and of those who do not, for example, and of beings whose emotional lives take very different forms. I want to argue that, although this may be true of purely theoretical rationality—logicality, instrumental rationality, scientific rationality—it cannot be true of *practical* rationality, including what is most relevant in the present context, namely, moral rationality. A being cannot meaningfully be said to be "rational" in any sense, of course, unless that being has at least one capacity in common with human beings, namely, the capacity to formulate thoughts, which can be true or false. But such a being does not need anything else in common with us—how he/she/it feels about the thoughts so formulated, for instance—in order to be capable of thinking logically—of recognizing and seeking to avoid inconsistencies between one thought and another. Nor are such common features necessary in order to be able to recognize instrumental, means–end, relations—for example, that hitting someone over the head is an effective method of rendering them unconscious; or to be able to see what empirical evidence tends to confirm or to refute a particular hypothesis.

However, something more in common does seem to be necessary if we are to talk of a being as *practically* rational. The possibility of practical rationality depends on our being able to develop a concept of a kind of reasoning which would be capable of *motivating* our actions. This seems to mean developing criteria for saying that some reasons for acting are more rational than others. It is a frequent criticism of Kantian ethics that it fails to provide such criteria, just because of his insistence that rational actions are not motivated by desires. Kant's picture, after all, as has been argued above, is of rational agency as a capacity which can be realized in a variety of types of species, which may have no particular desires in common. It seems to follow that it could be realized in a being who had no desires at all (if such a being is conceivable). To make a rational choice to act morally (or even prudentially) is then to make a choice independently of any desires. The problem with this view is expressed, for example, by Alasdair MacIntyre, when he says,

Kant's conception of moral motivation is flawed. On Kant's view, the basis of moral motivation lies not in one's desires, but in a recognition that some type of action is morally required or prohibited. But I was and am unable to understand how we could be motivated to act as we should by anything but our desires. (MacIntyre 2009: 116f.)

In view of this, it seems, Kant must somehow show, if he can, that the rationality of moral action is of the same type as cognitive rationality.

Some commentators (presumably, partly in an attempt to avoid this difficulty) have interpreted Kant's requirement of universalizability as meaning that maxims must accord with "what everyone wants done." If one attends to what Kant actually says, however (including in those passages already cited here), then it becomes obvious, as Onora O'Neill says, that this is a misinterpretation. As O'Neill says, Kant "asserts that [autonomous] agents need only to impose a certain sort of consistency on their actions if they are to avoid doing what is morally unacceptable" (O'Neill 1998, 505). Saying that morally acceptable maxims must be universalizable, according to O'Neill, is saying that the underlying principles by which we guide our more specific intentions must be consistently applicable to all relevant individuals (including, of course, the person proposing the maxim). This, she says, is "an uncompromisingly rationalist foundation for ethics" (O'Neill 1998, 505). If a maxim is consistently universalizable in this sense, she says, "we at least know that the action will not be morally unworthy, and will not be a violation of duty" (O'Neill 1998, 510).

On a later page, O'Neill gives a number of examples of maxims which can*not* be consistently universalized, and which are therefore "morally unworthy." Two of these are the maxims that everyone should become a slave, and that everyone should become a slaveholder. These, fairly clearly, could not become laws applying to everyone without logical contradiction. Action on either of them, O'Neill concludes, would reveal moral unworthiness, because "it could be undertaken only by one who makes of himself or herself a special case" (O'Neill 1998, 521). It should be said at this point, since it is relevant to the argument below, that O'Neill seems to be mistaken here. Individuals could logically accept such a maxim only if they were willing to formulate it in a way which allowed *exceptions*: but that need not mean that they made of *themselves* a special case. I could not, without self-contradiction, propose that everyone should be a slave, since one can be a slave only if there is someone else who is a slaveholder. However, I could logically propose that everyone else should be the slave of one person. That one person need not, however, be me—it could, for instance, be the Queen of England. There would be no *logical* problem with such a maxim, whatever other kinds of problems there might be.

Just because O'Neill's interpretation is true to Kant's own text, it reveals very clearly the deficiencies in Kant's conception of moral rationality. These deficiencies can be exhibited in various ways. First, as O'Neill herself implies, the most that the universalizability test *could* establish would be that certain maxims were *not* moral laws because they could not be consistently applied to all relevant cases. Thus, there could not be a moral law that everyone should be a slave. But there seems to be nothing irrational, in the sense of "logically self-contradictory," about the proposition that everyone else should be enslaved to one particular person. All that is necessary to achieve universalization without self-contradiction is to make the set of relevant beings mean the set of persons other than the one selected. O'Neill attempts to reinforce the connection with *moral* unworthiness by claiming that the exception must be the person proposing the maxim, but, as was argued above, there is no reason why the requirements of logic cannot be met without that being the case.

However, even apart from this, Kant's account is open to question because it seems to provide no means of rationally establishing that certain maxims are *positively* worthy. The positive maxim that no one should be anyone else's slave is certainly universalizable without self-contradiction, and virtually everyone would accept that it has moral worth. But there is equally no self-contradiction in the universal maxim that no one should wear brown shoes on Fridays, which seems like a clear instance of a morally arbitrary rule. Whatever makes the difference in their moral standing, therefore, it cannot be to do with consistent universalizability. In short, Kant's criterion may be, as O'Neill says, "uncompromisingly rationalist," but his notion of what this involves is defective.

3.4   The Turn to Aristotle

In order to develop an acceptable conception of *practical* rationality, it was earlier suggested, we need to provide a criterion or criteria, not of certain kinds of relation between the truth of one proposition and another, but of the rationality or irrationality of certain *actions*. And in order to speak of *moral* rationality, as a particular kind of practical rationality, we should have to show that there was a subclass of these criteria by which we could determine that certain kinds of action were rational in a specifically *moral* way. But how are we to arrive at such criteria? Actions can be "rational," surely, only if they are done *for good reasons*. For instance, it is rational for me to save money if I do so in order to have reserves in case of emergency, or to provide for my children when I am gone, or to put down the deposit on a house which I need. It is not rational for me to save money, however, if I do so simply because, like the miser in the story, I like to count it up every night (and never intend to use it for any good purpose). Good reasons for acting must be related, as MacIntyre implies, to our desires and wishes, and these in turn to our needs and purposes.

These needs and purposes that we have are, plainly, specifically *human*: If other types of being share any of them, then to that extent we can say that those beings are *human-like*. However, it follows that what counts as a rational action cannot be considered apart from the type of being that is being said to act, and the kind of life which that sort of being characteristically lives. In effect, this means that good reasons for acting must be intelligible as such to other beings of the same type. People act rationally, if this is right, to the extent that they intentionally act for reasons which can be generally seen to be "good" in the light of a shared conception of typically human needs. Their actions can in this case be regarded as "making sense" to anyone who shares this conception. So to be capable of acting rationally entails that one must oneself be able to understand this conception—to know what *counts* as making sense in the particular context in question.

Context is important. Human activity takes place in different contexts. Economic rationality is one such example. It consists in acting for what count as good reasons in this sphere, which is determined by the nature of that sphere. To be economically rational requires one to understand the nature of that sphere, and so what count as good reasons for acting in it. This understanding need not be explicit—people can be economically rational without having degrees in economics: In most cases, it will be intuitive, manifested more in one's actions than in one's statements. And it is possible for people whose behavior is economically *irrational* to have such understanding, while failing to act upon it. A case might be someone who, on an impulse, goes on a spending spree which consumes all his savings and leaves him with an unsustainable debt. Such a person can be criticized in economic terms, if he is capable of recognizing the economic irrationality of his behavior, even though, in a different context, one might admire him as bold and reckless. However, someone who had no idea (e.g., because of his cultural background) of how a market economy works—who did not, that is, have any conception of economic rationality in the required sense—could not be criticized, at least in these terms. Political rationality is another such sphere. It is arguable, for instance, that it is politically rational for the government of one nation-state to pass false information to the government of another, in order to gain some advantage for its own citizens. But someone who had no conception of what international politics was about would be unable either to act rationally in this context or to appreciate the rationality of someone else's actions. (Such a person might, for example, reject such action as "irrational" because this is not a *morally* good reason for acting.)

This brings us to our main concern, moral rationality. As well as asking whether someone is acting in an economically or politically rational way, we can ask whether someone has good moral reasons for acting as he or she does. And just as what count as economically good reasons is determined by the nature of economics, so what counts as moral rationality is determined by the essential nature of morality. For the sake of brevity, I shall say (dogmatically, but I think in accordance with most people's intuitions) that what distinguishes moral action is that it is action in which the desires and interests of others, or of society as a whole, are considered, as well as, or even in some cases in preference to, those of the agent: in short, an *unselfish* action. An action which is motivated, or mainly motivated, by a concern for someone else's well-being is done for a morally good reason. Examples might be giving someone a present because it would please the recipient, or taking risks to save someone's life, or devoting one's life to the service of others even though it means poverty for oneself. One which is motivated solely by a concern for the agent's own desires or interests, especially if it is intended to cause harm to those of other people, is done for a morally bad reason. Examples might be pursuing personal gain at the expense of others, or violently attacking someone because that person has made fun of one, or spreading malicious gossip about a rival candidate for a job in order to improve one's own chances. Pursuit of one's own self-interest is "rational" in the sense of being a generally intelligible motive for acting: but if one can pursue it only at the expense of other people's interests, feelings, wishes, and so forth, then it is not *morally* rational.

As in the other cases mentioned, to be a morally rational person requires one to be able to understand the concept of morality, and so what are, and what are not, morally good reasons for acting. However, one can be a morally rational person while still acting, occasionally or regularly, in a purely selfish or even deliberately malicious way. To act immorally logically requires one to understand what moral norms are, as much as to act morally. And again, of course, the understanding need not be explicit or theoretical. For most of us, most of the time, it is acquired by early upbringing and the habits of behavior thus instilled, including a recognition that we ought to feel shame or guilt for certain actions or motives. Someone who lacks this kind of understanding altogether, by definition, lacks what I am calling "moral rationality": He or she is not morally *ir*rational, so much as morally *non*rational.

Contrary to Kant, moral rationality, like other forms of practical rationality, cannot meaningfully be ascribed to beings who are not like human beings in relevant respects. It is the needs and typical structure of human beings, and the character of human life, on this account, which enable us to decide what count as morally good and bad reasons for acting. To put it differently, we should simply not be in a position to decide whether a being constituted in a totally different way from us, such that it related to conspecifics in a completely different way, had a "morality," or whether it had morally good or bad reasons for acting as it did. Given what was said just above, it seems that one human characteristic above all which is required for what we understand by a morality is indeed "empathy" in the sense of the ability to be aware that other human beings (and perhaps some nonhuman creatures) have thoughts, feelings, desires, plans, and so on like one's own. Without such awareness, we logically could not have concern for promoting the well-being and avoiding the harm of others. However, "empathy" in this sense is not to be *identified* with that concern: As was argued earlier, the possession of empathy in this sense is as much a logical requirement of sadism as of a moral concern for others. In order for us to have moral concern, we need in addition to learn that it is morally required that we should promote well-being and avoid harm, but this is a matter of how we *use* the knowledge gained by empathy. It does seem plausible, at least, to say that we could not understand the importance of moral concern unless we had some other typical characteristics of human beings, such as a Humean "feeling for the happiness of mankind, and a resentment of their misery." But this feeling is then a *precondition* for being able to possess moral rationality, not, as it was for Hume, a *substitute* for it. In order to be morally rational, we need to be able to understand the concept of morality; in order to understand that concept, we need to have empathy and to have feelings of concern for others (as most human beings do). Someone who is capable of moral rationality is capable of making a choice in cases in which there is a conflict between kinds of rationality. Such a person can, for example, choose between doing what is economically, politically, or selfishly rational and doing what is required for morally good reasons.

This account of moral rationality, and of practical rationality more generally, has been developed by reflection on some thoughts of Philippa Foot about "natural goodness" (Foot herself acknowledges the origins of these ideas in the work of Elizabeth Anscombe and Michael Thompson). It is possible, Foot argues, in the case of living things, to attribute a natural goodness to "living things themselves and to their parts, characteristics, and operations" (Foot 2001, 26–27). This goodness is "intrinsic or 'autonomous' … in that it depends directly on the relation of an individual to the 'life form' of the species" (Foot 2001, 27). To make the connection with evaluation, Foot goes on, we need to interpret the concept of a life form of a species in a *teleological* sense: a part, characteristic, or operation is naturally good to the extent that it is causally or teleologically related to the typical life of the species. That is, such parts "all have to do, directly or indirectly, with self-maintenance, as by defence and the obtaining of nourishment, or with the reproduction of the individual, as by the building of nests" (Foot 2001, 31). To the extent that a characteristic or operation achieves these purposes, it can be called "good." And, by applying such norms of goodness, and corresponding norms of badness, to an individual animal of the species, it can be judged either to "be as it should be" or as "defective" (Foot 2001, 34). And these judgments hold, Foot maintains, even although neither the animal or plant itself, nor we human beings as observers of it, endorse it. The term "goodness" in "human moral goodness" has the same meaning, according to Foot, as it does in "natural goodness," defined in terms of these natural norms. It relates to the conditions of life of the human species: though we must recognize the immensely greater complexity of human life, which cannot be limited to the purely biological needs of self-maintenance and reproduction. Interest in the (moral) goodness of human actions, Foot says, "has rather to do with the choice of lives, the education of children, or with decisions of social policy" (Foot 2001, 39). To live a good human life, people need such characteristics as the ability to communicate with each other and to respond to each other in typically human ways, together, of course, with the physical and mental preconditions of these abilities.

The important point, from our present point of view, is that a human being may be defective if he or she lacks one of the preconditions for living a fully "human" life. Anscombe, Thompson, and Foot all rightly agree that this line of thought is essentially Aristotelian. In determining what is the good for a human being—what Aristotle calls *eudaimonia* (misleadingly translated very often as "happiness," but better rendered as "well-being" or "flourishing")—we have, in Aristotle's view, to consider above all what the *function* of a human being is (Aristotle 2004, 25 [1097b]). This function must, he argues, be something which is proper to human beings as such—something which is, in other words, peculiar to the human species, as distinct from other kinds of being. Human beings share the characteristic of being alive with all other living beings, including plants and nonhuman animals. They share the property of sentience with many other animals. What is peculiar to human beings as such, Aristotle concludes, is neither life nor sentience, but a capacity to organize one's activities in accordance with a rational principle (practical rationality). The function of a human being is thus to act in accordance with a rational principle. Someone who consistently acts in this way exhibits an "excellence" or "virtue" of humanity. So "the conclusion is that the good for man is an activity of the soul in accordance with virtue" (Aristotle 2004, 26 [1098a]). The opposite of a "virtue" is a "vice": so to be a bad human being is to fail to act in accordance with rational principles. Unlike Kant, then, Aristotle defines moral goodness and badness, and so moral rationality, in terms of what is specific to human nature, which must be itself defined in relation to the specifically *human* mode of life, including typically human needs.

A clue to Aristotle's conception of this typically human mode of life can be found at the very beginning of the *Nicomachean Ethics*. He says there that the science which studies the supreme good for human beings must be politics, which is concerned with the good of the whole community, rather than that of any individual as such (Aristotle 2004, 4–5 [1094b]). The implication is that to govern one's actions by a rational principle is to act in accordance with what is necessary for living well together as human beings. Grant Gillett expresses this well by saying that moral consideration "for most of us, flows from a life of engagement with others" (Gillett 2010, 283). Someone is vicious, on this account, if they do not *wish* to act in accordance with the rational principles needed to govern our engagement with others, but they are pathological if they *cannot* act in accordance with such principles. The psychopath may be conceived as such a pathological type of human being.

We can now try to draw together some of the main threads of the argument. In this chapter, I have attempted mainly to do two things. First, I have sought to clarify the difference between psychopathic amoralism and "normal" immorality. Secondly, I have tried to use these reflections on psychopathy to shed light on what it means to be morally rational. On the first question, I have suggested that we can speak of "normal," nonpathological, immorality only when there is a genuine *alternative* to immoral action available to the agent. That is, it must be possible for the agent to recognize the force of moral considerations, or, as I would express it, to be "morally rational." A normally immoral person *chooses* in this sense to act immorally. The alternative to acting morally may be of various kinds. It may be to act on the basis of some other sort of practical rationality. Thus, the Macchiavellian politician may do terrible things on the basis of political rationality—*raison d'état*, the ruthless businessman may trample on the rights of his workers or customers in an economically rational pursuit—of profit, and the hedonist may exploit and manipulate others in pursuit of selfish pleasure. Or someone may be motivated to act immorally on *irrational* grounds—by pure impulse or blind passion, or by some irrational belief system, such as religious or antireligious fanaticism. (In the latter case, acting may require some self-deception—a belief that what the agent is doing is really based on moral grounds.) The important thing in all these cases is that there is nothing to prevent the person from being able to understand the relevance of moral considerations—however unlikely it may be in practice that he or she would allow such considerations to affect what he or she does. If we are to distinguish psychopaths from the normally immoral, therefore, it must be because there *are* obstacles to their being able to understand these considerations. What those obstacles may be in detail is a matter for empirical inquiry, but their general character follows from the nature of moral rationality, which brings us to the second question. I have sought to argue against the Kantian impersonal concept of moral rationality—the view that to act for moral reasons is to act in accordance with a rule which can be universally applied to any rational being, regardless of whether that being is human. That seems to me to ignore the fact that there are different ways of being practically rational, so that a being could be perfectly rational in the sense of being, say, instrumentally rational (what Max Weber called *zweckrational*) while not being morally rational. Moral rationality does seem to be, in a more Aristotelian way, dependent on certain specifically human features, such as the capacity for empathy and the ability which that makes possible to develop feelings of benevolence and resistance to causing harm to others. Researchers on psychopathy have suggested that some psychopaths may lack other kinds of rationality too—they may be impulsive or fail to consult their own long-term self-interest. However, there are clearly other psychopaths who are perfectly rational in the sense of being able to plan efficient means to achieve their ends. What seems essential to the concept of a psychopath is a lack of those abilities which most people have which make it possible for them to be morally rational.

References

Agich, G. J. 1994. Evaluative Judgment and Personality Disorder. In *Philosophical Perspectives on Psychiatric Diagnostic Classification*, ed. J. Z. Sadler, O. P. Wiggins, and M. A. Schwartz, 233–245. Baltimore: Johns Hopkins University Press.

American Psychiatric Association. 1994. *Diagnostic and Statistical Manual of Mental Disorders*. 4th ed. Washington, D.C.: American Psychiatric Association.

Aristotle. 2004. *The Nicomachean Ethics*, translated by J. A. K. Thomson, revised by H. Tredinnick, Introduction by J. Barnes. London: Penguin Books.

Baron-Cohen, S. 2011. *Zero Degrees of Empathy: A New Theory of Human Cruelty*. London: Allen Lane.

Blair, J., D. Mitchell, and K. Blair. 2005. *The Psychopath: Emotion and the Brain.* Oxford: Blackwell.

Charland, L. C. 2004. Character: Moral Treatments and the Personality Disorders. In *The Philosophy of Psychiatry: A Companion*, ed. J. Radden, 64–77. Oxford: Oxford University Press.

Foot, P. 2001. *Natural Goodness.* Oxford: Clarendon Press.

Gillett, G. 2010. Intentional Action, Moral Responsibility, and Psychopaths. In *Responsibility and Psychopathy: Interfacing Law, Psychiatry and Philosophy*, ed. L. Malatesti and J. McMillan, 283–298. Oxford: Oxford University Press.

Hare, R. 1993. *Without Conscience: The Disturbing World of Psychopaths among Us.* New York: Pocket Books.

Hume, D. 1975. *Enquiries Concerning Human Understanding and Concerning the Principles of Morals*, ed. L. Selby-Bigge, 3rd ed., with text revised and notes by P. H. Nidditch. Oxford: Clarendon Press.

Hume, D. 1978. *A Treatise of Human Nature*, ed. L. A. Selby-Bigge, 2nd ed., with text revised and notes by P. H. Nidditch. New York: Clarendon Press.

Kant, I. 1998. *Groundwork of the Metaphysics of Morals*, ed. M. Gregor, with Introduction by C. Korsgaard. Cambridge: Cambridge University Press.

MacIntyre, A. 2009. The Illusion of Self-Sufficiency. In *Conversations on Ethics*, ed. A. Voorhoeve, 111–131. Oxford: Oxford University Press.

Maibom, H. 2010. Rationalism, Emotivism, and the Psychopath. In *Responsibility and Psychopathy: Interfacing Law, Psychiatry, and Philosophy*, ed. L. Malatesti and J. McMillan, 227–241. Oxford: Oxford University Press.

O'Neill, O. 1998. Consistency in Action. In *Ethical Theory, Volume 2*, ed. J. Rachels, 256–281. Oxford: Oxford University Press.

4 Without Fellow Feeling

Heidi L. Maibom

The impoverished emotional lives of psychopaths capture the attention of most people. Psychopaths have impaired empathy, sympathy, guilt, remorse, shame, and love and their emotional experiences tend to be shallow (Cleckley 1982; Hare 2004).[1] What stands out most is their disregard for the well-being of others. Psychopaths are extraordinarily egocentric; they do not take the perspective of their victims and callously disregard their pain and suffering. They have no compunction about manipulating and lying to others. For psychopaths, an action's harmfulness does not appear to count against, and sometimes counts in favor of, performing it.[2] Psychopaths appear to care about the plight of others only when it is in their personal interests to do so; others are mere means to their ends. If they must hurt others to get what they want, so be it. Instrumental violence is particularly common in psychopaths compared to other violent offenders (Blair et al. 2005). This singular lack of a moral sense is unique among the mental disorders and has received much attention, not only by psychopathy researchers, but also by theorists from other fields hoping to gain knowledge that will shed light on their own area of research. Many philosophers, psychologists, and neuroscientists believe that understanding psychopathic immorality will give us tools for understanding ordinary morality, legal theorists hope that it will help to determine psychopaths' criminal responsibility, and the psychiatric profession that it will help provide better treatment options.

Adam Smith and David Hume famously thought that our propensity to feel with our fellow man, which I call empathy/sympathy, lies at the foundation of the moral sentiments, which, in turn, are the source of our moral judgments (Hume 1777/1975; Smith 1759/1976). Psychopaths are usually presented as being profoundly immoral or amoral individuals who are characterized by deficient emotions, particularly of the moral variety.

By comparison, their decision-making impairments have received relatively little attention, particularly in recent moral psychology (but see Maibom 2005). Psychopathy seems to lend strong support to classical sentimentalism, for in this condition we seem to find proof that lack of empathy or sympathy leads to a lack of a moral sense.

A number of theorists have been inspired by the sentimentalist interpretation of the psychopaths' moral impairment. Building on Seymour Feshbach's (1964) theory of aggression inhibition, James Blair (1997) proposed that psychopaths have a deficient violence inhibition mechanism (VIM). The VIM responds to signs of distress in others by inhibiting the ongoing actions of the agent. Under normal circumstances, this leads a person causing another distress to stop doing so. This is because it is highly aversive to witness distress in others. Ultimately, this mechanism causes prevention or inhibition of distress-provoking actions, gives rise to moral emotions, such as guilt and remorse, and is the source of our ability to make categorical moral judgments. Without a properly functioning VIM, a person will be unable to make true moral judgments and (properly) experience moral sentiments. In effect, the VIM is an empathy mechanism, implementing both a tendency to feel with others—as it is the aversive emotional reaction to others' pain that induces the subject to inhibit his or her aggression—and a benevolent attitude toward them. Though Blair no longer talks of a VIM, the basic idea remains; the defective neural wiring associated with the emotional responses characteristic of empathy plays a central role in psychopaths' moral deficit (Blair et al. 2005).

Shaun Nichols (2004) replaces the VIM with a concern mechanism (CM), which in combination with knowledge of norms produces moral judgment. Nichols's idea of empathy owes much to Daniel Batson's (1991) empathy–altruism hypothesis. Batson famously claims that empathic concern—"other-oriented emotion elicited by and congruent with the perceived welfare of someone in need" (Batson 2011, 11)—produces altruistic motivation. "Concern" for Nichols is much like "empathic concern"; it is a set of warm sympathetic feelings for the victim of some misfortune.[3] Nichols sees concern as the emotion(s) that backs harm norms. Psychopaths lack a CM though they have knowledge of norms. Therefore, the affective infusing of norms (by concern) that is required to produce categorical moral judgments—judgments of wrong and right—is not achieved in psychopaths. This explains their lack of moral sense. These sentimentalist readings of psychopaths' moral deficit—I call them "the empathy/sympathy hypothesis" for short—are compelling, but are they true? Here, I leave aside the decision-making deficits that also play an important role in psychopaths' immorality (Maibom 2005) and focus on the emotions. I argue that the role of empathy and sympathy in ordinary morality is not what we have been led to believe. Other emotions, traditionally not considered as relevant because they are not moral (enough), are likely to play a significant role in moral psychology. This changes the way we think about morally relevant emotions and has consequences for how to interpret psychopathy. First, however, we must consider what sorts of emotions empathy and sympathy are supposed to be and the evidence in favor of their playing an important role in preventing violence.

4.1 The Many Facets of Empathy (and Sympathy)

I am going to present what I take to be the most common characterization of empathy, sympathy, emotional contagion, perspective taking, and personal distress. There are divergent uses in the literature, but they are mainly terminological. What I ultimately argue will not depend on nomenclature, but on how characteristics of these emotions and capacities cluster together and the consequences thereof. One can therefore disagree with my particular choice of terms yet agree with my conclusions.

Empathy is a way of experiencing emotions. When we empathize, we feel happy, sad, or embarrassed not for ourselves, but for someone else because of what that person feels or is likely to feel in his or her situation (Davis 1994; Haidt 2006; Hoffman 2000; Sober and Wilson 1998). Roughly (Maibom 2009, 486),

S empathizes with *O's* experience of emotion *E* in *C* if *S* feels *E* for *O* as a result of believing that *O* feels *E*, perceiving that *O* feels *E*, or imagining being in *C*.

This characterization includes the most common routes to empathy: by belief, perception, and imagination or simulation. There may, however, be others (Hoffman 2000). Sympathy is usually taken to be an emotion, or a set of emotions, whose object is others' welfare (Maibom 2009, 487):

S sympathizes with *O* when *S* feels sad for *O* as a result of believing or perceiving that something bad has happened to *O*, or *S* feels happy for *O* as a result of believing or perceiving that something good has happened to *O*.

We note immediately a number of differences between empathy and sympathy. Empathy is a way of experiencing others' emotions whereas sympathy is less aligned with what people feel than with their welfare. Thus, although sympathy looks like a way of feeling for others, much like empathy, it is

actually quite different.[4] It does not, for instance, require emotion matching. Emotion matching involves feeling an emotion very close to the one
the other person experiences or is believed to experience (on the basis of
what someone plausibly would feel in that situation). The empathic emotion should, at a minimum, retain the same emotional valence (positive/
negative), tone, and relative intensity of that experienced, or thought to be
experienced, by the subject. I think we should require a closer fit. Though
we need not feel anger, exactly, to be empathizing with someone who is
angry, we should at least feel something like frustration or irritation and
not another negative emotion such as fear or sadness. It is sometimes
argued that because no clear or definite account is forthcoming on the
emotion matching required for empathy, we might as well think of empathy in terms of sympathy, pity, and compassion (Batson 2011). I think this
deploys a slippery-slope kind of thinking too easily, for there seem to be sufficiently many clear cases for us to have a reasonable grasp of the shape of
empathy, even if there are borderline cases. For instance, the neuroscience
literature claims that empathic pain and empathic disgust overlap with the
personal experience of pain and disgust (Singer et al. 2006).

Emotion matching and welfare orientation thus constitutes the two
main axes of difference between sympathy and empathy. Sympathy reflects
the welfare of the subject (roughly: good/bad), with little regard to the emotion she happens to be experiencing, whereas empathy matches the particular type of emotion experienced by the subject, in relative independence
of her actual state of welfare. Sympathy and empathy are commonly contrasted with two other ways of being sensitive to others' emotions: perspective taking and emotional contagion. Emotional contagion also involves
emotion matching between subjects—only, by contrast to empathy, it does
not involve *feeling for*. Briefly put,

S's feeling *E* is a case of emotional contagion if *S* feels *E* as a result of believing that *O* feels *E*, perceiving that *O* is *T-ing*, or of imagining being in the
C of *O*.

When we experience contagious emotion, we experience it, not as if for
someone else, but for ourselves, just like we experience most other emotions. It is personal and self-directed. Thus, although emotional contagion demonstrates sensitivity to others' emotions, it does not show the
other-directness that is characteristic of empathy and sympathy. Emotional contagion is not usually thought sufficiently oriented toward others or away from the self to be important to morality, except possibly as a
precursor to empathy (Darwall 1998; Hoffman 2000). When the inflicted

emotion is distress, it is often known as personal distress and is contrasted with empathic distress or concern as an egoistic or self-oriented emotion. Personal distress includes feeling "alarmed, bothered, disturbed, upset, troubled, worried, anxious, uneasy, grieved, and distressed" (Batson 2011, 103). Batson has demonstrated that people who experience more personal distress than empathetic concern are less likely (but still quite likely) to help others than those who preponderantly feel empathic concern (Batson 1991). If presented with an easy way of escaping the situation where they are exposed to someone's distress, people experiencing personal distress are more likely than people who experience empathic concern to do so. Batson takes this to demonstrate the essential self-interestedness of the motivation to help in personal distress. The subject helps the other in order to escape the unpleasant emotions that person's distress induces in her, not for the other person's sake, but for her own. Personal distress need not be the result of, or amount to, emotional contagion, since seeing a dead person, who is not in a position to feel anything, causes most people considerable personal distress. It is noteworthy that when people experience others as being in acute physical pain or very frightened, they are much more likely to feel personal distress than, say, empathy or sympathy (Eisenberg et al. 1988).

Perspective taking is also known as empathy. In perspective taking, we take up someone else's perspective on things, usually in order to understand him better. This type of activity is sometimes called "cognitive empathy" to distinguish it from the type of empathy discussed above, often referred to as "affective empathy." It is not clear that perspective taking is required for cognitive empathy, which is sometimes just described as understanding or representing what others think, want, or feel. Perspective taking is sometimes understood as simulation. As those familiar with this literature know, when we simulate someone, we imagine that we are in her situation and see what our reactions are. We then project our thoughts, feelings, and so forth onto her. Though we often correct for known differences between ourselves and the subject, simulation is essentially imagining how *we* would think, feel, and so on. To my knowledge, only one simulationist departs from this basic picture. Robert Gordon (1992) claims that we imagine ourselves in another's situation *as* that other person, not as ourselves. Something like this distinction is also made by Batson and colleagues (Batson et al. 1997). When we take someone's perspective, they argue, we either imagine how *we* would feel in their situation or how *they* feel in their situation. They call the former an imagine-self perspective and the latter an imagine-other perspective. Interestingly, the two perspectives evoke different emotional reactions and motivations (Batson et al. 1997).

If asked to consider how someone in need feels in his situation, a person generally comes to feel a preponderance of warm, compassionate, and sympathetic feelings for the other. This combination of feelings is what Batson calls empathic concern. Empathic concern induces motivation to help. The person also feels a degree of distress, including personal distress. If, on the other hand, you ask people to imagine *themselves* in the position of the other, that is, to imagine themselves to be in some sort of need, they experience a mix of sympathetic feelings and more acute, unpleasant distress. In fact, it seems that an imagine-self perspective on someone in need induces empathic concern *and* personal distress in about equal amounts. As Batson has shown, however, people who experience personal distress are more likely to escape the situation in which they are exposed to the other's distress, if it is relatively easy to do so, than people who experience a preponderance of warm, compassionate, and sympathetic feelings as a result of simply thinking about the others' emotions (Batson et al. 1997; Batson 1991). A number of functional magnetic resonance imaging studies support Batson's conclusions (e.g., Jackson et al. 2006). Perspective taking is, therefore, a relatively complex phenomenon associated with a variety of emotions.[5]

The above helps us see that the empathy item on the PCL–R most likely concerns affective empathy specifically *and* sympathy. It is also clear that what Batson calls empathy, as shorthand for empathic concern (Batson 2011), is what we, and most others, call sympathy. Not only does Batson require welfare matching, but he also characterizes empathic concern as feeling "sympathetic, kind, compassionate, warm, softhearted, tender, empathetic, concerned, moved, and touched" (Batson 2011, 103), none of which are likely to match what the person in need feels.[6] It is due to this sort of discrepancy of the use of terms that I sometimes talk of "empathy/ sympathy." With these distinctions in mind, we are in a better position to offer an answer to the question of what role deficient empathy/sympathy plays in psychopaths' moral deficiencies.

4.2   Measuring Empathy

The first problem facing anyone interested in establishing that deficient empathy or sympathy is at the core of psychopathic immorality is that empathy is usually not sufficiently distinguished from related, yet different, emotions and attitudes, including sympathy, emotional contagion, perspective taking, personal distress, emotional reactivity to others, general arousal, and social desirability. Many empathy indices measure many or all of these emotional reactions, either situationally or dispositionally. Situational empathy is measured in the situation, so it shows merely that a person feels empathy in a particular situation. This is helpful for discovering what types of situations typically give rise to it and what behaviors it motivates. This is the measure most used by someone like Batson, though, as we have seen, Batson tests for what we have called sympathy. Batson uses self-reports, but other people use physiological measures, such as skin conductance or the startle reflex. Dispositional empathy measures are meant to tap in to the propensities of people to respond empathically (or sympathetically) to others. Usually, self-report scales are deployed, though sometimes reports by others are used, mostly in the cases of children and psychopaths. As it turns out, all of these measures are flawed, though some much more than others.

Let us begin with tests of situational empathy. Skin conductance and startle reflex responses are relatively common ways of measuring empathy/sympathy in psychopaths. Using a startle reflex paradigm, Christopher Patrick and colleagues (Patrick et al. 1994) found that psychopaths react less to pictures of others in distress than controls do. This, however, does not show that psychopaths have reduced or absent empathy or sympathy specifically, since the startle reflex measures fear or anxiety more generally. He also found that psychopaths show the same abnormal startle reflex in response to directly threatening images (Levenston et al. 2000), raising the possibility that the deficit represents a generalized disorder in the initiation of defensive action from an orienting response. In other words, what is disordered could be their reaction to a potential threat; that is, their defensive reactions are delayed or impaired both in terms of affect and behavior. Thus, although the evidence shows that psychopaths have impaired negative reactions to others' distress, it does not provide evidence for an empathy or sympathy deficit specifically. In fact, it seems to demonstrate that psychopaths experience less fear, anxiety, or distress in response to seeing others in distress than nonpsychopatic individuals.

Like Patrick and colleagues, Blair and colleagues used physiological measures to test for reduced empathy in psychopaths. They found that psychopaths have reduced palmar sweating to pictures of people in distress compared to nonpsychopaths (Blair et al. 1997). The trouble with skin conductance tests, however, is that they measure arousal only and not, for instance, valence. Thus, increased skin conductance to people in distress, which is the common pattern in nonpsychopaths, can be interpreted as empathy, sympathy, emotional contagion, compassion, pity, personal distress, fear, shock, and stress. There are, however, some reason to think that skin conductance, like the startle reflex, captures personal distress and anxiety/shock/stress more than empathy, sympathy, or their compassionate cousins. Many of the pictures commonly used to stimulate skin conductance to the distress of others are of a rather dramatic kind, picturing extreme distress (weeping, grieving) or scenes of death and mutilation. The evidence suggests that the more distressed someone is, the more likely witnesses are to feel personal distress, to the point where personal distress is experienced more than empathic concern (Eisenberg et al. 1988; Hoffman 2000) or to the point of vicarious traumatization (Figley 2002). If this is correct, it means that much of what has been taken to be physiological measures of empathy are, in fact, physiological measures of personal distress or anxiety/shock/stress in response to harm to others. Predictably, psychopaths have deficient responses compared to nonpsychopaths, but what is measured is probably not empathy most of the time. So, though physiological measures of empathy are sometimes favored because they appear more objective, they are blunt instruments, often unable to yield the desired results.

Other, more indirect, measures are sometimes used to demonstrate lacking empathetic or sympathetic abilities in psychopaths, for example, lack of welfare justifications and impaired recognition of facial expressions of fear and sadness (Blair et al. 1997). Reduced tendency to give welfare justifications, particularly for harm norms, is a relatively decent measure of something like sympathy, but the evidence that it is significantly reduced in psychopaths is mixed (Dolan and Fullam 2010). In either case, even if welfare justifications are linked to sensitivity to the distress of others, they do not serve as reliable indicators of empathy or sympathy over, for instance, personal distress. Facial recognition of fear and sadness is tricky too. The ability to recognize sadness is reasonably thought to be involved in empathic sadness or guilt (Prinz 2007). Blair and colleagues (1997) found impairment in recognition of sad faces in children with psychopathic tendencies, but this finding has not been replicated with adult psychopaths. We can therefore conclude only that psychopaths suffer from impaired recognition of fear (Blair et al. 2005; Iria and Barbosa 2009). Some studies show sex offenders also have deficits in the recognition of the facial expression of fear; they often mistake it for surprise (Hudson et al. 1993). If psychopaths do suffer from deficits in fear recognition, this could play a role in their aggression, but more evidence is obviously needed. Thus, whereas there are many measures of negative responses to others' distress, understood broadly so as to include personal distress, sadness, fear, and so on, there are few that measure empathy or sympathy specifically. This means that there is little support for theories linking psychopathic immorality directly to emotions that are usually regarded to be *moral* emotions, such as empathy or sympathy. The difficulty, however, is not restricted to psychopathy but applies to empathy measures generally.

Most of the research on the relation between aggression and violence inhibition and empathy or sympathy use dispositional measures (Davis 1994; Jolliffe and Farrington 2004; Miller and Eisenberg 1988). The nature and validity of such measures are therefore important. Most dispositional measures of empathy are based on self-reports. Self-report measures, however, are notoriously unreliable (Nisbett and Wilson 1977; Paulhus and John 1998; Vernon 1964). People like to represent themselves positively, and most self-report scales make it pretty clear what is being measured. Furthermore, people often have only partial insight into their own motivations, attitudes, and so on (Ross and Nisbett 1991). Self-report measures of empathy have independently been found to be sensitive to social desirability and stereotyping. Eisenberg and Lennon (1983) found that girls outperformed boys on affective empathy measures but only when they were being observed, or tested by a female experimenter. Studies with adult women similarly indicate that they respond more empathetically than men on tests when it is clear that empathy is measured.[7] However, there is no difference between men and women on less obvious tests (Ickes et al. 2000) or when situational empathy is measured in other, non-self-report-based ways (Davis 1994).[8] This suggests that women present themselves as being more empathetic than they actually are—apparently because of social stereotyping—and/or that men present themselves as *less* empathetic. The concern that dispositional empathy scales reflect mainly social desirability continues to be voiced (Archer et al. 1981; Batson et al. 1986).

It is not only the ability of self-reports to measure what they are supposed to measure that is a source of concern. Empathy scales tend to measure a range of different emotional propensities and often show poor internal consistency. Scoring high on some items does not ensure that one will score high on others. As I've mentioned before, part of the problem is that theorists conceive of empathy in a great variety of ways. One of the main axes drawn in the literature is that between cognitive and affective empathy. Some empathy/sympathy scales measure only cognitive empathy, for example, Hogan's Empathy Scale (HES; Hogan 1969), or affective empathy (or sympathy), for example, the Questionnaire Measure of Emotional Empathy (QMEE; Mehrabian and Epstein 1972) or Bryant's Index of Empathy (BIE; Bryant 1982). Others explicitly set out to measure both, such as the Interpersonal Reactivity Index (IRI; Davis 1983) or the Basic Empathy Scale (BES; Jolliffe and Farrington 2006). Even within these types of empathy, many distinct cognitive and affective abilities and tendencies are conflated. For instance, HES measures not only the tendency to take others' perspectives, but also someone's patience, conservatism, personal tastes, and so on.[9] Davis (1994) suggests that HES is an assessment of "role-taking-mediated-social-skillfulness," but given the items included, this seems too charitable. HES appears to measure little of what is of interest to contemporary theorists of empathy (see also Jolliffe and Farrington 2006). Other measures of dispositional cognitive empathy are more promising, but they, too, are problematic.

As we saw when we discussed perspective taking, considering a situation from someone else's perspective can be interpreted as thinking in more detail about how he experiences his situation, including how he feels about it ("imagine-other" perspective). It might also involve taking someone's perspective by transposing oneself into it, that is, imagining oneself in the other's position ("imagine-self" perspective). The two approaches differ in how they engage the person's personal resources (is it a simulation or not?) and in their consequences (the degree to which they induce personal distress). However, perspective taking scales do not distinguish between the two. For instance, some of the questions on the IRI's perspective taking scale (PT) ask the subject to imagine how she would feel in the situation (Davis 1994, 57):

Before criticizing somebody, I try to imagine how I would feel if I were in their place.

Others seem to require an imagine-other perspective (Davis 1994, 56):

I try to look at everybody's side of a disagreement before I make a decision.

Since PT is connected to personal distress *via* its connection to an imagine-self perspective, it raises questions about what the IRI's subscales actually measure.

Affective empathy, as a category, often includes emotional contagion, emotional reactivity, empathy, sympathy and/or compassion, and personal distress. For instance, it is hard to figure out whether these items on the BES measure emotional contagion, empathy, or personal distress (Jolliffe and Farrington 2006, 593):

I get caught up in other people's feelings easily

and:

I usually feel calm when other people are scared (reverse scored).

The QMEE has similar items, for example (Mehrabian and Epstein 1972, 528):

The people around me have a great influence on my moods.

Even the IRI subscale empathic concern (EC) has an item which is difficult to interpret because it is compatible with sympathy, empathy, emotional contagion, emotional reactivity, and personal distress (Davis 1994, 56):

Other people's misfortunes do not usually disturb me a great deal (reverse scored).

As we have seen, personal distress is usually contrasted with empathy or sympathy in the literature, so a failure to partial out personal distress is a rather profound problem for empathy scales, and one that we shall return to. Many items measure the tendency to feel emotions consonant with those of another, but they do not distinguish between emotional contagion and empathy (Bryant 1982; Mehrabian and Epstein 1972, 528):

Even when I don't know why someone is laughing, I laugh too (BIE)

and:

I become nervous when others around me seem to be nervous (QMEE).

Perhaps the most serious problem with dispositional scales, from the perspective of empathy research, is their tendency to conflate empathy and sympathy. This is particularly significant when people attempt to link one or other of these emotions with the dual constructs of altruistic helping and violence inhibition. The QMEE, for instance, includes questions that test for both empathy and sympathy, for example (Mehrabian and Epstein 1972, 528):

I become more irritated than concerned when I see someone in tears (reverse scored)

and:

I don't get upset just because a friend is acting upset (reverse scored).[10]

By contrast, the BES and BIE do not include sympathetic items but, as we have seen, do not distinguish between empathy and emotional contagion. The IRI may be the only empathy test that does not test for what we have called empathy at all, but sympathy, perhaps due to the influence of Batson. For instance, the IRI–EC has questions like (Davis 1994, 56):

I often have tender, concerned feelings for people less fortunate than me

and:

Sometimes I don't feel very sorry for other people when they are having problems (reverse scored).

Two IRI items might measure empathy specifically:

Other people's misfortunes do not usually disturb me a great deal (reverse scored) (IRI–EC)

and:

In emergency situations, I feel apprehensive and ill-at-ease (IRI–PD),

but without further clarification it is hard to tell. It is notable, however, that one of those items is on the personal distress subscale (IRI–PD). The IRI, then, may be useful as a measure of sympathy and perspective taking generally, but probably not of empathy.[11] From the perspective of evaluating the empathy/sympathy hypothesis, then, the news is bad. Many measures used with psychopaths, in particular, only test for reduced emotional reactivity to the distress of others, and empathy scales measure a host of different constructs and often do not offer similar results for the same individuals. In the next section, I consider what this means for the empathy/sympathy hypothesis.

4.3   Psychopathy, Altruism, and Aggression Inhibition

Though Batson has always been very careful to define what he means by "empathic concern," his conclusions are often taken to show that something like empathy, as we have defined it, produces altruistic motivation. However, the emotion that appears to be most closely linked to altruism is what we have called sympathy. It is not, as Smith would have it, a fellow feeling where we feel what the other person feels, or something very close to it. We do not arrive at it by placing "ourselves in his situation … enter as it were into his body, and become in some measure the same person with him" (Smith 1759/1976, 9). Nor is it, as Hume suggests, "a psychological mechanism that enables one person to receive by communication the sentiments of another" (Cohen 2010), so that we "weep, tremble, resent, rejoice, and are inflamed with all the variety of passions" felt by others (Hume 1777/1975, 222). Instead, the feeling that is most likely to move us to help those in need is a warm, soft, and tender feeling most like sympathy, compassion, or pity, which is produced by focusing on the other person's situation and his or her feelings within it. This does not involve identifying with him or her, as this typically leads to a mix of sympathy and distress, part of which is personal and does not lead to altruistic motivation. Contrary to what is often thought, retaining a certain distance from the suffering of others, by clearly differentiating between what they are feeling and what one is feeling oneself, is ideal from the perspective of altruistic motivation and helping (Maibom 2009). It should be noted, however, that sympathy does not invariably lead to altruistic motivation; when the cost of helping is high, subjects who experience sympathy are more likely to escape the situation when it is easy to do so, just like people experiencing personal distress (Batson et al. 1983).[12]

By contrast to sympathy, the involvement of empathy in altruistic motivation is unclear. Since Batson's test for successful empathy induction tests for what we have called sympathy, and other studies use empathy scales of limited validity, it is hard to conclude much. However, empathy for someone in distress appears to be quite similar to the experience of personal distress, as it involves feeling "alarmed, bothered, disturbed, upset, troubled, worried, anxious, uneasy, grieved, and distressed" (Batson 2011, 103). The difference is supposed to be that in personal distress the individual focuses on her own distress whereas in empathic distress the focus is on the distress of the other. However, Batson notes that each of the imagine-perspectives (self and other) produces both sympathy and distress. The distress is felt both for the self and for the other. Clearly distress felt for the other is empathic distress. This suggests two things. First, people often feel both sympathy and empathy. Second, distress is felt simultaneously for the self and for the other. A certain degree of personal distress, therefore, may be part of the empathic response. This is independently plausible if we consider being an experimental subject asked to consider somebody else's distress or distressing situation. As a result of this imaginative process, *you* come to feel distressed. If an experimenter asks you how you feel, you will report feeling distressed or something very close to it (disturbed, anxious, etc.). If the experimenter then asks you whether you feel distressed for the other person or for yourself, I should imagine that the response would be mixed. Because *you* feel distressed, even if your distress is best described as empathic, it feels personal. However, since it is felt *because* the other is in the situation that she is in, or feels what she feels, it is also felt for her.[13]

If what I have said so far is correct, it leads to the rather paradoxical result that what is typically *contrasted* with empathy, or sympathy, is *part* of the empathic response. The issue here is not merely one of nomenclature. It requires us to rethink the categories empathy research has worked with over the last decades. And it raises doubts about the empathy part of the empathy/sympathy hypothesis. For empathy, understood as feeling what others feel for them because they feel what they feel (or are in the situation they are in), may not lead to *altruistic* motivation after all, despite being other-directed and involving concern for the other. This is suggested by the fact that personal distress is associated, at best, with motivation to help the other so as to alleviate one's own distress or, at worst, with escaping the situation when it is relatively easy to do so. What should not be forgotten, however, is that escape from the distressing situation is often not easy. This is particularly true when those in distress are our family, friends, coworkers, and neighbors. If I'm right that empathic distress usually involves a degree of personal distress, it is likely that empathic distress leads to a fair degree of helping. Should the fact that the motivation behind personal distress is that of relieving one's own distress count against personal distress as morally significant? I am inclined to say no.

Though technically speaking correct, calling the motivation associated with personal distress egoistic is misleading. It gives the impression of a narrow self-absorption, where the welfare and interests of others are insignificant. But while this may be true of psychopaths, it is not true of people who experience empathic or personal distress. As we have seen, it may be partly due to the fact that psychopaths do not feel empathic or personal distress that they exhibit this egoistic profile. It should not be forgotten that what induces empathic or personal distress is the distress of others. Empathic distress has as its focus the distress of others. What the subject aims to relieve is distress ultimately caused by others' distress (or distressing situation). Although the person is moved by the aversiveness of the distress that she feels, and even though that can lead to escaping the situation rather than helping the victim, it is nevertheless a fact that the distress or pain of others is aversive in its own right. This reflects a highly social, if not moral, orientation. In fact, one might even think that this capacity to be moved so strongly by the plight of others forms part of the appreciation of the wrongness of harming others and, perhaps, enables the feeling of a range of other morally significant emotions, such as pity, sympathy, and compassion. Since it is often not possible to distinguish personal distress that is part of an empathetic response from emotional contagion, one might add that emotional contagion too may lie at the root of responding to others morally.

The tendency to escape the situation when escape is easy is problematic (1) when you are trying to show that "true" altruism exists and (2) for the subject who needs help. Since we are not here concerned with altruism per se, but morally significant emotions more broadly, (2) is of greater concern. This issue is closely tied to an artificially created situation in which an unrelated subject needs help. It may not generalize, it seems to me. If you are the one causing the other person distress, your tendency to escape the situation if escape is easy could be extremely helpful to the other. Indeed, it could play a central role in curbing aggression. If we think back to Fesh-bach's and Blair's violence inhibition models, we see how close their con-ceptions of empathy are to personal distress. Blair, for instance, argues that the identification of fearful and sad facial expressions is essential to the proper operation of something like the VIM. Fearful and sad expressions are naturally aversive and can therefore serve as a natural "punisher." Being exposed to such expressions leads to retreat or to the cessation of the action that caused them. As a consequence, behaviors that become associated with these aversive stimuli become similarly aversive and thus preferentially avoided. This lies at the root of the moral capacities of the individual. But the best candidates for the emotion performing this job are empathic dis-tress or personal distress. Sympathy is not similarly aversive and is associ-ated with approach behavior, as in helping. By contrast, the desire to escape the distressing situation fits the violence inhibition model much better. By escaping the situation where the other is distressed, one often saves the subject from further distress, assuming that one is the aggressor. Egoistic or not, this kind of motivation may play an important role in the inhibition of violence and aggression.

The trouble with this suggestion is that the aggression literature suggests that the tendency to experience personal distress is associated with more aggression. For instance, some studies suggest that children more strongly emotionally aroused by others in distress experience more personal distress and more behavior problems (Strayer 1993; Cole et al. 1996). Psychopaths who have intact reactions to others' distress (Patrick 2007; Patrick et al. 1994) and score relatively low on affective and interpersonal impairments—so-called secondary psychopaths—are more aggressive and violent (Hicks et al. 2004) than so-called primary psychopaths, who experience more affect-related and interpersonal problems, including deficient aversive responses to others' distress (Blackburn 1998; Poythress and Skeem 2006).[14] Second-ary psychopaths also report greater amounts of stress, social alienation, and aggression. There are some reasons not to be overly impressed by these results, however. First, personal distress, when measured, seems to be a highly dysfunctional version of reactivity to others' distress, as indicated on the following item on the IRI-PD (Davis 1994, 57):

[w]hen I see someone who badly needs help in an emergency, I go to pieces

Being distressed, personally, by seeing somebody who badly needs help need not lead to someone's going to pieces or otherwise freaking out. And, of course, given the nature of these situations, we don't have any evidence about what people who are quite personally distressed by another's extreme need in a situation, that they are both in, actually do. It is also not easy to know how to compare degrees of personal distress found in the aggression literature with that in the altruism–helping literature. Rather than portraying a tendency to experience personal distress, scoring high on personal distress scales might reflect an individual's ability to deal with feeling personal distress. Second, secondary psychopaths experience a wide array of problems related to controlling their behavior and planning ahead, and they usually have lower IQs than primary psychopaths. Since their emotional reactions to others are relatively intact, it is therefore not unlikely that something like reduced ability to control or regulate emotions is responsible for this association between heightened personal distress and aggression. More research in this area is obviously needed. In the meantime, however, we are well advised to take more seriously the moral importance of empathic, personal, and contagious distress.

One last suggestion concerning how this research applies to psychopathy in particular: Perhaps secondary psychopaths have the basic affective building blocks to appreciate harm norms, but not the cognitive capacity to transform their affect into true concern for others, whereas primary psychopaths may be lacking in the ability to react vicariously to others' distress—be it emotional contagion or empathic distress. Without further research, we cannot know. However, if it were true, it would have significant consequences for how to think of the moral deficit of psychopaths, their legal responsibility, and treatment options.

Whatever one might think about the ways of measuring empathy-related constructs, it remains a fact that at this time the evidence that any such construct has an inhibitory effect on aggression is mixed (Batson 2011; Maibom, 2012). There is evidence of a negative relation between sympathy and aggression (Cohen and Strayer 1996), evidence of a positive relation between the two (Curwen 2003), and many studies showing no effect at all of sympathy (Jolliffe and Farrington 2004) or empathy on aggression (Bush et al. 2000). It is possible that the great variety of measures used in these studies (just think back on the number of dispositional empathy scales discussed here) can account for the confusion in this area. Another problem with this research is that it mostly measures people's response to distress in others that they have not caused themselves. However, there is evidence that children show much less sympathy ("empathic concern") toward their own victims than toward the victims of others' aggression (Zahn-Waxler et al. 1992), and that sex offenders only have problems empathizing with their own victims (Geer et al. 2000). But victim-specific episodes are the primary situations in which any kind of violence inhibition is supposed to operate. So to explore this suggestion further, more victim-specific research is required.

4.4 Conclusion, or Speculative Notes on Future Moral Psychology

There is little doubt that at least primary psychopaths have abnormal responses to people in distress, though this may be limited to their spontaneous reactions (cf. Meffert et al. 2013). To conceptualize this deficit as a deficit *only* in empathy or sympathy, however, is too hasty. Ordinary people are likely to experience at least empathic and personal distress, sympathy, fear and anxiety, and so on. The higher the distress felt by the other, the more personal distress a person is likely to feel (Figley 2002; Zeifman 1997). That tendency appears to be depressed in primary psychopaths, certainly. It is one of their better documented emotional impairments. Personal distress, however, may be a much more positive emotion than the literature suggests. It likely goes hand in hand with empathic distress (felt because *we* feel others' distress). Distress for others, particularly when it is also felt personally, may help us understand why harming others is wrong in the first place, because of its strongly aversive quality. And this very quality might inhibit our tendencies toward violence and aggression. Thus, it is quite possible that what forms the foundation for our appreciation of the badness of harming others and, therefore, our understanding of harm norms, is an emotion that causes motivation that is not, strictly speaking, altruistic. Since personal distress does not appear to give rise to altruistic motivation, but sympathy does, it is plausible that what inhibits aggression is not what causes altruistic behavior, like helping, and *vice versa*. Sympathy may play a more important role in what many regard as supererogatory action[15] than in violence inhibition (Maibom 2010), even if it is plausible that someone sympathetically inclined toward someone else is less likely to harm him. As things stand, however, there is little evidence that sympathy actually does inhibit aggression.

This way of thinking about part of psychopaths' moral deficit helps make sense of some interesting discrepancies in the literature. Many theorists think that a degree of cognitive empathy is required for affective empathy (Davis 1994), and it is usually assumed that psychopaths do not have deficits in the former area (Blair et al. 2005). However, psychopaths have been found to experience deficits in imagining themselves in distressing situations. Though their imaginative skills are unimpaired, their physiological reactions to what they imagine are flat (Patrick et al. 1994). If asked to imagine in detail being in the shower and hearing an intruder, psychopaths report much imaginative work, but they do not experience the stress/anxiety reaction that ordinary people do to this sort of imagery. This suggests that if psychopaths were to take an imagine-self perspective on others, it would not produce the distress reaction that such perspective taking does in ordinary people. So psychopaths do not feel for others when they imagine them in distressing situations, because they do not feel for themselves under similar circumstances. They can muster neither empathic distress nor personal distress in response to such imaginary scenarios. And some degree of feeling distress for yourself may be involved in the ability to feel distress for others. If it is true that there is such an interdependence between feeling for oneself and feeling for others, it is potentially very significant for philosophical conceptualizations of the psychological bases of morality. My point is not that psychopaths' moral deficit can be explained entirely in terms of emotional deficits. I merely suggest that to the extent that emotional deficits play a role in their moral impairment, their inability to feel distress in response to imagined scenarios might be quite important.

In conclusion, though the empathy/sympathy hypothesis enjoys considerable popularity, as far as I have been able to ascertain, it does not enjoy good empirical support. Furthermore, different proponents of the idea appear to have different emotional reactions to others in mind; Nichols is concerned with Batson-type sympathy and Blair with what appears to be empathic or personal distress. These are different reactions, with different consequences for behavior. Different imaginative activities are also associated with the two. Whereas one may involve a degree of identification (imagine-self), the other does not. One is associated with altruistic motivation, the other with egoistic motivation. What I have attempted to do here is to raise doubts about the centrality of altruistic motivation, and what causes it, to moral functioning. I pointed to empathic and personal distress as neglected candidates for emotions of great importance to moral psychology. Much more research is needed here, but I hope that this essay will stimulate different ways of thinking about this important area of research. In the case of psychopathy, it may be to empathic and personal distress that we should look in order to understand the impairment more fully, think of inventive new treatment options, and reach a more profound appreciation of legal and moral responsibility. In this way, the study of psychopathy also contributes to a fresh view of ordinary moral psychology.

Notes

The ideas in this chapter were presented at the conference Being Amoral: The Deficits of the Sociopaths at the University of Swansea. Thanks to Thomas Schramme for inviting me and to the audience and other participants for very helpful comments. Thomas also provided many helpful comments on the current paper, as did Dan Batson. Many thanks!

1. The Psychopathy Checklist—Revised (PCL–R) does not distinguish empathy from sympathy—so I include both—and does not include lack of shame or love. However, Hervey Cleckley (1982) thought lovelessness and shamelessness characterized the disorder.

2. Many psychopaths appear to take pleasure in inflicting pain and suffering as indicated by the degree of gratuitous and sadistic violence evidenced on the bodies of victims of psychopathic sexual violence (Porter and Porter 2007; Woodworth and Porter 2002).

3. Because the experimental literature rarely distinguishes between empathy and sympathy, Nichols prefers to call the emotional capacity or capacities that he has in mind "concern." "Concern" connotes an emotional reaction to another's distress that is experienced for the subject, whether it be consonant with that emotion (as in second-order distress) or not (as in sympathy) (Nichols 2004).

4. Most people think of sympathy only as feeling bad for someone in need. However, our idea of being sympathetic to someone does, it seems to me, include the propensity to feel good or happy for that person when good things happen to him (cf. also Batson 2011).

5. Davis (1994) report more mixed findings, which may or may not be compatible with Batson's once we consider that *both* sympathy and distress (both empathic and personal) are reported to be felt in the latter's studies (Batson et al. 1997).

6. At places, Batson has a more diverse list describing empathetic concern, which includes feelings of "sorrow, sadness, upset, distress, [...] and grief" (Batson 2011, 11). In most of his work, however, upset, grief, and distress are taken as signs of personal distress, not empathetic concern (e.g., 1991, 2011, 103). Batson stresses that what is central in the case of emotions such as upset, grief, and distress is the person who is the focus of the emotion. If that person is the other, we have a case of empathic concern; if it is the self, it is an instance of personal distress (Batson 2011, 12). The trouble is that if the test for whether individuals experience empathic concern or personal distress merely consists in asking them to report on the emotions that they are experiencing, without specifying their focus, different types of emotional experiences are potentially conflated. In particular, distress for someone else might be interpreted as personal distress.

7. Davis (1994) reports that this is particularly true when the Questionnaire Measure of Emotional Empathy is used.

8. See also Hyde (2005).

9. Items mentioned by Hogan include the following: "I enjoy the company of strong-willed people," "I frequently undertake more than I can accomplish," "I have seen some things so sad that I almost feel like crying," "It is the duty of a citizen to support his country, right or wrong" (reverse scored, i.e., a high score here means

low empathy), and "As a rule, I have little difficulty in 'putting myself into other people's shoes'" (Hogan 1969, 310).

10. Of course, this item tests for sympathy, empathy, or emotional contagion.

11. The full IRI includes perspective taking, personal distress, empathic concern (our sympathy), and fantasy (Davis 1983).

12. This occurs, for instance, when the cost is taking electric shocks for another that the experimenter claims are very painful. Batson (2011) argues that this is because the focus on the self replaces so-called empathic concern with self-concern.

13. How do we explain that the imagine-self perspective seems to induce more personal distress than the imagine-other perspective? I think this can be explained by the focus of the subject. In the imagine-self condition, the subject is asked to think of how *she* would feel in the situation. As a result, the subject's focus is more on the self and she is likely to interpret more of her distress as being personal, or direct, than the person in the imagine-other position who has been asked to focus on the other. Thompson et al. (1980) present some evidence that this is the case.

14. Primary psychopaths score high on PCL–R Factor 1 (i.e., lack of remorse, guilt, and empathy, shallow affect, manipulative, pathological lying, grandiose sense of self-worth), and secondary psychopaths score high on PCL–R Factor 2 (i.e., parasitic lifestyle, impulsive, irresponsible, poor behavior controls, early behavioral problems, juvenile delinquency).

15. Morally laudable, but not obligatory, action.

References

Archer, R., R. Diaz-Loving, P. Gollwitzer, M. Davis, and D. Fousheee. 1981. The Role of Dispositional Empathy and Social Evaluation in the Empathic Mediation of Helping. *Journal of Personality and Social Psychology* 40:786–796.

Batson, D. 1991. *The Altruism Question*. Hillsdale, N.J.: Erlbaum.

Batson, D. 2011. *Altruism in Humans*. New York: Oxford University Press.

Batson, D., M. Bolen, J. Cross, and H. Neuringer-Benefiel. 1986. Where Is the Altruism in the Altruistic Personality? *Journal of Personality and Social Psychology* 50:212–220.

Batson, D., S. Early, and G. Salvarini. 1997. Perspective Taking: Imagining How Another Feels versus Imagining How You Would Feel. *Personality and Social Psychology Bulletin* 23:751–758.

Batson, D., K. O'Quinn, J. Fultz, M. Vanderplas, and A. Isen. 1983. Self-Reported Distress and Empathy and Egoistic versus Altruistic Motivation for Helping. *Journal of Personality and Social Psychology* 45:706–718.

Blackburn, R. 1998. Psychopathy and the Contribution of Personality to Violence. In *Psychopathy: Antisocial, Criminal and Violent Behavior*, ed. T. Millon and E. Simonsen, 50–68. New York: Guilford.

Blair, J. 1997. A Cognitive Developmental Approach to Morality: Investigating the Psychopath. In *The Maladapted Mind: Classic Readings in Evolutionary Psychopathology*, ed. S. Baron-Cohen, 85–113. Hove, UK: Psychology Press.

Blair, J., L. Jones, F. Clark, and M. Smith. 1997. The Psychopathic Individual: A Lack of Responsiveness to Distress Cues? *Psychophysiology* 34:192–198.

Blair, J., D. Mitchell, and K. Blair. 2005. *The Psychopath: Emotion and the Brain*. Oxford: Blackwell.

Bryant, B. 1982. An Index of Empathy for Children and Adolescents. *Child Development* 53:413–425.

Bush, C., R. Mullis, and A. Mullis. 2000. Differences in Empathy between Offender and Nonoffender Youth. *Journal of Youth and Adolescence* 29:467–478.

Cleckley, H. 1982. *The Mask of Sanity*. St. Louis: Mosby.

Cohen, R. 2010. Hume's Moral Philosophy. In *Stanford Encyclopedia of Philosophy*, ed. E. Zalta, http://plato.stanford.edu/entries/hume-moral/.

Cohen, D., and J. Strayer. 1996. Empathy in Conduct-Disordered and Comparison Youth. *Developmental Psychology* 32:988–998.

Cole, P., C. Zahn-Waxler, N. Fox, B. Usher, and J. Welsh. 1996. Individual Differences in Emotion Regulation and Behavior Problems in Preschool Children. *Journal of Abnormal Psychology* 105:518–529.

Curwen, T. 2003. The Importance of Offense Characteristics, Victimization History, Hostility, and Social Desirability in Assessing Empathy of Male Adolescent Sex Offenders. *Sexual Abuse* 15:347–364.

Darwall, S. 1998. Empathy, Sympathy, Care. *Philosophical Studies* 89:261–282.

Davis, M. 1983. Measuring Individual Differences in Empathy: Evidence for a Multidimensional Approach. *Journal of Personality and Social Psychology* 44:113–126.

Davis, M. 1994. *Empathy: A Social Psychological Approach*. Boulder, Colo.: Westview Press.

Dolan, M. C., and R. S. Fullam. 2010. Moral/Conventional Transgression Distinction and Psychopathy in Conduct Disordered Adolescent Offenders. *Personality and Individual Differences* 49:995–1000.

Eisenberg, N., and R. Lennon. 1983. Sex Differences in Empathy and Related Capacities. *Psychological Bulletin* 94:100–131.

Eisenberg, N., M. Schaller, R. Fabes, D. Bustamante, R. Mathy, R. Shell, and K. Rhodes. 1988. Differentiation of Personal Distress and Sympathy in Children and Adults. *Developmental Psychology* 24:766–775.

Feshbach, S. 1964. The Function of Aggression and the Regulation of Aggressive Drive. *Psychological Review* 71:257–272.

Figley, C. (ed.). 2002. *Treating Compassion Fatigue*. New York: Routledge.

Geer, J., L. Estupinan, and G. Maguno-Mire. 2000. Empathy, Social Skills, and Other Relevant Cognitive Processes in Rapists and Child Molesters. *Aggression and Violent Behavior* 5:99–126.

Gordon, R. 1992. The Simulation Theory: Objections and Misconceptions. *Mind & Language* 7:11–34.

Haidt, J. 2006. *The Happiness Hypothesis*. New York: Basic Books.

Hare, R. 2004. *The Hare Psychopathy Checklist—Revised*, 2nd Ed. Toronto: Mental Health Services.

Hicks, B., K. Markon, C. Patrick, and R. Krueger. 2004. Identifying Psychopathy Subtypes on the Basis of Personality Structure. *Psychological Assessment* 16:276–288.

Hoffman, M. 2000. *Empathy and Moral Development*. New York: Cambridge University Press.

Hogan, R. 1969. Development of an Empathy Scale. *Journal of Consulting and Clinical Psychology* 33:307–316.

Hudson, S. M., M. D. Wales, E. McDonald, L. W. Bakker, and A. McLean. 1993. Emotional Recognition Skills of Sex Offenders. *Sexual Abuse: A Journal of Research and Treatment* 6:199–211.

Hume, D. 1777/1975. *Enquiries Concerning Human Understanding and Concerning the Principles of Morals*. Oxford: Clarendon Press.

Hyde, J. 2005. The Gender Similarities Hypothesis. *American Psychologist* 60:581–592.

Ickes, W., P. Gesn, and T. Graham. 2000. Gender Differences in Empathic Accuracy: Differential Ability or Differential Motivation? *Personal Relationships* 7:95–109.

Iria, C., and F. Barbosa. 2009. Perception of Facial Expressions of Fear: Comparative Research with Criminal and Non-Criminal Psychopaths. *Journal of Forensic Psychiatry & Psychology* 20:66–73.

Jackson, P., E. Brunet, A. Meltzoff, and J. Decety. 2006. Empathy Examined through the Neural Mechanisms Involved in Imagining How I Feel versus How You Feel Pain. *Neurpsychologia* 44:752–761.

Jolliffe, D., and D. Farrington. 2004. Empathy and Offending: A Systematic Review and Meta-analysis. *Aggression and Violent Behavior* 9:441–447.

Jolliffe, D., and D. Farrington. 2006. Development and Validation of the Basic Empathy Scale. *Journal of Adolescence* 29:589–611.

Levenston, G., C. Patrick, M. Bradley, and P. Lang. 2000. The Psychopath as Observer: Emotion and Attention in Picture Processing. *Journal of Abnormal Psychology* 109:373–385.

Maibom, H. 2005. Moral Unreason: The Case of Psychopathy. *Mind & Language* 20:237–257.

Maibom, H. 2009. Feeling for Others: Empathy, Sympathy, and Morality. *Inquiry* 52:483–499.

Maibom, H. 2010. Imagining Others. *Atelier de l'Ethique* 5 (1):34–49.

Maibom, H. 2012. The Many Faces of Empathy and Their Relation to Prosocial Action and Aggression Inhibition. In *Wiley Interdisciplinary Reviews: Cognitive Science (WIRE)*, ed. L. Nadel. Chichester: Wiley, 3, 253–263.

Meffert, H., V. Gazzola, J. A. den Boer, A. A. J. Bartels, and C. Keysers. 2013. Redued Spontaneous but Relatively Normal Deliberate Vicarious Representations in Psychopathy. *Brain* 136:2550–2562.

Mehrabian, A., and N. Epstein. 1972. A Measure of Emotional Empathy. *Journal of Personality* 40:525–543.

Miller, P., and N. Eisenberg. 1988. The Relation of Empathy to Aggressive and Externalizing Antisocial Behavior. *Psychological Bulletin* 103:324–344.

Nichols, S. 2004. *Sentimental Rules*. New York: Oxford University Press.

Nisbett, R., and T. Wilson. 1977. Telling More than We Can Know: Verbal Reports on Mental Processes. *Psychological Review* 84:231–259.

Patrick, C. 2007. Getting to the Heart of Psychopathy. In *The Psychopath: Theory, Research, and Practice*, ed. H. Hervé and J. Yuille, 207–252. Mahwah, N.J.: Erlbaum.

Patrick, C., B. Cuthbert, and P. Lang. 1994. Emotion in the Criminal Psychopath: Fear Image Processing. *Journal of Abnormal Psychology* 103:523–534.

Paulhus, D., and O. John. 1998. Egoistic and Moralistic Biases in Self-Perception: The Interplay of Self-Deceptive Styles with Basic Traits and Motives. *Journal of Personality* 66:1025–1060.

Porter, S., and S. Porter. 2007. Psychopathy and Violent Crime. In *The Psychopath: Theory, Research, and Practice*, ed. H. Hervé and J. Yuille, 287–300. Mahwah, N.J.: Erlbaum.

Poythress, N., and J. Skeem. 2006. Disaggregating Psychopathy: Where and How to Look for Subtypes. In *Handbook of Psychopathy*, ed. C. Patrick, 172–192. New York: Guilford.

Prinz, J. 2007. *The Emotional Construction of Morals*. New York: Oxford University Press.

Ross, L., and R. Nisbett. 1991. *The Person and the Situation*. New York: McGraw-Hill.

Singer, T., B. Seymour, J. O'Doherty, K. Stephan, R. Dolan, and C. Frith. 2006. Empathic Neural Responses Are Modulated by the Perceived Fairness of Others. *Nature* 439:466–469.

Smith, A. 1759/1976. *The Theory of Moral Sentiments*. Oxford: Oxford University Press.

Sober, E., and D. S. Wilson. 1998. *Unto Others*. Cambridge, Mass.: Harvard University Press.

Strayer, J. 1993. Children's Concordant Emotions and Cognitions in Response to Observed Emotions. *Child Development* 64:188–201.

Thompson, W. C., C. L. Cowan, and D. L. Rosenhan. 1980. Focus of Attention Mediates the Impact of Negative Affect on Altruism. *Journal of Personality and Social Psychology* 38:291–300.

Vernon, P. 1964. *Personality Assessment: A Critical Survey*. New York: Wiley.

Woodworth, M., and S. Porter. 2002. In Cold Blood: Characteristics of Criminal Homicides as a Function of Psychopathy. *Journal of Abnormal Psychology* 111:436–445.

Zahn-Waxler, C., M. Radke-Yarrow, E. Wagner, and M. Chapman. 1992. Development of Concern for Others. *Developmental Psychology* 28:126–136.

Zeifman, D. 1997. Predicting Adult Responses to Infant Distress: An Analysis of Cry and Adult Characteristics Related to Perception, Emotional Reaction, and Hypothetical Intervention. *Dissertation Abstracts International. B, The Sciences and Engineering* 57 (7-B):4789.

5 The Words but Not the Music: Empathy, Language Deficits, and Psychopathy

Gwen Adshead

5.1 Introduction

In the first edition of his famous work on psychopathy, *The Mask of Sanity*, Hervey Cleckley (1941) describes a group of men and women who lack the psychological capacity to engage in deep and enduring emotional relationships with others, and who use the language of emotion and feeling in a meaningless way. Cleckley called this "semantic dementia": although in a later edition, he made it clear that this lack of capacity was not a linguistic one but reflected a lack of deeper, more complex, psychological structures for the experience and communication of emotion (Kiehl 2006). This deficit was summarized poetically by Johns and Quay (1962), who described the "psychopath" as one who, in relation to emotional communication, "knows the words but not the music."

In this chapter, I want to explore the evidence that psychopaths "do not know the music" of emotional reasoning and communication. I will draw on the concept of "alexithymia," the inability to put feelings into words, and review the evidence that alexithymia is a feature of psychopathy. I will then review the connection between early childhood attachments and emotional language acquisition and will discuss whether this model helps us to understand the lack of emotional language in psychopathy. Finally, I will draw on research jointly carried out with Professor Jonathan Glover into how antisocial/psychopathic men talk about moral dilemmas and will suggest that we need more formal research into how such people talk, and what it is they think they are communicating.

5.2 Background: What's Wrong with Psychopaths?

For many years (before and after Cleckley's book was published), the term "psychopath" referred to people who were socially deviant in nonviolent terms, for example, incapable of holding down a job or maintaining relationships with others. They were not obviously mentally ill, in terms of obvious symptomatology such as abnormalities of sense perception, moods, or beliefs; rather, they seemed to lack a sense of how other people might experience them, and a failure to be concerned about this. Although likeable, they seemed to connect with others at a shallow level and be unaffected by others' mood states.

In Cleckley's original study, this lack of concern about others did not automatically result in criminal rule breaking; only a minority stole from friends or family, and an even smaller group committed acts of violence, usually in terms of drunken fights. However, in the 1990s, Robert Hare began to apply Cleckley's work to a group of people who had demonstrated their profound lack of interest in others' distress by hurting or frightening them. Hare (1999) developed a checklist of those features that seemed to distinguish a subgroup of cruel and violent individuals within criminal rule breakers. These men and women not only break the criminal law repeatedly and in a variety of ways; they also lack remorse for their actions, enjoy conning or deceiving others, and have little or no concern for vulnerability or weakness.

This work has made "psychopathy" synonymous with violence and cruelty to others. Yet Hare's work, and that of later researchers, shows that most criminals are not violent or psychopathic. "Psychopathy" is a personality constellation that can be divided into a number of factors: egocentricity and controlling attitudes toward self and others, impulsivity, and the willingness to break social rules (Hare 1999; Cooke and Michie 1999). These personality "factors" also include something described as "affective incapacity," that is, the capacity to be emotionally moved and engaged. There has been considerable debate as to how many factors there are, and to what extent people must demonstrate the presence of these factors to fulfill criteria for the category of "psychopath."

5.3   Emotional Incapacity and Interpersonal Attitudes

However many factors there are, most researchers agree that there is some kind of emotional deficit in psychopathy although it is heterogeneous in nature and expression. Some psychopaths appear to experience too little affect, especially fear (so-called primary psychopaths: Patrick 1994; Lander et al. 2012), while others experience uncontrolled negative affects of anger, hostility, and rage that contribute to their capacity for violence toward others (Blackburn 1988). Not all violence is associated with psychopathy: Only

25% to 30% of violent offenders in secure psychiatric units or prisons fulfill the criteria for psychopathy. In secure psychiatric settings, most "psychopaths" also meet diagnostic criteria for other psychiatric diagnoses, including mood disorders (Blackburn et al. 2003).

The paradigm of psychopathic emotional deficit might be best characterized as "predator" mode (Meloy 2006). In this state of mind, other people are seen as objects to be exploited for gain, and if they are vulnerable or needy, they are (literally) "fair game." The hunting metaphor is perfectly accurate: The psychopath is hunting for his or her prey because it meets his or her need to do so. Targeting those who are weaker and more vulnerable is preferable because it is easier to trap them and use for profit, and the hunter will preferentially seek out weaker prey and target those that will not be protected or cannot protect themselves.

It might be argued that it is not that psychopaths do not perceive affects in others; they are unmoved by them (see Cima et al. 2010). A predator is unmoved by his prey's distress although the predator may mark it: They belong to different worlds and have nothing in common. This lack of commonality means that there is no anxiety about deceiving or hurting the prey; indeed a psychopath might be puzzled at the suggestion (just as Cleckley described people who were puzzled at the idea that others were distressed by their actions). The predatory psychopath treats others as merely a means to an end and is puzzled at the suggestion that it could be otherwise.

There is a further subgroup of predatory psychopaths who seem to take pleasure in hurting others and exerting control over the vulnerable in terms of causing suffering. They are not indifferent to others' distress; they have a positive emotional response to it. This (thankfully small) subgroup demonstrate an *active derogation* for vulnerability and weakness: contempt, not just indifference. Such contempt facilitates cruelty, especially if combined with a belief in personal greatness. Such attitudes exist in the absence of criminality and may lead to harm in nonphysical, nonviolent ways: for example, those who con others out of their possessions or those in positions of authority who are cruel to those of lower status.

What seems to be crucial here is the psychopath's attitude to disparities of power and status and his or her detachment from the complexities of social relating that make us uniquely human. Humans are undoubtedly hugely influenced by social status and rank, like other primates (Sapolsky 2005): but unlike other primates, humans have devised complex ways of relating to those of lower status and also have developed social behavioral repertoires that allow flattening of hierarchies where possible and necessary. Like other primates, humans have a capacity for predatory behavior:

but almost every contemporary culture and group have abandoned the idea that other humans can be prey. Human cultures have gradually restricted the concept of legitimate human prey to animals and birds alone; since the gradual abolition of slavery, the spread of suffrage, and support for concepts such as universal human rights, there are almost no human cultures that socially license the use of vulnerable humans merely as a means to an end, and those that do are roundly criticized. I emphasize this change in social attitudes and policy because it demonstrates that there is nothing "natural" or at least immutable about treating other people as less than human.

5.4   Emotion and Language in Psychopathy

Cleckley (effectively) claimed that psychopaths could not "do" interpersonal emotions: Either they could not "read" emotions, or if they did, they seemed unmoved by them. Cleckley frequently gave examples of the limitations of their emotional language—for example, in the giving of promises to those who trusted them and in the shallow and superficial expressions of regret when these promises were broken.

There has been considerable research into the precise nature of any emotional deficit in psychopathy. One replicable feature seems to be a reduced experience of fear, with reduced startle responses and decreased perception of fear in the faces of others and impaired recognition of affect in the voice (Blair 1995; Blair et al. 1995; Blair et al. 2006; Wilson et al. 2011; Patrick 1994; Hicks and Patrick 2006; Iria and Barbosa 2009). However, there are contradictory results (e.g., Book et al. 2007): which would fit with the observations that some criminal psychopaths seem to be very attuned to fear and distress in their victims. It seems reasonable to conclude that there is a group that feel little or no anxiety or fear and another group who are sensitive to both in others but seem not to care or are derogatory. Both these groups differ from the typical case referred to secure mental health services, where there are elements of psychopathy combined with emotional dysregulation and distress.

There has also been considerable research into any language deficits that there might be in psychopaths (see Kiehl 2006 for a review). The consensus seems to be that, in research samples at least, there is some limited evidence for abnormalities of left-hemispheric language function, reduced processing of abstract words, and reduced interhemispheric integration (Hare and Jutai 1988; Hiatt et al. 2002). Such results would fit with speculations by neuroscientists such as McGilchrist (2010) who argue that the dominance of the left-hemisphere function results in excessive attention to categories and immediate consequences, and impaired attention to wider, deeper analyses of meaning, especially emotional meaning. Study of the word pattern usage of psychopaths indicates that they favor cause-and-effect language, which emphasizes material over social need (Hancock et al. 2011).

5.5   The Language of Emotions and Moral Decision Making

There is common ground between studies of emotional reasoning and language in psychopathy, and similar studies of the role of emotion in relation to moral reasoning. Psychopaths demonstrate failures/lapses in moral reasoning when they harm others; psychopaths have emotional deficits; ergo, emotional deficits are relevant to failures in moral reasoning. Of course, such an argument begs the question whether psychopaths are choosing not to reason morally or are unable to do so: a new-ish version of the much older question about how to judge intentions and apportion moral responsibility. This question cannot be explored here in depth; at this point, I wish only to note that there is common ground between studies, which I suggest is the role of emotion in moral decision making.

It is now accepted that emotional experience/reflection is one of a number of essential processes that make up the capacity for moral reasoning in humans (Oakley 1992; Glenn et al. 2009; Parkinson et al. 2011). Gilligan (1982) suggested that reasoning without attention to interpersonal feeling and emotion might lead to breaches of ordinary moral principles—a position to some extent borne out by research that suggests that decisions made without emotional intuition are incoherent and limited (Damasio 2000). Negative emotions are highly relevant to the experience of making moral decisions, especially emotions such as guilt, shame, and disgust (Nussbaum 2004). If these emotions are absent or reduced, then moral reasoning will be impaired.

It might also be argued that the study of psychopathy itself started with the observation that there must be something "wrong" with people who seem cognitively intact but who clearly have no feelings about others' distress. Paradigmatically, psychopaths should demonstrate abnormalities in moral reasoning processes that involve feeling and emotional connection to others. However, early studies of moral reasoning in psychopaths did not find much difference between psychopaths and nonpsychopaths (O'Kane et al. 1996; Blair et al. 1995) although these studies used measures of moral reasoning that were largely cognitive, which begs the question. A more recent study drew on Gilligan's (1982) work on different kinds of moral reasoning, finding that not all types of moral reasoning are impaired in psychopaths (Glenn et al. 2009). Yet another study found that psychopaths had no difficulty in making decisions relating to maximizing utility for material gain (Osumi and Ohira 2010) and in doing so, did not differ from nonpsychopaths.

5.6   Empathy and Relational Capacity

There seems to be some consensus that psychopaths either have reduced emotional responses, including the experience of negative feelings such as fear or distress, or they have no emotional response to others' distress, because they do not care or feel connected to others. The feeling of connection to other people, and affective responses to their mental experience as we perceive it, is the basis of *empathy*: a complex concept which is arguably part of the "social mind" that makes us human and allows us to live in relational groups over time (Gallese 2003; Dunbar 2003).

Empathy is both a phenomenological concept and a psychological capacity that makes possible knowledge of other minds as well as shared experience (Gallese 2003). In the experience of empathy, we become aware of others as embodied minds (MacIntyre 2006) and also become aware of something about ourselves (Fonagy et al. 1997; Singer et al. 1994; Moriguchi et al. 2007) through a mentalizing process. Empathy overlaps with Theory of Mind (ToM) but is separate from it (Singer 2006). Empathy involves both cognitive and affective appreciation of other's feelings, and one's own (Singer 1994; Shamay Tsoory et al. 2009): It involves a symbolic *sharing* of experience (Singer 2009).

Empathy is relevant to moral reasoning (Hoffman 2000; Decety and Moriguchi 2007) and makes explicit the role of personal emotional experience in moral decision making: Although emotions are not necessary or sufficient for moral judgment, there are many types of moral decision that do engage emotions, especially those that involve people with whom we have enduring relationships. Measures of empathy have been developed, and the neural basis of empathy is thought to involve a complex set of neural networks involving the limbic system, hippocampus, and orbitofrontal cortex (Gallese 2003; Moriguchi et al. 2006, 2007; Singer 2009).

To come full circle, it is arguably the lack of empathy as a relational capacity that Cleckley described in his "psychopaths" and which he suggested gave rise to antisocial and unkind behaviors toward others. It is often assumed that violent offenders lack empathy, and there have been many studies that have looked at empathy in those who hurt others, expecting to find evidence of lack of empathy. However, a review by Joliffe and Farringdon (2004) found less convincing evidence than might be expected. There is also no evidence that psychopaths lack ToM (Richell et al. 2003; Dolan and Fullam 2004). Some neuroimaging studies have claimed to find significant structural differences between the brains of criminal psychopaths and nonviolent comparison groups, specifically in those neural structures that support empathy (Raine and Yang 2006; Shamay-Tsoory et al. 2010). However, these studies have not yet demonstrated that these differences are *necessary* for the commission of cruelty.

5.7   "Speak What We Feel": Empathy and Language

In everyday social interactions, most of what we know about empathy and moral emotions comes through the use of *language*, especially metaphor (Lakoff and Johnson 1999; Pinker 2007). The power of language to generate feelings in humans has been known for millennia and is the essence of all those early poems, stories, and dramas: those early vehicles for moral discourse. The development of language is intimately connected with our anthropological development as group animals, which requires the development of what Dunbar (2003) calls "the social mind."

A key moment in the development of language skills is the move to representation of a feeling/experience as words (Bretherton and Beeghly 1982). The acquisition of a vocabulary of emotion and feeling is a process which takes place over many years and runs in parallel with the vocabulary of self-experience more generally. Babies recognize emotion in others by 9–12 months and are expressing emotional words by 24 months (Bloom 1998). The rate of acquisition of emotional words increases greatly in the third year; so that by nursery-school age, children have the beginnings of an emotional lexicon for their own emotional states and the states of others. Children as young as 18 months are able to articulate the distress of peers and their own distress in response, and this distress is linked to helping behavior (Eisenberg 1987; Zahn-Waxler and Radke-Yarrow 1990).

The capacity to acquire an "internal state lexicon" involves a developmental process, with stops and starts (Bretherton and Beeghly 1982): It takes time to acquire an adult capacity for articulating feelings (or to become "lexithymic"). There is a range of capacities in normal children and adults; not everyone is good at putting feelings into words, and some are much better/worse than others. In one study of language acquisition in a nonclinical sample of 4-year-olds, Lemche et al. (2004) found a range of internal-state language capacities. However, there is some evidence that impairment of emotional lexicon in children can be caused by environmental stressors such as abuse and maltreatment (Cicchetti and Beeghly 1987; Beeghly and Cicchetti 1994). Specifically, maltreated children lack the words for negative feelings, compared to children who have not been maltreated. Later studies found that these maltreated children have more negative representations of self as well as fewer words for negative feeling (Toth et al. 1997), suggesting a link between experience of self and emotional experience.

The inability to put feelings into words (alexithymia) has been recognized as a psychopathological phenomenon since the 1940s. It was noted to be a feature of the distress suffered by those who survived the Holocaust (Krystal and Niderland 1971), and subsequent studies have explored the relationship with post-traumatic stress disorder. Alexithymia is now recognized as a feature associated with a range of psychological conditions and abnormal behaviors. With the development of a self-report measure of alexithymia, researchers have been able to show a relationship between alexithymia and psychosomatic disorders, various physical disorders, and anxiety disorders (Taylor, Bagby, and Parker 2000).

If alexithymia is the lack of the capacity to symbolize feelings, and empathy involves the capacity to perceive and respond to the mental experience of others, then it might be supposed that there is a relationship between empathy and alexithymia. However, the relationship is likely to be complex, as suggested by Bird et al. (2010), who found that empathic responding was modulated by alexithymia but not by autism (where there are ToM deficits).

On Cleckley's analysis, psychopaths' inability to "read" other people's emotional states would suggest that they cannot read their own, so theoretically psychopaths should score highly on alexithymia. A counterargument, based on Hare's work, argues that psychopaths are verbally dextrous ("glib" is how they are described in the defining manual; Hare 1999) and may be actually quite good at simulating emotion and stimulating emotion in others, with the intention to con and deceive. On this analysis, they will score normally on a measure of alexithymia.

Studies of alexithymia and psychopathy are inconclusive and therefore tend to confirm Hare's view that there is not an obvious or strong relationship between psychopathy and alexithymia (Kroner and Forth 1995; Haviland et al. 2004; Pham et al. 2010; Grieve and Mahar 2010). There remains a real question as to the extent to which people (including those defined as psychopaths) may be highly empathic and verbally articulate but use these skills to cause distress to others and exploit their weaknesses—that is, that the problem lies not in a lack of capacity to feel, express, or share feelings but in *an attitude toward suffering and vulnerability in others* and an absence of any sense of relational connection.

5.8 Narratives and Emotional Language

Another way to look at empathy and emotional language might be to use a narrative approach to exploring moral decision making. Over the last two decades there has been a narrative "turn" in psychology, away from the mind-as-machine model of much cognitive research and toward a model of mind-as-meaning-maker (Bruner 1990). This has been mirrored by research methods in sociology that sees the "voice" of a speaker as a powerful social identifier and which recognize a narrative level of personal functioning and moral identity (McAdams 2009). Narratives are an important basis for the *development* of moral identity (Tappan 2000) and ethical reasoning (McCarthy 2003), which suggests that there may be a connection between the failure to generate moral narratives and failures in moral reasoning.

What a narrative approach brings is a demand for close attention, not only to the overall themes and nuances of *what* is being said, but also to *how* language is being used to convey emotional information. Obviously pauses, pace, and timing of language can convey mood or arousal, but where the stress on words is laid can change the meaning of a sentence considerably (readers may like to experiment with the different meanings generated by placing the stress sequentially on each word of the phrase "I wouldn't kill anyone").

Grice (1975) describes how language is a joint enterprise between speakers, and there are cooperative principles or *maxims* that underpin conversation. The maxim of *quality* requires that speakers provide some evidence for what they say, which they maintain consistently over time. The maxim of *quantity* requires that speakers do not impede discourse by either being too terse or speaking for so long that others miss their conversational turn. Similarly the maxim of *relevance* requires that speakers keep to their topic, or if they deviate are aware of it and return to the previous topic and finish their idea or reflection. Failure to observe these conversational maxims usually renders a narrative *incoherent* in Grice's terms—not that the narrative is incomprehensible, but that it is uncooperative (Hesse 2008).

Grice's concept of narrative coherence and incoherence has been used by researchers looking at the development of attachment bonds in adulthood and childhood. Using Grice's approach to rate narratives of recalled memory, researchers find that narratives that are low in narrative coherence are often found in speakers with an insecure sense of self and a variety of psychological problems (Hesse 2008; Steele and Steele 2008). Other researchers using a different method of analyzing coherence have found that a positive experience of psychological therapy (i.e., feeling better, feeling recovered) was associated with a greater coherence of self-narrative and an enhanced sense of agency (Adler et al. 2008).

What comes across in a coherent self-narrative is a rich and complex sense of a person who is able to recognize that things are not always what they seem and that a person's perspective (including his or her own) may change over time. Coherent narratives are high in self-reflective function, evidence that a person is able to mentalize and perceive not only his or her own intentions but the intentions of others. Poor mentalizers have little self-reflective function (Allen 2008), and this may be relevant to the ability to put feelings into words (Moriguchi et al. 2006, 2007).

The experience of being cared for in childhood is an important influence on the development of emotional language and coherent narratives of experience. In the first months and years, children lack language for their experience and need their caring adults to do this work for them (Meins 1997). The body is the default setting for the expression of distress, presumably because the parasympathetic innervation of bodily sensation is present from birth whereas the sympathetic neocortical connections take time to fully develop (Schore 2001). For this reason, children often use their bodies as metaphors for their distress: so that children will "feel" emotional distress as headaches and abdominal pain.

Children who do not receive good enough care in the first ten years or so of life often struggle to articulate emotional distress, and "externalize" it: often in the form of rule-breaking behaviors. Even controlling for IQ, psychologically insecure children seem to have reduced language competence compared with securely attached children (van IJzendoorn et al. 1995; Klann Delius and Hofmeister 1997). Lemche et al. (2004) suggest that it is the absence of the secure attachment relationship that leads to impairment of the internal state lexicon and subsequent alexithymia in adulthood.

Using an interview designed to look at psychological security Hesse (1999, 2008) describes three main forms of recognizable narrative incoherence associated with insecure states of mind. *Dismissing* narratives are often somewhat shorter than others because the speakers are often less engaged in interviews about themselves. They tend to use shorter sentences and close down discourse in ways that suggest that the whole topic of attachment or neediness or dependence is of little interest to them. The content of emotionally dismissing narratives often includes multiple claims to strength and normality, and speakers may emphasize the importance of independence. They have few memories of childhood, and these are rarely detailed. Despite this, speakers often violate the maxim of quality by describing their childhoods as "excellent" or "good" and appearing not to notice if the actual facts of their lives contradict their account. Such a failure to reflect or operate on the contradiction is a strong indicator of narrative incoherence.

Enmeshed or *preoccupied* speakers also seem unable to engage with interviews about themselves but in a different way. They speak at length, often in confused ways, and violate the maxim of relevance, as well as quantity. Speakers often wander off the topic and so fail to answer questions, which results in interviews that may be extra long. Sentences may falter and be incomplete, as if the speaker has lost his or her way, and there is often an absence of use of the personal pronoun. Speakers seem to take a passive, ineffective role in the construction of their narrative, and this passivity may be angry or vague. The content often contains marked oscillations of viewpoint about people and events from the past and often focuses on the present relationship (which is not the point of the questions). For example, enmeshed or preoccupied speakers may answer a question about their past relationship with their mother with a ten-minute diatribe about their mother's recent failure to help them.

Some narratives show evidence of both dismissing and enmeshed forms of linguistic incoherence throughout the interview, and these narratives may be categorized as *disorganized*. In some speakers, the narrative only becomes disorganized around one particular set of recalled experience, and this is usually suggestive of *unresolved trauma or loss*. Events from childhood that are particularly distressing/frightening, or cause attachment figures to be frightened and distressed, appear to be get "stuck" in the memory and are manifested as incoherence of speech in an otherwise coherent narrative of childhood. These "pockets" of disorganized narratives suggest that the speakers are having brief "lapses" of monitoring of the discourse when they are reminded of the loss or trauma and so are not aware that their language is becoming disorganized. The lack of awareness of how the language is failing is also an indicator of the degree of insecurity of mind.

Crittenden (1997) suggests that distressing and unprocessed feelings distort emotional language through the effect on semantic memory. Pillemer et al. (1998) also note how emotional "hot spots" in a narrative of past distress often are reflected in changes of verb tense: usually with the speaker moving from the past to the present tense without noticing, or appearing to do this deliberately for dramatic effect. The key issue here is that speakers' emotional stances may be unconsciously reflected in their use of language: the way they construct sentences, the grammar they use, and the metaphors they use.

5.9   Narrative Incoherence in Psychopathy

There have been a number of studies using narrative approaches with populations of psychopaths and other forms of criminal rule breakers. Most studies find that criminal rule breakers usually show low levels of coherence of narrative (Brinkley et al. 1999; see Adshead 2004 for review). Specifically, psychopathic and antisocial offenders dismiss and close down discussions of personal need and vulnerability and associated emotions (Frodi et al. 2001; Adshead 2004). They may also show active derogation of interpersonal situations where distress might be expected, such as bereavement.

I want now to quote two brief excerpts from a study using narratives of moral reasoning in patients detained in a high-secure hospital, who had all committed acts of serious violence (Adshead et al. 2008). All scored well above community norms on the Hare measure of psychopathy, although only a subgroup would score sufficiently to be considered a high-risk psychopath. We used two methods to generate text: the Ethic of Care Interview (ECI; Skoe 1993), which invites speakers to reflect on moral dilemmas involving family members or other emotionally significant people, and a "Socratic Interview" which invited speakers to reflect on a range of moral dilemmas, from unlawful parking to capital punishment (Glover, personal communication). The ECI has quantitative scoring methods, but we also rated the interview transcripts for coherence, using Grice's methods.

5.9.1   Example 1

Here is a section from an ECI transcript. The speaker has been asked to think about a hypothetical situation in which a man who likes living alone is visited by his elderly father, who makes it plain that he wants to come and live with his son. The speaker is a male patient; the interviewer's comments are in italics.

I think he should sit down and have a good chat with his father before he decides that he wants him even to live with him and I think before he even has his father living with him, he should bung him in a hotel or B&B.
Why should he do that?
Well, because it may be a mistake having his father living with him because he wants his privacy and his independence, you know, so er, he he should

like put his father in a B&B for a while and see how his father behaves himself, you know, you know because his father may be an old drunk now, you know you know what I mean, you know, so, er, yeah, you know...
What if it's your dad that wanted to live with you?
I wouldn't have my dad live with me
Why not?
He's dead [*laughs*]
If he was alive
If he was alive, I'd beat him up for what he's done to me, so but then again I don't know ... because I've never met my dad and I've never spoken to him or whatever, but I don't think my dad'd come to me anyway.... as far as I'm concerned, my dad's not part of me....

There are a number of markers of narrative incoherence here. Initially the speaker is very clear, but then his language begins to break up as he repeats "you know, you know, you know." It may be relevant that this happens after he has introduced the idea of the father being "an old drunk now," a detail about a completely imaginary father which he has inserted without any obvious reason or introduction. This is not criticism of the speaker, only to notice that "drunkenness" comes to mind unbidden when fathers are discussed.

Note that the speaker's language initially makes it unclear whether his father is dead or not, which suggests some degree of narrative incoherence. "I wouldn't have my dad live with me" implies that it is possible but that the speaker would not so choose. However, when the interviewer explores further, it becomes clear that it is impossible for the father to live with the speaker, and he knew this. A more coherent response to the question might have been:

"My dad's is dead so he couldn't live with me, but I wouldn't want him to because I have never known him."

The terse response, "He's dead" is typical of a dismissing stance, and it is noteworthy that the speaker still continues to talk about his father in the present tense as if it were possible for them to meet. The last phrase ("My dad's not part of me") is particularly interesting—partly because it is an interesting use of metaphor in terms of relationship, but also the use of the present tense suggests that the father is very alive to the speaker, even though he has just said that he is dead. A more coherent way of putting this would be as follows:

"As far as I'm concerned, my dad has never been part of me" (putting it in the past), or

"I don't feel that my dad is part of me" (adding self-reflection), or

"My dad would not be part of me" (mirroring the future conditional used in the question).

As it is, the speaker seems unaware that he has talked about his father as if he were alive, in direct contradiction of something else he just said. This passage also indicated incoherence in the form of laughter which is somewhat inappropriate in the context of discussion of a death, and in the absence of any explanation for or attempts to license the inappropriateness.

5.9.2 Example 2

In the next example, the speaker is asked to comment on the situation of a married man who is having an affair. His girlfriend becomes pregnant, but at the same time, he is offered a good job in a new city, which would be excellent for his wife and children. The speaker is asked what he thinks the man should do.

And he has been offered a permanent position for the next year, the next year, now if that permanent position is closer to the newborn child and the new wife, new girlfriend or whatever, he wasn't getting too much success from his married life, obviously felt the need to move away from home, I would feel if he went backwards, it may do him an injustice, it, you know, going against his grain of process (sic) of em....

This excerpt shows a number of indices of incoherence. It is generally harder to follow and there are odd repetitions of phrases, inferences without basis, and odd associations (what does "if he went backward" mean in this context?). Note that the overall meaning of this passage is not incomprehensible to the listener; we can make sense of it by context and inferential effort. However, there are unexplained pockets of words that hint at something that has meaning for the speaker but are not explained or licensed. What is the "it" that will do him an injustice? What is the "grain" of his "process," which has a poetic ring but leaves the listener unclear?

This text is the answer to a question about taking a course of action in which someone is likely to feel anxious, worried, angry, or upset. We found high levels of narrative incoherence in response to questions that generated emotions in the context of questions about the "right" way that people "should" treat one another. The violent offenders, including those who scored high for psychopathy, were more coherent on nonmoral questions but became less coherent on moral questions. This is consistent with a previous study by Blair (1995) which found that "psychopaths" were well able to make social conventional decisions but struggled with moral decisions.

Indices of incoherence included discussion of the imaginary protago-
nists in the present tense, as if they were real and active, and the making
of huge factual inferences about the states of mind of others, without any
evidence to back this up—sometimes to the point of weaving elaborate fan-
tasies about the players. Glover (personal communication) also notes that
speakers often became more incoherent when they made the shift from
considering a moral dilemma affecting an imaginary person to applying the
question to themselves (what would *you* do in this situation?).

5.10 Conclusion: Speaking Our Feelings

Speak what we feel, not what we ought to say.

—Lear

It seems that people who score highly on Hare's psychopathy checklist are
not the amoralists so beloved of thought experiments. Instead many appear
to be incoherent moral reasoners, who appeal to the same moral principles
as nonoffenders, and who make distinctions between moral principles and
social conventions. They do show some subtle language deficits around the
language of emotion in the context of interpersonal ethical decisions but
do not score high for alexithymia. Overall, the current research position
suggests that "psychopaths" are not a homogenous group who can be easily defined by their actions or their words and that they are not so distinct
from "normal" populations drawn from community samples of nonoffenders in terms of empathy, ToM, and alexithymia.

I make three points in closing for future researchers to consider. First,
there is a lack of agreement around definition of terms to be used in this
kind of research: The term "empathy" includes many different functions
and concepts, and not all researchers use the terms the same way (Preston
and de Waal 2002). Relatedly, not all research in "psychopathy" includes
participants who have offended: and it would seem likely that there may
be important differences between those psychopaths who are violent and
those who are not (Skeem and Cooke 2010).

Second, the normal "music" of human emotional communication is still
not well understood outside the domains of poetry, drama, and prose. In
order to understand more about authentic human emotional communication, it might be more helpful to study people who seem to be especially
skilled in emotional communication and/or ordinary lapses of emotional
communication in ordinary people.

Finally, it may be that the most psychopathic people are not in prisons
or secure hospitals, but are putting their cruel and antihuman attitudes

into practice in other ways. Although neuroimaging sometimes reveals intriguing details of neuroanatomical aberrations in the brains of criminal psychopaths, there is still no evidence that these aberrations have to be present for cruelty to take place. As I finish this chapter, I am mindful that we are still close to the seventieth anniversary of the Wannsee conference, at which a group of fifteen men planned the systematic murder of millions of innocent people. There is not much evidence that these men were psychopaths; in fact, they were deemed to be among the most effective of their day and were skilled in the use of emotional language to achieve success. At Wannsee, the "music" of emotional communication was played for a terrible purpose.

References

Adler, L. J., L. Skalina, and D. McAdams. 2008. The Narrative Reconstruction of Psychotherapy and Psychological Health. *Psychotherapy Research* 18:719–734.

Adshead, G. 2004. Three Degrees of Security. In *A Matter of Security: Attachment Theory and Forensic Psychiatry and Psychotherapy*, ed. F. Pfäfflin and G. Adshead, 47–66. London: Jessica Kingsley.

Adshead, G., C. Brown, E. Skoe, J. Glover, and S. Nicholson. 2008. Studying Moral Reasoning in Forensic Psychiatric Patients. In *Empirical Ethics in Psychiatry*, ed. G. Widdershoven, 211–230. Oxford: Oxford University Press.

Allen, J. 2008. What Is Mentalizing and Why Do It? In *Handbook of Mentalization in Clinical Practice*, ed. J. Allen, P. Fonagy, and A. Bateman, 311–321. Washington D.C.: American Psychiatric Press.

Beeghly, M., and D. Cicchetti. 1994. Child Maltreatment, Attachment and the Self-System: Emergence of an Internal State Lexicon in Toddlers at High Social Risk. *Development and Psychopathology* 6:5–30.

Bird, G., G. Silani, R. Brindley, S. White, U. Frith, and T. Singer. 2010. Empathic Brain Responses in Insula Are Modulated by Alexithymia but Not Autism. *Brain* 133:1515–1525.

Blackburn, R. 1988. On Moral Judgements and Personality Disorder: The Myth of Psychopathic Disorder Revisited. *British Journal of Psychiatry* 153:505–512.

Blackburn, R., C. Logan, J. Donnelly, and S. Renwick. 2003. Personality Disorders, Psychopathy and Other Mental Disorders: Co-morbidity among Patients in English and Scottish High Security Hospitals. *Journal of Forensic Psychiatry & Psychology* 14:111–137.

Blair, J. 1995. A Cognitive Developmental Approach to Morality: Investigating the Psychopath. *Cognition* 57:1–29.

Blair, R. J., L. J. Jones, F. Clark, and M. Smith. 1995. Is the Psychopath "Morally Insane"? *Personality and Individual Differences 19*: 741–752.

Blair, K. S., R. A. Richell, D. G. Mitchell, A. Leonard, J. Morton, and R. J. Blair. 2006. They Know the Words, but Not the Music: Affective and Semantic Priming in Individuals with Psychopathy. *Biological Psychiatry* 73:114–123.

Bloom, L. 1998. Language Development and Emotional Expression. *Pediatrics* 102:1272–1277.

Book, A. S., V. L. Quinsey, and D. Langford. 2007. Psychopathy and the Perception of Affect and Vulnerability. *Criminal Justice and Behavior* 34:531–544.

Bretherton, I., and M. Beeghly. 1982. Talking about Internal States: The Acquisition of an Explicit Theory of Mind. *Developmental Psychology* 18:906–921.

Brinkley, C., A. Bernstein, and J. P. Newman. 1999. Coherence in the Narratives of Psychopaths. *Personality and Individual Differences* 27:519–530.

Bruner, J. 1990. *Acts of Meaning*. Cambridge, Mass.: Harvard University Press.

Cicchetti, D., and M. Beeghly. 1987. Symbolic Development in Maltreated Youngsters: An Organizational Perspective. *New Directions for Child Development* 36:47–68.

Cima, M., F. Tonnauer, and M. Hauser. 2010. Psychopaths Know Right from Wrong but Don't Care. *Social Cognitive and Affective Neuroscience* 5:59–67.

Cleckley, H. 1941. *The Mask of Sanity*. 4th ed. St. Louis: Mosby.1964

Cooke, D., and C. Michie. 1999. Psychopathy across Cultures: Scotland and North America Compared. *Journal of Abnormal Psychology* 108:58–68.

Crittenden, P. 1997. Truth, Error, Omission Distortion and Deception: The Application of Attachment Theory to the Assessment and Treatment of Psychological Disorder. In *Assessment and Intervention Issues across the Lifespan*, ed. S. M. Clancy Dollinger and L. F. DiLalla, 35–76. Mahwah, N.J.: Erlbaum.

Damasio, A. 2000. *The Feeling of What Happens: Body and Emotion in the Making of Consciousness*. London: Heinemann.

Decety, J., and Y. Moriguchi. 2007. Empathy and Psychiatric Disorder: A Review. *BioPsychoSocial Medicine* 1:22.

Dolan, M., and R. Fullam. 2004. Theory of Mind and Mentalizing Ability in Antisocial Personality Disorder with and without Psychopathy. *Psychological Medicine* 34:1093–1102.

Dunbar, R. I. M. 2003. The Social Brain: Mind, Language and Society in Evolutionary Perspectives. *Annual Review of Anthropology* 32:163–181.

Eisenberg, N. 1987. The Relationship of Empathy to Pro-social and Related Behaviours. *Psychological Bulletin* 101:91–119.

Fonagy, P., M. Target, H. Steele, M. Steele, A. Levinson, and R. Kennedy. 1997. Morality, Disruptive Behaviour, Borderline Personality Disorder, Crime and Their Relationship to Security of Attachment. In *Attachment and Psychopathology*, ed. L. Atkinson and K. Zucker, 227–277. New York: Guilford.

Frodi, A., M. Dernevik, A. Sepa, J. Philipson, and M. Bragejo. 2001. Current Attachment Representations of Incarcerated Offenders Varying in Degrees of Psychopathy. *Attachment & Human Development* 3:269–283.

Gallese, V. 2003. The Roots of Empathy: The Shared Manifold Hypothesis and the Neural Basis of Intersubjectivity. *Psychopathology* 36:171–180.

Gilligan, C. 1982. *In a Different Voice: Psychological Theory and Women's Development.* Cambridge, Mass.: Harvard University Press.

Glenn, A., R. Iyer, J. Graham, S. Koleva, and J. Haidt. 2009. Are All Types of Morality Compromised in Psychopathy? *Journal of Personality Disorders* 23:384–398.

Grice, H. P. 1975. Logic and Conversation. In *Syntax and Semantics, Volume 3: Speech Acts*, ed. P. Cole and J. Moran, 41–58. New York: Academic Press.

Grieve, R., and D. Mahar. 2010. The Emotional Manipulation–Psychopathy Nexus: Relationships with Emotional Intelligence, Alexithymia, and Ethical Position. *Personality and Individual Differences* 48:945–950.

Hancock, J. T., M. T. Woodworth, and S. Porter. 2011. Hungry Like the Wolf: A Word Pattern Analysis of Psychopaths. *Legal and Criminological Psychology.* doi:10.1111/j.2044-8333.2011.02035.x.

Hare, R. D. 1991. *The Hare Psychopathy Checklist.* North Tonawanda, NY: Multi-Health Systems.

Hare, R. D. 1999. *Manual for the Hare Psychopathy Checklist—Revised.* Toronto: Multi-Health Systems. (2nd Edition 2003)

Hare, R. D., and J. W. Jutai. 1988. Language in Psychopaths. *Personality and Individual Differences* 9:329–337.

Haviland, M. G., J. L. Sonne, and P. A. Kowert. 2004. Alexithymia and Psychopathy: Comparison and Application of California Q-Set Prototypes. *Journal of Personality Assessment* 82:306–316.

Herpetz, S. C., U. Werth, G. Lukas, M. Qunaibi, A. Schuerkens, H.-J. Kunert, et al. 2001. Emotion in Criminal Offenders with Psychopathy and Borderline Personality Disorder. *Archives of General Psychiatry*, 58:737–745.

Hesse, E. 1999. The Adult Attachment Interview. In *Handbook of Attachment: Theory, Research, and Clinical Applications*, ed. J. Cassidy and P. R. Shaver, 395–433. New York: Guilford.

Hesse, E. 2008. The Adult Attachment Interview: Protocol, Method of Analysis, and Empirical Studies. In *Handbook of Attachment: Theory, Research, and Clinical Applications*. 2nd ed., ed. J. Cassidy and P. R. Shaver, 552–598. New York: Guilford.

Hiatt, K. D., A. R Lorenz, and J. P. Newman. 2002. Assessment of Emotion and Language Processing in Psychopathic Offenders: Results from a Dichotic Listening Task. *Personality and Individual Differences* 32:1255–1268.

Hicks, B., and C. Patrick. 2006. Psychopathy and Negative Emotionality. *Journal of Abnormal Psychology* 115:276–287.

Hoffman, M. 2000. *Empathy and Moral Development: Implications for Caring and Justice*. Cambridge: Cambridge University Press.

Iria, C., and F. Barbosa. 2009. Perception of Facial Expression of Fear: Comparative Research with Criminal and Non-criminal Psychopaths. *Journal of Forensic Psychiatry & Psychology* 20:66–73.

Johns, J. H., and H. C. Quay. 1962. The Effect of Social Reward on Verbal Conditioning in Psychopathic Military Offenders. *Journal of Consulting Psychology* 26:217–220.

Joliffe, D., and D. P. Farringdon. 2004. Empathy and Offending: A Systematic Review and Meta Analysis. *Aggression and Violent Behavior* 9:441–476.

Kiehl, K. 2006. A Cognitive Neuroscience Perspective on Psychopathy: Evidence for a Paralimbic Dysfunction. *Psychiatry Research* 142:107–128.

Klann Delius, G., and G. Hofmeister. 1997. The Development of Communicative Competence of Securely and Insecurely Attached Children in Interaction with Their Mothers. *Journal of Psycholinguistic Research* 26:69–88.

Kroner, D., and A. Forth. 1995. The Toronto Alexithymia Scale in Incarcerated Offenders. *Personality and Individual Differences* 19:625–634.

Krystal, H., and W. Niderland (eds.). 1971. *Psychic Traumatization*. New York: Little, Brown.

Lakoff, G., and M. Johnson. 1999. *Philosophy in the Flesh: The Embodied Mind and Its Challenge to Western Thought*. New York: Basic Books.

Lander, G., C. J. Lutz Zois, M. S. Rye, and J. A. Goodnight. 2012. The Differential Association between Alexithymia and Primary and Secondary Psychopathy. *Personality and Individual Differences* 52:45–50.

Lemche, E., G. Klann Delius, R. Koch, and P. Joraschky. 2004. Mentalizing Language Development in a Longitudinal Attachment Sample: Implications for Alexithymia. *Psychotherapy and Psychosomatics* 73:366–374.

McAdams, D. 2009. The Moral Personality. In *Personality, Identity and Character: Explorations in Moral Psychology*, ed. D. Narvaez and D. K. Lapsley, 11–29. New York: Cambridge University Press.

McCarthy, J. 2003. Principlism and Narrative Ethics: Do We Have to Choose between Them? *Journal of Medical Humanities* 29:65–71.

McGilchrist, I. 2010. *The Master and His Emissary*. London: Yale University Press.

MacIntyre, A. 2006. *Edith Stein: A Philosophical Prologue*. New York: Continuum Publishing.

Meins, E. 1997. *Security of Attachment and the Social Development of Cognition*. East Sussex, UK: Psychology Press.

Meloy, J. R. 2006. Empirical Basis and Forensic Application of Affective and Predatory Violence. *Australian and New Zealand Journal of Psychiatry* 40:539–542.

Moriguchi, Y., T. Ohnishi, R. D. Lane, M. Maeda, T. Mori, K. Nemoto, et al. 2006. Impaired Self-Awareness and Theory of Mind: An fMRI Study of Mentalizing in Alexithymia. *NeuroImage* 32:1472–1482.

Moriguchi, Y., J. Decety, T. Ohnishi, M. Maeda, T. Mori, K. Nemoto, et al. 2007. Empathy and Judging Other's Pain: An fMRI Study of Alexithymia. *Cerebral Cortex* 17, 2223–2234.

Nussbaum, M. 2004. *Hiding from Humanity: Disgust, Shame and the Law*. Princeton: Princeton University Press.

O'Kane, A., D., Fawcett, and R. Blackburn. 1996. Psychopathy and moral reasoning: Comparison of two classifications. *Personality and Individual Differences* 20:505–514.

Oakley, J. 1992. *Morality and the Emotions*. London: Routledge.

Osumi, T., and H. Ohira. 2010. Psychopaths Prefer Economic Utility over Fairness. *Personality and Individual Differences* 49:451–456.

Parkinson, C., W. Sinnott-Armstrong, P. E. Koralus, A. Mendelovici, V. McGeer, and T. Wheatley. 2011. Is Morality Unified? Evidence that Distinct Neural Systems Underlie Moral Judgments of Harm, Dishonesty and Disgust. *Journal of Cognitive Neuroscience* 23:3162–3180.

Patrick, C. 1994. Emotion and Psychopathy: Startling New Insights. *Psychophysiology* 31:319–330.

Pham, T., C. Ducro, and O. Luminet. 2010. Psychopathy, Alexithymia and Emotional Intelligence in a Forensic Hospital. *International Journal of Forensic Mental Health* 9:24–32.

Pillemer, D., M. Desrochers, and C. Ebanks. 1998. Remembering the Past in the Present: Verb Tense Shifts in Autobiographical Memory Narratives. In *Autobiographical Memory: Theoretical and Applied Perspectives*, ed. C. P. Thompson, D. J. Herrmann, D. Bruce, J. D. Read, and D. G. Payne, 145–162. Mahwah, N.J.: Erlbaum.

Pinker, S. 2007. *The Stuff of Thought*. New York: Viking Press.

Preston, S. D., and F. B. de Waal. 2002. Empathy: Its Ultimate and Proximate Bases. *Behavioral and Brain Sciences* 25:1–20.

Raine, A., and Y. Yang. 2006. Neural Foundations to Moral Reasoning and Antisocial Behavior. *Social Cognitive and Affective Neuroscience* 1:203–213.

Richell, R. A., D. A. Mitchell, C. Newman, A. Leonard, S. Baron Cohen, and R. J. Blair. 2003. Theory of Mind and Psychopathy: Can Psychopathic Individuals Read the "Language of Eyes"? *Neuropsychologia* 41:523–526.

Sapolsky, R. 2005. The Influence of Social Hierarchy on Primate Health. *Science* 308:648.

Schore, A. 2001. Effects of a Secure Attachment Relationship on Right Brain Development, Affect Regulation and Infant Mental Health. *Infant Mental Health Journal* 22:7–66.

Shamay-Tsoory, S. G., J. Aharon-Peretz, and D. Perry. 2009. Two Systems for Empathy: A Double Dissociation between Emotional and Cognitive Empathy in Inferior Frontal Gyrus versus Ventromedial Prefrontal Lesions. *Brain* 132:617–627.

Shamay-Tsoory, S. G., H. Harari, J. Aharon Peretz, and Y. Levkantz. 2010. The Role of the Orbitofrontal Cortex in Affective Theory of Mind Deficits in Criminal Offenders with Psychopathic Tendencies. *Cortex* 46:668–677.

Singer, T. 2006. The Neuronal Basis and Ontogeny of Empathy and Mind Reading: Review of Literature and Implications for Future Research. *Neuroscience and Biobehavioural Reviews* 30:855–863.

Singer, T. 2009. Understanding Others: Brain Mechanisms in Theory of Mind and Empathy. In *Neuroeconomics, Decision Making and the Brain*, ed. P. Glimcher, 251–270. London: Elsevier.

Skeem, J. L., and Cooke, D. J. 2010. Is Criminal Behavior a Central Component of Psychopathy? Conceptual Directions for Resolving the Debate. *Psychological Assessment* 22:433–445.

Skoe, E. 1993. *The Ethic of Care Interview Manual*. Unpublished manuscript. Available from the author on request. Oslo: University of Oslo.

Steele, H., and M. Steele. 2008. *Clinical Applications of the Adult Attachment Interview*. New York: Guilford.

Tappan, M. 2000. Autobiography, Mediated Action and the Development of Moral Identity. *Narrative Inquiry* 10:81–109.

Taylor, G., R. Bagby, and J. Parker. 2000. *Disorders of Affect Regulation: Alexithymia in Medical and Psychiatric Illness.* Cambridge: Cambridge University Press.

Toth, S., D. Cicchetti, J. Macfie, and R. Emde. 1997. Representations of Self and Other in the Narratives of Neglected, Physically Abused and Sexually Abused Pre-schoolers. *Development and Psychopathology* 9:781–796.

van IJzendoorn, M., J. Dijkstra, and A. G. Bus. 1995. Attachment, Intelligence and Language: A Meta Analysis. *Social Development* 4:115–128.

Wilson, K., M. Juodis, and S. Porter. 2011. Fear and Loathing in Psychopaths: A Meta-Analytic Investigation of the Facial Affect Recognition Task. *Criminal Justice and Behavior* 38:659–668.

Zahn-Waxler, C., and M. Radke-Yarrow. 1990. The Origins of Empathic Concern. *Motivation and Emotion* 14:107–130.

6 Psychopathic Comportment and Moral Incapacity

Kerrin A. Jacobs

6.1 Introduction

Meta-ethics has formulated types such as the moral free rider or moral nihilist, who are not motivated to be morally good persons or to be regarded as commendable members of the moral community. But do such prototypes fully account for the phenomenon Michael Smith has dubbed "real life psychopaths" (Smith 1994, 67)? The intentionality and phenomenality of psychopathic amoralism seem to be different from these other types: Psychopaths neither try to give arguments against morality in terms of a sophisticated nihilism as exemplified by Thrasymachus in Plato's *Republic*, nor do they seem to belong to that clever kind of free rider who is able to effectively calculate the costs and benefits and successfully avoids being detected.

The psychopath, in contrast, is someone who does not argue but tries to rationalize, who is not concerned about the possible negative consequences of his behavior, who is often characterized as being unable to follow any plan at all and gets engaged in high-risk behavior, whose charming appearance is evaluated by others at first glance as glib and superficial and so on, to mention just a few clinically relevant symptoms that might incline one to reassess the global myth of the "successful" psychopath. It rather seems that in psychopathy a particular kind of amoralism is involved which demands a discrete conceptualization within ethics.[1]

The purpose of this chapter is to describe the moral incapacity of psychopaths: In a first step, the concept of comportment (German: *Verhaltung*) is introduced, with the help of which I aim to explain the experiential unity of self-and-world disclosure. Secondly, I examine how the concept of comportment may contribute to an explanation of (psycho-)pathology in general, and how it refers to the entire gestalt of the psychopathic situation in particular. My hypothesis is that "comportment" provides a conceptual basis to describe the specific intentionality and phenomenality of the psychopathic condition, thereby contributing to an understanding of psychopathic amoralism. Psychopathic comportment is—among other alterations—characterized by a significant impairment of actual capacities for moral self-realization. On the one hand, psychopathic amoralism can be conceptualized in terms of a *restricted* individual realm of *moral* possibilities, yet, on the other hand, psychopathy also implies a pathologically *widened* space of possibilities. While the former points *ex negativo* to those capacities a person should probably have in order to be regarded as a moral person—and the psychopath appears as a contrasting figure incapacitated in terms of morality—the latter points to rigid patterns of self-realization outside the realm of the socially accepted, that is, to those antisocial and specific amoral modes of enacting that predominantly inform the clinical picture of psychopathy. The particular case of psychopathy makes it difficult to distinguish at first glance between the realms of the dissocial and psychopathology, especially on a phenomenological level of description. Since persistent patterns of dissocial and amoral behavior commonly underlie psychiatric diagnoses of psychopathy, however, such a conceptual demarcation is important to avoid conflating it with other cases of amorality or with other psychopathological conditions. Here the notion of comportment may provide some lines of demarcation, thereby accounting for the uniqueness of the psychopathic world-and-self-relation, its specific intentionality and phenomenality.

I suggest that psychopathy includes an altered *practical sense* of the world and a problematic self-relation, and accordingly I aim to specify the *lack of moral sense* as one subtype of an alteration of a general sense of evaluative self-and-world disclosure, which is then further specified in terms of incapacity. If one is prepared to grant such a fundamental alteration of self-and-world relation as characteristic for psychopathic comportment, one may furthermore be inclined to accept that psychopaths also have severe problems in areas other than exclusively the moral realm (cf. Maibom 2005). Indeed, psychopathic incapacity seems to transcend the moral domain as I attempt to demonstrate with respect to a particular distortion of self-reflexivity involved in psychopathy that supports the hypothesis of a changed practical sense, and give an illustration of in terms of volitional and evaluative incapacities of psychopaths. This not only explains their general lack of commitment but sheds light on the particular moral self-realization problems of concern in psychopathic comportment. I aim to exemplify this with reference to Harry Frankfurt's approach to self-reflexivity, according to which the disturbance of evaluative self-and-world relation and associated problems of volitional capacity in psychopaths can be understood as both a fundamental problem for their general encounters with the world and crucial for explaining their specific amorality.

6.2 Comportment

The notion of comportment (*Verhaltung*) was originally introduced by Martin Heidegger (1925/1985; 1927/1962).[2] One central aim of Heidegger's (1925/1985) *Prolegomena* is to prepare the ground for a broader notion of intentionality—further elaborated in his *Sein und Zeit* (*Being and Time*; Heidegger 1927/1962)—which contributes to capturing the experiential unity of individual self-and-world disclosure. Generally, "*Intentio* literally means directing-itself-toward. Every lived experience, every psychic comportment directs itself toward something" (Heidegger 1925/1985, 29). Consequently,

… it becomes clear that *comportment itself* … is in its very structure a *directing-itself-toward*. It is not the case that at first only a psychic process occurs as a non-intentional state (complex of sensations, memory relations, mental image and thought processes through which an image is evoked, where one then asks whether something corresponds to it) and subsequently becomes intentional in certain instances. Rather, the very being of comporting is a directing-itself-toward. (Heidegger 1925/1985, 31, italics original)

According to one line of differentiation, the class of explicitly self-reflective types of individual comportments form a particular subclass of lived experience, while others are rather prereflective types, which are normally not explicitly in the center of someone's attention or become objectified in intellectual consideration.[3] With such a broader notion of intentionality the concept of comportment captures a range of aspects of one's existential situation, such as one's situative awareness, especially those individual evaluations that go along with certain thoughts, beliefs, feelings toward, action tendencies, and bodily sensations (Jacobs 2013). In addition, it also addresses a range of rather tacit and prereflective modes of *Dasein*, such as a set of individual (pre-)dispositions, for example, incorporated body schemes, or what Matthew Ratcliffe has coined "existential feelings" (cf. Ratcliffe 2008), which form the affective background to the "foreground" of someone's more reflective intentional encounters with the world.[4] As such, with the notion of comportment we may refer to both the totality of someone's being engaged with the world and the way in which specific episodes of someone's life are singled out by specific comportments (Jacobs et al. in press). This points to the expressive dimension of comportments as lived experiences: While not all comportments are verbalized and, hence, narrated, they nevertheless might become observable in someone's gesture, posture, and so forth, as they are always expressed experiences. According to Heidegger,

we shall see that our comportments, lived experiences..., are through and through *expressed experiences*; even if they are not uttered in words, they are nonetheless expressed in a definite articulation by an understanding that I have of them as I *simply live in them* without regarding them thematically. (Heidegger 1925/1985, 48; emphasis added K. J.)

This illustrates, on the one hand, the dimension of spontaneity, vitality, and immediacy of lived experiences—as often enacted without any objectifying or intellectual stance we develop toward them in a specific situation. Furthermore, this quotation specifies the *habitual character* of comportment as including a set of incorporated predispositions and experiential patterns for world-disclosure, which rather seems to be taken for granted by individuals, inasmuch as these patterns are the incorporated basis for all encounters with the world.[5] On the other hand, the notion of comportment also refers to self-reflective modes of *Dasein* according to which agents develop a reflective stance upon their behavior and actions, and this

self-directedness toward our own experiential continuity is a new act which is called reflection. In such acts of reflection we find something objective which itself has the character of acts, of lived experiences, of modes of consciousness of something.... When we live in acts of reflection, we ourselves are directed toward acts. (Heidegger, 1925/1985, 96)

This living in acts of reflection points beyond the idea of simply becoming aware of having a particular thought, or being in a certain condition, or experiencing a certain feeling; self-directedness in reflection rather refers to a particular kind of self-relation, that is, individuals are able to develop an objectifying stance toward their thoughts, feelings, and acts (cf. Jacobs 2013, 3). It is this dimension of positioning oneself toward one's own experience in comportment that provides some further conceptual ground for illustrating how individuals constitute themselves as agents, by having the capacity to reflect on their actions, beliefs, feelings, and so on, that is, by having self-reflexive competence.[6]

According to my reading of it, comportment links together two inextricably intertwined dimensions that are associated with the prereflective and the more self-reflective intentional modes of being: Due to the *background* dimension, comportment includes individual predispositions (habituated, thus incorporated schemes of perception and practice etc.) and, as a prereflective awareness, a more implicit sense of self and world. The background has its counterpart in what I refer to as *foreground*, as the sphere of individual practice and those intentional encounters with the world which can be informed or are accompanied by self-reflection (Jacobs 2009/2012, 142ff.).[7] To the extent that the background dimension of comportment entails those evaluative patterns and embodied schemes of orientation which prestructure our specific reflective encounters with (and experiences of) the world and ourselves, it is the experiential basis according to which we perceive ourselves and events, situations, and objects in a certain way.[8] These implicit patterns apparently not only shape how we literally "feel" ourselves in the world, but moreover (pre-)structure *what we are able to do*, or what we actually evaluate as possible or impossible for us. In this regard, they are the prerequisite for all foreground activity and further reflective self-and-world disclosure.

Individuals are aware of their individual realm of possibilities provided by this background structure, that is, they are guided by a *practical sense* and normally experience their being in the world *as* a potential realm for individual action, feeling, and thought. Insofar as comportment carries a *space of individual possibilities*, it already entails an *account of ability*: While our individual abilities are already anchored as possibilities in the background, for example, in terms of individual predispositions, they become actualized in specific situations and, thus, are expressed in particular ways of enacting, which specifies someone's actual modus of being. Moreover, these experiences of being able or unable to do certain things in the light of one's self-reflective intentions—this sense for one's possibilities and ways of their particular actualization—is constitutive for someone's self-understanding as an agent.[9] To put it in other words, enacting the individual space of possibilities is already the way in which individuals constitute themselves in the world qua having certain abilities. This may happen in various forms and to corresponding degrees of self-reflexivity; the contemplation of one's own way of life, specific considerations of what might be worth striving for and so on count as examples for this particular form of self-relation that becomes relevant for autonomous agents and is often considered as central to being a moral agent.

From a conceptual perspective, the individual *realization* of one's space of possibilities involves a shift from someone's being merely enabled to *potentially* do *x*, to someone's *actually* being in the world, and the modes of how this is enacted in a specific situation.[10] The notion of comportment captures the dynamics of how individuals transform what is given to them as potentiality into the actuality of specific world encounters, which then shapes the gestalt of individual comportments in a particular situation. Central to the dynamics of background and foreground is that individual practice in the foreground dimension constantly *loops back* to the background, informing the more prereflective levels of the individual's situation. It is by these transitional dynamics between background and foreground that a circle is perpetuated according to which actual experience and individual practice manifest the experiential patterns for self-and-world disclosure.[11] These looping effects between both dimensions install the dynamics of individual potentiality and actuality, predisposition and enacted capacity, prereflexivity and reflexivity dependent on which specific comportments emerge and are expressed in action, thought, feeling, and specific forms of embodiment (such as gesture, posture, and speech).

6.3   Comportment and Psychopathology

The concept of comportment is sufficient to describe psychopathology in general, and for psychopathy, in particular:

1. According to a positive analysis, genuine pathological behaviors involving characteristic evaluative patterns, predominant affects, ways of embodiment, and characteristic modes of enacting are seen to form a characteristic gestalt of one specific psychopathological condition. The surface gestalt of psychopathic comportment is characterized by the prominent diagnostic criteria (American Psychiatric Association 2000, *Diagnostic and Statistical Manual of Mental Disorders*, fourth edition, text revision; World Health Organization [WHO] 2010, *International Classification of Diseases*, tenth revision [ICD–10]; Hare 1991, Psychopathy Checklist, revised [PCL–R]), while the spectrum reaches from aggressiveness, manipulation of others, glibness, and superficial charm to lying, incapacity to follow a life plan, lack of empathy, chronic violation of moral rules, strong rationalization tendencies and blaming others, and so on, thus illustrating the phenomenal heterogeneity of psychopathic comportment. These phenomena stand in close relation to a specific background structure that is not captured by the common classificatory systems. In stressing this background structure, one can furthermore account for alterations or a predominance of certain affects in psychopathy (existential feelings, emotional episodes, etc.), or specific incorporated experiences that eventually predetermine the psychopathic disposition, such as incorporated memories of physical and symbolic violence and social neglect in childhood, or learned aggressiveness that could probably explain a certain readiness for violent enacting in psychopaths, or

the existence of certain experiential patterns that amount to symptomatic psychopathic world-disclosure.

2. A determination *ex negativo*, in contrast, aims at specifying how certain pathologies diverge from *standard* comportments, which are stipulated as norms. A case in point is what Matthew Ratcliffe has dubbed a "given sense of reality" (Ratcliffe 2008), which is thought to be intact in healthy persons and, therefore, may function as a norm for the determination of both quantitative and qualitative deviations in individual experiences. A case in point are certain psychopathologies, such as schizophrenia, Cotard's syndrome, and also severe cases of depression (cf. Jacobs et al. in press ; Jacobs 2013), that present as conditions in which someone's experience of self and world alters in such a way that the world may appear as unreal, distant, and absurd or is experienced as if behind glass. Simultaneously, the experience of oneself may alter when the lived body (*Leib*) becomes conspicuous and feels alien, and/or is perceived as transforming into a corpse or a mere *Körper*—that is, the body becomes an object deprived of its feeling dimension—which can no longer function as a transparent and vital medium for world-disclosure.[12]

Another important alteration in many mental disorders is the loss of trust in one's own capabilities. One's intact sense of one's own abilities is replaced by experiences of being unable to go through one's daily routines, thus shaping an individual reality which stands in sharp contrast to one's sense of self and world before the onset of a mental disorder. This may amount to an existential situation reminiscent of Karl Jaspers's (1950) notion of *Grenzsituation* (*border situation*).[13] In depression, for instance, incorporated patterns required for daily encounters can no longer be actualized (e.g., getting out of bed in the morning is an unperformable task for the severely depressed). The whole system of practical world orientation is shaken, and the individual space of possibilities and the ability to perform in familiar ways is restricted, which may, in severe cases, lead to a fragmentation of the vital continuity of individual experience.[14]

The following section demonstrates that even if psychopathy does not, from a first-person perspective, involve predominant experiences of suffering from the condition of illness, an alteration of experiential patterns for world-and-self-disclosure—thus an altered practical sense—seems to be crucial for psychopathic comportment. The psychopathic self-relation and world orientation can be described as a deviation of such standard comportment and shows a unique intentionality and phenomenality due to a positive analysis of comportment.

6.4   Psychopathic Comportment—Lack of Moral Sense

Psychopaths are usually conceived not as merely immoral, but rather as amoral persons, as they lack the capacities relevant to adopt a moral point of view. Psychopaths are not "incapacitated" like those people who can adopt the moral view in principle, but fail from time to time to actually do so, or who intentionally refuse to adopt it in a given situation as an optional point of view. Apparently, psychopaths must then somehow be set apart from other types of amoralists, to whom a much higher degree of moral potential and actual capacity for moral understanding may be ascribed. But how can one defend such a difference between psychopaths and moral wrongdoers with reference to the concept of comportment, and to what extent does the particular hypothesis of a restricted realm of moral possibilities and actual capacity in psychopaths account for the specificity of psychopathic amoralism?

In general, an individual space of possibilities has been introduced with the notion of comportment and is associated with those underlying experiential patterns for self-and-world disclosure that have been addressed above in terms of a background dimension that provides individuals with a kind of practical sense of self and world. This is the basis for the discussion of psychopathic amoralism, inasmuch as such a general space of individual possibilities (background) also includes the *moral potential* of individuals and, accordingly, predetermines someone's actual moral capacity, in particular. The parlance of someone's "moral possibilities" refers more precisely to those psychic dispositions, incorporated schemes of practice, and respective abilities of individuals that seemingly contribute to whether someone actually is able to experience self and world from a moral point of view and to act in the ways required. If background, as the realm of individual potentiality, generally determines the actual capacity of individuals, it must also determine someone's capacity to regard the world from a moral point of view and to some extent also to be motivated to act respectively.[15] This particular enactive dimension in comportment is captured by certain (e.g., rational, emotional, volitional, evaluative) capacities individuals possess, which allow for their moral self-realization and, subsequently, their self-constitution as moral agents.

My hypothesis is that the realm of moral possibilities is severely restricted in psychopathy and, consequently, that psychopaths are fundamentally incapacitated for moral self-constitution, thus being amoral agents. The specificity of psychopathic comportment is based on a pathological alteration of experiential patterns that prestructure the practical encounters with the world. This can be concluded by considering the persistent problems with respect to actual moral self-realization in thought and action in psychopaths (Jacobs 2009/2012). Accordingly, I would like to suggest that even if psychopaths fully actualize their moral potential, they still operate on a level below common standards of morality, given their pathologically altered background structure.

In the following, *the lack of moral sense* in psychopaths is addressed as a specific disturbance of *practical sense*, that is, as grounded in an alteration of the background structure, which leads to symptomatic expressions of thought and action. These implicit structures—constitutive for a certain way of perceiving oneself and relating to the world and others in terms of those meaningful relations—that shape moral practice are seen as inaccessible forms of experience for psychopaths. Respectively, the lack of moral sense, as forming a subtype of a distortion of practical sense, can now be further specified as grounded in alterations of genuine evaluative patterns for self-and-world relation. Psychopathic comportment lacks a moral horizon and apparently discloses the world with a different kind of sense for, and sensing of, perception of social and thus moral practice. This can be assumed with respect to the phenomenal dimension, that is, those characteristic expressions of behavior that reflect the internal world of psychopaths. If one is inclined to grant my account of practical sense as that which tacitly prestructures individual self-and-world disclosure on the one hand, and which, moreover, shapes the sense of one's capacities on the other, a moral sense may be best conceptualized as already embedded in an individual's more general (embodied) schemes for self-and-world disclosure.[16] By means of incorporated, educationally mediated processes, it is, for instance, normally possible for individuals to learn to overcome the egocentric stance, to recognize when certain kinds of behavior should be displayed, and so on. These developmental processes allow for an adoption of a prosocial and later explicitly moral perspective, which opens a space of individual moral possibility. This acquired sensing of and for moral practice is part of our individual set of predispositions, patterns of evaluation, and self-reflective practice. It is a necessary prerequisite for being able to take the moral point of view, which can furthermore become integral—as *moral stance or attitude* (German: *Haltung*)—to someone's self-understanding. It offers some stable patterns for self-and-world orientation and modes of individual commitment, which contribute to how someone actually constitutes himself or herself as a *moral* agent. There is a difference between being able to adopt a moral perspective and the development of an individual moral stance. The latter implies a certain kind of self-reflection according to which someone adopts or affirms the moral view as part of one's self-image. A moral perspective may have a primacy to a moral stance, as it is associated with the evaluative, cognitive (etc.) schemes which are necessary but not sufficient prerequisites to acquire something like a full-blown moral stance. There might be, however, cases of dissociation, that is, someone might be occasionally able to adopt a moral perspective but is unable to develop a consistent moral stance that guides his or her course of action in the long run, while someone who already has developed a moral self-image may predominantly act according to it. This might explain the difference between free riders and psychopaths, that is, my claim that free riders have greater moral potential than psychopaths: Although free riders do not actualize this moral point of view to such an extent that it constantly determines their daily course of action—apparently there is also nothing like a solid moral stance—a moral perspective however remains an open possibility to them, an optional perspective for thought and action, which then is often rejected or employed to maximize their benefits. At least free riders successfully use this perspective to make predictions of behavioral schemes of others "playing the moral game," which they then successfully exploit for their own needs. If it is necessary to reach some ends, a moral perspective can in principle be adopted in specific situations although a constant moral stance is not developed.

One might object that this cannot account for what it really means to adopt the moral point of view, because this would imply taking morality seriously, in the sense of not only randomly behaving in a moral way or just adapting to moral demands when it pays off but developing something like a full-blown moral stance. Since the free rider also shows no sincere commitment to morality in terms of a personal moral stance, the line of demarcation between free riders or "classic" amoralists and psychopaths again seems to become blurred. Still, the qualitative disturbance of moral sense and the difference in the phenomenality and intentionality of both conditions can offer lines of demarcation on a conceptual level. For one could argue that a free rider at least differs from a psychopath in having greater sensitivity and skills for understanding the moral game without getting all too easily detected as a rule breaker, for having a more intact practical sense for the spectrum of the social game, for ways to bend the rules, a sense for timing in social interaction, and even an ability to be loyal to others (e.g., due to a criminal code) that may give strength to the intuition that their space of moral possibility is not as restricted as is the case in psychopathy.[17]

While free riders display a greater flexibility for "dealing" with situations, psychopaths, in contrast, rather tend to show rigidity in their patterns of self-and-world orientation that may explain why they often act in a way that is far from maximizing their benefits. In psychopathy, the individual widened space for amoral self-realization builds a contrast to the restricted moral realm: While the moral realm is constantly closed on the one hand, psychopaths often enact in a way that dramatically exceeds common, socially set thresholds of aggressiveness, manipulation, cruelty, cold-bloodedness, and so forth on the other. This pathological deviation of practical sense in psychopaths finds a certain parallel to what Harry Frankfurt (2006, 32) as well as Pierre Bourdieu (1992/1996, 235) have dubbed the "unthinkable," that is, what normally would never be considered as a real option for action and thought in a particular situation (e.g., given volitional necessities, according to Frankfurt, or as provided by the categories of perception constitutive of a certain habitus in Bourdieu's account) but actually is an option for a psychopath and leads to persistent amoral self-realization (Jacobs 2009/2012, 251). Unlike for the free rider, for the psychopath a moral perspective does not allow for an alternative view in terms of a perspective that can from time to time successfully be used for realizing evil intent. Even if it is proclaimed that amoral self-realization in free riders resembles some realization structures in psychopathy, one can put emphasis on an altered background structure in psychopaths, according to which moral incapacity and amoral self-realization are to be conceptualized in terms of *gradual* as well as *structural* differences that allow one to set psychopathy apart from other forms of amoralism.

Psychopaths cannot take the moral point of view and thus are unable to develop a moral stance, but they show other characteristic patterns for self-and-world disclosure that become manifest during the course of their lives. These rigid patterns predispose them to characteristic ways of self-realization in behavior, thought, and action that are pathological and amoral. The development and manifestation of antisocial self-and-world relation follow the logic of the looping effects between background and foreground: It seems that the more often one gets engaged in amoral self-realization, the more one practically behaves in an aggressive, manipulating, cold-blooded way, the more these experiences become woven into one's personality structure, which then contributes simultaneously to the (re-)production of certain behavioral patterns. It is this kind of vicious circle by which psychopathy manifests itself in relatively stable patterns for world-and-self-disclosure. Consequently, the therapeutic aim is to alter both incorporation and enacting of these structures, by appealing to some sort of self-reflexive capacity or introspection of the individual in order to eventually reshape these perpetuating dynamics.[18]

The focus of analysis has hitherto targeted the background structure in order to sketch the impairment of practical, and thus moral, sense in psychopaths. This can finally be addressed in terms of incapacity as one way to exemplify the lack of moral sense in psychopathic comportment due to a restricted space of moral possibility. The absence of a moral perspective and a moral stance in psychopathy can be specified in terms of an incapacity for *caring* that prevents self-realization as a moral agent. The notion of caring offers one way to refer to those evaluative patterns that normally provide one with a relatively stable practical orientation in life and that have been alluded to with the notion of a "personal (moral) stance." It is finally suggested that psychopathic comportment involves an inability to care, also in terms of an inability to meaningfully relate oneself to others, that may explain the particular amoral orientation of psychopaths toward the world and sheds light on their problematic self-relation, too.

6.5   Inability of Moral Self-Realization in Psychopathic Comportment

Harry G. Frankfurt's approach of *self-reflexivity*[19] offers several points of departure to explain a moral lack in psychopathic comportment. According to one line of argumentation, one could address problems of self-reflexivity with respect to Frankfurt's (1988) account of wantonness. A *wanton* is someone who has no second-order volition or preference as to which desire should determine his or her will. Prototype wantons are young children and severely retarded adults, thought to be incapable of caring about their will and showing a lack of self-reflexivity insofar as they remain simply indifferent toward what action shapes their course of life. One could claim that psychopaths are *generally* not able to form second-order volitions, that is, that they are wanton, because second-order desires do not "effectively" determine their will in such a way that they actually act according to them. This seems to offer one reasonable explanation for the impulsivity, recklessness, and unstable orientation in the life of a psychopath. One could also claim that psychopaths show this structural deformation at least exclusively with respect to morality and have to be considered as *moral* wantons insofar as their alleged desire to be a morally good person does not effectively determine their will.

It has to be addressed as a general problem when one states a structural impairment of the will in psychopathic comportment (e.g., in terms of wantonness) that one is specifying the moral lack on one hand, but apparently also has to account for those occasions in which the structure of volition in psychopaths seems to be intact on the other. I am rather skeptical when it comes to claims about a structural deficit of the will exclusively for morality whereas the volitional structure is regarded as remaining unimpaired in all other realms of self-and-world disclosure. With regard to the idea of an individual realm of possibility that is both fundamentally restricted and pathologically widened in psychopathy, it seems one cannot fully rule out that even a psychopath may occasionally show concern from time to time and, thus, is not always a typical wanton. It appears more important in this context that these moments in which psychopaths are not indifferent or indecisive seem to be rather transitory episodes in an otherwise incoherent life. I therefore suggest characterizing psychopathic world-disclosure as being deprived of long-term commitments, which cannot be fully grasped in terms of the merits of *synchronic unity of self* as accessible to someone decisive and able to spontaneously enact due to an unimpaired will, or consistent in will in one specific situation (Frankfurt 1988, 166; 2006, 19). Rather, one may focus on a particular kind of self-constitutive practice that provides a *diachronic unity of the self*, thus coherence in life, which is what seems to be essentially missing in psychopathy.[20]

Psychopathy indeed includes a kind of incapacity that affects the general self-and-world orientation and therefore also moral capacity. In order to specify this incapacity and, moreover, relate it to what has been previously outlined, one has to focus on the notions of caring and love, and impairments in self-reflexive processes in psychopaths. Additionally, wantonness may come into play as one feature of psychopathic comportment that sometimes disturbs effective deliberation. I am not predominantly concerned with psychopaths as being able or unable to make individual decisions but am more interested in those structures that normally integrate individual decisions and contribute to a coherent way of life that is essential for a meaningful self-and-world relation. The incapacity for committed care and love deprives psychopaths from adopting the moral perspective and developing a personal moral stance. The notion of caring also serves to illustrate in a much better way than the reference to mere "desiring" that individuals get deeply involved with things, invest themselves in what they do, and come to a kind of self-understanding in which the things that matter to them mirror what kind of persons they are or want to be:

It is by caring about things that we infuse the world with importance. This provides us with stable ambitions and concerns; it marks our interests and goals. The importance that our caring creates for us defines the framework of standards and aims in terms of which we endeavor to conduct our lives. A person who cares about something is guided, as his attitudes and his actions are shaped, by his continuing interest in it. Insofar as he does care about certain things, this determines how he thinks it important for him to conduct his life. The totality of the various things that a person cares about—together with his ordering of how important to him they are—effectively specifies his answers to the question of how to live. (Frankfurt 2004, 23)

This process of self-constitution through caring presupposes that individuals are able to acquire certain motifs, take a preliminary objectifying stance toward certain motifs, and finally come to a decision as to what their will should be, whereby an individual hierarchy of volition gets implemented. Respectively, it can be assumed that even if the psychopath "might *believe* that he had cared about certain things, and that those things mattered to him" (Frankfurt 2004, 22; italics original), he practically undermines "caring" as it turns out to be an empty promise to himself and others.

The characteristic aspect of caring is that individuals normally go beyond mere desiring by continuing to want certain things. Caring installs the difference between a mere transitory affirmation of a motif and a long-term commitment, that is, choosing all further means for an end by which a particular process of caring is sustained. Caring then has the potential to function as a structuring principle for all further desires or motifs concerned with a particular volitional complex. Respectively, "caring about something implies a diachronic coherence, which integrates the self across time" (Frankfurt 2006, 19). In the framework of Frankfurt's theory, this volitional continuity provided by caring is the pivot for the act of individual self-constitution and deeply shapes the identity of an agent. Moreover, caring involves also a certain kind of *flexibility* in self-reflexive practice, according to which we are able to question certain continuities of our caring in reassessing what has been of import for us so far, and whether we really want to go on caring about something also in the future (cf. Wolf 2009, 426).

An important variant of caring is "love" as "the originating source of terminal value. If we loved nothing, then nothing would possess for us any definitive and inherent worth" (Frankfurt 2004, 55). With respect to the concept of love, one can once more explain how certain dispositions for action get structured. While caring rests on a reflexive identification with one's desires, which allows one to follow certain motifs in the long run—and thus to take them seriously—"loving" implies a long-term commitment, too. It further implies that lovers defer from their own interests in favor of the needs and interests of the beloved. While caring refers to the things a person regards as being of importance given their instrumental value, loving is a kind of caring about things or people for the sake of their own intrinsic worth (Frankfurt 2004, 42ff.). In analogy to caring as a structuring principle that integrates single motifs in time, love has the potential to structure particular modes of caring. What qualifies love as a specific variant of caring is that it also enthralls us in such a way that someone cannot help loving what he loves; and second, he therefore cannot help taking the expectation that an action would benefit his beloved as a powerful and often decisively preemptive reason for performing that action. Through loving, then, we acquire final ends to which we cannot help being bound; [...]. (Frankfurt 2006, 42)

Respectively, we are provided with reasons for action that appeal to us as compelling. This marks a point in self-reflexive processes when one becomes clear about what one loves with necessity (cf. Frankfurt 1999), which in turn allows one to enter a stage of *self-acceptance*. Self-acceptance is reached by accepting what has been revealed as *authentic* expression of one's self. Finally, the concept of *self-love* becomes central to the approach of self-reflexive practice: According to Frankfurt, "self-love consists, then, in the purity of a wholehearted will" (Frankfurt 2004, 96), which means that no part of one's will is experienced as alien or opposed to oneself, and so a unity of will is reached. As it is actively acquired by individuals, someone is not "passively intruded upon or imposed upon any element of it" (Frankfurt 2004, 96). Furthermore, "loving ourselves is desirable and important for us because it is the same thing, more or less, as being satisfied with ourselves" (Frankfurt 2004, 97). This specifies the kind of self-acceptance described above, by which one endorses one's *volitional identity* (as a loving person). Consequently, self-reflexivity is a practice that constitutes identity in terms of the capacity to reach a volitional unity. This unity makes us aware of that kind of decisive identification that has been shown as being necessary to form second-order volitions and now reflects a decision to accept those things we cannot help but dedicate ourselves to. Frankfurt points out that these "fundamental necessities of the will are not transient creatures of social prescription or of cultural habit" and furthermore are not "constituted by peculiarities of individual taste or judgment" (Frankfurt 2006, 38). According to the scheme of someone's background disposition explained above, I suggest regarding them as also influenced and shaped by habitus, but this does not imply that we are simply exposed to this background structure or passively enact the space of possibilities; rather we are able to acquire stable patterns of behavior for which we can also be held responsible, insofar as we are actively positioning ourselves toward them, and thus are free to accept or reject certain underlying motifs and to alter our behavior and actions, respectively (see also note 8). The approach of self-reflexive practice provided by Frankfurt helps to specify my account of how individuals constitute themselves as autonomous agents in the face of a prestructuring background, which entails the dimension of individual (volitional) necessities.

The problems of moral self-constitution in psychopaths might be explainable due to a certain proneness to wantonness, but this does not justify a general assimilation of psychopaths to the type of the wanton, as their problem of self-constitution seems to be more complex. Basically, I consider psychopaths not as merely incapacitated for a decisive identification with genuine moral motifs but regard their problem predominantly as anchored in their lacking the potential for a structural integration of self by processes of caring. Moreover, what has been described as self-acceptance by means of love seems also essentially missing in the lives of psychopaths. Given the assumption that they are not predominantly wanton, it seems that they have rather fewer problems deliberating singular motifs for action, but more with long-term commitment to something or someone, which is integral for developing a diachronic unity of self and thus a consistent volitional identity. Psychopaths show, in a trivial sense, a synchronic unity of self—due to their being capable of spontaneous deliberation—but apparently show no diachronic unity in terms of those long-term structures generated by caring and love that would provide them with those sufficiently stable orientations according to which single modes of their transitory self-realization become meaningfully integrated in the long run. Respectively, meaningful practice of self-constitution as a (moral) person in terms of caring and love is out of the experiential reach in psychopathic self-and-world disclosure. Although psychopaths can eventually achieve a preliminary affirmation of certain motifs and may also effectively deliberate according to single decisions that may give them a moment of self-unity, this however does not lead to the development of a stable, long-term orientation in life. Their kind of decisiveness cannot fully count as a mode of real identification, that is, what is essentially missing is this kind of identification constitutive of caring for something or loving someone. This explains why they do not acquire certain motifs integral to their self-understanding that could enable them to actually constitute themselves as agents in the same way others can. Psychopaths do not realize their potential for action in the same ways as persons for whom certain things and other people are close to their hearts. The mere knowledge—and this is something we hardly can deny in psychopaths—which motifs are present-at-hand, as well as an effective realization of these motifs in certain situations, is not a substitute for this particular kind of self-reflexive practice Frankfurt accounts for with caring and love. This implies that for psychopaths the experience of freedom—in the strong sense of an experience of unity in terms of wholeheartedness—may be something that is, as lived experience, fundamentally restricted. Due to this restricted space of possibility, they cannot enter the relevant stages of self-reflexive practice that are constitutive for being able to experience one's life as meaningful. Psychopaths do not experience motifs with the absolute necessity that enthralls other agents, and so lack an understanding for both the instrumental and intrinsic value of caring and love for the good life. Psychopaths neither realize that they cannot have certain things if they do not continuously care for them, nor are they capable of that kind of fundamental identification that shows itself in "disinterested" (Frankfurt 2004, 82) caring about the well-being of others. This qualifies as a deformation of the will, insofar as the psychopath seems oddly fixed to a level of discrete realization of oneself—having the potential to experience some sort of synchronic unity—but is unable to enter a stage of self-reflexivity according to which the diachronic unity of self can be actually achieved and maintained and that normally provides stable structures for action orientated to the long-term and thus a coherent life. It is just because psychopaths do not have a sufficient potential for identification with long-term structuring configurations of will that they also fail to take the moral perspective; to the extent that moral concern is nothing close to their hearts, they cannot experience it as having import. It is especially with reference to persistent antisocial patterns of behavior that psychopaths do not acquire a prosocial attitude, especially not in terms of a capacity for disinterested care due to the modes of love.

Applying Frankfurt's theory, we can relate the competence for (self-) love to the moral competence of agents, and this might finally explain the moral incapacity, thus specifying problems of self-realization with regard to morality. Frankfurt emphasizes a strong volitional unity, which actually is captured by the concept of self-love, as self-love *is* already the unity of will. Consequently, this unity of the will may not only function as a criterion to set apart mentally healthy individuals from the mentally impaired (cf. Frankfurt 2004, 95), but, moreover, provides a solid normative source and, therefore, is relevant for an explanation of moral behavior. Insofar as the loving person identifies—by the very processes of caring—with the beloved object, this simultaneously qualifies as one mode of caring for one's own well-being. Caring for others and for oneself are not just morally neutral concepts to explicate the structures of volition but are furthermore bound to considerations about the good life in Frankfurt's theory. Developing a reflexive self-relation, which manifests itself in acts of love and caring, then, indeed, involves moral self-realization: Inasmuch as we can achieve volitional identity, especially by our being related to others, the practice of caring and love includes a practical sense for our own well-being and that of others, which qualifies as a mode of being a morally good person.[21] As this allows for self-constitution, it is not only necessary to care and to love, but it appears as self-evident to do good to oneself and to others (whether this predominately arises out of an insight into the instrumental value of caring and love or rests on appreciating them as being of intrinsic value then seems secondary). The specific moral incompetence of psychopaths then is characterized as an incapacity to experience the necessities of will—that becomes apparent in the particular mode of love as a source of normativity—to the depths of lived experiences. As psychopaths are not capable of identification, especially disinterested identification with others, they are deprived of the fundamental source of moral self-constitution and thus cannot take the moral point of view or develop a moral stance. These processes of caring and love do not count as experiential horizons of a psychopath and are not vital sources of moral motivation and meaning in psychopathic encounters with the world and their being with others, and so psychopathic comportment is characterized in terms of a rather trivial and empty life.

I have focused in this section on volitional incapacity to map its potential for a specification of a lack of moral sense in psychopaths, which provides a rather preliminary scheme for further considerations on psychopathic comportment. Although this analysis is restricted in scope, I believe that I have provided reasons to accept that in order to take the moral perspective, one has to have the competence for caring and loving, something psychopaths cannot obtain because of their restricted space of moral possibility.

6.6   Conclusion

I have examined in this chapter moral incapacity in psychopathic comportment. The concept of comportment captures and unites the intentional (prereflective and reflective) with the phenomenal dimension to account for the experiential unity of self-and-world disclosure. This is achieved by introducing the dimensions of background and foreground as the two sides of the coin of one's existential situatedness. I have argued that mental illness can include a distortion of practical sense, given certain alterations of these underlying structures (including evaluative patterns) for self-and-world experience that respectively contribute to particular experiences of inability and/or manifest themselves in certain ways of incapacity. Respectively, I put emphasis on the idea that psychopaths show an impairment of practical sense that explains the heterogeneity of deviation from normal comportment. This alteration of the underlying structure that predetermines self-reflective and moreover self-reflexive intentional encounters with the world involves, in particular, an impairment of moral sense. Inasmuch as moral sense has become specified as one subtype of one's practical sense for self and world, a moral dimension has been installed into the concept of comportment. I have further attempted to define this lack of moral sense as preventing psychopaths from taking the moral point of view or developing a personal stance in terms of being able to actively develop stable evaluative patterns for self-and-world disclosure. This provides some line of demarcation for setting apart the psychopath from the free rider, to whom a greater moral potential and actual capacity can be ascribed, as the free rider is able to occasionally utilize a moral perspective for his or her egoistic concerns. I then have outlined how one can describe moral incapacity in more detail and stressed the notions of caring and love as accounting for these fundamental alterations of evaluative self-and-world relation in psychopaths. Psychopaths can be described as being incapable of those modes of individual commitment and self-reflexive practice that are integral for caring and for love. Finally, this proves helpful to readdress their specific amorality as deeply rooted in a problematic self-and-world relation, which is the conceptual core of psychopathic comportment.

Notes

1. This chapter is based on my Ph.D. thesis (Jacobs 2009/2012), which focuses on the interplay of emotional, rational, volitional, and evaluative incapacities and their explanatory power for addressing the problem of moral motivation in psychopaths. I have presented several drafts of the scheme of an existential situation as the interplay of background and foreground and its application for explaining impairments of agency and other modes of altered evaluative self-and-world orientation in mental disorder at several workshops since September 2009.

2. Martin Heidegger introduces the term in his *Prolegomena* (cf. 1925/1985, section 5, 51) and discusses it in a slightly different way in *Sein und Zeit* (*Being and Time*; Heidegger 1927/1962) and six months later in the 1927 Marburg Lecture "Problems of Phenomenology" as "ways of behaving/behaviour" (p. 26, 37), "factual attitude" (p. 238), and "ways in which Dasein comports itself" (p. 176). In the following, I quote from the respective English translations.

3. "This implies that the so-called logical comportments of thinking or objective theoretical knowing represent only a particular and narrow sphere within the domain of intentionality, and that the range of functions assigned to logic in no way exhausts the full sweep of intentionality" (Heidegger 1925/1985, 78).

4. Of course, some of these background patterns can also become themselves an object of reflection and/or shift from the subject's background to the foreground of awareness in a specific situation. Sartre (1939/1962, part III) stresses the different ways in which a state can be conscious in his differentiation of "prereflectively con-

scious" and "reflectively conscious" states. While the former is conscious insofar as the subject's attention on its intentional object is focused without the subject's having to be aware of being in that state, the latter is conscious in that the subject is conscious of having a conscious state—for instance, of experiencing a certain emotional episode like fear—that is, the subject is self-aware of being in a certain conscious state, which normally simultaneously becomes the object of attention, thus becoming "foregrounded."

5. A similarity to Pierre Bourdieu's (1979/1984, 1980/1990) work becomes evident here: Inasmuch as comportment accounts for these patterns for self-and-world disclosure, this resembles Bourdieu's *habitus*. Habitus is the totality of learned habits, bodily skills, styles, tastes, and other nondiscursive forms of knowledge which shape social practice, and it becomes observable in its incorporealized form as *hexis*. According to Bourdieu, habitus allows one to intuitively adapt to the social games one plays in particular social fields, that is, it provides the individual with a kind of practical sense for self and world, which has been illustrated as an integral dimension also of comportment. Bourdieu's habitus and Heidegger's comportment both refer to those underlying structures according to which world and self are perceived, and they are also the structures enacted in individual practice. Both notions already presuppose an individual space of possibilities that predetermines the actual capacity of individuals, thus providing practical orientation in the world. Maurice Merleau-Ponty also emphasizes this practical sense in his *Phenomenology of Perception* (1962, part I, chap. 3, section 19, 159): "Consciousness is in the first place not a matter of 'I think that' but of 'I can.'" This sphere of practice is further accounted for in Heidegger's idea that the world is experienced as a place of practical affordances— that is, that the things of the world appear to individuals not only as "present-at-hand," but also normally as "ready-to-hand." This is central to the conceptualization of comportment in *Being and Time* (cf. Heidegger 1927/1962, 114, section 18). Moreover, the implementation of a "world of possibilities" could be further elaborated by looking at Husserl's (e.g., Husserl 1960) and Merleau-Ponty's (1962) concepts of *horizon* (cf. Jacobs 2013, 7).

6. To avoid confusion between "reflection" and "reflexivity," the terms have to be clarified: For the purpose of this chapter, I use the term "self-reflective" to refer to a certain form of self-relation that has been introduced in the most basic sense as a specific way of being directed toward one's own experiences and particular actions in Heidegger's notion of intentionality. Normally, self-reflection is understood as a mode of individual comportment that improves future practice through a *retrospective* analysis of action, that is, through a post facto relating to completed stages of action, thought, and so on. Although it can also be concerned with seeking to further improve one's practice, it nonetheless remains rather connected to the past. The difference from "self-reflexivity" becomes relevant with regard to when the process of introspection exactly takes place. Self-reflexivity is rather referring to the ongoing process of evaluation. Both modes of self-directedness respectively contribute to clarifying what might be impaired in psychopaths.

7. As one aim of my approach is to account for the well-known dichotomy of possibility and ability as central for a conceptualization of moral incapacity in psychopathy, the idea of an existential background as a space of experiential possibilities (Ratcliffe 2008) has led me to emphasize in my analysis of moral (in-)ability a foreground dimension, which has its counterpart in such a background, a sphere of individual possibility.

8. As prestructuring conditions for our encounters with the world, these implicit evaluative patterns can be further specified with reference to an explicit *affective* dimension (this is the idea of an explicit affective background; cf. Ratcliffe 2008). In contrast to approaches that focus predominantly on background *feelings* as providing these evaluative patterns, or which place *affective* intentionality in the center of self-world-relation (Slaby and Stephan 2008), I would like to emphasize, with the notion of comportment, a broader concept of intentionality, which can account for the phenomenal heterogeneity and intentionality of individual situatedness. Respectively, comportment refers to the whole range of individual predispositions, perceptional schemes, embodied memories, skills and abilities, and so forth that (pre)structure individual self-world-relation (cf. Jacobs et al. in press). These experiential patterns for self-and-world disclosure cannot—with respect to their rich evaluative dimension—be reduced to a mere affective or "felt" sphere, albeit affectivity certainly is *one* way to address specific modes of evaluative self-world-relation (cf. Jacobs 2013).

9. Individuals constitute themselves as the person they are, or want to be, by the things they actually (can) do. This implies that someone is not merely exposed to one's existential situation, or just passively enacts certain (bodily, mental, etc.) predispositions, but that something quite the opposite becomes relevant: Being able to develop a kind of self-reflective stance toward one's being in the world (with others), and toward specific courses of one's action in particular, is, besides other capabilities, one way to bring individual autonomy and responsibility into play. This might help to counterbalance the idea of the background as determining in such a way that people cannot help but enact in a particular way. Individual dispositions or habitus clearly predetermine one's actual capacities and thus are prestructuring conditions for more reflective encounters with the world, but they do not rule out autonomy in general. However, it becomes clear with respect to comportment in mental illness that structural alterations of one's existential background can fundamentally restrict one's possibility and actual capacity to experience oneself as enabled or as a particularly autonomous agent (cf. Jacobs and Thome 2003; Jacobs 2009/2012, 142ff). It remains to be ascertained whether such structural alterations point toward a diminished responsibility in psychopathy (Jacobs 2009/2012, 255–270).

10. I have already mentioned that Bourdieu's concept of habitus—like the notion of comportment—refers to a double structure of the existential situation of individuals. In scholastic times, it was Aquinas who—relying on Aristotle's dichotomy of *energeia* and *dynamis* (or potentiality and actuality) pointed out that habitus "*est medium*

inter potentiam puram et puram actum" (Krais and Gebauer 2002, 26). This says that habitus mediates between the sphere of potentiality (*potentia pura*) and the sphere of actual practice (*purus actus*) and thus is describable in terms of the vital transformation processes according to which something given to individuals as potentiality becomes actualized, while the modes of actuality simultaneously impregnate (loop back to) the sphere of individual possibility. To the extent that comportment also generates forms of social practice due to the underlying structure of evaluative, perceptual, and cognitive schemes for individual orientation, it resembles habitus as *modus operandi*, and insofar as comportment is analyzable as a product of these generative patterns, it is simultaneously also analyzable as *modus operatum*.

11. I have explained elsewhere, regarding the case of depression, how relatively stable as well as rigid habitual patterns become implemented due to these looping dynamics (cf. Jacobs 2013). The concepts of comportment and habitus both explain those ways in which agents incorporate or inhabit the structures and techniques relevant to their individual sphere of practice. Objective social structures and individual practices deeply shape our bodies and can become part of our set of (bodily) dispositions. It is via constant repetition and mimetic reading of bodies, things, rooms, and various other experiences in social space that relatively stable comportments, including schemes of movements, skills, individual preferences, and so on, are acquired and become incorporated. This is how they become integrated into the personality structure of individuals (cf. Fuchs 2006).

12. Basically *Körper* refers to the body as an object of one's experience, that is, it is the observable body (and respectively designates what I have referred to with *hexis* in terms of the works of Pierre Bourdieu). The body as *Körper* expresses also several forms of incorporated practice or roles. An actor can, for instance, incorporate (*verkörpern*) a certain role (e.g., a ballerina, a warrior, etc.). While this kind of incorporation is the product of intentional processes, it is just one specific form of incorporation. There are, of course, other forms that impregnate and "enter" the body through education, social structures, and so forth and, as such, rather tacitly (pre-) structure our situation as embodied individuals (see: *habitus*). Contrastingly, *Leib* refers to the lived or felt body. *Leib* is a medium for evaluative world-disclosure and respectively is that through which we are enabled to be (for instance, affectively) engaged in our actual encounters with the world. In several mental disorders especially the dimension of the lived body is disturbed and contributes as well as already expresses a changed sense of oneself. Someone may experiences his or her body as opaque, dead, alien or robot-like, that can be explained as shifts toward pathogenic forms of experiencing oneself just as a *Körper* or just as having a *Körper* deprived of its vitality and thus of its self-and-world-disclosing function. This feeling oneself as *being* a *Leib* and perceiving oneself as *having* a *Körper*, as well as the ability to shift in one's awareness between both experiential dimensions, can become unbalanced in psychopathology. It moreover amounts to particular pathological forms of one's self-and-world orientation that shape the specific experiential dimension of the

respective disorders (e.g., Svenaeus 2000; Ratcliffe 2008, 2009a, 2009b; Warsop 2009; Jacobs 2013; Jacobs et al. in press).

13. The German term *Grenzsituation*—translated *limit situation* (cf. Chris Thornhill 2011), *boundary situation* (cf. Ronny Miron 2012), or *border situation* (cf. Jacobs and Thome 2003)—can be used to describe psychiatric disorders as an exceptional state of existence, converting *Alltagssituationen* (situations of daily life) to *Grenzsituationen*, inasmuch as fundamental shifts in one's experiential patterns are involved (cf. Jacobs 2013, 2). It has to be discussed elsewhere in greater detail how to specify the notion of comportment in relation to a particular kind of experiential stance that is associated with Karl Jaspers's conceptualization of *Grenzsituation*: The concept of comportment then may be further specified as including particular experiences of the unconditioned (*das Unbedingte*), which is a characteristic of the border situation in Jaspers's notion and which is associated with a certain kind of self-reflexive stance. This shows when individuals face the unconditioned in particular modes of anxiety or experience their actual situation in the light of death and illness. It can imply that one puts into question one's own perceptual schemes, the implicitness of one's daily routines, and so forth. This furthermore includes, in Jaspers's account, the possibility of transforming experiences. Individuals may seek not only to transcend the limits of reason in the sophisticated ways Jaspers emphasizes with the idea of an "existentially open consciousness" but may moreover cope with such experiences also by virtue of a force that literally "keeps them going." This most basic sense of vitality, a conatus or a basic drive or striving, is associated rather with prereflective conditions of someone's existential situatedness. It might be further elaborated in its relation to those higher cognitive forms of intentionality involved in self-reflexive processes of contemplating the possibilities and actual restrictions of one's own existential situation.

14. While depression and most of the personality disorders are seen to involve ego-dystonic experience, psychopathy, in contrast, rather goes along with ego-syntonic experience. That is, the experience of suffering due to a felt mismatch or devaluation of respective patterns of behavior and symptoms of illness in the light of one's self-image is not predominant. With reference to an objective perspective one can, however, claim that psychopathy goes along with fundamental incapacities that are symptomatic for the disorder. Moreover, most symptoms of psychopathy can be reassessed as being themselves expressions of incapacity or as at least bringing with them the risk or actual condition of suffering for the individual.

15. Moral capacity, in the most basic sense, already includes the realm of respective practice. So I indeed refer here to the idea that someone who is able to take a moral stance not only as one point of view among others, but has developed a moral *stance* as one modus of comportment that becomes integral to one's self-understanding, normally is already predisposed to act according to it. Thus, it seems that taking the moral point seriously determines the continuity and constancy of a respective individual moral practice. Consequently, I consider the motivational dimension as

anchored in the notion of comportment since it accounts for the transformational dynamics from possibility to actuality (ability).

16. My account of moral sense diverges from classic sentimentalism insofar as I do not single out moral sense as one distinctive faculty that accounts for moral understanding solely in terms of moral feeling or particular affective responsiveness. I rather opt to regard moral sense as emerging from the grounds of the totality of lived experience. It essentially involves the idea of experiential patterns as incorporated structures according to which we can *intuitively* adapt to the social sphere, and respectively also to the subsphere of the "moral game," which simultaneously is instantiated and sustained by individual practice. This may be a starting point for a further discussion on the interplay of different kinds of evaluation involved in moral judgment. Moral sense might furthermore include a sensibility for a possible disharmony between different kinds of evaluations someone might have in a certain situation: for instance, a possible difference between one's spontaneous feelings and the rational assessment of that very situation.

17. Paul E. Mullen (1992) also stresses this difference: The psychopaths are "as incapable of consistently behaving in accordance with the codes that govern the behaviour of prisoners or of other offender groups as they are incapable of consistently complying with the wider society's requirements. It is for this reason that they tend to be isolated among their criminal peers as well as in wider society. Such individuals cannot be trusted and are unpredictable within any social context and any set of ethical and moral imperatives" (Mullen 1992, 239). Studies that empirically support the distinction between free riders and psychopaths are provided by Campagna and Harter (1975), Fodor (1973), and Jurkovic and Prentice (1977). Although Lee and Prentice (1988) and Trevethan and Walker (1989) came to contrasting results in their comparative study on moral reasoning in nonpsychopathic offenders and psychopaths—and one has to admit additionally that the free rider must not be assimilated to the offending type in general—the higher rate of recidivism in psychopaths in comparison with nonpsychopathic offenders after therapeutic treatment (Rice et al. 1992; Hare et al. 2000; Hemphill et al. 1998), their poor adjustment to therapeutic programs (Hobson et al. 2000; Ogloff et al. 1990), and their particular problems in processing information about future response requirements and choosing the right strategy to successfully avoid punishment (Elliott and Gillett 1992; Newman et al. 1987) may lend credibility to the thesis that psychopaths fundamentally differ from several types of free rider and that their various functional impairments amount to a unique form of altered practical sense. This is a view which I also see addressed in Hervey Cleckley's description of the psychopathic dissociation due to "a persistent lack of ability to become aware of what the most important experiences of life mean to others" and respectively this is something which lies out of a psychopath's "mode of experience" (Cleckley 1941, 228ff.).

18. From what has been said so far, it seems rather implausible to account for these moments of insight due to a self-reflexive stance in psychopaths, which can be

related to the hypothesis that psychopaths neither benefit from treatment nor are able to adjust to the therapeutic setting for several reasons (e.g., incapacity of forming the emotional bonds to a therapist required for therapeutic success). Cleckley (1941), McCord (1982), and Hare (1970) conclude that there is no evidence for efficacious treatment of adult psychopaths while "therapeutic pessimism" is rejected by Salekin (2002) and Skeem et al. (2002; for a critical review of more recent studies, see Harris and Rice 2005). Specific cognitive–behavioral therapy interventions based on a social skills training and anger-management program (e.g., Hare et al. 2000), principles of good correction treatment (Seto and Barbaree 1999), or treatment which directly targets personal characteristics seen as correlative with recidivism (Wong and Hare 2005) rely on this idea of changing behavioral patterns that eventually have an impact on experiential patterns, and they may respectively aim to increase self-reflexive competence in psychopaths.

19. Self-reflexivity is rather referring to the ongoing process of evaluation and refers in Frankfurt's theory to those stages of self-directed practice in which individuals become aware of what is of importance for them.

20. One might further examine how recent empirical studies may support this phenomenological hypothesis and how these findings amount to an explanation and specification of the lack of diachronic unity. One can highlight, for instance, functional impairments, for example, impairment in selective attention and information processing (cf. Zuckerman 1978; MacCoon and Newman 2006; Blair et al. 2001; Blair et al. 2002; Kosson 1996), altered responsiveness to distress cues (Blair et al. 1997), and differences in emotional learning (Newman and Kosson 1996; Newman et al. 1987; Newman et al. 1997; Thornquist and Zuckerman 1995). These aspects amount to specifying an altered practical sense in psychopaths and respective changes in experiential patterns that also shape individual predispositions and one's actual modes of orientation in the world. If one is moreover inclined to accept that such fragments of unity can be further evidenced with respect to a phenomenological perspective on psychopathy, the characteristics of psychopathy captured by diagnostic criteria are likely to support the idea of incoherence and incapacity for long-term commitment: Low tolerance to frustration, a low threshold for discharge of aggression and violence, and impulsiveness may count as factors that prevent psychopaths from properly adjusting to specific situations that require stable, long-term commitment (at work, in relationships, etc.). With reference to the PCL–R (Hare 1991; cf. Cooke and Michie 2001 and Frick and Hare 2001) items such as "lack of realistic, long-term goals" refer to the incoherent style in psychopaths. The incapacity to maintain enduring relationships (though having no severe difficulty in establishing them, i.e., to merely transitorily affirm a relationship with someone), mentioned by the ICD–10 (WHO 2010) for dissocial personality disorder (F60.2, 160), may—from a *phenomenological level of description* that regards psychopathy not as equivalent with antisocial personality disorder or dissocial personality disorder, but accounts for the similarity in the surface criteria of the conditions—further show

as a specific mode in which the lack of diachronic self-realization in psychopaths manifests itself in particular. It points toward a fundamentally restricted possibility for caring and love in psychopathy, a distortion of a practical sense for self that becomes most transparent in relation to others.

21. In principle, someone can also be wholeheartedly devoted to the morally bad and respectively take care of amorality, which might offer at first glance an optional path for the reconstruction of psychopathic amoralism within Frankfurt's account. By taking a closer look, one might however object that this would not fit in the picture of psychopaths drawn here as lacking the capacity to care. Consequently, a psychopath is incapacitated to care for what is morally bad, too. Moreover, such a kind of practical identification with and commitment to what is morally bad does not really illustrate amoralism but rather corresponds to a radical variant of immoralism, which accounts for doing the morally wrong for the sake of it, thus implying simply a value orientation under reversed signs.

References

American Psychiatric Association. 2000. *Diagnostic and Statistical Manual of Mental Disorders*. 4th ed., text revision. Washington, D.C.: American Psychiatric Association.

Blair, R. J. R., E. Colledge, L. Murray, and D. Mitchell. 2001. A Selective Impairment in the Processing of a Sad and Fearful Expression in Children with Psychopathic Tendencies. *Journal of Abnormal Child Psychology* 29:499–511.

Blair, R. J. R., L. Jones, F. Clark, and M. Smith. 1997. The Psychopathic Individual: A Lack of Responsiveness to Distress Cues? *Psychophysiology* 34:192–198.

Blair, R. J. R., D. Mitchell, S. Kelly, R. Ritchell, A. Leonard, C. Newman, and S. Scott. 2002. Turning a Deaf Ear to Fear: Impaired Recognition of Vocal Affect in Psychopathic Individuals. *Journal of Abnormal Psychology* 111:682–686.

Bourdieu, P. 1979/1984. *La Distinction: critique sociale du jugement.* Paris: Les Editions de Minuit; transl.: *Distinction: A Social Critique of the Judgement of Taste Translated by Richard Nice.* London: Routledge Kegan & Paul.

Bourdieu, P. 1980/1990. *Le sens pratique.* Paris: Les Editions de Minuit; transl.: *The Logic of Practice.* Cambridge: Polity.

Bourdieu, P. 1992/1996. *The Rules of Art: Genesis and Structure of the Literary Field,* trans. S. Emanuel. Cambridge: Polity.

Campagna, A. F., and S. Harter. 1975. Moral Judgements in Sociopathic and Normal Children. *Journal of Personality and Social Psychology* 31:199–205.

Cleckley, H. M. 1941. *The Mask of Sanity: An Attempt to Clarify Some Issues about the So-called Psychopathic Personality.* 5th ed. St. Louis: Mosby.

Cooke, D. J., and C. Michie. 2001. Refining the Construct of Psychopathy: Towards a Hierarchical Model. *Psychological Assessment* 13:171–188.

Elliott, C., and C. Gillett. 1992. Moral Insanity and Practical Reason. *Philosophical Psychology* 5:53–67.

Fodor, E. M. 1973. Moral Development and Parent Behaviour Antecedents in Adolescent Psychopaths. *Journal of Genetic Psychology* 122:37–43.

Frankfurt, H. G. 1988. Freedom of the Will and the Concept of a Person. In *The Importance of What We Care About*, 11–25. New York: Cambridge University Press.

Frankfurt, H. G. 1999. *Necessity, Volition, and Love*. Cambridge: Cambridge University Press.

Frankfurt, H. G. 2004. *The Reasons of Love*. Princeton: Princeton University Press.

Frankfurt, H. G. 2006. *Taking Ourselves Seriously and Getting It Right*, ed. D. Satz, Stanford, Calif.: Stanford University Press.

Frick, P. J., and R. D. Hare. 2001. *The Antisocial Process Screening Device (APSD). Technical Manual*. Toronto, ON: Multi-Health Systems.

Fuchs, T. 2006. Gibt es eine leibliche Persönlichkeitsstruktur? [Is there a bodily-lived personality structure?] *Psychodynamische Psychotherapie* 5 (2):109–117.

Hare, R. D. 1970. *Psychopathy: Theory and Research*. New York: Guilford.

Hare, R. D. 1991. *The Psychopathy Checklist—Revised [PCL-R]*. Toronto, ON: Multi-Health Systems.

Hare, R. D., D. Clark, M. Grann, and D. Thornton. 2000. Psychopathy and the Predictive Validity of the PCL–R: An International Perspective. *Behavioral Sciences & the Law* 18:623–645.

Harris, G. T., and M. E. Rice. 2005. Treatment of Psychopathy: A Review of Empirical Findings. In *Handbook of Psychopathy*, ed. J. C. Patrick, 555–572. New York: Guilford.

Heidegger, M. 1925/1985. *Prolegomena zur Geschichte des Zeitbegriffs (Sommersemester 1925)*, GA Bd. 20, hrsg. von Petra Jäger, 3., durchgesehene Aufl., 1994, Frankfurt am Main: Klostermann; transl.: *History of the Concept of Time: Prolegomena*, trans. T. Kisiel. Bloomington: Indiana University Press.

Heidegger, M. 1927/1962. *Sein und Zeit*. Tübingen: Niemeyer; transl. *Being and Time*, trans. J. Macquarrie and E. Robinson, Oxford: Basil Blackwell.

Hemphill, J. F., R. D. Hare, and S. Wong. 1998. Psychopathy and Recidivism—A Review. *Legal and Criminological Psychology* 3:737–745.

Hobson, J., J. Shine, and R. Roberts. 2000. How Do Psychopaths Behave in a Prison Therapeutic Community? *Psychology, Crime & Law* 6:139–154.

Husserl, E. 1960. *Cartesian Meditations: An Introduction to Phenomenology*, translated by D. Cairns. The Hague: Martinus Nijhoff.

Jacobs, K. A. 2009/2012. *Soziopathie—Eine Untersuchung moralischer Unfähigkeit [Sociopathy—An Analysis of Moral Incapacity]*. Uelvesbüll: Der Andere Verlag.

Jacobs, K. A. 2013. The Depressive Situation. *Frontiers in Psychology* 4:1–11.

Jacobs, K. A., and J. Thome. 2003. Zur Freiheitskonzeption in Karl Jaspers' Psychopathologie [The Concept of Liberty in Jaspers' Psychopathology]. *Fortschritte der Neurologie-Psychiatrie* 71:509–516.

Jacobs, K. A., A. Stephan, A. Paskaleva, and W. Wilutzky. in press. Existential and Atmospheric Feelings in Depressive Comportment. *Philosophy, Psychiatry & Psychology*.

Jaspers, K. 1950. *Einführung in die Philosophie*. Zürich: Artemis. English transl.: *Way to Wisdom: An Introduction to Philosophy*, trans. R. Manheim, New Haven, Conn.: Yale University Press, 1951.

Jurkovic, G. J., and P. M. Prentice. 1977. Relation of Moral and Cognitive Development to Dimensions of Juvenile Delinquency. *Journal of Abnormal Psychology* 86:414–420.

Kosson, D. 1996. Psychopathy and the Dual-Task Performance under Focusing Conditions. *Journal of Abnormal Psychology* 105:391–400.

Krais, B., and Gebauer, G. 2002. *Habitus*. Bielefeld: transcript Verlag.

Lee, M., and N. M. Prentice. 1988. Interrelations of Empathy, Cognition, and Moral Reasoning with Dimensions of Juvenile Delinquency. *Journal of Abnormal Child Psychology* 16:127–139.

MacCoon, D. G., and J. P. Newman. 2006. Content Meets Process: Using Attributions and Standards to Inform Cognitive Vulnerability in Psychopathy, Antisocial Personality Disorder, and Depression. *Journal of Social and Clinical Psychology* 27:802–824.

Maibom, H. L. 2005. Moral Unreason: The Case of Psychopathy. *Mind & Language* 20:237–257.

McCord, J. 1982. Parental Behavior in the Cycle of Aggression. *Psychiatry* 51:14–23.

Merleau-Ponty, M. 1962. *Phenomenology of Perception*, trans. C. Smith. London: Routledge.

Miron, R. 2012. *Karl Jaspers: From Selfhood to Being; Value Inquiry Book Series*. Amsterdam: Rodopi.

Mullen, P. E. 1992. Psychopathy: A Development Disorder of Ethical Action. *Criminal Behaviour and Mental Health* 2:234–244.

Newman, J. P., and D. Kosson. 1996. Passive Avoidance Learning in Psychopathic and Non-psychopathic Offenders. *Journal of Abnormal Psychology* 95:252–256.

Newman, J. P., C. M. Patterson, and D. S. Kosson. 1987. Response Perseveration in Psychopaths. *Journal of Abnormal Psychology* 96:145–148.

Newman, J. P., W. A. Schmitt, and W. D. Voss. 1997. The Impact of Motivationally Neutral Cues on Psychopathic Individuals Assessing the Generality of the Response Modulation Hypothesis. *Journal of Abnormal Psychology* 106:563–575.

Ogloff, J., S. Wong, and A. Greenwood. 1990. Treating Criminal Psychopaths in a Therapeutic Community Program. *Behavioral Sciences & the Law* 8:81–90.

Ratcliffe, M. 2008. *Feelings of Being: Phenomenology, Psychiatry and the Sense of Reality.* Oxford: Oxford University Press.

Ratcliffe, M. 2009a. Belonging to the World through the Feeling Body. *Philosophy, Psychiatry, & Psychology* 16:205–211.

Ratcliffe, M. 2009b. Understanding Existential Changes in Psychiatric Illness: The Indispensability of Phenomenology. In *Psychiatry as Cognitive Neuroscience*, ed. M. Broome and L. Bortolotti, 223–244. Oxford: Oxford University Press.

Rice, M. E., G. T. Harris, and C. Cormier. 1992. A Follow-up of Rapists Assessed in a Maximum Security Psychiatric Facility. *Journal of Interpersonal Violence* 5:435–448.

Salekin, R. T. 2002. Psychopathy and Therapeutic Pessimism—Clinical Lore or Clinical Reality? *Clinical Psychology Review* 22:79–112.

Sartre, J.-P. 1939/1962. *Esquisse d'une théorie des émotions.* Paris: Les Editions Scientifiques, Herrmann; transl. *Sketch for a Theory of Emotions.* London: Routledge.

Seto, M. C., and H. Barbaree. 1999. Psychopathy, Treatment, Behavior, and Sex Offender Recidivism. *Journal of Interpersonal Violence* 14:1235–1248.

Skeem, J. L., J. Monahan, and E. P. Mulvey. 2002. Psychopathy, Treatment, and Subsequent Violence among Civil Psychiatric Patients. *Law and Human Behavior* 26:577–603.

Slaby, J., and A. Stephan. 2008. Affective Intentionality and Self-Consciousness. *Consciousness and Cognition* 17:506–513.

Smith, M. 1994. *The Moral Problem.* Oxford: Blackwell.

Svenaeus, F. 2000. The Body Uncanny—Further Steps towards a Phenomenology of Illness. *Medicine, Health Care and Philosophy* 3:125–137.

Thornhill, C. 2011. Karl Jaspers. In *The Stanford Encyclopedia of Philosophy* (Spring 2011 Edition), ed. E. N. Zalta, http://plato.stanford.edu/archives/spr2011/entries/jaspers.

Thornquist, M. H., and M. Zuckerman. 1995. Psychopathy, Passive-Avoidance Learning and Basic Dimensions of Personality. *Personality and Individual Differences* 19:525–534.

Trevethan, S., and L. J. Walker. 1989. Hypothetical versus Real-Life Moral Reasoning among Psychopathic and Delinquent Youth. *Development and Psychopathology* 1:91–103.

Warsop, A. 2009. Existential Feeling, Touch and "Belonging." *Philosophy, Psychiatry, & Psychology* 16:201–204.

Wolf, U. 2009. Reflexion und Identität: Harry Frankfurts Auffassung menschlichen Handelns. [Reflection and Identity: Harry Franfurt's Account of Human Action.] In *Sozialphilosophie und Kritik. Axel Honneth zum 60. Geburtstag*, ed. R. Forst, M. Hartmann, R. Jaeggi, and M. Saar, 409–432. Frankfurt am Main: Suhrkamp Verlag.

Wong, S., and R. D. Hare. 2005. *Guidelines for a Psychopathy Treatment Program.* Toronto, ON: Multi-Health Systems.

World Health Organization. 2010. *International Classification of Diseases*, tenth revision [ICD 10].

Zuckerman, M. 1978. Sensation Seeking and Psychopathy. In *Psychopathic Behaviour: Approaches to Research*, ed. R. D. Hare and D. Schalling, 165–186. Chichester: Wiley.

7 Not Caring: Sociopaths and the Suffering of Others

Piers Benn

I begin with an intuitive and rather obvious fact about suffering. This is that when you suffer, you want that suffering to end, other things being equal. Even if you consider your suffering as justified in some way—for example, as punishment or because it is the lesser of two evils—there is still something intrinsically aversive about it. Admittedly, there have been suggestions that certain neurological interventions allow people to experience pain but somehow "not mind" it. This is intriguing and not to be ruled out a priori. However, I shall stick with the normal case of suffering: a state experienced as nasty and as crying out for its own termination.

This may seem to be a statement of the obvious. There is, admittedly, a puzzle, in the philosophy of psychology concerning *what it is* about suffering that makes it so awful, about how there can be a state that cries out for its own destruction in this way. The same question can be raised about pleasure, about what is it about pleasure that makes us seek it. However, it is hard to see what could count as a good, informative answer. I shall take it simply as given that there are such states. Such experiences are intrinsically reason giving: My suffering gives me a prima facie reason to put a stop to it. Of course, suffering of one kind (e.g., sensations of pain) can arouse pleasure of another kind (e.g., sadomasochistic sexual pleasure), and so it might be sought out for that reason. But this is not an objection to the general point.

So much for one's own suffering. But what about the suffering of other people and perhaps all other sentient beings? There are writers, notably Thomas Nagel (1970), who think that if my own suffering provides me with a reason to extinguish it, then knowledge of the suffering of others must also provide me with a reason to end their suffering. And if I act on this reason, that shows I can be motivated by knowledge of another's pain—that I can altruistically desire that his or her pain should end. Some people doubt this; they think that whenever people seem to be acting out of concern for others, they are really acting only out of self-interest. For example, they suppose that if I obtain satisfaction from helping another person, then I help the other person only for the sense of satisfaction it gives me. However, if I didn't genuinely care about the other person, it would be hard to explain why I would obtain any satisfaction from their being helped.

Nagel defends the possibility of altruism and takes any suffering, whoever's it is, to be reason giving; the suffering of anyone—and many would add, of any sentient creature—provides a reason to end it. In this, he is, of course, far from alone. He finds it hard to see how this could be otherwise. What, objectively considered, is the relevant difference between me and someone else? Is it not clear that if I have such an obvious reason to end my own suffering, then anyone else who knows of it also has a reason to end it?

However, although altruistic motivation is clearly possible and often explains our behavior, it is obvious that at other times we are pretty indifferent to the suffering of others. We witness the suffering of a stranger, and though we might be moved by it to some extent, we are not moved as we are by our own suffering or that of people close to us. Almost none of us is an altruistic saint. However, my focus will be on people who are so unusually lacking in such concern that they seem qualitatively different from most other people in this respect. In particular, they display a marked lack of concern for those with whom they come into regular contact and for those with whom they appear to have close relationships. It is sometimes said that they are unable to put themselves into the shoes, or minds, of normal people when it comes to personal concern for others. But what does this mean? And if it is true, does it mean they are so different from us "normal" people that we cannot put ourselves into *their* shoes? In other words, should we follow the popular idea that there is something so alien about such people—who are sometimes called sociopaths or psychopaths, especially in the popular media—that we cannot make any real sense of their motivations?

7.1 "Normal" Indifference to Suffering

However, consider first some of the reasons why most of us don't care as much as we might about the suffering of others. I see the emaciated face of a starving child in Somalia, where there is, as I write, a famine. Then I try to remember that the appalling suffering in famine-ridden areas, torn apart by cruel and stupid wars, is only a tiny detail of the picture of human suffering. There is the fear suffered by people at great risk of random violence. There is the grief and rage suffered by those who love them. There is the terror and agony of the millions who suffer torture. Then there are, millions of times over, the unspoken minutiae of suffering, the unfathomable small details of people's lives, and the human monsters who cause many of these horrors. And there are the ordinary heartbreaks of everyday life, nothing to do with famine or cruelty. So what do I feel? What should I feel? The sense of "compassion fatigue" quickly comes over me; I watch the news but still look forward to the next "happy" item, when I shall pour some wine and think about the coming weekend. I may vaguely reprimand myself for this, but I find myself thinking that I cannot take all these horrors on board emotionally, and that I am not greatly to blame for this. I might donate a paltry amount of money to a charity, and then find myself paying less attention to the continuing news bulletins because I have now "done my bit."

Compassion fatigue, or a sense of emotional burnout, affects almost everyone with the capacity for compassion. This is not particularly surprising. Just as we cannot remember a numerical sequence with more than a certain number of digits or make sense of sentences containing triple or quadruple negatives, so there seem to be inbuilt limits when it comes to compassion. At the same time, we can be aware of this. Intellectually speaking, I recognize that the many hundreds of millions of suffering people are no less worthy of compassion than a particular suffering person whom I am thinking about now. I recognize, likewise, that the death of a stranger's child is objectively no less of a calamity than the death of my child would be. For many of us, this is where reason—here meaning knowledge and understanding—comes to the rescue of moral motivation. I may be almost unmoved emotionally by the suffering of another, but this is no excuse for not acting; my reason tells me that this suffering is at least a prima facie reason for trying to alleviate it, whether or not it distresses me. Emotional burnout is no excuse. The existence of suffering provides a reason for anyone to alleviate it who can.

However, turn now to another kind of case of not being moved to act, which touches on Nagel's thoughts. Imagine someone who is in close proximity to another person, who he knows is suffering terribly—perhaps this other person has intense claustrophobia and is trapped in a small enclosed space, or perhaps he is suffering from awful, clinical depression. Imagine he knows that by doing something extremely simple and virtually effortless, like pulling a lever, he can put an instant stop to that suffering. Suppose also that he has no reason to want the suffering to continue—for example, he doesn't think the suffering is deserved in any way or will lead to a greater good. Moreover, he is neither a sadist nor bears any personal grudge—he gets no personal gratification from the other person's suffering. He merely says that he *sees no reason* to end the torment. If he can be shown a good reason why he should, he will act on it without hesitation. Until then, he will leave him as he is.

How might we make sense of this? We would almost certainly find this man disturbing—he appears *radically perverse*. He perversely, rather than stupidly or unimaginatively, fails to see an incontrovertible reason for pulling the lever. He is a bizarre figure in a thought experiment. However, let us speculatively call him a "rational amoralist"—at least, with respect to others' suffering. He is in the grip of a perverse conception of practical reasoning but is quite prepared to be proved wrong and would willingly relieve the suffering if he found a sound reason to do so.

In this way, it is possible to understand the man's stance in terms of an unusually austere and penetrating devotion to rationality. On this interpretation, he is more rational than most of us are able to be. He has bitten a very unusual bullet and has followed his reason where he thinks it leads. Nevertheless, in practice his "rationality" would be considered simple perversity, to the point that we would find it impossible to regard him as "one of us" in our dealings with him. We would, in real life, see him as someone whose intellectual clarity masks either a deeply abnormal personality or a deeply flawed moral character. We think he is demanding what is a priori impossible when he keeps asking why he should end the torment and thus has set the standard impossibly high; he perversely agrees with us but sees this as confirming his position. In short, and especially if much of the rest of his behavior showed the same pattern, we would conclude that we were dealing with an intelligent sociopath.

7.2 Sociopaths and the Rest: Swapping Shoes

Of course, this character is a far cry from the real people usually called sociopaths. He was introduced to suggest that although he presents us with a temptation to describe him in other terms, for example, as a highly rational man with a tenaciously defended philosophical approach, his radical lack of concern for others' interests puts him in the same class as ordinary sociopaths. However, the terms "sociopathy" and "psychopathy" abound in psychiatric and philosophical literature, with no complete consensus about their diagnostic criteria or the real psychological essences they refer to if they do so at all. For example, Adam Morton (2004, 47) distinguishes sociopaths from psychopaths, reserving the latter term to describe sociopaths who are also violent. (In this respect, I am following Morton.) Others think that sociopaths (if the term is appropriate at all) are simply evil people. But what is generally agreed is that persons to whom such terms apply lack certain emotions and may also be *unable* to experience, or even understand, these emotions. That is why sociopaths are frequently defined as lacking empathy, as deficient in imaginative understanding of the joy or suffering of others.

Sociopathy and lack of empathy are strongly connected, but in addition, it is important to distinguish empathy from sympathy. Empathy, I suggest, is an imaginative recognition of what another is feeling, while sympathy is an emotional reaction to what another is feeling, even if this reaction is quite calm. It is hard to be sympathetic without empathy, and the two are usually closed linked. Yet it seems possible to behave with due concern for others' feelings, even if one *either* has a poor general imagination of what it is like to have those feelings *or* if one does have this general understanding but is inept at detecting them in particular situations. Indeed, the moral philosophy of Immanuel Kant might be of comfort to people like this: Kant says that a morally admirable deed must come from the motive of duty, regardless of whether the agent also has natural sympathy for others, or any other inclination to do the good deed (Kant 1964). Conversely, a sadist could be empathic, with his empathy allowing him to devise subtle, bespoke torments for those unfortunate enough to come his way. He is not unmoved by the suffering of others—on the contrary, it excites him. He is not a sociopath, if sociopathy entails lack of empathy. We are far more likely to call him evil instead and explain this in terms of his extraordinary lack of appropriate sympathy; the sympathetic person has empathy and is moved by this to experience some distress at the suffering of another and to try to alleviate it if possible.

Empathy, then, is not sufficient for sympathy. It is also, arguably, possible to act in a sympathetic manner, without deception, yet also without much empathy. However, given that there is usually a close connection between empathy and sympathy, I stipulate that sociopaths are best described as lacking the hybrid quality of *empathic sympathy*. A sociopath may not be sadistic. He may not obtain gratification from other people's suffering, for its own sake. But he has little or no concern for the suffering, wrong, or harm that he inflicts upon others. He lacks conscience, guilt or remorse. Characteristically, he is deceitful, manipulative, and self-centered. He may be charming, and able to simulate remorse and sympathy when it is useful. No doubt there are degrees of sociopathy. But near one end of the spectrum, there is a small cluster of people who display these traits consistently. And we want to ask, do these people really share our moral or social world? Is a sociopath—as opposed to someone who is properly described as bad—able to grasp what it is to be normal?

From this comes the idea that the sociopath's lack of sympathy arises from his or her failure of empathy, albeit that these are two different things. Morton suggests,

The psychology of most kinds of dangerous people involves some deficit in the grasp of what it is to be another person. The violent individual has difficulty understanding that people do not rank others favourably in terms of their capacity to inspire fear. The sociopath has difficulty understanding that many human acts are performed either for the sake of the interaction itself or in order to benefit others. One might conjecture that sociopaths have difficulty with tasks that require one to put oneself imaginatively in another person's situation, especially when that situation is an essentially social one. (Morton 2004, 51)

The idea of grasping "what it is to be another person" is more suggestive than precise. However, it echoes the widely accepted idea that there is something about human interactions that sociopaths simply don't grasp. For that reason, sociopathy has been compared with autism, though, of course, autistic people are no more antisocial than anyone else, and probably less so, because they find it difficult to deceive. It might be said that sociopaths don't understand sympathetic human interaction, much as tone-deaf people don't understand music. Those who are tone-deaf may become experts in music theory, just as some sociopaths are expert in simulating sympathy and remorse and are shrewd about others' motivations. But beneath this veneer, there is a deep, disturbing emptiness.

What is particularly interesting, however, is whether the incomprehension is one-sided or whether in reality there is mutual incomprehension between sociopaths and the rest of us. People often think of sociopaths as radically apart from the rest of us, such that they are disturbingly incomprehensible. This adds to their aura of alien dangerousness. But is this true? We might ask, can we put ourselves into the shoes of people who can't put themselves into *our* shoes, emotionally speaking? Can we properly understand what it is, or what it would be like, to have no understanding of the things that, in reality, we do understand?

I maintain that it is too simple to declare that the inner worlds of sociopaths are radically incomprehensible. Though it may disturb us to contemplate it, it is within the power of normal people to put themselves into the shoes of people who lack empathic sympathy—at least on a particular occasion—and even into the shoes of people who delight in atrocity and evil. To see this, we need some account of the difference between wallowing in a terrible act or desire and imaginatively identifying with someone who does. We need also to see how precarious the line between these two things can be.

Take the example of violence. Only a minority of sociopaths are habitually violent, and most habitually violent people are not sociopaths. However, it is helpful to use the example of violence in order to understand how ordinary people can depart from accepted moral norms against violence. Morton suggests that many violent people have been through a process of "violentization," which has conditioned them to react violently in situations when most people would not. Often, the process starts in early childhood, when children are subjected to, or witness, regular violence from family members and learn to see this as normal. Later on in childhood they learn that violence brings immediate rewards; they are feared, and others comply with them. In adulthood this becomes integrated into the rest of their personality, and they manage social situations with violence or the threat of violence. This becomes essential to their functioning. They like being feared and think that if they aren't feared, they aren't respected. They cannot see that most people manage their social interactions perfectly well without inspiring fear through the use or threat of violence.

Other cases of violentization are different. Morton uses an example of an ex-paratrooper suffering from post-traumatic stress disorder due to his experience of extreme fear and danger on the battlefield. He has witnessed the horrible deaths of men with whom he had tightly bonded, and this leads to intense rage. This may cause him to go berserk later on, in completely peaceful situations; perhaps he becomes a spree-killer who randomly shoots passersby in a shopping mall.

The point about both cases—children for whom violence becomes a learned behavior and the previously peaceful adult who becomes violent—is that their dangerousness is the end result of a process. Most people have a "violence inhibiting mechanism," as described by James Blair (1995), and a few of us learn to overcome that mechanism. Normal adults can be conditioned to be violent in certain particular circumstances. Soldiers are conditioned to kill the enemy, and security police serving repressive regimes are often trained to overcome their natural aversion to torturing and murdering, sometimes by being very roughly treated during the training. Violent sociopaths, on the other hand, are different. It is possible that they never had a violence inhibiting mechanism to be overcome in the first place. And likewise, nonviolent sociopaths—the majority—never had inhibitions about disregarding the rights and interests of others when it suited them.

They have always acted as if other people were things to be manipulated. No special conditioning was ever needed for them to behave in this way.

So can we imagine what it is like to be them? In the case of people who have been made violent by the processes described, there is certainly one sense in which we can understand them—we can understand that their experiences were unusual or highly stressful, that they greatly contributed to their violent dispositions, and hence we might say, "There but for the grace of God go I." Most of us do have a threshold at which we become violent, although it is thankfully much higher than it is for violent individuals, and we can imagine that threshold being lower. However, there is another sense of "understanding" that goes to the core of sociopathy. Our answer to the question posed partly depends on our initial theory of sociopathy. Difficulties arise from supposing that a sociopath has no understanding of what motivates normal people. For example, there seems to be a tension between being, on the one hand, a successful manipulator of others, and on the other hand, lacking any ability to get into their shoes. For accomplished manipulators are uncannily adept at imagining themselves in the position of their intended victims; they must have a shrewd grasp of what they are thinking, of what motivates them in various situations. If they didn't have this grasp, they would not know which "buttons" to push.

Much hangs, therefore, on what it means to understand another person's mind. Even if empathy is genuinely lacking in the sociopath, the sociopath may still learn about other people's motivations by means of accumulated observation of how they usually react in a wide variety of situations. The sociopath knows that if he or she does one thing, the intended victim will react in one way, and if he or she does something else, the intended victim will react in another way. That is, this individual knows that certain triggers produce certain responses, and he or she can use this knowledge to produce responses in others that are advantageous to himself or herself. Furthermore, as Morton notes, sociopaths do have some normal emotions; they can experience excitement, joy, anger, and disappointment. It is fair to assume, then, that they do know what it is for others to experience at least some emotions. What is lacking is human sympathy, which is at least partly caused by their lack of empathy, and of imaginative grasp of certain emotions—most obviously guilt. They might know their treatment of their victims will cause hurt and anger. The problem is that they don't care.

Can we "normal" people (as we hope we are) imagine what it is like to be like this? To at least some extent, I think we can—for all of us, to different degrees and in different circumstances, lack concern for others when we ought to have it. We might fail to feel pity for someone who has encountered a terrible misfortune. As we saw, we might not be much moved by natural disasters which cause disease and starvation. If we hear of a casual friend who is in hospital with a serious illness, we may not be much moved emotionally even if we dutifully visit her. And when we do things we know are wrong, we find ways to dim guilty feelings. I think to myself, I know I shouldn't be doing this, but since I've decided to do it, I can live with the moderately uncomfortable sense that I shouldn't. I'll find some way to appease my conscience later on; in the meantime, present desire has its reasons, of which conscience knows nothing. If I let conscience speak too loudly, it might cause me to change course—and that would be frustrating. I *can* tell this lie, or break this promise, and probably get away with it, so I shall. This surely is a common human experience, and it gives us *some* insight into what it is like to be a sociopath. The main difference is that sociopaths have little or no conscience, so acting on temptation does not present this sort of internal struggle. Normal people can dim down their conscience, so to that extent they can understand what it is to act without being hindered by it. Sociopaths have little or no conscience to dim down in the first place.

7.3 Imagination

The fact that humans have imagination, that almost indefinable multilayered faculty, is an important key to the question facing us. How could we get stuck in a novel or a play, empathizing with fictitious characters and caring about what happens to them, if we did not have this faculty? Why should I care how the plot culminates if I know that the events related never happened? In the early days of the novel, some puritans regarded novels with suspicion. They seemed to consist of a pack of lies since they related events that never occurred. Of course, this was naive—novelists do not pretend to be relating events that really happened. Readers know this yet are still absorbed by them. We may say that they "suspend their disbelief," but if that is the right way to think of it, it is not a matter of temporarily believing that the events in a novel are real, but rather of not being prevented from enjoying the work by the knowledge that it is fiction. It is imagination that enables readers to do this, as well as to take an interest in the characters in the novel, in their motivations, personalities, and psychological and moral characteristics.

In many other areas, too, we are normally capable of suspending disbelief, or of imaginatively entertaining a feeling or supposition that we do not believe to be rooted in reality. The line between experiencing an emotion

and entertaining an emotion in imagination is quite hard to draw. In con-
sciously trying to recall intense emotions once felt, like those experienced
when falling in love, you are reminded of what this was like. Should we
say that you are in love with that person again, as long as you recall the
experience in all its intensity? This does not seem right, yet recalling a past
love sometimes tempts people to try to recreate it in reality and pursue the
person in question once again. The experience of an emotion and its imaginative recreation become very hard to separate psychologically.

However, detachment is also possible, as other examples suggest. Suppose you have no religious beliefs or commitment, yet you find yourself
drawn to religious services or to a religiously inspired way of life. There are
times when you suspend doubt, when you deliberately set aside the question of whether you believe the relevant theological propositions, and try
to adopt the committed believer's perspective. You might then find yourself
with a partial understanding of how the teachings, liturgies, and practices
make sense to believers, appreciating subtle meanings and insights in scrip-
ture or the transcendent quality of liturgical music. If suddenly challenged
as to whether you really believe it, you answer that you don't, or are not
sure—but sense the challenge as an unwelcome intrusion into a real imaginative identification with the true believer's point of view. It is not that you
ever *forget* that you don't believe it. It is rather that you direct your attention away from the fact that you don't believe it. You set aside your doubts,
rather than deny them.

But if such exercises of imagination are possible in these arguably positive areas of life, what of the darker side of human motivation? Can we
put ourselves into the shoes, psychologically speaking, of those whose
behavior appalls us? Could crime authors successfully write literary crime
fiction if they did not have some such capacity? Of course, the murders
committed in crime fiction spring from all too familiar and understandable human motives—like greed, jealousy, or revenge. Sometimes they are
carefully planned. At other times they are committed in fits of sudden,
explosive rage. Most murders in real life spring from motives like these,
and crime fiction reflects this. However, some fictitious criminals found
at the more literary end of the genre are more subtle; the crime author
Ruth Rendell, for example, presents us with uncanny portraits of characters (sometimes female) whom we might regard as sociopathic—intelligent,
attractive, scheming individuals who plan heinous crimes with a complete
absence of conscience. Presumably it is possible for such crime writers to
enter imaginatively into the scheming of such sociopaths without themselves having such traits. A writer might ask herself, how would I go about

achieving certain goals, if I myself were cunning, highly plausible, and entirely untroubled by scruples? We have already seen that most of us can bypass the promptings of conscience and sometimes manage to set them aside, at least partially. To that extent, we know what it is to act without a conscience. Furthermore, as Morton suggests, people who do terrible things have many of the same desires as others—what is different about them is in the way they put their desires into action.

Everyone is guilty of immoral acts and omissions. Sometimes they occur in spite of a strong sense of wrongdoing, sometimes with a weaker sense, as when we set it aside, and some occur, more rarely, with little or no protest from conscience. When we do bad things, we often act from perfectly intelligible desires—desires which in other circumstances could have led to perfectly acceptable behavior. Given that most of us have these desires at times—for money, for "getting even," and so on—it is not difficult to understand the motives of those who act on them. It is important to notice, as Morton points out, that even sociopaths are not completely unintelligible to us; we share some perfectly ordinary emotions and desires with them. The difference is that they are prepared to act on some of them, without being troubled at all by guilt. In trying to put ourselves in their shoes, then, we are often imagining acting on these desires, but without imagining the restraining sense of guilt that would normally stop us from acting on them. In imagination, we simply put this sense aside. To that extent, we can imaginatively identify with at least some sociopathic individuals.

However, there comes a subtle point when this becomes difficult or troubling. The disturbing brakes of conscience start to be applied when we catch ourselves crossing the line between the imaginative suspense of conscience and its actual loss. This appears to occur when we contemplate a situation in which the excitement or attraction of an act cannot be imaginatively detached from a sense of its appalling nature. Some things can be found thrilling precisely because of their forbidden nature—obscenity is a good example. In averting our gaze, or feeling utterly repelled by the idea of committing a certain atrocious deed, we are somehow aware of how attractive it could be, if only we let ourselves go and did away with our usual restraints. The sense of revulsion that is rooted in the very thought that something is obscene—as opposed to undesirable or dangerous for some extraneous reason—coincides with the fear that we could be aroused by it, that we understand uncannily well how we could find it fascinating or attractive. In other words, when we apply the brakes of self-restraint when tempted to immerse ourselves in some illicit pleasure, and recoil in horror at being the kind of person who does this sort of thing, it is sometimes because we understand all too well the attraction of it, and how easy it could be to become that kind of person. And the fear *of losing our fear* of becoming that sort of person constitutes an additional horror. People like that are the ones we call sociopaths, and the last thing we want is to be like them.

We all have an interest in identifying sociopathic people when we can, if only to protect ourselves from them. It is helpful to be aware that a few people, possibly among our acquaintances, have strongly antisocial character traits that are very unlikely to change. We need to realize that generous behavior toward them, even if morally admirable, will never be reciprocated. Yet there are also difficult ethical, psychiatric, and legal questions to be addressed about how they should be dealt with by society. These issues largely concern moral responsibility, the use and relevance of psychiatry, and the proper role of the criminal justice system in dealing with them after they have committed crimes.

The problems about moral responsibility that arise from sociopathy are the most fundamental and difficult since they affect our approach to the other issues. We have seen that the motivations of sociopaths are not always as alien as we like to think, and this makes it attractive to conclude that we can use the language of wrongdoing and vice to describe their behavior, just as we can with respect to ordinary people. At the same time, we cannot dismiss the thought that there is something radically different about them. How might we do justice to both these intuitions? In what follows, I shall present some possible positions starkly and with the risk of oversimplification, in order to see the genuine difficulties confronting them.

7.4   A Traditional Framing of the Problem: Free Will and Its Absence

First, then, there is a robust, metaphysical account of moral responsibility, based on the belief that most people, in ordinary circumstances, possess free will;[1] that they often freely choose to do what is morally wrong, and that when such acts are crimes, justice requires, or at least permits, retribution. Free will is crucial to this approach to responsibility. For such retribution to be just, the crimes must have been committed freely. If they were not, then there is no justification for retribution—though it may be necessary to deprive offenders of their liberty, in order to protect others and perhaps the offenders themselves from their harmful behavior. So on this approach, the crucial question when it comes to dealing with those alleged to be criminal sociopaths is whether their criminal acts proceed from the exercise of free will. This, in turn, leads us to the question of whether we should think of sociopathy as a condition that, by nature, greatly diminishes or even eliminates free will. If we say that these criminals act from free will, and also regard sociopathy as a condition that excludes free will, then we shall conclude that such criminals are not sociopathic and are better described as bad. However, if we judge that such criminals do not act from free will, then it may be right to describe their behavior as exhibiting sociopathy.

But ought we to regard sociopathy as incompatible with free will? This question highlights a significant problem: namely, whether we should use terms like "sociopath" or "psychopath" such as to exclude free will as if *by definition*, or rather use them to designate a cluster of behavioral dispositions that are so distinct and remarkable as to *make especially apt* the question of whether people who behave in these ways possess free will when they so behave. It is tempting to reserve such designations for people whom we judge to be so different from most other people that there *must* be some special explanation—etiology, even—for their behavior; this is bolstered by the fact that the term "sociopath" has a "medical" ring to it, suggesting a psychiatric disorder. However, we should resist the "definitional" route to this conclusion. We should not assume *at the outset* that sociopathy and free will are incompatible. It is much better to start by observing the descriptive differences between these people and others—that is, the fact that those we call sociopaths are markedly antisocial, lacking in concern for others or remorse (and so on)—and then go on to ask whether they have a special condition that excludes or severely diminishes their free will, while allowing that this may not be the case. This leaves open the conclusion that the attribution of sociopathy is fundamentally a moral one, which designates a moral category—a category of people who are strongly disposed to do seriously bad things.

Such a view is defended by Louis C. Charland (2004), and it has its merits. For him, although there may be some personality disorders that negate moral responsibility—for example, the paranoid, schizoid, obsessive, and others—there is also a "moral group" of personality disorders, notably the antisocial, narcissistic, histrionic, and borderline disorders. The standard psychiatric descriptions of antisocial disorder (e.g., disregard for the feelings of others, impulsivity, lack of guilt) and narcissistic disorder (e.g., morbid self-admiration, attention-craving, lack of reciprocity) (Gelder et al. 1994) are paradigmatic targets for moral censure—after all, people with these traits are hardly likeable and we tend to blame them for their atrocious behavior. Thus when narcissistic or histrionic people insist that they can't help their behavior and demand sympathy (for remember, they have very special qualities) we naturally dismiss their pleas, seeing them as manipulative excuses for demanding and unreasonable carryings-on. This is our natural response; however, the question remains open as to what extent it is justified. We shall return to this a little later.

7.5   The Strawsonian Maneuver

Second, there is an approach which seeks to bypass the metaphysical problems of free will and determinism, claiming instead that certain moral reactions toward others are inevitable in practice, and that it is conceptually misguided to subject them to such metaphysical scrutiny. This is an approach brought to our attention by P. F. Strawson, in his influential paper "Freedom and Resentment" (Strawson 1962). Crucial to this is the fact that most of us have "participant reactive attitudes" (PRAs)—for example, moral admiration, gratitude, resentment, and blame—and that these are irremovably central to meaningful human interaction. The "participant" perspective is our default position in our relations with others as rational and feeling beings, and only special circumstances incline us to adopt an "objective" perspective instead, as we might if we discover that someone is psychotic, has dementia, or is simply under exceptional stress. Our PRAs encompass not only the obviously moral ones, but also the attitudes and emotions involved in interpersonal relationships in general. Strawson correctly surmises that it would be impossible, in practice, to get rid of such attitudes wholesale, and thinks that life would be greatly impoverished if we did. However, the fundamental point is that we cannot make sense of any perspective upon ourselves that purports to require the abolition of the PRAs. A partial parallel can be drawn with radical skepticism in epistemology. Although decisive refutation of "the skeptic" arguably remains elusive, or at least the nature of such refutation remains controversial, hardly anyone wonders seriously whether he or she may be the only person who exists or whether the past is unreal. Most people who entertain these ideas at all end up with something like Hume's position (Hume 1975, section XII), which may crudely be summed up as common sense realism in life, even if not in philosophy. Radical skepticism does not come naturally to us, any more than radical doubt about the appropriateness of certain PRAs to our own and others' behavior. Criticism of some attitudes is appropriate according to the circumstances, but the framework as a whole is not up for serious challenge.

In an earlier paper (Benn 1999), I suggested that even if we take this framework as given, there may be room within it for suspending some of our PRAs toward genuine sociopaths. I hypothesized that there is a strongly communicative aspect to the expression of such attitudes. For example, when we express anger toward someone, we are often trying to induce guilt or shame, to bring about an acknowledgment of responsibility. But if some people are incapable of experiencing such reactions, to the point that they cannot understand what we are trying to induce, then perhaps we should not regard them as proper targets for such expressions. This was connected with my speculation that sociopaths themselves may be markedly deficient in the PRAs, and in particular that they may not experience moral anger toward others. To that extent, dealing with them is more like dealing with dangerous animals than with normal adults.

I remain broadly sympathetic to this approach; at least part of the point of expressing gratitude and resentment is to be understood by recipients *as* expressing exactly these attitudes. Hence, *if* there is a special class of antisocial people, broadly different from "ordinary" ones, who really don't understand this language, then this should affect the attitudes we take toward them. However, I may have been speculating about sociopaths "from the armchair," and overhasty in supposing that they had little or no grasp of such attitudes. In fact, people who are classed as sociopaths can experience some emotional reactions, such as jealousy, pride, and perhaps even moral indignation (at least, when they are at the receiving end of what they think is other people's bad treatment of them!). What is different about them is the significant *gaps* in their grasp of such reactions. However, more fundamentally, I am less sure that the Strawsonian approach adequately addresses some difficult metaphysical questions of free will and responsibility. In terms of the traditional dispute between compatibilists and incompatibilists, Strawson belongs roughly in the compatibilist camp, in that he regards determinism as largely irrelevant to the rationality of the PRAs. But his dismissal of the traditional framing of the problem of responsibility may itself be overhasty. And this is where the first approach I outlined above—that which sees the issue as turning upon a more traditional question of free will—may be necessary after all. To say—probably correctly—that the PRAs are an indispensable "given," from a practical point of view, is not to prove that their ultimate rational basis cannot properly be challenged.

7.6 A Cautious, Pessimistic Conclusion

There is a real difficulty here. When it comes to attributing responsibility, and especially to questions of criminal justice, many of our intuitions seem to arise from precarious attempts to grapple with issues that are not well understood, despite their enormous importance. It is essential that the punishment of criminals should not be unjust, and this entails not only that an *actus reus* should have been committed by the defendant, but that

it should have been committed with *mens rea*. If it is really the case that
certain findings in, let us say, neuroscience or genetics cast proper doubt
on some criminals' responsibility for what they do, then we should take
this very seriously, in order to satisfy an essential requirement of retributive justice—that those who act without adequate *mens rea* should not be
punished. It will not be enough to shrug our shoulders and declare that our
retributive practices are so deeply ingrained in society that we shouldn't
think of changing them. We shouldn't assume that just because most people, for instance, will always regard the "my-brain-made-me-do-it" defense
as absurd, we should never treat it as a serious theoretical problem. We need
to look at both the scientific data themselves and the input of philosophers (among others) as to the relevance of such data and their conceptual
groundwork. We should boldly admit that the issues are both genuine and
difficult, but that too much is at stake to justify letting the problems go, or
retreating into ordinary accepted practice merely because that is the easiest
thing to do.

What, then, of those deemed sociopaths? If we decide that these people
are *not* importantly different from ordinarily antisocial people, with respect
to moral responsibility, we still have the traditional problem of free will,
which is relevant to all human action. However, if we accept that there may
be significant differences between these individuals and the rest of us, then
we need to ask what these differences are, how they are to be explained,
and whether such explanations bear on the responsibility issue.

The most plausible characterization (at least, that I know of) of the
putative difference is that sociopaths are *incapable* of empathic sympathy
whereas "ordinarily" antisocial people do not lack that capacity. Possession
of this capacity is, no doubt, a matter of degree. But if a person genuinely
lacks capacities that are necessary for being morally blameworthy for the
bad things he or she does, then on the robust account of free will outlined
above, it is unjust to blame that person—as well as almost certainly futile
from the point of view of rehabilitation. Moreover, if the findings of genetics or neuroscience can shed light on how the lack of capacity arose, then
these sciences are relevant to whether we should morally blame, or legally
punish, the offenders in question.

There is no obvious reason, in principle, why we cannot understand how
brain-based explanations of behavior might threaten our notions of responsibility. For example, we can accept that if someone who starts behaving in
a strange or antisocial way is discovered to have a brain tumor, it is reasonable to revise our judgment of him. We also know that brain damage can

radically alter behavior, and this could be used as a legal defense. Of course, it is very likely that all behavior is intimately related to states and processes of the brain, but the point is that certain brain abnormalities (however that is to be understood) diminish our *capacity* for normal behavior. In the case of sociopaths, there is evidence that emotional deprivation in early childhood, especially when combined with violence, can prevent certain cortical structures from ever developing properly. It would be overhasty to dismiss such factors as irrelevant to the issue of responsibility, since they seem to affect the capacity for moral development, and not just the direction of such development.

At the same time, we have good reason to be wary of what Stephen J. Morse calls "Brain Overclaim Syndrome" (Morse 2006), of looking to neuroscience to explain away more and more of the spheres of life once occupied by notions of freedom, responsibility and control. Explanations along the lines of "Jones thought he was choosing to do X, but in reality his brain was choosing to do it" have a triumphantly debunking air but are philosophically obscure—most obviously because "Jones's choosing" and "Jones's brain choosing" appear for present purposes to be the *same* event or process. And a general appeal to a combination of determinism and mind–brain identity and/or strict interactionism raises a general problem for free will, which has nothing intrinsically to do with either psychopathology or neuropathology.

Where does this leave us, then? We have stipulated that genuine sociopaths are likely to lack a capacity for empathic sympathy that most people possess, that this deficiency shows itself partly in a lack of imaginative understanding of what is communicated when PRAs are expressed to them, and that this lack of capacity is likely to have special neural causes or correlates. However, we are almost certainly in no position to know all the relevant facts about the mental–neural correlations, or to map our everyday talk of psychopathology onto the neuroscientist's talk of neuropathology. At the same time, everyday interpersonal relations and indeed criminal proceedings require fairly clear categories and boundaries—concerning responsibility, *mens rea*, and psychological abnormality. Such practices could not properly function without them, and criminal justice morally requires (as I have stipulated) that these practices avoid injustice. The great problem, and one which should leave us feeling somewhat confused and pessimistic, is that in our present state of understanding of both the scientific and the philosophical issues, we cannot be sure of avoiding such injustice. In a practical sense, we have to live with this; at the same time, this fact should trouble us.

Note

1. Broadly speaking, philosophical defenders of free will divide into compatibilist and incompatibilist camps. Compatibilists believe that free will is compatible with causal determinism whereas incompatibilists deny this. I am not taking sides in this dispute here, since both are likely to agree that if sociopathy is a condition that negates free will, it does so in a special way, distinct from ordinary causal determinism.

References

Benn, P. 1999. Freedom, Resentment and the Psychopath. *Philosophy, Psychiatry, Psychology* 6:30–39 and 57–58.

Blair, R. J. R. 1995. A Cognitive Developmental Approach to Morality: Investigating the Psychopath. *Cognition* 57:1–29.

Charland, L. C. 2004. Character: Moral Treatment and the Personality Disorders. In *The Philosophy of Psychiatry: A Companion*, ed. J. Radden, 64–77. Oxford: Oxford University Press.

Gelder, M., D. Gath, and R. Mayou. 1994. *Concise Oxford Textbook of Psychiatry*, 79–80. Oxford: Oxford University Press.

Hume, D. 1975. An Enquiry Concerning Human Understanding. In *David Hume, Enquiries Concerning Human Understanding and Concerning the Principles of Morals*. 3rd ed., ed. P. H. Nidditch, 1–165. Oxford: Oxford University Press.

Kant, I. 1964. *Groundwork of the Metaphysic of Morals*, translated and analyzed by H. J. Paton. New York: Harper & Row.

Morse, S. J. 2006. Brain Overclaim Syndrome and Criminal Responsibility: A Diagnostic Note. *Ohio State Journal of Criminal Law* 3:397–412.

Morton, A. 2004. *On Evil*. London: Routledge.

Nagel, T. 1970. *The Possibility of Altruism*. Princeton, N.J.: Princeton University Press.

Strawson, P. F. 1962. Freedom and Resentment. *Proceedings of the British Academy* 47:1–25. Also in *Free Will*, ed. G. Watson. Oxford: Oxford University Press, 1982, 59–80.

II Issues in Moral Psychology

8 Do Psychopaths Refute Internalism?

Walter Sinnott-Armstrong

Many moral philosophers endorse some version of motivational internalism about moral judgment. In response, their opponents often cite psychopaths as counterexamples to such internalism. In my view, they are both wrong: Internalists are wrong to claim an internal relation between moral judgment and motivation (Brink 1989; Sinnott-Armstrong 1993), and their critics are wrong to claim that psychopaths refute motivational internalism about moral judgment.

Here I will focus on the claim that psychopaths refute internalism. First, I will define internalism and psychopathy. Then, I will survey the scientific literature on psychopaths' moral judgments and their motivations. Next, I will discuss whether psychopaths are irrational in a relevant way. Finally, I will draw conclusions for motivational internalism about moral judgment.

8.1 What Is Internalism?[1]

Motivational internalism about moral judgment is formulated in various ways, including these:

Price (1787/1969, p. 194): "When we are conscious that an action is fit to be done, or ought to be done, it is not conceivable that we can remain uninfluenced, or want a motive to action."

Harman (1977, p. 33): "To think you ought to do something is to be motivated to do it."

Nagel (1970, p. 7): "Internalism is the view that the presence of a motivation for acting morally is guaranteed by the truth of ethical propositions themselves."

Blackburn (1984, p. 188): "It seems to be a conceptual truth that to regard something as good is to feel a pull toward promoting or choosing it."

Darwall, Gibbard, and Railton (1997, p. 308): "Judgment internalism holds that if S judges (or believes, or sincerely asserts) that she ought to do A (or that she has reason to do A), then, necessarily, she has some motivation to do A."

The shared idea is that morality has something built into its insides—hence the name "internalism." But what is built into what? And what is it for that to be built into that? Internalisms differ in these details.

8.1.1 What Is It Built Into?

Although some internalists (such as Nagel, quoted above) claim that moral facts or truths have motivation built into them, internalism is usually formulated instead as a claim about what is built into moral judgments, understood as concrete mental states rather than abstract propositions. Some internalists extend their internalism to all normative judgments, including aesthetic, prudential, and perhaps even epistemic judgments. However, it is the moral judgments of psychopaths—rather than their prudential or aesthetic judgments—that are supposed to cause trouble for internalism, so the relevant position here is internalism about moral judgment in particular.

Which moral judgments? It would not be too surprising if abstract moral judgments that do not apply to any situation at hand or that apply only to other people did not have any detectable motivation built into them (Kennett and Fine 2008), so I will assume that internalism is mainly or only about first-person present-tense in situ moral judgments. I will also assume that the thesis of internalism is about judgments of what is morally obligatory, wrong, or ought not to be done rather than judgments of what is morally ideal, good, or virtuous.

8.1.2 What Is Built In?

Internalists then claim that something is built into such moral judgments, but what? There are two main alternatives: motivations and reasons (meaning normative or justificatory reasons rather than explanatory reasons and reasons for action rather than reasons for belief). Of course, if reasons always include motivation, then reasons cannot be built into moral judgments unless motivations are also built into moral judgments. In any case, nobody should deny that psychopaths have reasons not to commit murder, rape, theft, and fraud unless they assume (falsely, in my view) that such reasons must include motivation. Thus, the basic issue raised by psychopaths is about motivation.

Still, internalism about motivation comes in several strengths, including the following:

Overriding-motivation internalism Moral judgments have overriding motivations built into them.

Some-motivation internalism Moral judgments have some motivation built into them.

Since a motivation can fail to be overriding, overriding-motivation internalism is much stronger than some-motivation internalism.

This stronger view is also implausible. People normally act on their overriding motives, so overriding-motivation internalism makes it hard to see how anyone could ever do what they know is morally wrong or bad. Overriding-motivation internalism can also be refuted by common conflicts between self-interest and moral judgment. Even if I judge that it is wrong to steal money, I might go ahead and steal money because my desire for money (and what it can buy) overrides any motivation from my moral judgment. My moral judgment provides some impartial motivation not to steal, but that motivation might not be as strong as my conflicting partial motivation to get money. This common kind of example refutes overriding-motivation internalism, but it is compatible with some-motivation internalism. That is why most internalists endorse only some-motivation internalism (see the quotations above, especially the one from Darwall, Gibbard, and Railton). It is also why I will focus on some-motivation internalism. If psychopaths refuted only overriding-motivation internalism, they would be just one among many other counterexamples to that overly strong thesis. It is more interesting to ask whether psychopaths refute the weaker and more plausible claim of some-motivation internalism.

8.1.3 What Is It to Be Built In?

We still need to unpack the metaphor of being built in. To claim that motivation is built into moral judgments is to claim some necessary relation between what is built in (motivation) and what it is built into (moral judgment). Although all internalists refer to necessity (cf. Darwall, Gibbard, and Railton, quoted above), different versions of internalism claim different kinds of necessity:

Psychological some-motivation internalism It is psychologically necessary that every person who makes a moral judgment has some motivation to act accordingly.

Conceptual some-motivation internalism It is conceptually necessary that every person who makes a moral judgment has some motivation to act accordingly.

The issue here is whether internalism is supposed to hold by virtue of human nature—the way human minds or brains work—or, instead, by virtue of abstract moral concepts independent of contingent facts about human nature.

Most internalists hold the conceptual version (cf. the quotations from Price, Harman, and Blackburn above). However, we do not need actual psychopaths to refute the conceptual view. All we need is a possibility, not an actual case. Nichols has presented survey evidence that most common folk believe it is possible for an agent (even a rational agent) to believe a moral judgment and not have any motivation to act accordingly (Nichols 2004, chapter 3). Some critics respond that philosophers should not care what common folk think since common folk are probably confused about such issues. In this view, all that matters is what trained philosophers believe. However, philosophers can be misled by prior commitments to abstract theories, including internalism. Thus, it is at least not clear why philosophers are more reliable than common folk or why we should care more about what philosophers think than about what common folk think. In any case, the current chapter is about the specific challenge raised by psychopaths. Although actual psychopaths might be sufficient to refute conceptual some-motivation internalism, actual examples are not necessary to refute that version of internalism. Hence, I will focus instead on the psychological version of internalism, except where noted.

Psychological some-motivation internalism claims that the nature of our human minds or brains is what makes motivation accompany moral judgment. The main challenges to this view come from mental illnesses and irrationality. Consider the claim that humans by nature want to survive. This common claim about human nature might not be refuted by a teenager who is depressed enough to be suicidal, because such teenagers are dismissed as mentally ill and irrational. Similarly, if depressed people lose any motivation to avoid what they think is morally wrong, then these cases might not refute the psychological claim that it is part of human nature for people to have some motivation to avoid what they judge to be morally wrong. The most common way to make such cases irrelevant is to limit the definition of internalism to rational people:

Rational psychological some-motivation internalism It is psychologically necessary that every person who is rational and who makes a moral judgment has some motivation to act accordingly. (Compare Smith 1994.)

Of course, many more distinctions could be drawn, but this view is strong enough to be interesting and not too strong to be plausible.

For psychopaths to refute this view, three theses must be true: (1) Psychopaths really do make moral judgments, (2) psychopaths really do lack any motivation to be moral, and (3) psychopaths are not irrational in any way that could justify dismissing them as irrelevant (like suicidal teenagers). Sections 3–5 will survey the evidence and arguments for these three theses in turn. But first I must define psychopathy.

8.2   Who Is a Psychopath?

Psychopathy is officially diagnosed using the Psychopathy Checklist–Revised, or PCL–R (Hare 1991). The PCL–R uses a semi-structured interview plus a background check to verify information provided during the interview. The interviewee is assigned a score of 0, 1, or 2 (with + or –) on each of 20 items. Total scores range from 0 to 40. Eighteen of the 20 items can be divided thematically and statistically into four facets:

Factor 1:

Interpersonal Facet 1:

Item 1: glibness/superficial charm
Item 2: grandiose self-image
Item 4: pathological lying
Item 5: conning/manipulative

Affective Facet 2:

Item 8: callous/lack of empathy
Item 7: shallow affect
Item 6: lack of guilt or remorse
Item 16: failure to accept responsibility

Factor 2:

Lifestyle Facet 3:

Item 3: need for stimulation/proneness to boredom
Item 14: impulsivity
Item 13: failure to have realistic long-term goals
Item 15: irresponsibility
Item 9: parasitic lifestyle

Antisocial Facet 4:

Item 10: poor behavior control
Item 12: early behavior problems
Item 18: juvenile delinquency
Item 19: revocation of conditional release
Item 20: criminal versatility

Sexual items:
Item 11: promiscuous sexual behavior
Item 17: many "marital" relationships

Within Facet 1, items 1 and 2 can be thought of as representing narcissism whereas items 4 and 5 can be understood as Machiavellianism. Within Facet 2, items 8 and 7 can be seen as insensitivity to other people (although item 7 also includes lack of fear) whereas items 6 and 16 suggest insensitivity to one's own past. Within Facet 3, items 3, 14, and 13 represent instability (see also item 10 in Facet 4) whereas items 15 and 9 suggest parasitism. Items 12, 18, 19, and 20 of Facet 4 can be seen as behavioral results of the personality traits in Facets 1–3. The sexual items (11 and 17) do not load statistically with the other facets but can be seen as a separate problem. Considering all of these items and groupings together, extreme psychopathy can be thought of as a complex amalgamation of many socially undesirable personality traits.[2]

Although there is still much debate over whether psychopathy is a discrete kind (or category) or, instead, a dimension (or spectrum), a psychopath is officially defined as anyone who scores 30 or above on the PCL–R. Unfortunately, most published studies of moral judgment in psychopaths have few, if any, participants who score above 30, and many studies redefine "psychopath" to indicate a significantly lower PCL–R score. In addition, clinicians who have interviewed psychopaths report that psychopaths who score 34 or above are qualitatively very different from those who score around 30. Hare notes this impression and describes those who score 34 or above as "high psychopaths" (Hare 1991, 2003). Almost no studies of moral judgment in psychopaths have participants who score above 34. Thus, moral judgment has been assessed very little in clinical psychopaths and even less in high psychopaths.

8.3 Do Psychopaths Make Moral Judgments?[3]

Because of their deviant behaviors (especially item 20) and shallow emotions (items 6–8), many commentators assume that psychopaths do not make normal moral judgments. However, deviant behavior might indicate lack of motivation rather than lack of moral judgment. Psychopaths might not know that their acts are immoral, or, alternatively, they might know that their acts are immoral but not care about avoiding wrongdoing (except when they might be caught and stopped). To decide between these hypotheses, we need to look carefully at the scientific data.

8.3.1 Kohlberg's Tests

The first studies of moral judgments in apparent psychopaths used Kohlberg's Moral Judgment Interview. Contrary to expectations, Link, Scherer, and Byrne (1977) found that psychopaths had *improved* moral reasoning compared to both control groups, despite no significant differences in age, IQ, or education.

A second test within the Kohlberg tradition is the Defining Issues Test (DIT). O'Kane et al. (1996) found no correlation between total PCL–R scores and DIT scores in 40 incarcerated individuals in a British prison once IQ was accounted for. Lose (1997) found similar results in an American sample of inmates.

Kohlberg later developed a third test—the Moral Judgment Task (MJT). Kiehl's research group[4] administered the MJT to 74 inmates in New Mexico. This study is currently being prepared for publication, so it should not be relied on too much, but analyses so far do not indicate any significant correlations between responses on the MJT and PCL–R Total scores or Factor scores. Thus, Kohlberg's tests have not revealed any evidence that psychopaths are deficient in moral judgment.

8.3.2 Turiel's Moral/Conventional Test

Turiel's Moral/Conventional distinction provides a different perspective on moral judgment. In Turiel's view, moral violations are seen as (a) serious, (b) based on harm to others, and (c) independent of authority and geography in the sense that what is morally wrong is supposed to remain morally wrong even if authorities permit it and even if the act is done in some distant place or time where it is common. In contrast, merely conventional violations are seen as (~a) not serious, (~b) not based on harm to others, and (~c) dependent on authority and geography.

To test whether an individual distinguishes moral from conventional violations, experimenters ask participants the following questions about various scenarios:

1. *Permissibility*: "Was it OK for [agent] X to do [act] Y?"
2. *Seriousness*: "On a scale of 1 to 10, how bad was it for X to do Y?"
3. *Justification*: "Why was it bad for X to do Y?"
4. *Authority dependence*: "Would it be OK for X to do Y if the authority says that X is allowed do Y?"

Children by age 4 tend to say that wearing pajamas to class is wrong but would *not* be wrong if the teacher allowed it, whereas it *would* still be wrong to hit other children even if the teacher said hitting was allowed.

Four-year-olds also tend to say that hitting other children is more serious than wearing pajamas to class and that what makes it more wrong is harm to those children, whereas harm to individual victims is not what makes it wrong to wear pajamas to class.

Blair et al. published two studies of the moral/conventional distinction in adult psychopaths. In the first study, Blair (1995) administered the moral/conventional test to 10 psychopaths and 10 nonpsychopaths. Blair reported that 6 of 10 psychopaths drew no moral/conventional distinction (and 2 drew only a mild distinction), whereas 8 of 10 nonpsychopaths drew a clear distinction between moral and conventional violations. More specifically, nonpsychopaths cited harm and justice to explain why moral violations are wrong (in Question 3), but psychopaths cited conventions or authorities to explain why moral violations are wrong. In addition, psychopaths failed to make the distinction on dimensions of permissibility (Question 1), seriousness (Question 2), and authority independence (Question 4). Surprisingly, psychopaths rated conventional violations to be serious and impermissible even if society and authorities allowed the act. In this respect, they treated conventional violations as moral, whereas they had been expected to treat moral violations as conventional. These results were mostly replicated in a second study (Blair et al. 1995).

Readers might think that psychopaths can make moral judgments even if they cannot distinguish moral judgments from conventional judgments. However, if an art dealer cannot distinguish aesthetic value from financial value, then he cannot make real aesthetic judgments. Similarly, one might argue, if psychopaths cannot distinguish moral from conventional judgments, then they cannot make real moral judgments. This implication makes Blair's results crucial here.

However, these highly cited results are subject to competing interpretations. Blair (1995) proposes that psychopaths really see both moral and conventional norms as authority dependent but call them both authority independent in order to impress investigators. An alternative explanation is that psychopaths do believe that moral wrongness is more authority independent than conventional wrongness, but they promote conventional wrongs to authority independence in order to impress investigators. Blair's data cannot decide between these hypotheses.

To decide this issue, Kiehl's research group presented our own set of moral and conventional violations to 109 inmates and 30 controls (Aharoni et al. 2012). Unlike previous tests, participants were told that 8 of the acts were prerated as morally wrong (that is, wrong even if there were no rules, conventions, or laws against them), and 8 were prerated as conventionally wrong (that is, not wrong if there were no rules, conventions, or laws against them). This design removed any incentive to rate all violations as moral, because participants knew that this response would misclassify half of the violations. Aharoni et al. (2012) found that PCL–R scores had no relation to inmate performance on this task. These results might seem to suggest that psychopaths do have the ability to distinguish moral from conventional transgressions.

The design in Aharoni et al. (2012) might, however, change the question. Their participants might have reported what they think that other people (the preraters) believe about moral issues rather than what they themselves (the participants) believe about those issues. If so, then participants are describing generally accepted norms rather than endorsing those norms or making moral judgments themselves. Thus, the issue remains unsettled.

8.3.3 Tests from Philosophy

Philosophers have constructed many moral dilemmas, including trolley cases (Foot 1978; Thomson 1976, 1985), that psychologists have adapted to study moral judgment. This method took off when Greene et al. (2001) published a battery of 40 nonmoral scenarios, 40 "impersonal" moral scenarios, and 40 "personal" moral scenarios (defined as scenarios where an agent causes harm to an identified victim not merely by redirecting a preexisting threat).

Five published studies have used these scenarios to test individuals whom they call "psychopaths." In two reports from the same group (Glenn et al. 2009b; Glenn et al. 2009c), there were no significant differences in the responses between high and low scorers on the PCL–R, both of whose responses distinguished personal from impersonal scenarios and matched healthy controls. Similarly, Cima et al. (2010) found no significant difference between high-scoring offenders and either low-scoring offenders or controls in the percentage of endorsed acts of impersonal or personal harm or in any subset of acts of personal harm (such as those serving the interest of the agent vs. other people). Again, Pujol et al. (2012) discovered no differences between high scorers and low scorers in personal moral dilemmas as a whole. These null results line up nicely.

Unfortunately, these studies did not use the standard diagnosis of psychopathy. Glenn et al. and Cima et al. both used 26, rather than the standard 30, as their cutoff for diagnosing "psychopaths." Pujol et al. included participants as low as 16 on the PCL–R. Thus, these studies do not rule out the possibility that true psychopaths might represent a discrete group with differences in moral judgment.

A fifth study by Koenigs et al. (2012) used a PCL–R cutoff of 30 and found that psychopaths said they would perform the actions described in impersonal moral dilemmas significantly more often than nonpsychopaths. They also found that psychopaths with low anxiety were more likely than either high-anxiety psychopaths or nonpsychopaths to say they would perform the actions described in personal moral dilemmas. These results conflict with the others.

All of the studies described in this section face two big problems. One is that they did not ask participants explicitly moral questions. Koenigs et al., Cima et al., and Pujol et al. asked their subjects "Would you … ?" The question of what someone *would* do asks for a prediction of actual behavior rather than a moral judgment about what they *ought* to do. Psychopaths could easily respond that they would not do an act even if they thought that the act was not morally wrong. They could also respond that they would do an act, even though they thought it was morally wrong, especially if they did not care whether the act was morally wrong. The two studies by Glenn et al. avoided this problem by asking their participants, "Is it appropriate to X?" Still, it was not clear whether their participants reported what they thought was morally wrong or what they thought was required by local nonmoral conventions.

The second big problem is that many psychopaths are pathological liars or conning and manipulative (PCL–R items 4 and 5). None of these studies adequately controlled for deception by participants.[5] Hence, even if the above studies had asked participants explicitly about what they thought was morally wrong, psychopaths' responses still might not reflect their real moral beliefs. Thus, these data cannot determine whether psychopaths really have different moral beliefs than nonpsychopaths or any moral beliefs at all.

8.3.4   Tests from the Law

Another kind of moral judgment concerns how much punishment is deserved. To test these judgments, Robinson and Kurzban (2007) constructed 24 scenarios with standard crimes, including theft, fraud, manslaughter, murder, and torture. Their participants agreed 92% of the time that no punishment was deserved for 4 scenarios and 96% of the time about how to rank pairs among 20 other scenarios.

Kiehl's research group administered Robinson and Kurzban's test to 104 adult male inmates (Schaich Borg et al. 2013). These results are currently being prepared for publication, so they should not be relied on too much. Nonetheless, the level of agreement in these inmates was close to that in Robinson and Kurzban's nonincarcerated sample. The analyses so far suggest no significant correlation between total PCL–R scores and judgments of deserved punishment. However, this overall correlation was insignificant because Factor 1 (especially Facet 1) correlated positively and Factor 2 (especially Facet 4) correlated negatively with task performance. These opposing correlations canceled each other out in the PCL–R total score. One possible explanation of these findings is that Facet 1 of Factor 1 includes items about pathological lying and being conning or manipulative, so psychopaths who are high in this Facet might be less likely to reveal what they really believe about moral issues.

8.3.5 Tests from Anthropology

The tests so far focus on moral judgments about harming. Haidt (2012) has argued that morality extends beyond harm to include five "foundations" of morality: (1) Harm/care, (2) Fairness/reciprocity, (3) Ingroup/loyalty, (4) Authority/respect, and (5) Purity/sanctity. Haidt's Moral Foundations Questionnaire (MFQ) tests judgments in these five areas of morality.

Glenn et al. (2009a) investigated the relationship between MFQ scores and psychopathic personality traits in the general population, assessed by the Levenson Self-Report Psychopathy Scale (SRPS). SRPS scores correlated negatively with endorsement of the moral foundations of Harm and Fairness in this study and correlated slightly negatively with endorsement of the Purity moral foundation. They also found a positive correlation between SRPS scores and endorsement of the In-group moral foundation and failed to find any correlation between SRPS scores and endorsement of the Authority foundations.

To investigate this issue in clinical psychopaths, Kiehl's research group administered the MFQ to 222 adult male inmates (Aharoni et al. 2011). Like Glenn et al. (2009a), they found that total PCL–R scores were negatively correlated with ratings for the Harm and Fairness foundations but not correlated with the Authority foundation. However, unlike Glenn et al. (2009a), they did not find any correlation between total PCL–R scores and ratings of the Purity or In-group foundations.

Two twists need to be considered. On average, the inmate population studied by Aharoni et al. (2011) rated the Harm and Fairness foundations as highly as the nonincarcerated populations studied by Graham et al. (2009). Curiously, however, the In-group, Authority, and Purity foundations were rated as much more important by Aharoni et al.'s incarcerated population than by Graham et al.'s noncarcerated population. These differences suggest that moral foundations may play different roles in incarcerated populations than noncarcerated populations, but these differences are not well understood yet.

8.3.6   Tests Using Brain Scans

All of the studies so far depend on verbal self-reports of moral judgments. However, psychopaths' tendencies to deceive (PCL–R items 4 and 5) suggest reasons to doubt that psychopaths' self-reports reveal what they really believe. Moreover, even if psychopaths really do believe what they say about morality, they still might not make those moral judgments in the same way as nonpsychopaths.

These hypotheses receive some preliminary support from recent studies that have used functional magnetic resonance imaging (fMRI). The first studies (Glenn et al. 2009bc) found that psychopaths' judgments of a subset of Greene's moral scenarios did not differ significantly from those provided by nonpsychopaths, but higher psychopathy scores did correlate with reduced activity in the left amygdala (Glenn et al. 2009b) and increased activity in the dorsolateral prefrontal cortex (Glenn et al. 2009c) in response to personal moral scenarios compared to impersonal moral scenarios. Another study (Pujol et al. 2012) found that psychopaths' judgments of a subset of Greene's moral scenarios did not differ significantly from those by nonpsychopaths, but psychopathy scores correlated with decreased activity in the posterior cingulate and right angular gyrus. These results lend some support to the hypothesis that psychopaths make moral judgments differently than nonpsychopaths, even if their moral judgments are rarely abnormal. However, as discussed above, these studies had very few real psychopaths (30+ on the PCL–R) and did not ask explicitly moral questions.

In another study, Kiehl's research group showed pictures of moral violations (such as a Ku Klux Klan rally), emotional scenes without moral violations (such as an automobile accident), and neutral scenes that were neither moral nor emotional (such as an art class) to 16 psychopaths (PCL–R: 30+) and 16 nonpsychopaths (Harenski et al. 2010). While undergoing fMRI, participants were asked to rate the moral violation in each picture on a 1–5 scale. Similar to behavioral studies, the psychopaths rated the depicted moral violations just as severely as did nonpsychopaths. However, the psychopaths had abnormal brain activity while rating moral violations. In particular, compared to nonpsychopaths, psychopaths had reduced activity in the ventromedial prefrontal cortex and anterior temporal cortex. Moreover, amygdala activity was parametrically related to moral severity ratings in nonpsychopaths but not in psychopaths. Perhaps most interestingly, activity in the right posterior temporal/parietal cortex correlated negatively with moral severity ratings in psychopaths but not in nonpsychopaths. Increased activity in this brain area has been associated with ascriptions of beliefs to other people (Saxe 2006), so this finding might be explained by the process of psychopaths thinking about what other people believe instead of forming or expressing their own moral beliefs. However, the correlation is negative rather than positive, which makes it hard to interpret. Nonetheless, these few brain studies of psychopaths tentatively suggest that psychopaths might not reach moral judgments in the same way as nonpsychopaths, even if they do reach the same moral judgments.

8.4 Emotion and Motivation in Psychopaths

Some critics might reply that, no matter how psychopaths answer moral questions, psychopaths cannot make real moral judgments because they lack emotions that are necessary for real moral judgment. On some sentimentalist theories, one cannot make a moral judgment if one lacks certain sentiments or emotions (e.g., Prinz 2009). These views imply that psychopaths cannot make moral judgments if they lack the required sentiments or emotions.

Some evidence of psychopaths' emotions is how they talk about their actions. The detailed interviews behind a PCL–R score are supposed to investigate whether an interviewee has (6) lack of guilt or remorse, (7) shallow affect, and (8) callousness/lack of empathy. However, to say that a person has shallow affect or is callous is not to say that the person does not feel emotions at all. It is only to say that he feels less emotion in important areas than normal people. Similarly, interviewees can receive the highest score (2 out of a possible 2) for lack of empathy and for lack of remorse even if they show some signs of limited empathy or remorse.

Of course, psychopaths can and do lie about their emotions. Sometimes their talk suggests lack of understanding: "when asked if he experienced remorse over a murder he'd committed, one young inmate told us, 'Yeah, sure, I feel remorse.' Pressed further, he said that he didn't 'feel bad inside about it'" (Hare 1993, 41). Such confusions suggest to some observers that psychopaths feel no remorse or any relevant emotions, despite what they say. However, such confusions could result from shallow emotions or from a lack of reflection on emotions rather than from a total lack of emotions.

How can we tell whether psychopaths really feel what they say they feel? One indirect method uses physiological measures, such as galvanic skin responses while observing people in physical distress. Two studies found that psychopaths show little to no change in skin resistance in response to observing a confederate get shocked (Aniskiewicz 1979; House and Milligan 1976). A third study found that psychopaths actually show

increased changes in skin resistance in response to observing a confederate get shocked (Sutker 1970). These first three studies assessed psychopathy with the Minnesota Multiphasic Personality Inventory. The only study
of galvanic skin responses to employ the PCL–R found that psychopaths
did demonstrate significant galvanic skin responses to pictures of distress
cues, but these responses were much lower than in nonpsychopaths (Blair
et al. 1997). These studies together suggest that psychopaths are much less
aroused than nonpsychopaths when they observe others in pain or distress,
but psychopaths still might be aroused to some degree.

If such physical signs of arousal are sufficient evidence for empathy,
then psychopaths seem to feel at least some morally relevant emotions.
That makes it hard to see why they could not be credited with real moral
judgments, even according to sentimentalist theories. Of course, some high
psychopaths (PCL–R score of 34+) still might feel no empathy or remorse
or any morally relevant emotion at all. If so, then these extreme psychopaths cannot make moral judgments, according to sentimentalists. Nonetheless, they can still make moral judgments if sentimentalists are wrong
about moral judgment. And there is plenty of room to suspect that emotions are not necessary for moral judgments (cf. Joyce 2008). If not, then
psychopaths can make moral judgments without any feelings of empathy
or remorse.

What about motivation? Emotion is distinct from motivation, but similar issues arise for motivational internalism. On conceptual versions of
motivational internalism (see quotations above), a person cannot make a
real moral judgment if that person lacks motivation to act according to the
judgment. We already saw why such views are plausible only if they require
only some motivation but not overriding motivation. However, conceptual
some-motivation internalism rules out moral judgments by psychopaths
only if psychopaths have no motivation at all to behave morally. It might
seem obvious that psychopaths lack moral motivations. How else could
they do what they do to their victims? However, many people do things for
personal gain even though they feel some reluctance to do them. Similarly,
people can have strong motivations not to do certain acts but still do those
acts because they have even stronger contrary motivations. They also might
fail to apply their general concerns to particular situations when distracted
or confused, but that would not show that those general concerns are never
effective. Thus, as with other people, psychopaths' immoral behavior by
itself does not show that they entirely lack all moral motivations.

We simply do not have enough evidence to decide between the hypothesis that psychopaths have no motivation at all to be moral and the contrary

hypothesis that psychopaths have some (but little and often overridden) motivation to be moral. If the latter hypothesis is correct, then psychopaths cannot refute some-motivation internalism in either the conceptual or the psychological version. Hence, we do not have enough evidence to settle this issue.

8.5 Are Psychopaths Irrational?

Despite these uncertainties, let's suppose that at least some psychopaths do make real moral judgments but have no motivation at all to act according to those judgments. Then psychopaths would refute unqualified psychological (and conceptual) some-motivation internalism. Nonetheless, they still would not touch *rational* psychological some-motivation internalism (Smith 1994) if psychopaths are irrational in a relevant way. To address that version of internalism, we need to ask whether psychopaths are irrational and, if so, how.

Psychopaths seem not to lack cognitive or theoretical rationality. They are almost never delusional, and the average IQ of psychopathic inmates is as high as nonpsychopathic inmates (Blair et al. 2005, 23–24). PCL–R items are almost all decision-making deficits about what to do, not cognitive deficits about what to believe. The only exceptions are grandiose self-image (item 2) and failure to accept responsibility (item 16). Psychopaths' emotional deficits (item 7) might also lead to "cognitive-perceptual shortcomings in the *recognition* of certain emotions in others' faces and voices" (Maibom 2005, 242). However, psychopaths "are renowned for their successful manipulation of people, including parole boards and psychiatrists" (Maibom 2005, 243), so they seem to be good at detecting some beliefs and feelings in other people. In any case, these cognitive deficits hardly amount to any kind of irrationality that could explain psychopaths' lack of motivation to be moral or justify dismissing them as irrelevant to internalism.

Other deficits in psychopaths do seem more relevant to motivation. First, psychopaths have "narrowed attention span, limiting how many things they can pay attention to at the same time and how long they can sustain attention" (Maibom 2005, 239). These attention problems might explain why psychopaths disregard risks of punishment during their pursuit of reward (Newman et al. 1990) and why psychopaths also have trouble with response reversal (Maibom 2005, 244–245; cf. Blair et al. 2005, 51–52). These attention deficits are relevant to practical rationality because they can lead to irrational action when psychopaths cannot attend to all of the risks in complex situations. However, psychopaths' attention deficits are evident only under time pressure. Their performance is close to normal when they are forced to pause between trials (Maibom 2008, 176a). Often psychopaths have had a long time to think about their moral views, especially because psychopathy arises relatively early (item 12). Hence, their lack of motivation cannot be explained by their attention deficits.

Second, psychopaths "are intransigent to certain forms of conditioning" (Maibom 2005, 242). Specifically they have difficulty learning how to avoid painful shocks and learning which decks to avoid in the Iowa gambling task (Maibom 2005, 242; cf. Blair et al. 2005, 115–122). These learning deficits might involve cognitive errors about what causes painful shocks or how probable harm is. However, it is also possible that psychopaths are aware of the pain and the risks but do not care about them. Moreover, in the Iowa gambling task, the risky decks are also more exciting, because they gain more and lose more, so choosing these decks might satisfy psychopaths' need for stimulation (item 3). Then their choice of the risky decks might not be irrational.

Third, psychopaths "frequently act in their own worst interest" (Maibom 2005, 242). Most studies of real psychopaths are done in prisons, so it is no surprise that most studied psychopaths have committed crimes. In addition, they seem to be more likely to die early from violence, accidents, and disease, such as AIDS (Black 1999, cited in Maibom 2005, 247, note 11). This tendency to act against their own interest suggests practical irrationality. This practical irrationality can stem from impulsivity (item 14) and justifies classifying psychopathy as a mental disease (Nadelhoffer and Sinnott-Armstrong 2013). As a result, this kind of irrationality is just the kind that could justify dismissing psychopaths as irrelevant to rational psychological some-motivation internalism.

Of course, psychopaths are not totally irrational. They can sometimes be scarily effective at getting what they want. Some opponents of rational internalism might dispute whether their practical irrationality is severe enough to dismiss them as irrelevant to rational internalism. Still, at the very least, it is not clear that psychopaths would count as rational people in the way that they need to be in order to refute rational psychological some-motivation internalism.

8.6   Conclusions

This discussion leads to negative results. Actual psychopaths are not needed in order to refute conceptual versions of internalism or even psychological versions of overriding-motivation internalism about moral judgment.

For psychopaths to refute psychological some-motivation internalism, we would need to know that (1) psychopaths make real moral judgments and (2) psychopaths do not have even some motivation to be moral. My survey of current scientific research reveals little evidence for either (1) or (2). Moreover, even if future research did establish both (1) and (2), psychopaths still could not refute rational psychological some-motivation internalism because there is independent reason to suspect that psychopaths are irrational in practical ways that could explain their lack of motivation and make them irrelevant to rational psychological some-motivation internalism.

Overall, then, actual psychopaths do not have any clear implications for these particular issues in philosophy.[6] As I said at the start, there are other strong reasons to reject motivational internalism (Sinnott-Armstrong 1993). However, psychopaths are not among them.

Notes

1. This section is based on Sinnott-Armstrong (2009), which contains more details.

2. Psychopathy needs to be distinguished from antisocial personality disorder (ASPD). Almost all psychopaths have ASPD, but not all people with ASPD are psychopaths. Experts estimate that 80% or more of medium-security inmates meet the ASPD diagnostic criteria in the *Diagnostic and Statistical Manual of Mental Disorders* (fourth edition, text revision; American Psychiatric Association 2000) whereas 20% or fewer from the same population should be diagnosed with psychopathy (Serin 1996).

3. This section and the next summarize Schaich Borg and Sinnott-Armstrong (2013). See that chapter for more details. Many thanks are due to Jana Schaich Borg.

4. Kent Kiehl's research group includes Jana Schaich Borg, Rachel Kahn, Carla Harenski, Eyal Aharoni, Elsa Ermer, various collaborators, and the research staff in Kiehl's laboratory at the Mind Research Institute.

5. Cima et al. (2010) did try to control for lying by giving a Socio-Moral Reflection questionnaire, but that method is problematic.

6. Of course, psychopaths still might teach lessons in other areas of philosophy. See Sinnott-Armstrong (forthcoming) on implications for moral epistemology.

References

Aharoni, E., O. Antonenko, and K. Kiehl. 2011. Disparities in the Moral Intuitions of Criminal Offenders: The Role of Psychopathy. *Journal of Research in Personality* 45:322–327.

Aharoni, E., W. Sinnott-Armstrong, and K. Kiehl. 2012. Can Psychopathic Offenders Discern Moral Wrongs? A New Look at the Moral/Conventional Distinction. *Journal of Abnormal Psychology* 121:484–497.

American Psychiatric Association. 2000. *Diagnostic and Statistical Manual of Mental Disorders*. 4th ed., text revision. Washington, D.C.: American Psychiatric Association.

Aniskiewicz, A. S. 1979. Autonomic Components of Vicarious Conditioning and Psychopathy. *Journal of Clinical Psychology* 35:60–67.

Black, D. 1999. *Bad Boys, Bad Men*. New York: Oxford University Press.

Blackburn, S. 1984. *Spreading the Word*. Oxford: Oxford University Press.

Blair, R. J. R. 1995. A Cognitive Developmental Approach to Morality: Investigating the Psychopath. *Cognition* 57:1–29.

Blair, R. J. R., L. Jones, F. Clark, and M. Smith. 1995. Is the Psychopath "Morally Insane"? *Personality and Individual Differences* 19:741–752.

Blair, J., L. Jones, F. Clark, and M. Smith. 1997. The Psychopathic Individual: A Lack of Responsiveness to Distress Cues? *Psychophysiology* 34:192–198.

Blair, J., D. Mitchell, and K. Blair. 2005. *The Psychopath: Emotion and the Brain*. Oxford: Blackwell.

Brink, D. 1989. *Moral Realism and the Foundations of Ethics*. New York: Cambridge University Press.

Cima, M., F. Tonnaer, and M. D. Hauser. 2010. Psychopaths Know Right from Wrong but Don't Care. *Social Cognitive and Affective Neuroscience* 5:59–67.

Darwall, S., A. Gibbard, and P. Railton (eds.). 1997. *Moral Discourse and Practice*. Oxford: Oxford University Press.

Foot, P. 1978. The Problem of Abortion and the Doctrine of the Double Effect. In *Virtues and Vices and Other Essays on Moral Philosophy*, ed. P. Foot, 19–33. Oxford: Blackwell.

Glenn, A. L., R. Iyer, J. Graham, S. Koleva, and J. Haidt. 2009a. Are All Types of Morality Compromised in Psychopathy? *Journal of Personality Disorders* 23:384–398.

Glenn, A. L., A. Raine, and R. A. Schug. 2009b. The Neural Correlates of Moral Decision-Making in Psychopathy. *Molecular Psychiatry* 14:5–6.

Glenn, A. L., A. Raine, R. Schug, L. Young, and M. Hauser. 2009c. Increased DLPFC Activity during Moral Decision-Making in Psychopathy. *Molecular Psychiatry* 14:909–911.

Graham, J., J. Haidt, and B. Nosek. 2009. Liberals and Conservatives Use Different Sets of Moral Foundations. *Journal of Personality and Social Psychology* 96:1029–1046.

Greene, J. D., R. Sommerville, L. E. Nystrom, J. M. Darley, and J. D. Cohen. 2001. An fMRI Investigation of Emotional Engagement in Moral Judgment. *Science* 293:2105–2108.

Haidt, J. 2012. *The Righteous Mind: Why Good People Are Divided by Politics and Religion.* New York: Pantheon.

Hare, R. D. 1991. *The Hare Psychopathy Checklist—Revised (PCL–R).* Toronto, ON: Multi-Health Systems.

Hare, R. D. 1993. *Without Conscience: The Disturbing World of Psychopaths among Us.* New York: Guilford.

Hare, R. D. 2003. *Manual for the Revised Hare Psychopathy Checklist.* 2nd ed. Toronto, ON: Multi-Health Systems.

Harenski, C. L., K. A. Harenski, M. S. Shane, and K. A. Kiehl. 2010. Aberrant Neural Processing of Moral Violations in Criminal Psychopaths. *Journal of Abnormal Psychology* 119:863–874.

Harman, G. 1977. *The Nature of Morality: An Introduction to Ethics.* New York: Oxford University Press.

House, T. H., and W. L. Milligan. 1976. Autonomic Responses to Modeled Distress in Prison Psychopaths. *Journal of Personality and Social Psychology* 34:556–560.

Joyce, R. 2008. What Neuroscience Can (and Cannot) Contribute to Metaethics. In *Moral Psychology, Volume 3: The Neuroscience of Morality*, ed. W. Sinnott-Armstrong, 371–394. Cambridge, Mass.: MIT Press.

Kennett, J., and C. Fine. 2008. Internalism and the Evidence from Psychopaths and "Acquired Sociopaths." In *Moral Psychology, Volume 3: The Neuroscience of Morality*, ed. W. Sinnott-Armstrong, 173–190. Cambridge, Mass.: MIT Press.

Koenigs, M., M. Kruepke, J. Zeier, and J. P. Newman. 2012. Utilitarian Moral Judgment in Psychopathy. *Social Cognitive and Affective Neuroscience* 7:708–714.

Link, N. F., S. E. Scherer, and P. N. Byrne. 1977. Moral Judgement and Moral Conduct in the Psychopath. *Canadian Psychiatric Association Journal* 22:341–346.

Lose, C. A. 1997. Level of Moral Reasoning and Psychopathy within a Group of Federal Inmates. *Dissertation Abstracts International. B, The Sciences and Engineering* 57 (7-B):4716.

Maibom, H. 2005. Moral Unreason: The Case of Psychopathy. *Mind & Language* 20:237–257.

Maibom, H. 2008. The Mad, the Bad, and the Psychopath. *Neuroethics* 1:167–184.

Nadelhoffer, T., and W. Sinnott-Armstrong. 2013. Is Psychopathy a Mental Disease? In *Neuroscience and Legal Responsibility*, ed. N. A. Vincent, 227–253. New York: Oxford University Press.

Nagel, T. 1970. *The Possibility of Altruism*. Oxford: Oxford University Press.

Newman, J., C. Patterson, E. Howland, and S. Nichols. 1990. Passive Avoidance in Psychopaths: The Effects of Reward. *Personality and Individual Differences* 11:1101–1114.

Nichols, S. 2004. *Sentimental Rules: On the Natural Foundations of Moral Judgment*. New York: Oxford University Press.

O'Kane, A., D. Fawcett, and R. Blackburn. 1996. Psychopathy and Moral Reasoning: Comparison of Two Classifications. *Personality and Individual Differences* 20:505–514.

Price, R. 1787/1969. A Review of the Principal Questions in Morals. Excerpted. In *The British Moralists*, ed. D. D. Raphael. New York: Oxford University Press.

Prinz, J. 2009. *The Emotional Construction of Morals*. New York: Oxford University Press.

Pujol, J., I. Batalla, O. Contreras-Rodriguez, B. J. Harrison, V. Pera, R. Hernández-Ribas, E. Real, et al. 2012. Breakdown in the Brain Network Subserving Moral Judgment in Criminal Psychopathy. *Social Cognitive and Affective Neuroscience* 7:917–923.

Robinson, P. H., and R. Kurzban. 2007. Concordance and Conflict in Intuitions of Justice. *Minnesota Law Review*, 91:1829–1907.

Saxe, R. 2006. Uniquely Human Social Cognition. *Current Opinion in Neurobiology* 16:235–239.

Schaich Borg, J., R. E. Kahn, W. Sinnott-Armstrong, R. Kurzban, P. H. Robinson, and K. A. Kiehl. 2013. Subcomponents of Psychopathy Have Opposing Correlations with Punishment Judgments. *Journal of Personality and Social Psychology* 105:667–687.

Schaich Borg, J., and W. P. Sinnott-Armstrong. 2013. Do Psychopaths Make Moral Judgments? In *Handbook of Psychopathy and Law*, ed. K. Kiehl and W. Sinnott-Armstrong, 107–128. New York: Oxford University Press.

Serin, R. C. 1996. Violent Recidivism in Criminal Psychopaths. *Law and Human Behavior* 20:207–217.

Sinnott-Armstrong, W. 1993. Some Problems for Gibbard's Norm-Expressivism. *Philosophical Studies* 69:297–313.

Sinnott-Armstrong, W. 2009. Mackie's Internalisms. In *A World without Values: Essays on John Mackie's Moral Error Theory*, ed. R. Joyce and S. Kirchin, 55–70. Dordrecht: Springer.

Sinnott-Armstrong, W. Forthcoming. Moral Disagreements with Psychopaths. In *Challenges to Moral and Religious Belief: Disagreement and Evolution*, ed. M. Bergmann and P. Kain. Oxford: Oxford University Press.

Smith, M. 1994. *The Moral Problem*. Oxford: Blackwell.

Sutker, P. B. 1970. Vicarious Conditioning and Sociopathy. *Journal of Abnormal Psychology* 76:380–386.

Thomson, J. J. 1976. Killing, Letting Die, and the Trolley Problem. *Monist* 59:204–217.

Thomson, J. J. 1985. The Trolley Problem. *Yale Law Journal* 94:1395–1415.

9 Psychopathic Resentment

John Deigh

Hitchcock, in *Shadow of a Doubt*, introduced a new kind of villain into his films. His previous villains, while conventionally ruthless and sinister, were largely plot devices. His most successful earlier films were about espionage, reflecting the growing political tensions in Europe at the time, and the villains in those films were spies and assassins whose intrigues created the suspense for which Hitchcock had become famous. In *Shadow of a Doubt*, by contrast, the suspense comes from the villain himself: one Charles Oakley, masterfully played by Joseph Cotten. Oakley, to his sister and her family, is the worldly Uncle Charlie, a man who exudes boyish charm, displays impeccable manners, and is attentive to all in his company, especially the women. And they in turn adore him. He is also, as we see in the opening scenes, in flight from the law, and as we later learn, a serial killer who preys on widows and who has sought refuge in the small California town of Santa Rosa, where his sister and her family live. As the film progresses and Oakley comes under the suspicion of his niece, he becomes increasingly secretive, manipulative, and menacing toward her. Slowly we come to realize that this charming, debonair fellow connects with no one and has no conscience. He is Hitchcock's first major attempt at exploring the chilling personality of a psychopath.

Hitchcock continued this exploration in *Rope*, which is loosely based on the infamous Leopold and Loeb case,[1] and then in *Strangers on a Train*, which is based on Patricia Highsmith's eponymous novel. The villain in the latter film, Bruno Anthony, is, if anything, an even more gripping example of a psychopathic killer. Robert Walker, who gives a brilliant performance as Bruno, endows the character with a naive egocentricity, like that of a child, and in doing so bids us to see his lack of conscience and inability to connect with others as products of a severely arrested moral development. Bruno, who has murdered the estranged wife of the film's protagonist, Guy Haines, in the belief that he and Guy have entered into a compact in which in return for his killing Guy's wife, Guy would kill Bruno's father, becomes enraged when it becomes evident to him that Guy has no intention of killing his father. Feeling double crossed, Bruno seeks revenge. The last part of the film is then taken up with his repeatedly frustrated attempt to return to the scene of the murder so as to plant evidence against Guy and Guy's attempt to stop him. Bruno's displays of resentment and anger in this part of the film seem entirely in keeping with his personality. They match, in this respect, the resentment and bitterness Oakley exhibits in a scene in which he suddenly and vehemently denounces the world as a "foul sty" and belittles his niece as a know-nothing. It is, I believe, no accident that Hitchcock made the capacity for these volatile, retributive emotions part of both villains' personality profile.

While the anger and resentment these villains exhibit seems entirely in place in Hitchcock's portrayal of them, their having a capacity for these emotions may nonetheless seem incongruous to those who are familiar with what has become the standard view in Anglo-American philosophy about their nature. Resentment, in particular, is now commonly understood as an emotion a person cannot experience unless he or she is capable of moral judgment, and indeed rather complex moral judgment. Stephen Darwall's recent treatment of the emotion in his book *The Second Person Standpoint* is representative.[2] Darwall writes, "Resentment ... is felt in response to apparent injustice, as if from the victim's point of view. We resent what we take to be violations against ourselves or those with whom we identify. If you resent someone's treading on your foot or, even more, his rejecting your request or demand that he stop doing so, you feel as if he has violated a valid claim or demand and as if some claim-exacting or responsibility-seeking response by you, or on your behalf, is justified."[3] What makes such accounts of resentment seem ill-suited to the resentment displayed by the villains in Hitchcock's films is not so much the complexity of the judgment that the emotion is represented as containing as the moral orientation that they presuppose. It is not an orientation one would think was available to someone like Oakley or Bruno. It is not, one would think, the orientation of a psychopath. Yet it is essential to these accounts.

On Darwall's account, for instance, resentment is one of a set of emotions that he calls, following P. F. Strawson, reactive attitudes.[4] The set also includes gratitude, moral indignation, guilt, and forgiveness, and to have the capacity for these emotions one must, according to Darwall, see oneself and others as members of a moral community in which every member has authority to address any other, to make obligation-creating claims on him or her, and to hold that person responsible for failures to meet those obligations.[5] Accordingly, the injustice to which or to the appearance of which Darwall characterizes resentment as a felt response consists in a failure to meet some such obligation. And similarly for the two other emotions, moral indignation and guilt, that Darwall takes to be felt responses to injustice. What differentiates each of these emotions from the other two, then, is the viewpoint from which the injustice is seen. Thus, when one feels resentment toward another, one takes oneself to have been treated unjustly by him or her; when one feels moral indignation toward another, one takes the person to have acted unjustly toward a third party on whose behalf one is taking this retributive attitude; and when one feels guilt, one takes oneself to have acted unjustly toward another. Consequently, on Darwall's view, to be liable to any of these emotions is to be capable of making moral judgments that reflect a view of oneself as joined together with others in mutual relations defined by reciprocal rights and obligations.[6] And this means, given the capacity of psychopathic killers like Hitchcock's villains for resentment, that they too are capable of making such moral judgments. Yet the lack of a conscience and inability to connect with others that are principal marks of this type of personality imply that they are not.[7]

Explaining how such killers could have a capacity for resentment consistently with Darwall's account of the emotion may not, however, seem all that problematic. For it requires explaining how they can regard themselves as victims of injustice though they lack a conscience and are unable to connect with others, and one might give such an explanation by appealing to their egocentricity. After all, being egocentric does not obviously imply that one is incapable of judging that another has treated one unjustly, even if there is no question that it implies that one lacks a conscience and cannot connect with others. Accordingly, since the primary evidence for taking the lack of a conscience as a principal mark of psychopathy is that psychopaths exhibit no guilt or remorse for their crimes and since the absence of these emotions is also evidence of their inability to connect with others, it may suffice for understanding Darwall's account as consistent with acknowledging the capacity of psychopaths for resentment to point out that a capacity for resentment requires only that a person be capable of making moral judgments from his viewpoint. Hence, that psychopaths are incapable of making moral judgments from others' viewpoints need not be a problem on Darwall's account. Or so one might argue.

Of course, if one makes this argument, one must abandon the common characterization of psychopaths as incapable of moral judgment. But this departure from settled opinion may not seem that worrisome. As long as it is understood that psychopaths are incapable of taking the viewpoints of others and making moral judgments from those viewpoints, one might think that it is possible to attribute to them, consistently with accounts of resentment like Darwall's, a limited capacity for moral judgment. Thinking this, however, would be a mistake. On such accounts, the capacity for moral judgment cannot be limited in this way.

The reason is that the capacity for moral judgment that these accounts presuppose is a capacity for judgments that reflect an understanding of oneself as belonging to a moral community in which one's relations to the other members are relations of *reciprocal* obligation. Because of this fact, one cannot, according to these accounts, judge, when another fails to meet an obligation he owes one, that he has acted unjustly toward one unless one is also able to judge, when one has failed to meet a similar obligation that one owes him, that one has acted unjustly toward him. Or to put the point in the language Darwall favors,[8] the obligations that any member of a moral community has are reasons to do that which he is obligated to do, and therefore, if one sees oneself as a member of a moral community, whatever reasons one thinks these obligations give others to act are reasons one also recognizes oneself as having. Consequently, if one expects others to meet their obligations to one in view of these reasons and likewise demands of them that they make amends if they don't, one must then see oneself, in view of the same reasons, as required to meet the obligations one has to others and be disposed to demand of oneself that one make amends if one doesn't. Resentment, on Darwall's account, that one feels toward someone who has not met his obligations to one implies both that one expects him to meet those obligations and that one demands of him that he make amends since he didn't. And it does so because the moral judgment it contains reflects an understanding of oneself as a member of a moral community. So, on this account, resentment implies that one expects the same of oneself and is disposed to make similar demands on oneself if one fails to meet one's obligations. Plainly, then, it is not possible, on this account, to be liable to resentment if one is incapable of taking the viewpoints of others. The resentment of which psychopaths are capable remains, therefore, inexplicable.[9]

No doubt, this problem will seem to many to be merely an issue of labeling. Surely, they will think, we can restrict the term "resentment" to that species of anger that is moral in character and felt in response to one's being treated unjustly or at least to what one takes to be unjust treatment. To say that it is moral in character is to say that the judgment about being treated unjustly it implies is a moral judgment. And it follows, then, that the anger toward others of which psychopaths are capable, while it may be similar to resentment, should not be called "resentment" since psychopaths are incapable of making genuine moral judgments. After all, the standard view in Anglo-American philosophy about the nature of resentment emerged in the process of our regimenting our terms for moral emotions so as to have a precise way of discussing the emotions distinctive of moral agency. Such regimentation is necessary because language is used loosely in everyday speech. The standard view, then, once one understands that it has come about through stipulation necessary for making discussions of the psychology of moral agents precise, is not threatened by the anger displayed by psychopaths toward those whom they see as having betrayed them.

The problem, however, with this way of understanding the standard view is that it makes any representation of the liability to resentment as a mark of moral agency vacuous. This result is especially problematic for accounts of resentment like Darwall's, for the apparent force of these accounts comes from their representing the liability as such a mark.[10] Typically, their proponents put forward the liability to resentment and other emotions like guilt and indignation as an essential feature of being a moral agent so that the accounts of these emotions they propose are seen as illuminating the nature of moral agency. Such illumination, however, would be illusory if the emotions were defined in advance as the emotions of a moral agent. Hence, to be genuinely illuminating, an account of resentment, like accounts of other natural phenomena, must presuppose that one can identify the emotion prior to giving the account. For to give an illuminating account of some natural phenomenon one must first be directly acquainted with the phenomenon, which is to say, one must first know how to identify it by name. Having so identified the phenomenon, one then brings its nature to light by developing an account that fits it. One cannot, therefore, understand the liability to resentment as a mark of moral agency unless the attribution of resentment to psychopaths is a misidentification.

Yet nothing supports taking such attributions to be misidentifications apart from the thesis in question, that the liability to resentment implies a capacity for moral judgment. While the source of the anger Oakley expresses when he denounces the world as a "foul sty" is obscure,[11] it is clear that Bruno's anger at Guy is due to his belief that Guy has double-crossed him. He is not, therefore, merely furious with Guy for thwarting his plan to end his father's life. His anger, that is, is more than the fury of someone whose efforts are frustrated by another's refusal to do what he wants him to do. Such fury is no different from anger at some machine or beast for refusing to work as it should. The farmer who beats his mule mercilessly because it refuses to pull the plow may thereby show anger amounting to rage that is due to the mule's obstinacy and the farmer's frustration at being unable to get the mule to move, but because the farmer need not see the mule as having betrayed him, the farmer's anger need not be vengeful or retributive. Bruno's, by contrast, is, which is why we readily identify it as resentment.

Bruno's sense of being betrayed by Guy comes from an attachment he has formed to Guy. His fondness for Guy develops during the conversation they have on the train that sets the story in motion and continues afterwards. He thinks of Guy as his friend and expects that this new found friend will follow through on the agreement he imagines they have made. His attachment to Guy is childlike to be sure, but even small children regard their playmates as friends. A psychopath is not necessarily a loner. Thus Bruno's anger, when he realizes that Guy does not plan to follow through on the agreement he imagines they have made and, indeed, is not his friend, is anger at what he feels to be a betrayal. It is resentment.

The standard view in Anglo-American philosophy about the nature of resentment is therefore mistaken. A capacity for moral judgment is not necessary to be capable of the emotion. Someone whose personality is entirely egocentric may be capable of it as well. Consequently, its place in human psychology is different from that of the other emotions that are commonly explained in conjunction with it as emotions that imply judgments about injustice and that differ from each other according to the viewpoint with respect to the injustice from which the emotion is experienced. Thus, think again of Darwall's account of these emotions according to which resentment is a response to injustice experienced from the viewpoint of the victim, indignation a response to it experienced from the viewpoint of a third party, and guilt a response to it experienced from the viewpoint of the perpetrator. While the symmetry among these emotions that structures this account neatly fits the underlying thesis that each emotion is distinctive of moral agency, it is belied by the psychopath's liability to resentment. Only indignation and guilt imply moral judgments. The question then is how resentment, which does not imply such judgment, is related to them.

Ironically, the work that exponents of the standard view about the nature of resentment usually cite as its source, Strawson's "Freedom and Resentment," offers an answer. It is embedded in Strawson's explanation of the role of these emotions in the dynamics of interpersonal relations. The emotions belong to a set whose members, as we've already noted, Strawson calls reactive attitudes, and the insight on which Strawson proceeds in this essay is that the dispute over whether determinism threatens the soundness of our practice of attributing moral responsibility to people for their actions can be resolved through a study of these emotions. Strawson's explanation of their role in the dynamics of interpersonal relations consists mostly of his description of the conditions of their arousal and expiration, and to see the answer to our question that Strawson's essay offers, the question, that is, about the relation of resentment to the other reactive attitudes, requires elaboration of his explanation. The explanation begins with some plain, natural facts—what Strawson calls commonplaces—about men and women as social beings. The facts he adduces are these.[12]

A central concern of people who live together in communities is what their intentions and attitudes are toward each other. They place great importance on these intentions and attitudes, and they interact with each other with an expectation that generally their fellows behave with good-will toward them. The goodwill each expects of others consists in the others' keeping, as best they can, from harming him in their conduct toward or interactions with him and in their being responsive to harm they may nonetheless cause him by being solicitous of his injury and feelings. Such goodwill may be basic to human personality generally (though not universally), or it may derive from more basic emotions and primitive attachments. Either is compatible with the general fact that Strawson means to emphasize: that people are highly sensitive to and greatly concerned with whether others are well- or ill-disposed toward them. This sensitivity and concern gives rise in a person to certain attitudes and feelings when others—particularly certain others—behave in ways that manifest good or ill will toward him. Thus, while one naturally takes pleasure in benefits that come one's way on account of another's behavior, one responds, not just with pleasure, but with gratitude too, when one sees that the other intended to benefit one through his actions and because of his affection, esteem, or goodwill toward one. Likewise, while the harm inflicted on one by another's actions is disagreeable, one will feel, not just displeasure, but also resentment if one recognizes in his actions malice or ill will toward one. Gratitude and resentment are Strawson's initial examples of reactive attitudes that result from one's seeing in another's actions evident good or ill will toward one. Other examples are love, forgiveness, and hurt feelings. He calls these personal reactive attitudes.

One cannot overstate the importance to Strawson's explanation of the distinction between being benefited or harmed inadvertently or accidentally and being benefited or harmed intentionally out of evident good or ill will toward one. It is essential to how he conceives of the personal reactive attitudes. They are, on his conception of them, emotional responses in which one discerns (or thinks one discerns) in the beneficial or harmful action of another the person's good or ill will, regard or indifference toward one. Hence, they differ from one's merely being pleased or delighted with the benefit, pained or aggravated by the harm. They differ in that the cognition implicit in the response in either case, the cognition by virtue of which the response is an intentional state, is an awareness of the attitude toward one that is expressed in the action to which one is responding. The ability to discern in actions that benefit or harm one the actor's dispositions and attitudes toward one is, therefore, necessary to one's being liable to the personal reactive attitudes.

Indeed, the ability, by virtue of the feelings and attitudes it makes possible, is basic to human sociability. Strawson makes this point implicitly when he invites us to "think of the many different kinds of relationship which we can have with other people – as sharers of common interest; as members of the same family; as colleagues; as friends; as lovers; as chance parties to enormous range of transactions and encounters" and to think, "in turn ... of the kind of importance we attach to the attitudes and intentions toward us of those who stand in these relationships to us, and of the kinds of reactive attitudes to which we ourselves are prone."[13] A decade later, John Rawls, in A Theory of Justice, makes it explicitly. Concerning the three psychological laws that, on his theory of moral education, explain the transitions between the stages of moral growth in a child's development of a sense of justice, Rawls writes, "[T]he three laws are not merely principles of association or of reinforcement. While they have a certain resemblance to these learning principles, they assert that the active sentiments of love and friendship, and even the sense of justice, arise from the manifest intention of other persons to act for our good. Because we recognize that they wish us well, we care for their well-being in return. Thus we acquire attachments to persons and institutions according to how we perceive our good to be affected by them. The basic idea is one of reciprocity, a tendency to answer in kind.... [T]his tendency is a deep psychological fact. Without it our nature would be very different and fruitful social cooperation fragile if not impossible."[14]

The depth of this fact (and so the ability to discern the dispositions and attitudes of others toward one) was observed two centuries earlier by Rousseau, whom Rawls acknowledges as his predecessor.[15] For Rousseau, the fact has to do with the transition in the very young child from the solipsism characteristic of infancy and the corresponding regard for others as mere instruments of or threats to the satisfaction of its needs to its uniting with or setting itself in opposition to others and the corresponding regard for them as fellows or foes. "Every child," Rousseau writes, "is attached to his nurse.... At first this attachment is purely mechanical. What fosters the well-being of an individual attracts him; what harms him repels him. This is merely a blind instinct. What transforms this instinct into sentiment, attachment into love, aversion into hate, is the intention manifested to harm us or be useful to us. One is never passionate about insensible beings which merely follow the impulsion given to them. But those from whom one expects good or ill by their inner disposition, by their will – those we see acting freely for us or against us – inspire in us sentiments similar to those they manifest toward us. We seek what serves us, but we love what wants to serve us. We flee what harms us, but we hate what wants to harm us."[16]

While Rousseau takes account of both relationships of mutual affection and of mutual enmity as products of our awareness of and responsiveness to the attitudes of others toward us, Strawson concentrates on the former. In general, Strawson thinks of these relationships as based on the parties to them expecting and demanding "some degree of goodwill or regard" from each other.[17] This is another of the plain, natural facts about us as social beings he adduces. The personal reactive attitudes occur, then, against the background of these expectations and demands. They and the responses they elicit in turn are evidence of them. Resentment is Strawson's prime example. Thus, when one party in a relationship of mutual regard injures another and the injured party feels resentment in response, the offender may try to remove these feelings with expressions of regret or apologies and such explanations as "It was an accident," "I didn't mean to," "I didn't see you coming" or similarly "I couldn't help it," "I slipped," or "I had no choice." Each of these explanations is typically offered to assuage resentment by denying that the offending action manifested ill-will. They are meant, that is, to restore the relationship to the prior state of mutual goodwill or regard by giving the injured reason to abandon his belief that the offender acted with indifference or malice toward him. The offender in making such pleas is in effect saying that he did not, despite his having committed the offense, lack the goodwill toward the person he injured expected of him. He is saying, in other words, that while he is an appropriate object of reactive attitudes particularly at the time he committed the offense, the resentment the injured feels is misplaced in this case.

Strawson compares such pleas with pleas that are offered to assuage resentment by denying that one was even, at the time one committed the offense, an appropriate object of reactive attitudes. "I lost my head," "I was only a child," "It happened during a psychotic breakdown," "I was in a complete trance" etc. Each of these explanations is meant to exempt the offender, at least at the time of the offense, from the class of people of whom one expects some degree of goodwill in their dealings with one. It is in effect a plea to look on the offender, not as a fellow participant in the kind of friendly or cooperative relations that presuppose mutual goodwill and regard, but rather objectively as someone to be managed, controlled, or handled. In taking this outlook toward someone, one ceases to see his actions as manifesting good or ill will toward one and consequently one loses one's disposition to feel resentment, gratitude, or any of the other reactive attitudes toward him. One may of course still be liable to some feelings toward him. That one looks on the offender objectively does not mean that one becomes incapable of feeling sympathy, fear, or irritation toward him. What it means, though, is that one no longer engages with him with an attitude of goodwill or regard and an expectation of its being reciprocated. While his actions can, then, provoke in one emotional responses, these responses do not belong to the class Strawson defines as that of the reactive attitudes. Hence, the objective view of someone that pleas of this second type invite is sharply opposed to the view one takes of another with whom one participates in an interpersonal relationship.

Strawson makes this comparison between the two types of plea to bring out the difference between our viewing someone as a participant in an interpersonal relationship with us and our viewing him as an object whose behavior is the product of the external forces and conditions to which he is subject and who is to be managed or controlled accordingly. The latter is consistent with the view we would take of people and their actions if we were to accept the thesis of determinism and regard them in its light. We are disposed to take such a view of someone when we see him as immature or dysfunctional in a way that incapacitates him for normal interpersonal relationships. In that case, we abandon the view of him as a participant with us in such relationships and regard him, instead, with detachment of a sort that an objective view of him entails. Nor is this the only occasion on which we would view someone objectively. We also, typically, take such a view of people generally when we are making social policy or designing a program to provide certain services to a given population. And we sometimes take such a view when, because of the strain of our relations with someone, we need to put distance between him and us of the sort that a detached attitude toward him creates. In each of these cases, we maintain an objective view only temporarily or only toward certain individuals. We could not, Strawson argues, permanently hold such a view of all people, for doing so would require our doing something we cannot in fact do, namely, cease to have interpersonal relationships. Nor, to continue Strawson's argument, would it be wise permanently to adopt the objective view even if we could, for to do so would mean giving up human life as we know it, and abandoning our humanity is an unreasonable sacrifice. Determinism, Strawson concludes, is therefore no threat to the personal reactive attitudes. We would not cease to be liable to them even if we did accept its truth, nor would we have good reason to suppress them.

Whether Strawson's argument, at this point, succeeds in vanquishing the bogey of determinism is not our concern, however. What we are after is how Strawson explains the relation of resentment to the moral emotions of indignation and guilt. To make this explanation he adds to the class of reactive attitudes vicarious analogs of the personal reactive attitudes. These analogs are attitudes one takes toward the goodwill or ill will of another, not in reaction to the manifestation of that will in the person's actions toward one, but in reaction to its manifestation in his actions toward others. Specifically, Strawson calls the vicarious analog of resentment "indignation" or "disapproval." Plainly, his use of "indignation" and "disapproval" is, as he notes, somewhat stipulative. In common speech, for instance, we are as comfortable with saying that one feels indignation at one's own mistreatment as that one feels it at the mistreatment of another. But since his point is to have distinctive names for vicarious resentment and not to give an independent account of indignation or disapproval, the stipulative use of these terms is unproblematic.

Strawson also remarks that the vicarious character of indignation, that one can conceive of it as "resentment [felt] on behalf of another, where one's own interest and dignity are not involved," makes the adjective "moral" an apt modifier of the attitude.[18] Strawson, in other words, takes indignation to be a moral attitude in virtue of its being impartial or disinterested. He does not, then, in conceiving of it as a third party analog of resentment, suppose that to feel it in response to someone's injuring another in a way that shows a lack of due regard for the victim one must have a special attachment to or specially identify with the victim. Rather he supposes that people's expectations of and demands for a reasonable amount of goodwill toward each other that form the backdrop of interpersonal relationships generalize as they, as individuals, come to recognize that everyone reasonably expects and demands such goodwill and regard on the part of others toward himself or herself in his or her transactions with them. The recognition of this general fact, Strawson further supposes, naturally disposes a person to respond with indignation or disapproval when, say, the person witnesses an injury done to someone to whom he has no special attachment by another, who manifests attitudes toward the injured that fall short of the goodwill and regard for others that is generally expected of people in their transactions with others. Strawson, apart from a quick reference to human connection, does not say why it is natural for people's expectations of and demands for a reasonable amount of goodwill from others toward themselves to generalize in this way. Nonetheless, one could, to explain this development, appeal in the way Hume did to something like our general sympathy with humankind.

Strawson, in fact, seems to be tacitly following Hume in this part of his essay. Hume too distinguished attitudes that reflect a disinterested view from those reflecting an interested one and took the former to be moral because they reflected this view and occurred in response to a perception of the quality of the will manifested in the action that is their object. Indeed, Hume took the distinction between the personal or interested view and the general or disinterested view to be crucial to the explanation of our praising some people for their moral virtue and censuring others for their moral depravity. Such praise and censure, Hume held, express the sentiments of moral approbation and blame that we experience in response to our perceiving behind the actions of those whom we praise and censure such motives as kindness and compassion, on the one hand, envy and malice, on the other, and for our perception of such motives to give rise to these sentiments we must perceive them from a general or disinterested view. We could not otherwise, Hume argues, explain our praising and censuring the heroes and villains of the ancient world, like the Roman senators who defended the republic at the time of its crumbling and the Roman emperors who came later and whose cruelty and injustice are infamous, since their actions can hardly affect our interests.[19] What Strawson then adds to Hume's account is the idea of certain moral feelings and attitudes being analogs of feelings and attitudes that reflect a personal or interested view.

In addition to the vicarious reactive attitudes, Strawson introduces reflexive ones into the class of reactive attitudes. He calls these "self-reactive attitudes." They naturally arise, he suggests, as a result of one's generalizing the expectations of and demands for goodwill on the part of others toward one and thereby coming to expect and demand such goodwill of others toward each other in their transactions with themselves. For once one has generalized these expectations and demands, one realizes that they apply to oneself as well, that one is no different from others in being someone of whom such goodwill in interpersonal relations is expected and demanded. Accordingly, one becomes liable to feeling obliged or bound to act as the goodwill toward others that is expected and demanded of one requires, to feeling compunction, and to feeling guilt or remorse if one fails to meet this requirement. These are what Strawson refers to as the self-reactive attitudes.

He mentions them, he says, for the sake of completing the picture.[20] But he also notes that an agent who was not liable to the self-reactive attitudes would be abnormal in a way that supported, were he to injure another, a plea like the pleas of immaturity and derangement that invite taking an objective view of him and thus suppressing the resentment or indignation toward him that otherwise would be forthcoming.[21]

Strawson, having completed his picture of the reactive attitudes, returns to the dispute over whether determinism poses a threat to our practice of attributing moral responsibility, and to show that it doesn't, he reprises the argument he gave to show that accepting the thesis of determinism would not affect our being liable to the personal reactive attitudes. The argument, he believes, applies mutatis mutandis to the vicarious reactive attitudes, since they are analogs of the former. At the same time, he suggests that we can directly see in the argument's application to this subclass of the reactive attitudes that our accepting the thesis of determinism is no threat to our practice of attributing moral responsibility. The argument, as applied to the vicarious reactive attitudes, affords this observation, he argues, because our susceptibility to these attitudes, unlike our susceptibility to the personal reactive attitudes, is the same as our expecting and demanding of everyone in our community some degree of goodwill or regard toward others generally in his or her dealings with them, and this generalized, impersonal expectation and demand amounts to an understanding of everyone in the community as lying under moral obligations to act with some degree of goodwill toward others generally in his or her dealings with them and as therefore someone to whom moral responsibility for failures to meet these obligations and for harms that result from some such failures is, in the absence of an exculpatory plea, properly attributed. Attributions of moral responsibility, according to Strawson, require an understanding of people as moral agents and as members of a moral community, and the interpersonal relationships in which one participates are seen as falling among the relationships that a moral community comprises only when one regards people in one's community from a general or disinterested standpoint.

Strawson initially makes this point by supposing someone whose view of himself and others is entirely interested or personal.[22] Such a person is liable to the personal reactive attitudes but not to the vicarious ones. He is someone, then, who expects and demands from others a degree of goodwill toward himself in their dealings with him but does not expect of or demand from others such goodwill or regard in their dealings with each other. Such a person, Strawson contends, would be a moral solipsist. He would not, that is, see the interpersonal relationships in which he participates as embedded within a moral community. He would not see the demands he makes on others that they act with a degree of goodwill or regard toward him as general requirements to act with that degree of goodwill toward others to which everyone is subject and that as such represent moral obligations under which everyone lies. The ideas of belonging to a moral community, of having in common with others reciprocal moral obligations to act with a degree of goodwill toward one another, and of being, as everyone else is, morally responsible for actions that affect others do not arise, then, until one takes up the standpoint of others in one's community and their expectations and demands on those with whom they interact.[23] These ideas do not arise, in other words, until one regards oneself and others from a general or disinterested standpoint.

Here too Strawson may be meaning to follow Hume in supposing that perceptions and judgments of moral relations and moral conduct must come from a view we share with others. The intelligibility and practical force of the language of morals, Hume argued, presuppose a common point of view, and therefore we must vacate our respective interested or personal viewpoints, which are peculiar to each of us, and take up a disinterested or impersonal one (or suppose that we have), which is common to all, to take in the moral character of people's relationships and actions within them and to speak properly of it. Nonetheless, though Strawson may be meaning to follow Hume here, he departs, I think, from Hume in supposing that we get our ideas of moral obligation and moral responsibility directly from generalizing the expectations of and demands for goodwill toward ourselves that we make on others, which is to say, by vacating our personal view and taking up an impersonal or disinterested one. For Hume does not think we come to have these ideas until we apply the generalized expectations and demands that we acquire in taking up the impersonal view to ourselves in those circumstances in which we find ourselves lacking the natural motives by which we typically manifest goodwill or due regard in our dealings with others.

Specifically, Hume thinks we acquire these ideas as a result of a kind of indignation with ourselves for lacking the motives of goodwill toward others that we come to demand of everyone including ourselves when we take up the impersonal or disinterested view.[24] That is, seeing that we lack the motive of benevolence, say, or fellow feeling that in our dealings with another would show us to bear goodwill toward him and at the same time expecting and demanding on his behalf that we so act, we reproach ourselves for our lack of benevolence and fellow feeling and are thereby moved by a sense of duty to do the action that we would have done had we been naturally moved by either to do it. It is this experience of self-reproach for lacking the proper natural motive of goodwill and the consequent sense of duty to do what we would naturally do if we had that motive that gives us the idea of moral obligation, the idea that acts displaying goodwill or due regard for others in our dealings with them are obligatory even when we lack in ourselves the motives of benevolence or fellow feeling that would naturally produce them. And presumably, though Hume does not expressly say this, the same experience that gives us the idea of moral obligation gives us as well the idea of being morally responsible for doing or failing to do what we now understand as obligatory. Be this as it may, the important point is that Strawson, like Hume, holds that the acquisition of these ideas occurs only after one becomes liable to the vicarious reactive attitudes. Being liable to the personal reactive attitudes is by itself insufficient for having them.

Let us distinguish, then, between Strawson's original account of the reactive attitudes and that account modified to reflect Hume's view of how we come to see ourselves as having moral obligations. I will refer to the latter as the modified Strawsonian account. Clearly, either account shows how someone might be liable to resentment though not to indignation. Such a person, while capable of experiencing personal reactive attitudes, would be incapable of experiencing the vicarious ones. To be capable of the former he must be able to form attachments to others, to regard them as friends, mates, pals, or the like, and thus to have some affective tie to them. Such attachments are possible, though, even if one is incapable of experiencing the vicarious reactive attitudes. For one can form an attachment to another without being able to understand the other's interests sympathetically, and on either account, to be capable of the vicarious reactive attitudes means that one can take an impartial view of others, a view in which one regards their interests sympathetically and thereby feels personal reactive attitudes on their behalf. A person who is incapable of taking such a viewpoint is thus incapable of experiencing the vicarious reactive attitudes. On the modified Strawsonian account, such a person is also incapable of experiencing the self-reactive attitudes, for on this account, a person can experience such attitudes only if he is capable of experiencing the vicarious reactive attitudes. Being capable of experiencing the latter attitudes, in other words, is a necessary condition for being capable of experiencing the former. Hence, at least on the modified Strawsonian account, a thoroughly egocentric person, someone lacking a conscience and incapable of empathy, could nonetheless be liable to resentment. This account, in short, supports an understanding of psychopaths as capable of resentment.[25]

If psychopaths, by virtue of their lacking a conscience, are the paradigm of human agency that is incapable of moral judgment but otherwise rational, then the modified Strawsonian account yields the better explanation of this incapacity and thus yields a better understanding of the nature of moral agency. The two accounts differ in identifying the capacity for moral judgment with the acquisition of different liabilities to reactive attitudes. The modified Strawsonian account identifies it with the acquisition of a liability to the self-reactive attitudes. Strawson's original account, by contrast, identifies it with the acquisition of a liability to the vicarious reactive attitudes. On his account, acquiring the capacity for these attitudes is independent of one's acquisition of a liability to the self-reactive attitudes. Yet if the hallmark of the capacity for moral judgment is the ability to see oneself as others see one and to react accordingly, then Strawson's original account, in identifying the capacity for moral judgment with the liability to experience the personal reactive attitudes vicariously, falls short. A general sympathy with others that gives rise to one's being liable to the vicarious reactive attitudes is, in other words, insufficient for understanding oneself as joined with others in relations of reciprocal moral obligations and for understanding, in consequence, the moral responsibility that can attach to failures to meet those obligations. Hence, only with the development of the self-understanding that comes from being able to see oneself as others see one and of the liability to the self-reactive attitudes that is consequent to it does one acquire a capacity for moral judgment. Such development marks a significant advance over the development of a capacity for experiencing vicarious attitudes.[26] The modified Strawsonian account of the reactive attitudes captures this advance. By doing so it explains, as Strawson's original account does not, the moral deficit that is so memorably displayed by Hitchcock's villains in *Shadow of a Doubt* and *Strangers on a Train*.

Notes

Editor's note: This chapter was reprinted from A. Konzelmann Ziv, K. Lehrer, and H. B. Schmid (eds.), *Self-Evaluation: Affective and Social Grounds of Intentionality* (Philosophical Studies Series 116), with kind permission from Springer Science+Business Media, copyright 2011.

1. The film is an adaptation of Patrick Hamilton's play *Rope*.

2. Darwall (2006). See also G. Watson (1988), and R. J. Wallace (1996).

3. Ibid., 68.

4. P. F. Strawson (1962). All references to the reprint.

5. Darwall (2006, 67).

6. Ibid., 66–68.

7. See R. D. Hare (2003).

8. Darwall, 74–79.

9. For further discussion of what it means to say that psychopaths lack the capacity for moral judgment see Deigh (1995, 743–63).

10. Darwall, 17.

11. Hitchcock plants in the film's dialogue the suggestion that the cause of Oakley's anti-social personality is a childhood injury to the brain.

12. The following is taken from part I of my essay "Reactive Attitudes Revisited" in *Morality and the Emotions*, edited by Carla Bagnoli (Oxford: Oxford University Press, 2011).

13. Strawson, 76.

14. Rawls (1971, 494–95).

15. Rawls (1963, 281–305).

16. Rousseau (1979, 213).

17. Strawson, 76.

18. Ibid., 84.

19. Hume (1975, 215–18).

20. Strawson, 84.

21. Ibid., 86.

22. Ibid., 85.

23. Strawson then reaffirms the point in considering how pleading, in response to injuring someone, that one was at the time incapacitated for normal participation in interpersonal relationships ("I was suffering hallucinations, undergoing a psychotic breakdown, in a trance, etc.") affects our susceptibility to moral indignation. Thus, Strawson, after introducing the case by writing of seeing the agent in a different light, "as one whose picture of the world is an inane delusion; or as one whose behaviour ... is unintelligible to us" etc., goes on, "[A]bstracting now from direct personal interest, we may express the facts with a new emphasis. We may say: to the extent to which the agent is seen in this light, he is not seen as one on whom demands and expectations lie in that particular way in which we think of them as lying when we speak of moral obligation; he is not, to that extent, seen as a morally responsible agent, as a term of moral relationships, as a member of the moral community." Ibid., 86.

24. See Hume (1978, 479).

25. Strawson's characterization of the moral solipsist is that of someone who is capable of experiencing the personal reactive attitudes but not the vicarious ones, and Strawson allows that such a person might also be capable of the self-reactive attitudes. Consequently, the moral solipsist, as Strawson characterizes him, does not fit the profile of a psychopath. At the same time, Strawson raises the possibility of a moral idiot, who does. See Strawson, 85.

26. See Hoffman (2000, 93–112).

References

Darwall, S. 2006. *The Second Person Standpoint: Morality, Respect, and Accountability.* Cambridge, MA: Harvard University Press.

Deigh, J. 1995. Empathy and Universalizability. *Ethics* 105:743–763.

Deigh, J. 2011. Reactive Attitudes Revisited. In *Morality and the Emotions*, ed. C. Bagnoli. Oxford, New York: Oxford University Press.

Hare, R. D. 2003. *Manual for the Revised Psychopathy Checklist.* 2nd ed. Toronto, ON: Multi-Health Systems, Inc.

Hoffman, M. 2000. *Empathy and Moral Development: Implications for Caring and Justice.* Cambridge: Cambridge University Press.

Hume, D. 1975. *Enquiries Concerning Human Understanding and Concerning the Principles of Morals.* 3rd ed., ed. P. H. Nidditch. Oxford: Clarendon Press.

Hume, D. 1978. *A Treatise of Human Nature.* 2nd ed., ed. P. H. Nidditch. Oxford: Clarendon Press.

Rawls, J. 1963. The Sense of Justice. *Philosophical Review* 72:281–305.

Rawls, J. 1971. *A Theory of Justice.* Cambridge, MA: Belknap Press.

Rousseau, J. J. 1979. *Emile or On Education.* Bloom, A., (trans.). New York: Basic Books.

Strawson, P. F. 1962. "Freedom and Resentment." *Proceedings of the British Academy*, 48, 1–25. Reprinted in G. Watson (ed.), *Free Will*, 2nd ed. Oxford: Oxford University Press, 2003, 72–93.

Wallace, R. J. 1996. *Responsibility and the Moral Sentiments.* Cambridge, MA: Harvard University Press.

Watson, G. 1988. Responsibility and the Limits of Evil: Variations on a Strawsonian Theme. In *Responsibility, Character, and the Emotions*, ed. F. Schoeman, 256–286. Cambridge: Cambridge University Press.

10 Being a (A-)Moral Person and Caring about Morality

Thomas Schramme

In the philosophical debate on the foundations of morality, a specter is lurking: the figure of the amoralist. This is a person who entirely rejects morality's normative power. Such persons are not simply immoral, but rather a-moral, in the sense that moral rules, norms, and standards have no influence on their behavior. In philosophical ethics, it is sometimes argued that we must give the amoralist a reason for adhering to morality, or risk endangering the very bases of morality as an institution of behavioral control (Bayertz 2004).

Psychiatric practice, meanwhile, is concerned with the diagnostic description and therapeutic treatment of people who are apparently true amoralists, namely, those labeled psychopaths and sociopaths, and those with a dissocial (or antisocial) personality disorder. A closer analysis of this terminology will follow, for it is particularly debatable whether all people suffering from an antisocial personality disorder may be considered morally incapable. In this essay, I use the terms "psychopathy" and "psychopath" primarily as shorthand for moral incapacity and morally incapable persons—although I would also allow for psychopaths to be severely deficient, and not really incapable, in this regard. My aim is to incorporate psychiatric terminology without simply adopting a particular conceptual framework for this language; that is, I want to leave room to discuss the appropriateness of various psychiatric classifications. This use of terminology is also meant to imply that the psychiatric research on psychopathy has significance for the philosophical question of the amoralist.

I will proceed in three stages that are organized into four sections: I will first clarify what it means to be amoral by asking what it means to be a moral person. I believe we should distinguish between people who are fundamentally capable of morality and those who are incapable of it. Philosophical discussions usually present amoralists as people who choose not to be moral, although they would be capable of morality in principle. In the second section, with the help of a little-known argument from Gilbert Ryle, I will identify the essential, overall capacity for taking a moral perspective with the idea of *caring about* morality. In the second stage, which is contained in the third section, I will take a closer look at the psychiatric concept of psychopathy and related categories. I aim to show why I believe that psychopaths are morally incapable, and why they do not actually correspond, in this respect, to the figure of the amoralist within moral philosophy. Psychopaths lack certain capacities, or are severely deficient in these respects—most important here is the significant limitation or loss of fellow feeling—that are essential for being a moral person. In my view, a morally capable person cannot help but to care about morality; this effectively results from the capacity itself, which cannot simply be "put on hold." For the philosophical debate, this means that the amoralist specter is perhaps not so threatening as sometimes assumed. That topic will be my focus in the fourth and final section.

10.1   What It Means (Not) to Be a Moral Person

We can ask what it means to be a moral person, or we can ask what it means *not* to be a moral person. In what follows, I hope to demonstrate that these two questions cannot, in every sense, be regarded merely as slightly different formulations of the same problem. They do not simply address the same topic from positive and negative perspectives. Instead, I argue that the phrase "not being a moral person" encompasses a meaning not found in the description "being a nonmoral person." There are people who are not moral persons in the strong sense, as they lack the capacities necessary to take a moral perspective. This means they are "not moral persons" in the sense that they *cannot* be moral, and not because they are not *being* moral people. They must be distinguished from people who simply act immorally, or reject the guidance of moral considerations, because people who are truly morally incapable do not even have this ability. Morally incapable people really do exist, I wish to argue. They are not identical with the so-called amoralists discussed so frequently in philosophical ethics. Amoralists are people who do not accept the guidance of moral considerations although in principle they would be capable of doing so. In ethics, they are usually presented as a challenge to the possibility of justifying morality or a moral perspective. Should I be moral at all? This is the question sometimes expressed. The amoralist is a person who poses this question on a fundamental level and answers in the negative. If we cannot give this person any reason to be moral, it would appear that moral obligations have no secure foundation.

Admittedly, the figure of the amoralist is often understood in purely hypothetical terms. Many moral philosophers propose that the amoralist need not actually exist. However, according to my argument, the idea of a morally capable amoralist, even in the hypothetical sense, appears inconceivable. For phenomenological reasons, that is, reasons that make it "practically inconceivable" (Strawson 1962, 12), this figure becomes implausible, if not entirely impossible. The amoralist is inconceivable, I argue, because learning to take a moral perspective is equivalent to caring about it, and this leads me to doubt the possibility of ever ceasing to care about it. Thus, according to this theory, someone is "not a moral person" only if he or she is incapable of taking a moral perspective.

I do not wish to claim, of course, that a morally capable person always makes the right moral choices, or is at least motivated to do so. Being a moral person seems comparable to me to the idea of being a rational person. To be a rational person does not mean that one always acts in a rational manner, or is even persistently inclined to do so. Instead, it means having the capacity to think and act rationally.

Let us begin by briefly considering what we mean by a moral person. In this way, we can discard uses that are not relevant for our purposes here. First, one might imagine a person who usually, or perhaps always, acts in line with moral obligations. However, this person is not necessarily a moral person, I would argue. Such persons may act in a morally required manner, certainly, but that does not necessarily mean they understand the institution of morality, or the reasons why they should act as they do. Even a machine could observe moral rules.

Second, one could therefore understand a moral person to be someone who does the right moral thing based on the right motivation. Kant, for instance, identified the good will as the source of moral conduct. But again, this is not the term "moral person" I am after; in fact, Kant's notion probably more accurately refers to a morally *good* person. In my understanding, a morally bad person is still a moral person. Granted, there appear to be limits here: It would seem somehow misplaced to regard a person as moral if he or she engaged only in wrongdoing. However, in such cases, we might rather begin to doubt this person's moral capacity, according to my theory. In any case, it seems plausible to argue that, in order to count as a moral person, one need not be a particularly good person, nor do the right thing, morally speaking, in every situation.

As mentioned earlier, I am concerned here with an idea of the moral person that can be conceptualized in terms of a capacity, similar to the idea of the rational person. In this interpretation, a moral person is someone capable of understanding moral considerations and allowing these to guide his or her actions. The opposite concept is that of moral incapacity. Someone who is not a moral person in this regard is often considered a psychopath. As we will see, it seems that the idea of the moral person has to do with a specific type of moral knowledge, namely, knowledge of the difference between right and wrong, which inevitably implies caring about this difference.

However, it seems undeniable that we understand a moral person to be someone who not only is morally capable, but who also uses that capacity. Being a moral person, in this view, means being disposed to do the right thing, or to be virtuous. One also speaks here of "moral character." The opposite of a moral person in this sense is the amoralist. Not being a moral person, according to this interpretation, is the same as being morally indifferent. However, as already mentioned, a key question I wish to ask is whether it is actually possible for a morally capable person not to have a moral character. It should be emphasized here that the amoralist need not be an immoral person. For the latter can indeed accept moral dictates and norms, and can certainly have a moral character, but choose not to act in accordance with them. The amoralist, on the other hand, does not accept the very institution of morality and does not consider it binding.

10.2   Ryle: "On Forgetting the Difference between Right and Wrong"

We now come to the problem of what it means to be a moral person, more positively described. I have already suggested that we can understand the adoption of a moral perspective as the acquisition of knowledge about the difference between right and wrong. In this context, Gilbert Ryle offered the following scenario in an article published in 1958: Let us suppose that someone asks another person, perhaps in a reproachful tone, "*Don't you know the difference between right and wrong?*" The reply: "*Well, I did learn it once, but I have forgotten it.*" Ryle goes on to claim, "This is a ridiculous thing to say" (Ryle 1958, p. 147). Ryle thus finds it absurd to suppose that one could forget the difference between right and wrong. However, why is the idea of moral forgetfulness ridiculous? By addressing this question with Ryle's help, we will see, I hope, why the claim I made earlier—that being a morally capable person inevitably means orienting oneself by morality—is perhaps not so absurd as it may seem at first.

Ryle first dismisses an explanation of this absurdity that is important because it is common, but also inadequate. One could maintain that knowing the difference between right and wrong is a type of skill, that is, a kind of *knowing how*. However, skills can become rusty and may ultimately be forgotten or unlearned. This does not hold true for knowledge of the difference between right and wrong. As Ryle notes, for instance, we cannot excuse a malicious action by pointing to our lack of practice in fair-mindedness and generosity. Knowing the difference between right and wrong seems to be a form of knowledge, but not a kind of *knowing how*. It also does not seem like propositional knowledge, that is, knowledge that something is the case, because that type of knowledge may certainly be forgotten while moral knowledge may not.

Let us pause here and consider what kind of a problem Ryle addresses. I am reluctant to say that his puzzle is a conceptual one although that seems to follow from what he claims. In addition, Ryle explicitly declares that his question is "Why will 'forget' and 'be reminded of' not go with 'the difference between right and wrong'?" (Ryle 1958, 149). Nevertheless, I doubt that he is merely concerned with the meaning of words. He rather addresses a problem of how to make sense of an aspect of our moral life, or more specifically, of how we ought to conceive of ourselves as moral agents. Although it is true that there seems to be a linguistic error involved in applying "forget" to "the difference between right and wrong"—still, to acknowledge the error does not solve the riddle of the inconceivability of forgetting the difference between right and wrong. I believe that this distinguishes Ryle's problem from plain conceptual problems, which are, for instance, based on category mistakes and dissolve by conceptual analysis.

I am laboring this point because an obvious solution to the puzzle could be that the very definition of forgetting implies that something that can be forgotten has to be a kind of knowledge. Thus, if the notion of forgetting the difference between right and wrong does not make sense, then, one might claim, there can be no such thing as moral knowledge. The problem would dissolve—the linguistic error would be due to the false assumption that the term "moral knowledge" has meaning. Once we had grasped that there is no moral knowledge, we could easily see why it makes no sense to speak of forgetting the difference between right and wrong. But this is not how Ryle argues. He actually allows for moral knowledge, although, as we will see, not in the same way as it is often conceived in modern moral philosophy. More importantly, he sees the inconceivability of forgetting the difference between right and wrong as being based not on a conceptual error but on a phenomenon in real life. The puzzle calls for an explanation that is not merely sorting out conceptual mistakes, but gives an account of an important aspect of human morality.

Ryle draws an analogy comparing knowledge of the difference between right and wrong to a developed sense of taste. Having a developed palate means knowing the difference between good and bad. According to Ryle, this includes two aspects. On the one hand, it involves knowing the evaluation standards (*standards of superiority*) in a certain domain of taste, whether it be an aesthetic domain, such as art, or a culinary domain, such as enology. On the other hand, it also involves caring about these evaluation standards. To know the difference between good and bad means to care about this difference. Ryle argues, "There seems to be a sort of incongruity in the idea of a person's knowing the difference between good and bad wine or poetry, while not caring a whit more for the one than for the other; of his appreciating without being appreciative of excellences" (Ryle 1958, 152).

A person correspondingly does not really know the difference between right and wrong if he or she is not disapproving of wrong acts. "Here, too, there seems to be an incongruity in the idea of a person's knowing that something wrong had been done, but still not disapproving of it or being ashamed of it" (ibid.). I believe this second element, that is, caring, is the decisive aspect of Ryle's explanation of the inconceivability of forgetting the difference between right and wrong. Although we can lose morality, just like our tastes can deteriorate, we do not regard this as forgetting. It is rather an instance of ceasing to care. If this is applied to the analogous case of the knowledge of the difference between right and wrong, then we can only be said to possess this moral knowledge, following Ryle, when we also take this difference seriously, that is, when we care about it. That does not seem so implausible if we consider, for example, the connection between this knowledge and that which is called the conscience of a person. To have a conscience means to care about things that might come into conflict with it. "Conscience is not something prior to or posterior to moral convictions; it is having those convictions in an operative degree, i.e. being disposed to behave accordingly" (cf. Ryle 1940, 189).

So Ryle maintains that one can indeed lose the difference between right and wrong, just as one can lose a developed sense of taste, but that this is not forgetting. Instead, one ceases, in this case, to take the moral standards seriously, or to *care* about them. Conversely, to possess knowledge of the difference between right and wrong means to care about this difference and to be motivated accordingly. Knowledge, caring, and motivation are one here, and Ryle, in this article and other writings, consequently opposes the usual separation of cognition, emotion, and volition. "In our abstract theorizing about human nature we are still in the archaic habit of treating ourselves and all other human beings as animated department stores, in which the intellect is one department, the will is another department and the feelings a third department" (Ryle 1972, 442). In this respect, knowledge of the difference between right and wrong is an integral aspect of a person's character. Someone who ceases to care about the difference between right and wrong does not lose a piece of information—an item of propositional knowledge—or a skill, but instead alters his or her very self. This can be referred to as experiencing a *change of heart* (Wallace 1986, 47). One might infer that to know the difference between right and wrong is an aspect of the character of a person and not a contingent feature like having certain information or skills.

This might also account for another aspect of Ryle's explanation: People can differ in the strength of their caring about the difference between right and wrong, but they do not thereby show differences in knowledge. It is not the case that the person who is very resentful about vicious acts knows the difference between right and wrong better than the person who is only slightly indignant about the same act. Moral education, if successful, ignites in persons the appreciation of the difference between right and wrong, but it does not need to light a bonfire. Ryle puts it this way: "So even if, in some domains, to teach is, *inter alia*, to kindle, still we do not think of what is taught as varying in magnitude with the heat of the fire. The match is the same, but the fuels are different" (Ryle 1958, 158).

It might seem wrong or at least unusual to include appreciation or even enjoyment as part of knowing something, in our case of knowing the difference between right and wrong, because it seems that this element of caring cannot be learned but is an effect of getting to know something. First we learn the difference; then, if all goes well, we appreciate it. Ryle objects to this rigid distinction between knowing and appreciating the difference between right and wrong by pointing out that on this account it would need to be possible to interrupt the causal connection by some intervention, similar to preventing seasickness as an effect of the rolling of a ship by taking some drug. However, to assume that such an intervention might work seems a ludicrous idea in the realm of morality. More importantly, appreciation of the difference between right and wrong for Ryle is an elementary part of moral education. In fact, it is this particular aspect that seems to be the reason why there is something special to teaching the virtues. Although to appreciate or to admire is to learn something, it is not to gain information or learn a skill. Ryle insists: "The notions of learning, studying, teaching and knowing are ampler notions than our academic epistemologies have acknowledged. They are hospitable enough to house under their roofs notions like those of inspiring, kindling and infecting" (ibid., 154). So a person who does not care about the difference between right and wrong has not yet learned the difference (ibid., 155).

It should be noted that, in speaking of the knowledge of the difference between right and wrong, we are faced with an element of ambiguity that I have not yet addressed. This phrase can refer, on the one hand, to knowledge of the difference between right and wrong in terms of moral rules. One example would be the knowledge that truthfulness is morally right while lying is wrong. However, this would, in Ryle's terms, concern the standards of moral superiority, thus would be a kind of information—about the content of morality—that can indeed be forgotten. Hence in the first reading, to know the difference between right and wrong means that one knows the moral evaluation standards and thus possesses moral information. Still, this would not be the kind of moral knowledge Ryle is addressing, and indeed, it seems clear that psychopaths can have this kind of propositional knowledge (Cima et al. 2010; cf. Morse 2008, 209).

The expression can also mean that someone knows of the *existence* of a difference between right and wrong. In this second interpretation, awareness of the difference between right and wrong is tantamount to an acknowledgment that something such as morality even exists. Again, it is probably not what Ryle means. For him, to know the difference between right and wrong is rather a mode of being. To know the difference between right and wrong is therefore identical, in a more awkward expression, to having virtues—in contrast to knowing what the virtues consist in. In short, to have moral knowledge in Ryle's sense is to be a moral person.

To summarize, since Ryle included in the very notion of knowing the difference between right and wrong an element of caring, it might seem awkward to refer to it as an instance of knowledge at all. It might be better, then, to slightly change terminology and reserve "moral knowledge" for moral information and skills. "To be a moral person" could replace what Ryle means by "knowing the difference between right and wrong." According to this terminology, we cannot forget to be virtuous and Ryle's paper would have better been called "On Forgetting to be a Moral Person."

The question I have raised—of whether it is possible to cease being a moral person—does not concern the question of whether, in the sense of the first interpretation, one can stop caring about a certain conception of what constitutes vice and virtue; one can certainly do that. It is possible, for example, to stop caring about the prohibition against lying. But is it possible to stop caring about morality? I doubt that this is possible, because the specific nature of moral capacity makes it impossible to cease caring about morality or to simply stop using one's moral capacity. In this context, I will focus on our capacity for fellow feeling. I will make the argument that a morally capable person cannot turn into an amoralist.

10.3   Psychopathy as Psychiatric Category

However, before we take a closer look at the question of whether one can, as it were, entirely cease to acknowledge the institution of morality, we will first return to the phenomenon of psychopathy introduced at the beginning. Psychiatric classification systems offer three categories of particular relevance: The *International Classification of Diseases* (ICD) describes dissocial personality disorder as "a personality disorder characterized by disregard for social obligations and callous unconcern for the feelings of others." The American *Diagnostic and Statistical Manual of Mental Disorders* (DSM–IV) allows for a diagnosis of antisocial personality disorder under the following conditions:

There is a pervasive pattern of disregard for and violation of the rights of others occurring since age 15 years, as indicated by three (or more) of the following: (1) failure to conform to social norms with respect to lawful behaviors as indicated by repeatedly performing acts that are grounds for arrest; (2) deceitfulness, as indicated by repeated lying, use of aliases, or conning others for personal profit or pleasure; (3) impulsivity or failure to plan ahead; (4) irritability and aggressiveness, as indicated by repeated physical fights or assaults; (5) reckless disregard for safety of self or others; (6) consistent irresponsibility, as indicated by repeated failure to sustain consistent work behavior or honor financial obligations; (7) lack of remorse, as indicated by being indifferent to or rationalizing having hurt, mistreated, or stolen from another.

Finally, the Psychopathy Checklist (revised; PCL–R) created by the well-known psychologist Robert Hare proposes a range of factors, including personality factors such as "aggressive narcissism" and case history factors such as "socially deviant lifestyle." The checklist features a total of 20 criteria to be tested by at least one trained diagnostician using a points system. Persons who test with 30 points or more are considered psychopaths under this classification. Hare's checklist is not part of official psychiatric nosology, but its use is growing, especially in forensic contexts (Hare and Neumann 2010).

I lack the space to examine these psychiatric categories in detail here (but see my introduction, this volume). I must simply warn against uncritical acceptance of the "data" that I find so relevant for my philosophical enquiry. It is first striking to note that these psychiatric classifications are closely connected to violations of norms and are thus concerned with manifest behavior. To this are added rather vague indications of emotional disturbance, such as lack of remorse, low tolerance for frustration, and aggressiveness. However, this is problematic because deviant behavior can have many different causes. We must determine whether a person behaving in this way is not *able* or not *willing* to act in compliance with norms. Only in the first case—a lack of, or severe deficit in, ability—can we speak of a genuine mental disorder. We thus find ourselves asking the old—if slightly misleading because simplifying—question, "Mad or bad?" (Reznek 1997). This calls for research into the nature of the deficit, that is, the specific mental dysfunction underlying the antisocial personality. The cited classification systems describe psychopathy and similar categories as psychiatric categories that are, relatively speaking, highly unusual; they also feature language of a strongly and explicitly normative nature, as in the references to "callousness" (ICD), "reckless disregard" (DSM), and "parasitic lifestyle" (PCL–R).

For my purposes, it would be necessary to further differentiate between psychopaths, who are in fact morally incapable, and people with restricted moral capacities. I here use the term "psychopath" as shorthand for morally incapable persons, not in the sense found in Hare's checklist, even if our uses may well overlap. It now seems clear that a simple adoption of psychiatric findings would not be adequate for answering philosophical questions. In fact, the analytical insights of the philosophical debate should also be used to inform empirical scientific research; our aim should be a genuinely interdisciplinary perspective.

Even in the context of that long-term project, we may already note that the psychiatric approach, regardless of the many differences among its classification systems, generally seems willing to conclude that psychopaths—understood as extreme cases of antisocial personality—do not possess the capacity to take a moral perspective. The reasons for this have in turn been discussed in both the psychiatric and philosophical literature, without agreement on any particular explanation. I will not be concerned here with the causal explanation, that is, the etiology of this mental disorder, but rather with determining the nature of the deficit found in psychopaths. Regarding the first question of why psychopaths are incapable of morality, there are two fundamentally differing explanations. First, there may exist an organic or mental deficit that renders the person incapable of taking a moral perspective. Second, the moral incapacity may be caused by deficient moral education. Both explanations appear plausible to me, and they are not mutually contradictory. In the first case, the person lacks the biological mechanisms necessary for moral capacity, and in the second case, these mechanisms have not been developed into a capacity.

There are also no uniform theories on the specific deficit found in psychopaths. However, many approaches agree that psychopaths have no difficulty understanding that societies have normative expectations regarding human behavior. They are also able to name concrete moral obligations. What is more, they can anticipate moral reactions in others, such as reproach or shame, and factor this into their considerations. This means that they can certainly act in a morally compliant manner; they need not necessarily violate moral norms or break laws, although if it happens that is probable due to their disorder. Psychopaths seem rather to lack a true comprehension or understanding of such moral reactions, as they themselves seem not to be capable of them. It is not in their instrumental thought and action that we find an essential deficit, but rather primarily in their lack of fellow feeling, or emphatic concern. Many theories of psychopathy agree on this point (cf. Blair, Mitchell, and Blair 2005). Although there is, of course, a lot of scope for disagreement and additional explanation, for my purposes, this deficit is crucial, and I will therefore focus on it. In the view I present here, psychopaths suffer from a genuine "lack of moral sense." The question of whether they also suffer from other disturbances will not be pursued here, although it is quite likely that they do.

Empathic concern has been called the "cement of the moral universe" (Slote 2010, 14). I wish to argue that empathy, here interpreted as a capacity, not as a present feeling, is indeed a necessary requirement of morality. Morality, as explained before, is understood as taking the moral point of view, or being a moral person. In virtue of gaining access to the minds of others via empathy, we also develop the capacity to care about others. However, this is not the end of the story. I believe in the final analysis to be moral means to care about morality, or to care about being moral, not to care about others (though we probably have to care for some people in order to become moral persons).

Psychopaths indeed seem to lack empathy (see, e.g., Baron-Cohen 2012). But we first need to clarify what "empathy" means, exactly. In the last few years there has been a lot of debate about, and attempts to distinguish between, different aspects of empathy. I will use some of these distinctions in order to clarify what aspect might eventually be pertinent to moral issues. Empathy, according to a common definition, is "a motivating psychological mechanism" (Slote 2010, 5) that involves "having the feeling of another (involuntary) aroused in ourselves" (ibid., 15). It is to be distinguished from sympathy, where a person feels *for* someone. To experience empathy, therefore means to have a shared feeling or emotion, usually one that has a negative quality, such as pain and anguish. Obviously, we may also share a positive emotion with others, but it seems plausible to use examples of negative emotions since these are usually related to prosocial, beneficial behavior. Empathy might also be felt vicariously (in addition to the vicariously *shared* feeling of other examples of empathy), for instance, when we learn about a friend's being left by her partner before she herself gains knowledge about it. We then might feel shocked and tormented when thinking about her and how she might feel.

This seems like a straightforward description of a common and well-known phenomenon, but one might ask whether we always, or even normally, feel what someone else feels when we empathize with them. Indeed, do we need to feel anything at all when empathizing? It has, for instance, been pointed out that we can empathize with a depressed person without ourselves being or becoming depressed (Darwall 1998; see Slote 2010, 16). Someone might, of course, respond to this particular example that we indeed do not feel empathy toward a depressed person but sympathize with the person, that is, feel sorry for him or her. But, again, we might, in all honesty, say to a depressed person, "I know how you feel," because we have had similar experiences before, say, phases of feeling low and being disheartened. This seems possible without necessarily feeling for the depressed person, that is, without sympathizing with her. Yet to know how someone else feels does not require being in any particular emotional state at all; it simply requires some kind of acquaintance with the particular emotional state the other person is in.

Maybe here is the right moment to pause briefly and to consider the notion of empathy from the perspective of its history. As is well-known, empathy was first used in the English language as a translation of the German term *Einfühlung*, which had been introduced as a word to describe an epistemic mechanism of gaining access to other minds (Coplan and Goldie 2011, xiii). It seems that humans can "feel into" a target without actually feeling something at that time. Arguably, to be able to gain access to another person's mental condition requires general emotional capacities because it seems likely that we learn the capacity of "mind reading" at least partly in virtue of our ability to feel what the other feels. In contrast, a robot does not seem able to empathize because it does not have experience of *any* feelings. To be sure, a robot might be able to "read" the mind of other people by deducing certain mental states from the behavior of a target, but this would not constitute empathy proper because it would not involve any aspect of the target's mental state. In other words, for a robot, it is not the mental state of a target that is in focus, but the target's behavior. The mental state of the other is a piece of information that is deduced from studying the respective behavior. However, in empathy, the mind of a target is the object of our mental state, and not simply the deduced data of studying overt behavior.

All this is, of course, familiar to scholars interested in simulation theory within the philosophy of mind, which contrasts with "theory-theory." The latter is a theory, or family of theories, which argues that understanding other minds—to have a theory of mind—works like applying a theory, hence the unusual title. In simulation theory we find an interest in empathy as a capacity to "step into the shoes" of others. This can, in principle, be a purely cognitive mechanism, hence implying a belief about a mental state of another person, though simulation theorists regularly include sharing affect as part of this process. It does not seem surprising, then, that in (neuro-)psychology we can find a distinction between cognitive and emotional, sometimes called affective, empathy (e.g., Shamay-Tsoory et al. 2009; Smith 2006). As regards this distinction, I have just claimed that cognitive empathy does not require the presence of emotional empathy, but that it does require emotional empathy as a general capacity of the (cognitively) empathizing person. This claim is an empirical one, and it would need to be supported by respective findings.

It seems unlikely that we always need present emotional empathy to be motivated to act morally. For instance, there are cases of helping behavior, where one indeed cannot have the feeling of another aroused in oneself at all, because the target is unconscious and hence does not feel anything. And there are examples of moral reactions where our feelings and the target's feelings are incongruent, as in the already mentioned case where we help someone who is depressed. Finally, there are cases of moral behavior where we actually should attempt to suppress any shared emotion, or emotional empathy—for instance, when we have to decide between two people whom to help.

Thus, emotional empathy might trigger moral behavior, but it might not be required for morality and might potentially even be detrimental to it. In line with this, emotional empathy does not seem to be the main aspect of morality, but "empathic concern." The latter term was introduced by psychologist Daniel Batson (2011), and it can also be found in Martin Hoffman's developmental story of how the ability of empathy matures in humans (Hoffman 2000).

Empathic concern seems to have an element of sympathy as part and parcel because the concern aspect seems to be calling for a moral point of view, that is, implying sympathy, which arguably is again to be explained by empathy. In other words, it seems to be potentially circular reasoning if we explain sympathy, that is, a genuine moral feeling, by empathy but define empathy as concern for the other. However, it seems indeed impossible, when referring to a mature capacity to empathize, to distinguish it from fellow feelings such as sympathy. Hoffman, for instance, explicitly refers to a "sympathetic component" in empathy (Hoffman 2011, 234f.; see also Darwall's notion of "proto-sympathetic empathy"; Darwall 1998, 271f.).

Hence empathy, I take it, has an important role for, and cannot be completely separated from, sympathy, although they are surely distinct phenomena. Sympathy, that is, feeling for someone else, is again arguably a necessary requirement of being able to take the moral point of view. This way of putting it entails a particular thesis about the role of empathy and sympathy for morality that implies that both capacities are necessary for morality, but that they don't always need to be present as actual feelings in order for a person to be morally motivated. Through the development of (our capacities for) empathy and sympathy we are able to take the moral point of view, but once we are moral persons, we don't have to actually empathize and sympathize in order to appreciate the morally right thing (Slote 2010, 88). In other words, we should see empathy and sympathy as capacities or skills that can be developed, that is, generally and potentially universally applied.

I have just described the notion of empathic concern in a way that brings it close to what I have called the moral point of view, in virtue of including a sympathetic component. So, again, there is potentially circular reasoning: (1) Taking the moral point of view means to have empathic concern; (2) psychopaths are unable to take the moral point of view; (3) psychopaths lack empathic concern. However, I do not believe that here we have a vicious circle since this line of reasoning seems more like an empirical backing of a conceptual thesis, established in the first claim. After all, at least the third claim is partly an empirical one, and it might prove false in the future. Accordingly many philosophers, not just me, study psychopathy as an interesting phenomenon for basic issues in moral philosophy.

When we consider the role of empathy for morality, it seems difficult to think of either cognition or emotion by itself as a sufficient element of the moral standpoint because empathy already contains both elements. Accordingly, to be a moral person seems to require both aspects. We need emotional empathy to appreciate that certain behavior is bad for others, and we need cognitive empathy to appreciate that all persons have needs and interests that are protected by morality, even those people we do not emotionally empathize with, and even in relation to those needs and interests that do not raise any emotional concerns (cf. Decety and Meltzoff 2011, 78ff., for further considerations regarding cognitive capacities in prosocial attitudes).

Although we can analytically distinguish between emotional and cognitive empathy, we need to be wary of such a distinction when talking about morality. Indeed, we might go further in undermining the very distinction between cognitive and emotional aspects of our minds more generally, as Gilbert Ryle has done in the quote above. Obviously, much more needs to be said and scrutinized in order to make good such a basic and general claim, but at least the phenomenon of empathy should bring us to question our distinctions of different mental realms.

In summary, I have tried to establish that the most basic aspect of morality is to take the moral point of view. I have argued that we can only be moral persons if we have certain capacities. These capacities can be determined by studying psychopaths, who arguably are morally incapacitated. Empirical research concerning psychopathy and related research regarding empathy calls into question the neat distinction between cognition and emotion but underlines the importance of empathy for morality.

Now people who gain the capacity for empathy also acquire "moral ballast," as it were. They are then able, among other things, to put themselves in the position of others; they know that people are vulnerable, and that their own actions can cause pain. They are also motivated to avoid such harmful actions whenever possible, so as not to violate their conscience. Moral education also includes other aspects, of course, but I will largely omit these here in order to concentrate on empathy. It should be clear by now that the very formation of this specific capacity relies on complex developments that are in no way limited to the affective domain. This offers support for Ryle's critique of the separation of cognition, emotion, and motivation. These reflections also lead us to consider that the lack of empathy found in psychopaths may well originate in a cognitive deficit, such as a deficient understanding of the consequences resulting from actions. For that reason, I find it incorrect to view psychopathy as a purely emotional disturbance, as it is sometimes presented. It is, in fact, to be regarded as a conglomeration of various deficits, even when merely focusing on lack of empathy, and ignoring other potential deficits that might be involved in psychopathy.

10.4 Moral Capacity and Caring about Morality

Let us now return to the question following from Ryle's observations: Is it conceivable that someone who has acquired the capacity for morality, who thus, in Ryle's phrasing, knows the difference between right and wrong, can cease to care about morality? In short, can a moral person turn into an amoralist? It is naturally conceivable, I think, that an originally moral person might turn into a psychopath—for instance, if certain brain regions were damaged in an accident. However, we have a different case before us. A person who ceases to care about morality does not lose the ability to take a moral perspective, but instead simply ceases to value it. But is that possible? This seems inconceivable to me for at least two reasons. First, this would mean ceasing to care not only about the capacity for morality, but also other capacities. As we have seen, the adoption of a moral perspective and the development of empathy, in particular, are linked to a complex network of capacities. To cease caring about the whole package of moral capacities, as it were, would require giving up much more than one's moral perspective. Second, humans are social creatures. A decision to stop valuing morality as an institution for coordinating behavior would carry immense social costs, as it concerns our identity and, indeed, integrity (Schmidtz 1993, 63). This is clearly demonstrated by the social situation of psychopaths; whether or not they have committed offenses, they are indeed social outsiders. For these two reasons, I argue that it is virtually impossible to lose one's moral perspective. The impossibility of imagining that someone could cease caring about morality altogether—with the reminder that we are not speaking only of specific norms—stems from consideration of what it means to be a morally capable person.

In a final illustration of this inconceivability, we can consider a group of criminals frequently regarded as amoralists, namely the National Socialist mass murderers, such as Adolf Eichmann or Amon Göth. In my view, these people did not entirely disregard the institution of morality, for they did indeed act morally, if only toward certain persons. This makes it all the harder to understand how they could commit such crimes, at least from the perspective of modern morality, which usually claims to be universal. We also know, however, that an important psychological factor in atrocities is the denial of the victims' human status. The Nazi example shows us, I think, how difficult it is—perhaps inconceivable—to jettison all moral scruples. As I mentioned at the outset, to be a moral person does not mean that one is incapable of even the most serious crimes. The Nazis were moral persons, although extremely bad moral persons.

Let us then summarize our results: Being a moral person primarily means being a morally capable person. I have attempted to argue that a morally capable person of this kind cares about morality as an institution and is inclined to be guided by it. Once moral capacity has been acquired, there is no way back, so to speak, apart from a return to moral incapacity, such as caused by brain injury after an accident. It seems inconceivable to me that one could cease caring about the institution of morality after having learned to value it, because that would mean losing not only the capacity to empathize with other people, but also other capacities essential for living our lives. It would also be tantamount to ejecting oneself from the social context. Morality thus seems to be an inherent aspect of the *conditio humana*. Ernst Tugendhat once objected to the idea of conceptualizing morality as an element of human biology, as if it were a body part like the heart or spine (Tugendhat 1993, 97). I would agree. However, the adoption of a moral perspective results from our education by others who harness our innate biological mechanisms. Being a moral person is therefore an integral aspect of human nature—or, maybe better, an aspect of our second nature.

Acknowledgments

Many people have commented on earlier versions of this chapter. I would specifically like to thank Hugh Upton, Heidi Maibom, and Neil Roughley for valuable discussions.

References

Baron-Cohen, S. 2012. *Zero Degrees of Empathy: A New Theory of Human Cruelty*. London: Penguin.

Batson, C. D. 2011. *Altruism in Humans*. Oxford: Oxford University Press.

Bayertz, K. 2004. *Warum überhaupt moralisch sein?* [Why be moral at all?]. Munich: Beck.

Blair, J., D. Mitchell, and K. Blair. 2005. *The Psychopath: Emotion and the Brain*. Malden, Mass.: Blackwell.

Cima, M., F. Tonnaer, and M. D. Hauser. 2010. Psychopaths Know Right from Wrong but Don't Care. *Social Cognitive and Affective Neuroscience* 5:59–67.

Coplan, A., and P. Goldie. 2011. Introduction. In *Empathy: Philosophical and Psychological Perspectives*, ed. A. Coplan and P. Goldie, IX–XLVII. Oxford: Oxford University Press.

Darwall, S. 1998. Empathy, Sympathy, Care. *Philosophical Studies* 89:261–282.

Decety, J., and A. N. Meltzoff. 2011. Empathy, Imitation, and the Social Brain. In *Empathy: Philosophical and Psychological Perspectives*, ed. A. Coplan and P. Goldie, 58–81. Oxford: Oxford University Press.

Hare, R. D., and C. S. Neumann. 2010. Psychopathy: Assessment and Forensic Implications. In *Responsibility and Psychopathy: Interfacing Law, Psychiatry and Philosophy*, ed. L. Malatesti and J. McMillan, 93–123. Oxford: Oxford University Press.

Hoffman, M. L. 2000. *Empathy and Moral Development: Implications for Caring and Justice*. Cambridge: Cambridge University Press.

Hoffman, M. L. 2011. Empathy, Justice, and the Law. In *Empathy: Philosophical and Psychological Perspectives*, ed. A. Coplan and P. Goldie, 230–254. Oxford: Oxford University Press.

Morse, S. 2008. Psychopathy and Criminal Responsibility. *Neuroethics* 1:205–212.

Reznek, L. 1997. *Evil or Ill? Justifying the Insanity Defence*. London: Routledge.

Ryle, G. 1940. Conscience and Moral Convictions. *Analysis* 7:31–39.

Ryle, G. 1958. On Forgetting the Difference between Right and Wrong. In *Essays in Moral Philosophy*, ed. A. I. Melden, 147–159. Seattle: University of Washington Press.

Ryle, G. 1972. Can Virtues Be Taught? In *Education and the Development of Reason*, ed. R. F. Dearden, P. H. Hirst, and R. S. Peters, 434–447. London: Routledge.

Schmidtz, D. 1993. Reasons for Altruism. *Social Philosophy & Policy* 10 (1):52–68.

Shamay-Tsoory, S., J. Aharon-Peretz, and D. Perry. 2009. Two Systems for Empathy: A Double Dissociation between Emotional and Cognitive Empathy in Inferior Frontal Gyrus versus Ventromedial Prefrontal Lesions. *Brain* 132:617–627.

Slote, M. 2010. *Moral Sentimentalism*. Oxford: Oxford University Press.

Smith, A. 2006. Cognitive Empathy and Emotional Empathy in Human Behavior and Evolution. *Psychological Record* 56:3–21.

Strawson, P. F. 1962. Freedom and Resentment. *Proceedings of the British Academy* 48:1–25.

Tugendhat, E. 1993. *Vorlesungen über Ethik* [Lectures on ethics]. Frankfurt am Main: Suhrkamp.

Wallace, J. D. 1986. *Virtues and Vices*. Ithaca, N.Y.: Cornell University Press.

III Social Aspects: Blame, Transgression, and Dangerousness

11
Psychopathy, Responsibility, and the Moral/Conventional Distinction

David W. Shoemaker

In many current discussions of the moral and criminal responsibility of psychopaths, the moral/conventional distinction bears a great deal of weight, albeit for strikingly different conclusions. For some theorists, psychopaths' failure to distinguish between moral and conventional transgressions suggests that they are not capable of the sort of moral understanding necessary for either moral or criminal responsibility. Because we cannot justifiably blame them, says Neil Levy, we also cannot expose "them to those aspects of the criminal justice system which are expressive of blame."[1] For others, psychopaths' responses to the moral/conventional distinction ground just the opposite conclusion: while their viewing all transgressions on an evaluative par exhibits *some* impairment in practical reason—indeed, it exhibits a moral disorder—it also exhibits an ability to recognize and respond to at least one category of reasons against acting in certain ways (those derived from conventional norms), and this ability is sufficient to ground both their criminal and moral responsibility. In Heidi Maibom's words, psychopaths are "more bad than mad"[2] and excusing the morally bad is not warranted by the facts about psychopaths as we know them and would "contravene the entire point of our legal system."[3]

I will attempt to lay the groundwork for defending a "hybrid" view: psychopaths may be criminally responsible but not, in an important way, morally responsible.[4] I will begin by advocating skepticism about the strategy of putting weight on "the" moral/conventional distinction in reaching conclusions in moral philosophy, because, as I hope to show, this distinction is far too fractured to do the kind of philosophical work the above theorists seem to want. I then intend to focus on just one aspect of the distinction to reveal a heretofore underappreciated feature of psychopathic psychology that may ground differing treatments of their criminal and moral responsibility.

1. The Moral/Conventional Distinction

In 1995, James Blair published two landmark articles investigating the psychopath's response to the moral/conventional distinction.[5] In doing so, he applied a test originally developed and deployed by Larry Nucci and Elliot Turiel in 1978.[6] The original idea was to see if preschool children could track what was taken to be a crucial distinction between what Nucci and Turiel called "social conventional" and "moral" events. Social conventions "are behavioral uniformities which coordinate interactions of individuals within social systems," and "in themselves are arbitrary in that they do not have an intrinsically prescriptive basis."[7] By contrast, "within the moral domain, actions are not arbitrary, and the existence of a social regulation is not necessary for an individual to regard an event as a (moral) transgression."[8] Because the original study was on children, the task's 263 scenarios involved regulations with which children would be familiar, so examples of conventional transgressions included playing or working at the wrong time or in the wrong area of a classroom, failing to engage in an assigned group activity, or violating various other classroom rules (e.g., standing, rather than sitting, while eating a snack). Moral transgressions included hitting another child, stealing another child's belongings, or refusing to share.[9]

The task was eventually developed to elicit four sorts of judgments in response to a scenario describing a child's transgression. First, was what the child did *permissible*? (Was it right or wrong for X to do Y?) Second, how *serious* was the transgression (On a scale of one to ten, how right [or wrong, depending on the first answer] was it for X to do Y?) Third, what was the *justification* for the answer to the permissibility question (Why was it right [or wrong] for X to do Y?) Fourth, if what X did was wrong, how *modifiable* were those first judgments upon the removal of authority from the equation? ("Would it be OK for X to Y if the teacher says X can?"[10])

Regarding the first two judgments, the children took moral transgressions to be more serious than conventional transgressions roughly just as adults did, and while both sorts of transgression were generally judged impermissible, conventional transgressions were "more likely to be judged *permissible* than moral transgressions."[11] Regarding justifications, children (and adults) typically appealed to what are called "normative" reasons—"those are the rules" or "it is just not acceptable"—to justify the impermissibility of conventional transgressions, whereas they would most often refer to the welfare of others to ground their reasoning about the impermissibility of moral transgressions.[12] Regarding modifiability, conventional transgressions were judged to be more authority-dependent than moral transgressions, that is, if the teacher said it was okay for the child to perform the act, conventional "transgressions" were thought then to be permissible, whereas moral trans-gressions were not.[13] This moral/conventional distinction has been found worldwide in children from as early as thirty-nine months.[14]

Blair's insightful advance was to study how psychopaths did on the task. He originally studied ten incarcerated psychopaths and ten incarcerated controls (nonpsychopaths), giving them the same task with the same sto-ries from the early studies on children.[15] The breakdown of the main results looked as follows:

There were two important findings (the second of which was rather surprising). First, unlike both nonpsychopathic children and adults, psy-chopaths typically did not make the moral/conventional distinction with respect to the modifiability judgments, and their justifiability judgments for both types of transgression made reference far more often to "the rules" than to others' welfare.[20] Second, while psychopaths evaluated moral and conventional transgressions under the authority modification as more or less on a par, they "treated conventional transgressions like moral trans-gressions"[21] and so viewed them both as authority-*independent*.[22] This result was taken merely to have been a function of the inmates' desire to prove they had reformed and learned the rules. These general findings were repli-cated in another study of incarcerated psychopaths (with more subjects),[23] and it was also replicated in certain respects in children with psychopathic tendencies: when authority was removed from an act's prohibition, while subjects did tend to note a distinction between the moral and conventional transgressions, it was far less marked than it was for controls.[24]

2. Alleged Payoffs for Responsibility

Several theorists have taken these findings to have great import for moral philosophy. While most have deployed them in investigations into the debate between internalists and externalists about moral judgment,[25] some have been tempted to explore what they mean for questions of moral responsibility, with widely varying results. For example, Levy takes psycho-paths' failure to draw the moral/conventional distinction to be evidence for a crucial failure of moral understanding. While the results of the task reveal that psychopaths know their actions "are widely perceived to be wrong..., they are unable to grasp the distinctive nature and significance of their wrongness."[26] In a similar vein, Cordelia Fine and Jeanette Kennett suggest that, "while psychopathic offenders certainly appear to know what acts are prohibited by society or the law (and therefore know that their transgres-sions are legally wrong), they do not appear to have the capacity to judge an act to be *morally* wrong."[27] In both cases, then, what psychopaths lack

Table 11.1

	(Im)Permissibility[16]		Seriousness[17]		Modifiability (Im)permissibility[18]	
	Moral	*Conventional*	*Moral*	*Conventional*	*Moral*	*Conventional*
Psychopaths	.98	.93	8.28	6.42	.95	.80
Nonpsychopaths	1.00	.75	8.04	4.72	1.00	.38

Justifiability[19]

	Others' Welfare		*Normative*		*Disorder*		*Lack of Change*		*Rudeness*		*Other*	
	M	*C*	*M*	*C*	*M*	*C*	*M*	*C*	*M*	*C*	*M*	*C*
Psychopaths	17.5	0.0	52.5	42.5	0.05	22.5	12.5	7.5	0.0	17.5	12.5	10.0
Nonpsychopaths	52.5	0.0	35.0	25.0	2.5	32.5	2.5	12.5	2.5	17.5	5.0	12.5

is the capacity for moral understanding. Fine and Kennett think that this—the failure to meet the epistemic condition—in and of itself is the source of psychopaths' lack of moral responsibility; Levy thinks that their lack of moral understanding excuses them from moral responsibility by preventing them from meeting the *control* condition.[28] But at any rate, insofar as moral responsibility is itself thought by these authors to be an essential condition for criminal responsibility, psychopaths are also not criminally responsible.

Maibom argues in the opposite direction. She notes the standard legal distinction between actions that are *malum in se* (bad in themselves) and those that are *malum prohibitum* (bad because prohibited by law) and then she simply asserts that psychopaths "clearly have an understanding of *malum prohibitum*."[29] What she takes to be the crucial question, then, is whether or not this sort of understanding is sufficient for *mens rea*, being regarded for purposes of criminal responsibility as having a "guilty mind."[30] It has been claimed that a significant roadblock to its sufficiency is that psychopaths lack empathy, which is itself taken by some to be necessary for moral understanding, for example, the understanding of why it is wrong to harm others, a welfare-based justification psychopaths typically fail to deploy in the moral/conventional task. Maibom's reply is twofold. First, she shows that we actually do not have very clear evidence at all that psychopaths (or at least all types of psychopaths) lack empathy. But even if they do, she argues secondly, this does not yet show that they lack moral understanding thereby. Indeed, one might come to moral understanding in a variety of ways, justifying not harming others via appeal to, for example, God's law, Kantian duties, or declarations of rights, but none of these clearly moral justifications require empathy.[31] If, then, the empirical evidence yields the conclusion that psychopaths are merely *impaired* in their abilities for practical reasoning and empathy, not lacking in them, and at any rate their performance on the moral/conventional task does not reveal any incapacity for coming to moral understanding via alternative—that is, nonempathic—routes, then such impairments are insufficient to undermine the possibility of their criminal responsibility, and, for similar reasons, she "hints," such impairments would be insufficient to undermine the possibility of their moral responsibility as well.[32]

3. Doubts about the Moral/Conventional Distinction

The assumptions behind the moral/conventional task have come under serious attack in recent literature. These are, quite generally, the theses that (1) transgressions involving harm, rights-violation, or injustice yield judgments—pan-culturally, and emerging as early as thirty-nine months in the nonpsychopath—that they are both authority-independent and more serious than conventional rules; and (2) transgressions that do not involve harm, rights-violation, or injustice yield judgments—pan-culturally, and emerging as early as thirty-nine months in the nonpsychopath—that they are both authority-dependent and less serious than moral rules.[33] Both theses are questionable, however.

Thesis (2) seems to be undermined by several studies. For instance, children in Arab villages in Israel view many so-called conventional transgressions as serious and authority-independent.[34] And the same seems to be true of many in lower socioeconomic groups: Jonathan Haidt, Silvia Koller, and Maria Dias found that actions that were not harmful, unjust, or rights-violating, like cleaning the toilet with a flag or having sex with a chicken, were nevertheless judged by members of such groups in the United States and Brazil as being on a par with moral transgressions, viewed as being quite serious and authority-independent.[35] Even advocates of the task have found reason to wonder about it. Nucci and Turiel found that U.S. Orthodox Jewish children judged several religious rules that nevertheless did not involve harm, etc., to be authority-independent.[36] Shaun Nichols also found that merely disgust-inducing scenarios were judged by Americans (children and college students) to be serious and authority-independent (at least by those with higher levels of "disgust sensitivity").[37]

Regarding thesis (1), Daniel Kelly et al. devised a series of surveys designed to test (a) whether or not so-called moral transgressions (involving harm/ injustice/rights-violation) would be viewed as noncontextually wrong or as wrong only specific to contemporary culture, and (b) whether or not there were some so-called moral transgressions that were viewed as authority-dependent. In both cases, they found reason to doubt the general thesis. Regarding (a), many subjects found whippings and slavery to be permissible long ago, but not today (or in the recent past). Regarding (b), many subjects judged that the permissibility of a teacher spanking her students depended on whether or not spanking was prohibited by rule or authority (i.e., her principal). Furthermore, and more disturbingly perhaps, many subjects judged that physical abuse of military trainees was also authority-dependent, permissible when there were no Pentagon orders prohibiting it.[38] Consequently, "a substantial number of subjects [do] not judge harm transgressions to be authority independent."[39]

There are more general problems. For one thing, it is not obvious that children do have clearly demarcated conceptual domains at work after all. For instance, Elizabeth Fitton and Ann Dowker found that when the so-called conventional transgressions matched the so-called moral transgressions in perceived seriousness ("jumping the queue" and "boys wearing girl's clothes to school" for conventional transgressions, "lying to someone" and "not sharing sweets" for moral transgressions), eight- to ten-year-old children failed to differentiate the domains "in terms of rule contingency, perceived obligations and the justifications used."[40] Indeed, these children tended to judge that the conventional behaviors were *more* obligatory than the moral ones.

Finally, a foundational assumption of the task—that there is indeed a distinction between moral and conventional transgressions based partly on the distinction between the authority-independent and the authority-dependent—may simply beg the question against some reflective, theoretically grounded participants. Were one a committed divine command theorist or cultural relativist, say, according to which moral rules depended on, respectively, God's commands or cultural mores, removing the relevant authority in each case would render one's transgression of the rules nonmoral, given the assumptions of the task. But this would implausibly imply that what one took to be moral judgments were really just conventional. And the same could well hold true for a reflective contractualist, one who took the right-making feature of moral rules to depend ultimately on the authority of all her reasonable fellows.[41] (I will say more on a point in this neighborhood below.)

At any rate, all of these problems might well seem to add to what Kelly et al. call a "growing body of evidence justifying substantial skepticism about *all* the major conclusions that have been drawn from studies using the moral/conventional task."[42] If this is right, then it would seem that moral philosophers have no business depending on results from the task at all.

4. Clarifying the Distinction

This conclusion strikes me as far too quick, however, for weathering this torrent of criticism is the fact that there is *some* sort of distinction we make that psychopaths do indeed fail to track. Whether or not it is labeled 'moral/conventional' or is universally recognized or is tracked by all children from thirty-nine months is beside the point. A distinct possibility for moral philosophy, then, is that the psychopath's failure to track a distinction like this (whatever it consists in, precisely) could still reveal to us something about both his and our capacities and places in the moral community.

Getting clear on what this revelation is, though, is the sticky wicket. We need to start with the nature of the distinction itself. What becomes apparent upon closer inspection is that "the" moral/conventional distinction is actually a set of only occasionally overlapping distinctions. First, there is the "permissible–impermissible" distinction, or as it is put in the task, "the OK–not OK" distinction.[43] Second, there is the "more serious–less serious" distinction. Let us start with the latter and consider how it is supposed to map onto the "moral" and the "conventional." True enough, when presented with transgressions like drinking soup out of a bowl (a "conventional" transgression) versus killing someone (a "moral" transgression) the consensus (including that of psychopaths) is that killing someone is certainly the more serious infraction. Nevertheless, as has been shown already, jumping the queue ("conventional") versus failing to share ("moral") yields judgments of roughly *equal* seriousness (among British children, anyway).[44]

Now consider the "relation" between the first two distinctions. They are simply orthogonal to one another, for permissibility and impermissibility apply to both serious and nonserious actions: helping someone in distress is serious and permissible, while killing someone is serious and impermissible; failing to share is less serious but impermissible, while donating to charity is less serious but permissible.

Next, consider the justification distinctions, of which there are many. When transgressions occur, the wrongness may be attributed to considerations of (a) welfare (It will hurt him.); (b) rules (It is against the rules/ unacceptable to do that.); (c) rudeness (It is bad manners.); (d) disruption (It is distracting to the class.); (e) rights (It is not *his*.); (f) justice (It is not fair.); or (g) other.[45] But it again should be obvious that these sorts of distinctions do not necessarily map onto the seriousness or permissibility distinctions in the assumed way. To take just one example, welfare-based justifications may well attach to relatively nonserious (and what were typically taken to be conventional) transgressions: One should not slam a door in someone's face *because it might hurt him*. Furthermore—and this is merely speculative, albeit plausible—it is quite possible that many subjects view transgression-justifications as being "overdetermined," as having multiple sources. Thus, some action may be both distracting *and* hurtful, both a violation of the rules *and* unfair. Where one justification seems more serious than another, then, that justification may be exclusively expressed, but that surely does not render it an exclusive justifier. Indeed, this point could be relevant to Maibom's argument that psychopaths' failure at making the moral/conventional distinction does not yet demonstrate their lack of moral understanding, for there could be multiple possible justifiers for wrongness, and psychopaths may simply have nonstandard justifiers, which, when expressed, do not tell us anything about whether they do not have other justifiers that remain unexpressed.

Another aspect of "the" moral/conventional distinction is the authority dependence–authority independence distinction. But once again, there seems to be no necessary overlap between this distinction and the previous ones. For example, Kelly et al.'s research seems to reveal that harming activities may be considered authority-dependent. Further, some religious conventions, as well as some merely disgust-inducing activities, are viewed as authority-independent, despite no obvious connection to harm, justice, or rights. It would also seem distinctly possible for there to be nonserious authority-independent transgressions (e.g., white lies) as well as serious authority-dependent transgressions (e.g., jumping the queue). And it could be that removal of authority does not alter judgments of permissibility but does alter judgments of *seriousness*: perhaps hitting someone is, while still viewed as impermissible, also viewed as less seriously wrong if there is no rule against it.

Finally, there is the general distinction that was taken to ground the original categorization of moral and conventional transgressions: a distinction between actions that are "shared behaviors (uniformities, rules) whose meanings are defined by the constituted system in which they are embedded" and those that fall under the rubric of "how persons ought to relate to one another."[46] But not only does this distinction not necessarily overlap with the previous ones (for by-now familiar reasons), it is also not an exhaustive dichotomy, for there are surely moral assessments we may make that fall into neither category, including duties to self and aretaic judgments.[47]

So where does this leave us? To make reference to "the" moral/conventional distinction is to conjure up a phantom: there is no such general distinction. Rather, there are simply several more specific subdistinctions in the neighborhood, some of which sometimes overlap to some extent with some others. "The" distinction should thus bear no weight for moral philosophers, it would seem.

That is not to say, however, that none of the more specific subdistinctions should not. The seriousness people take various transgressions to have, the justifications to which people appeal in their judgments that some conduct is not OK, the degrees of obligation people may attach to various activities—all of these are surely relevant to an accurate description of our moral psychology and moral practices. And here the fact that these distinctions are made orthogonally to one another may also reveal something to us about both our psychology and our categorization of morally relevant concepts. What I wish to suggest in the remainder of this essay, however, is how it might still be possible to generate something more robust by focusing on just one specific subdistinction in particular.

5. Authority

The subdistinction I am most interested in exploring is the so-called authority dependence–authority independence distinction. This is the one most relevant, after all, to the study of psychopaths and children with psychopathic tendencies, for it is the one to which they most clearly seem to provide different answers than nonpsychopaths. There are two results of interest here: first, psychopaths tended to view all the transgressions in these studies as roughly on an evaluative par, regardless of whether or not an authority said it was OK, and second, they viewed them to be on a par in terms of remaining impermissible (not OK), regardless of the authority's ruling. Now this second point is the one discounted by Blair (and others), under the assumption that the incarcerated psychopaths responding this way were "faking good." I am not so sure this is the right explanation, however.

Consider why someone might fail to distinguish between the permissibility of one child hitting another, say, and the permissibility of a child's turning her back on the teacher, even after authority was removed in each case. One answer is that this person just does not trust the so-called voice of authority, believing that what the authority *says* about the relaxation of a rule does not necessarily indicate whether or not it remains in place. This could be the case, for instance, for agents who have been, or are wary of being, tricked. Imagine being in a relationship with a passive aggressive person who says, "No really, it is okay for you to spend the evening out with friends this evening; we can skip our usual movie night." Being "better safe than sorry" may counsel sticking with the judgment that going out is in fact *not* OK, regardless of the announcement that the rules have been relaxed. Similarly, psychopaths could be wary that what some authority says about the rules means nothing about whether the rule remains in force; indeed, it would be unsurprising if this were a sort of inductive conclusion drawn from past interactions with capricious prison authorities, in combination with a recognition of the psychopath's own capriciousness with others: he himself is out to get everyone, so why not assume everyone else is out to get him as well?[48]

Here is another way in which authority might be thought irrelevant to waiving impermissibility for "conventional" transgressions: authority (it could be imagined) has nothing to do with the *establishment* or the *grounding* of these norms in the first place, so why should it be relevant to their removal? Rules, one might think, simply exist, just in virtue of their being rules, and while authorities may voice them, they can neither create nor destroy them, because rules are not the kinds of things that *can* be created or destroyed. (I will say more on this below.)

Finally, there is a crucial ambiguity in the modifiability prompt that could explain the psychopath's thought that both hitting and turning one's back remain on an impermissibility par despite a teacher's licensing them. The prompt, again, is this: "Would it be OK for X to Y if the teacher says X can?"[49] One understanding of the question could be this: Do *you* think it is in fact OK for X to Y if the teacher says X can? The other understanding could be this: Would it *generally be thought* to be OK for X to Y if the teacher says X can? These are very distinct questions, however: the first asks for the subject's own moral judgments, whereas the second asks merely for the subject's judgment about others' (or perhaps society's) moral judgments. If the psychopath were to adopt the first sort of interpretation, he might then—due to his holding one or the other views of the authority–permissibility relation just discussed—respond that so-called conventional transgressions are indeed not OK (e.g., he will stick with his "better safe than sorry" thought). If he were to adopt the second sort of interpretation, though, it is not at all clear that we could draw *any* conclusions about his moral capacities, for he would simply be mistaken about nonmoral facts—in this case, mistaken about what others generally think of these sorts of transgressions. This might be true in virtue of his projecting his own judgments about the status of the transgressions onto the general populace, or it might be true in virtue of his judging there really to be a difference between the "moral" and the "conventional" but also believing all others are dumber than he is and they thus fail to see the distinction! Under either interpretation, though, we would have a plausible explanation for why psychopaths claim that "conventional" transgressions absent authority remain impermissible alongside "moral" transgressions, without taking psychopaths who make these judgments to be "faking good" at all.

Turn, then, from the question of why the psychopath thinks both sorts of transgressions remain impermissible absent authority to the question of why they are both thought to be *on an evaluative par generally*. Obviously, the assumption behind this aspect of the moral/conventional task is that if the teacher says it is OK, then turning your back on her *really is* OK, whereas hitting someone is never OK, even if the teacher says it is. The rest of us can make this distinction without batting an eye. What exactly is it, though, that *we* are recognizing that the psychopath is not? Given the make-up of the task, researchers likely think the following: the *justifications* to which we appeal in each case are different. For us, the thought may go, it is wrong for one child to hit another for reasons having to do with the victim's welfare, whereas it is typically wrong for a child to turn her back on the teacher because it is rude, or simply because there is a rule against it. In the latter case, then, the teacher's announcement that it is OK purportedly eliminates this justification: because she says it is OK, there is no longer a rule against it, and perhaps this alone renders it not rude as well. As a consequence, goes this line of thinking, because our justifications for each action are different, we view their transgressions in the modifiability variations as evaluatively distinct. But because psychopaths are "significantly less likely to justify items by references to the *victim's welfare*,"[50] their justifications for transgressions will not be that different from those on the so-called conventional side of the map, and so they will be more likely to rank all transgressions on an evaluative par despite the teacher's license to transgress.

I do not think this is the right story, though, and instead I want to advance what I think is an important alternative explanation. We have already seen how some "conventional" transgressions could nevertheless be thought to involve victims (such that welfare justifications become relevant). In fact, it seems to me quite plausible to think that there is a victim in *all* of the cases that were presented to the psychopaths. These were (1) the back-turning case, (2) children talking in class, (3) a child leaving the class without permission, and (4) a boy wearing a skirt.[51] Insofar as all of these could be disruptive to learning or to classroom decorum, they could all plausibly be construed as instances of rudeness *to the teacher*.

Let us focus, then, on the back-turning case, where it is especially easy to think of the teacher as the victim. The fact that she could be viewed as both the classroom authority *and* the victim of the rude behavior yields the distinct possibility that, in the modifiability prompt, normal individuals judge the back-turning to be permissible because the teacher—in an exercise of her authority *as the potential victim*—has granted permission to the behavior. But then this point suggests that to truly investigate the authority distinction, we need to explore what would happen if the same sort of authority were exercised in the hitting case: what if the potential victim there were to sincerely say that it was OK for the other child to hit him (or to pull his hair, or to smash his piano, etc.)? In other words, what have been overlooked in the task are additional sources of authority that may well be essential to our making the modifiability distinction. And once we recognize these additional sources, it is no longer clear that even non-psychopaths make the modifiability distinction in terms of authority-independence, for they may actually view the so-called moral transgressions as authority-*dependent* as well.

Here we can only consult our intuitions (given that the relevant questions have not been part of any official empirical inquiry yet). So would it be OK (i.e., not impermissible) to hit someone who said it was OK to do so? What about pulling someone's hair if she agreed? Smashing her piano? Taking her property? In every case, my intuition—one I can only assume is widely shared—is that the behavior at that point, while certainly not obligatory, would also not be wrong (assuming the permission was sincere, informed, and rational, which I take to be assumptions as well of the authority-exemptions provided in the standard moral/conventional task[52]). The reason is that performing the action post-permission would no longer warrant a *complaint* on the part of the victim. "You said I could!" is all the justification necessary to block such a reply and to undermine any associated resentment. What I am suggesting, then, is that we may not view so-called moral transgressions as authority-independent after all. Instead, we may see an important kind of authority in the potential victim, such that *her* voice may indeed (at least partially) determine what counts as a moral transgression in the first place.[53]

What, then, grounds our making the distinction we obviously do in the modifiability cases if we are not necessarily making a distinction between authority-dependence or authority-independence? I think that what we are making instead is a distinction between transgressions over which a certain subset of practical reasons—authority-based reasons—governs. Very briefly, authority-based reasons (what Stephen Darwall calls "second-personal reasons") are claims we make on one another, implicitly or explicitly, and they are agent-relative considerations (derived from our relations to one another) that are valid only on the presupposition of "authority and accountability relations between persons and, therefore, on the possibility of the reason's being addressed person-to-person."[54] Commitment to such address commits one to a certain sort of accountability relation to all those who can grasp and respond to such demands, so that a violation of (only) that sort of demand renders the expression of resentment or other reactive emotions appropriate.[55]

In the conventional scenarios, then, the authority of the ostensible victim has been explicitly voiced to express a second-personal reason for why the previously impermissible behavior (turning your back on her) was now OK, namely, the reason *that she said it was OK.*[56] In the "moral" scenarios, however, the authority of the ostensible victim has been implicitly voiced to express a second-personal reason for why the previously impermissible behavior (hitting her) remained impermissible, namely, *that she has not said it was OK* (or that she says it is *not* OK).[57] In these latter cases, then, we (nonpsychopaths) view ostensible victims as implicitly addressing second-personal reasons against certain sorts of treatment to those whose actions may affect them. These reasons may be eliminated, but only at the authority—via (implicit or explicit) authorization—*of the reason-giver*. This is precisely why the *teacher's* saying it is OK for one child to hit another is irrelevant for us to change our perception of its wrongness, for the teacher's authority is not viewed as relevant to its wrongness in the first place. But the fact that the wrongness of the action is not *teacher's*-authority-dependent does not mean it is not nevertheless *authority*-dependent, namely, dependent on the authority of the targeted victim.

On my alternative explanation of the relevant data, then, it could be precisely this distinction between authority-based reasons for and against that the psychopath cannot make, simply because the psychopath is insensitive to the category of authority-based reasons in the first place.[58] The fact that someone may say that an action is OK or not OK with her—insofar as she has the authority to do so—simply does not seem to register with the psychopath. Instead, he remains focused exclusively on what he perceives the *rules* to be, and any expression of authority ostensibly lifting them makes no dent in his perception that they are still in place. But this is just to fail to recognize or respond to the *reasons* for the rules. If, as I have suggested, these are claim-based (second-personal) reasons that are grounded in the authority of potential victims, then psychopaths fail to recognize or respond to such reasons.

To see why, we need to look at his incapacities, which are rather well known. Psychopaths have both emotional incapacities and empathetic incapacities.[59] Start with the former. They have been shown not only to have serious deficits in fear (which is thought to contribute heavily to moral development) and guilt but also to have serious deficits in the more mature emotions involved in love, remorse, and shame. Their emotional deficiencies undermine any real ability to care about other people. To care about someone is to be emotionally vulnerable to her up-and-down fortunes.[60] But without the necessary emotional resources, there can be no such vulnerability.

Their caring deficiencies are directly related to their empathic deficiencies. In discussing empathy, however, it is important to distinguish between two different forms. On the one hand, there is "detached empathy," which simply involves understanding what some other person is thinking or feeling, that is, forming a representation of the mental states of others.[61] Think of this as the empathy the psychologist has for her patients: in order to help them best, she must at least understand what they are going through psychologically (e.g., what their various emotional reactions to the events of their lives consist in). But this is different from "identifying empathy," which involves *feeling* what the other person is feeling in at least a roughly similar way to how that person feels it. In the most vivid circumstances, when I empathize with you in this latter sense, it is almost as if what has happened to you has happened to me as well. If you are exhilarated at some victory, so am I; if you are grieving a loss, so am I. A psychologist who engages in this more robust form of empathy with her clients would likely burn brightly but burn out quickly.

Psychopaths evidently have the capacity for detached empathy: they are able to anticipate and delight in what their dastardly deeds will be like for their victims. They can describe the various emotions being experienced by others and manipulate them with great success.[62] What they lack, however, is the capacity for identifying empathy. This is simply because to empathize with someone in this sense requires that one be able to *share the cares* of the other person, to be emotionally vulnerable in the same way as the other person is to her up-and-down fortunes. To the extent that psychopaths lack this capacity, then, they cannot empathize with others in this crucial way.

The psychopath's emotional and empathic incapacities seem to be perfectly sufficient to explain his insensitivity to second-personal reasons. If I lack the ability to care about others and so lack the ability to projectively feel what they are going through, then it will be no surprise when I fail to be able to sense or appreciate their demands about how they are to be treated, or to appreciate those demands as *reasons* even when they are explicitly expressed. It would be for the rest of us as if we had encountered a robot out of whose speaker box came the words, 'Don't call me names'. The words themselves would likely fail to establish any authoritative reasons for us, at least in part because of our inability to "feel" what it is like to be a robot or to care about the robot for its own sake. What "that thing" demands of me will more likely be taken as something of a joke.

So too it is, I suggest, for psychopaths and us: they fail to be sensitive to the subset of practical reasons we point to or express via our claims on one another—either implicitly or explicitly—so that the words coming out of our speaker boxes are irrelevant to what they take themselves (and perhaps others) actually to have reason to do. They likely fail the modifiability aspect of the moral/conventional task not because they fail to see that only some norms are grounded in authority-independent reasons but, rather, because they fail to see authority-*dependent* reasons as grounding norms at all.

Nevertheless, psychopaths seem to maintain that there are norms against *both* "moral" and "conventional" transgressions. If these are not thought to be grounded in authority, though, what would they be grounded in? Psychopaths' justifications for their judgments of wrongness in so-called moral transgressions were significantly less victim-based than they were *rule-based*, for example, "It is wrong," or "It is not socially acceptable."[63] This suggests that psychopaths see the various rules themselves as perhaps ungrounded (or self-grounded), seeing them instead as simply the Rules of Society.[64] If psychopaths indeed view them in this way (not being sensitive to the reasons we take to ground them), then it is obvious why these Rules of Society would be thought to remain in place regardless of anyone's (implicit or explicit) dictates about them: they are The Rules, after all, and they answer to no one.

6. Criminal and Moral Responsibility

This last point finally puts us in a position to address the psychopath's criminal and moral responsibility. What I have already suggested is that the psychopath's failure to draw the authority distinction implies an incapacity with respect to a certain class of reasons, namely, authority-based, second-personal reasons. This insensitivity, I want to suggest now, is nevertheless compatible with criminal responsibility, while being incompatible with a significant realm of moral responsibility. This is of course a very large and provocative thesis, and I cannot hope to defend it adequately here. Rather, I will simply wave my hands vigorously for a bit, toss out some stipulations, and hope to begin to make a not entirely implausible presumptive case for this position.

To be criminally responsible is to meet the conditions warranting conviction in a criminal court. And what are these conditions? Victor Tadros, in a very compelling account, argues that there are three: (a) one must have status-responsibility, (b) one must be attributability-responsible for the specific criminal action, and (c) one must be culpable for that action. Having status-responsibility means meeting the minimal conditions for responsible agency generally, and this requires the capacity to form true evaluative beliefs about the world.[65] An agent is attributability-responsible for some action just in case it reflects on the agent *qua* agent, where this means that the desire motivating the agent is appropriately connected to the agent's system of values (met minimally if the agent has simply *failed to attempt to reject* the desire or her values).[66] Attributability-responsibility establishes merely that the agent is now *open* to assessment for her action, but it does not imply anything about what that assessment is to be. In order to be criminally responsible, then, one must in addition be culpable for the action, where this involves being the appropriate target of moral criticism by the state. To be such an appropriate target, one must have displayed a moral vice in one's conduct (one must have expressed some bad aspect of one's character).[67] What this suggests is that a criminal conviction communicates a moral judgment to the defendant: he is a 'murderer', say, or a 'rapist', where these predicates express a kind of public moral criticism.

Our question, then, is whether or not, if the psychopath were truly incapacitated with respect to recognizing authority-based, second-personal reasons, he would also thereby be incapacitated from being criminally responsible, and on a theory like Tadros's the only arena in which this might be so is in the establishment of his status-responsibility. After all, psychopaths can surely be attributability-responsible: when they act, we have no reason whatsoever to believe that they are not motivated by desires that are appropriately connected to their values. Further, they can be culpable, displaying vices in their conduct. Indeed, when they act, they often express their bad ends to us, for example, cruelty, callousness, manipulativeness, and the like. This may be why, for instance, Robert Hare calls psychopathy an "aggravating" factor in the criminal law.[68] They are truly out to get us.

Do they have the capacity for status-responsibility, then? The answer depends on what counts as the relevant sort of evaluative beliefs. It seems to me that all that matters to be eligible for criminal responsibility is that one be able to arrive at correct deontic verdicts, that is, correct beliefs about what one should do, given one's awareness of the rules and penalties of the criminal law. It matters less or not all that one is sensitive to all of the various reasons that may ground the rules or penalties (more on this point below). Even if we suppose, therefore, that authority-based, second-personal reasons do ground the core *moral* areas of the criminal law (e.g., murder, rape, assault, theft, etc.), the psychopath's insensitivity to those reasons does not render him incapable of coming to the correct evaluative verdict that the actions picked out in these areas are ones he should not perform.[69] As long as he has sufficient cognitive development to come to an abstract understanding of what the laws are and what the penalties are for violating them,[70] it seems clear that he could arrive at the conclusion that these actions are not worth pursuing for purely prudential reasons, say. And with this capacity in place, he is eligible for criminal responsibility, where his insensitivity to a certain subset of practical reasons could actually be grounds for *both* attributability and culpability, that is, insofar as he judges that my demand that he not treat me a certain way is not reason-giving, his violation of that demand grounds a certain sort of moral criticism of him—callousness, say—that attributes the action to a flaw in his character.[71]

What, then, about the psychopath's moral responsibility? In this realm, I believe that being insensitive to authority-based reasons *is* sufficient for an exemption from a core area, namely, from the sort of accountability-demands we make of one another, the violation of which renders resentment (or other sorts of moral emotions or expressions) fitting. Considerations in favor of this view are complicated, and they deserve a much fuller treatment (which I hope to provide elsewhere), but I will just briefly lay out the main ideas here.

On one of the most popular conceptions of this core area of moral responsibility, to be accountable to others is just for one to be susceptible to various sorts of reactive attitudes to the quality of one's will.[72] If one expresses ill will to others, one is susceptible to expressions of resentment or indignation (or one's own guilt); if one expresses good will, one is susceptible to expressions of gratitude or love.[73] Such reactive attitudes, however, seem to be conceptually tied to moral "wrongings," to one party disrespecting the (presumed to be valid) demands of another. And as Darwall points out, these attitudes respond to the exercise of specific capacities, namely, those exercised by someone "who can recognize, freely accept, and act on the distinctive second-personal reasons the demand addresses."[74] Moral accountability, then, presupposes the capacity to recognize authority-based reasons. To the extent that psychopaths cannot recognize these reasons, they are not morally accountable. If they are indeed nonculpably blind to our second-personal demands, they simply cannot disrespect them.

Of course, one might well think that authority-based demands are essential to the heart of the criminal law as well. The wrongness of murder and rape and theft must surely be grounded on second-personal reasons (they are wrongings, after all). But if psychopaths cannot recognize such reasons, then how could they be criminally responsible for failing to respond to them? The answer is that it is just not a requirement of the criminal justice system that people respect the moral grounding of the criminal law. For one thing, not all moral wrongs are actually criminal wrongs and vice versa. But even in cases where immorality and criminality do overlap, this is due to the political reasons to render some behavior criminal, that is, the reasons there are to deem it a public wrong.[75] There are obvious reasons to render certain actions (those that also fall under the rubric of the immoral) criminal, the most general one being that they manifest an insufficient concern for those interests of citizens worthy of legal protection.[76] Criminal prohibitions may thus be overdetermined, having two groundings, namely, second-personal (moral) reasons, and the agent-*neutral* reasons related to those citizenry interests deemed worthy of legal protection. The latter are not authority-based, though: it is not just insofar as the state demands it of you that, ultimately, it is illegal for you to murder someone; rather, it is illegal for anyone to murder anyone, given that every citizen has an interest in not being harmed, and this interest is worthy of legal protection on a politically liberal framework, say, given the state's obligation to protect the liberty of its citizens to pursue various goods. It seems implausible, therefore, that the ability to recognize the second-personal reasons grounding distinctively moral obligation is at all essential to recognizing some other of the variety of reasons that might ground the criminal law.

These sorts of considerations thus make at least a presumptive case that psychopaths could be criminally responsible without being morally accountable. Another way of describing the view I have in mind amounts to thinking of criminal responsibility as being about the having and expressing of evaluative ends, whereas moral accountability requires the ability to be accountable *to* one another, where this latter involves sensitivity to the special sort of reasons we give to each other.[77] What thus seems to be implied by the psychopath's failure to distinguish between the authority-based judgments we have drawn from the remnants of the moral/conventional task is that he is perhaps incapable of being accountable *to us*, but this does not yet render him ineligible for the kind of moral predication that is constitutive of criminal convictions.

One may wonder, however, about the justification for holding psychopaths criminally responsible, that is, for punishing them. Thus far, I have merely suggested a possible justification for judging psychopaths criminally responsible, where this consists in the issuance of a conviction, the point at which the defendant is labeled a criminal. While this might constitute a sanction for the defendant, it also might not (some people clearly revel in the criminal label), and anyway, that does not necessarily seem to be its aim; rather, the verdict of guilt is merely a finding (a judgment). Punishing the criminal, however, is definitely a sanction, and may, on a communicative theory of punishment, involve the expression of society's resentment or indignation toward the criminal. But if it turns out that such expressions conceptually presuppose that the target has the second-personal capacity, punishment will be senseless to a psychopath who lacks this capacity, just as it would be senseless to hold a psychopath morally accountable. Perhaps my view implies, then, that we would not be warranted in punishing the psychopaths we find criminally responsible (and so perhaps I have been too hard on Fine and Kennett, who seem to focus just on this aspect of criminal responsibility).[78]

Addressing this worry adequately would require another paper, but for now I want to offer just a suggestion for how we might resist it. Consider the fact that no one seems to find it at all objectionable to penalize psychopaths for violations of merely regulatory offenses (those rendered criminal

solely by statute), for example, driving over the speed limit, public intoxi-
cation, selling tainted meat, carrying a concealed weapon, insider trading,
or unlawful disposal of toxins. The penalties here may range from fines to
incarceration. All that matters, it seems, is that the offenders are capable of
recognizing, and conforming their actions to, the requirements of the law,
regardless of the reason. Indeed, the primary reason most people probably
adhere to these regulatory laws is prudential: that it might get me a stint in
prison is sufficient reason to avoid these actions. We might wonder, then,
why it would suddenly become inappropriate to penalize those who violate laws that have moral grounds in addition to statutory grounds.[79] Why
should the inclusion of additional reasons against performing the action
undermine the justification for penalization when the action is performed?
While theorists have seemed to want a robustly moral justification for punishment, it is far less clear that we need one for penalties,[80] in which case
holding the psychopath responsible for his "moral" crimes could simply
consist in doling out some publicized penalty in response. Of course, there
may be no communicative element attached to the penalty, a communication to which the psychopath would be deaf anyway, but it is not at all clear
to me why, if this element can justifiably be absent with respect to merely
regulatory offenses, it needs to be present in criminal offenses that have an
additional moral grounding.

Just a few more remarks on this last point may be in order. Most of us
refrain from murdering and raping others solely by being sensitive and
responding to their implicit demands (i.e., our moral obligations) that we
not do so. That these actions have been rendered criminal, in addition, is
irrelevant for us. Further, what matters to us in the moral realm is that we
not treat one another with ill will, and to do so we must take one another's
legitimate demands as reason-giving. In the criminal realm, though, where
it is the protection of the legitimate interests of citizens that is paramount,
it would require far too much of citizens to demand that they take others'
interests or claims themselves as reason-giving. Indeed, this would render
the merely insensitive among us criminal, right alongside those who do the
right things for the wrong reasons. Instead, all that is necessary to protect the
interests of citizens is that the state requires us to treat others *as if* we took
their interests or demands as reason-giving. The state cannot ask that you *be*
a moral agent; it can only ask that you *act like* a moral agent. Failing to act in
this way gets you penalized (just like holding the linebacker in a certain way
in football gets you penalized). While most of us do take others' interests or
demands as reason-giving (and so we are hardly ever motivated by thoughts
of penalties), there remain those of us who do not, and for them the penalties are intended to provide prudential reasons to treat us *as if* we mattered.

There is nothing at all we have seen about the psychopath to indicate that he cannot at least treat us in this fashion, and so no reason I can see that undermines our warrant for issuing penalties on him when he fails to do so.

7. Conclusion

I have tried to make three general points in this paper. First, it is unlikely that there is such a thing as "the" moral/conventional distinction, neatly carving out two conceptual domains. Instead, "the" distinction is at most just a set of several different distinctions that may not even partially overlap. Moral philosophers are thus ill-advised to put much, if any, weight on "the" distinction in drawing conclusions about the moral judgments or agential capacities of psychopaths. Second, there does remain some sort of distinction that psychopaths cannot seem to track. While this has been thought to be a distinction between authority-dependent and authority-independent norms, I have suggested instead that the actual distinction may well be between authority-based permissions and impermissions, and, further, I have suggested that the reason psychopaths fail to track this distinction is because they fail to recognize authority-based reasons altogether, given their empathic and emotional incapacities. Third, then, I pointed the way toward how my interpretation might favor a hybrid theory of the criminal and moral responsibility of psychopaths, according to which the core of moral responsibility—accountability—requires facility with authority-based reasons, whereas criminal responsibility does not. What counts as an aggravating factor in the criminal arena, therefore, may, interestingly enough, count as an exempting factor in the moral arena.[81]

Notes

Editor's note: This chapter was reprinted with permission from *The Southern Journal of Philosophy* 49 (Spindel Supplement):99–124, 2011. © 2011 The University of Memphis.

1. Neil Levy, "The Responsibility of the Psychopath Revisited," *Philosophy, Psychiatry, and Psychology* 14 (2007): 129–38, at 136. A very similar view was expressed a few years earlier in Cordelia Fine and Jeanette Kennett, "Mental Impairment, Moral Understanding and Criminal Responsibility: Psychopathy and the Purposes of Punishment," *Law and Psychiatry* 27 (2004): 425–43. For verdicts about psychopaths similar to this one (albeit not necessarily driven by consideration of the moral/conventional distinction), see also Jeffrie Murphy, "Moral Death: A Kantian Essay on Psychopathy," *Ethics* 82 (1972): 284–98, and Christopher Ciocchetti, "The Responsibility of the Psychopathic Offender," *Philosophy, Psychiatry, and Psychology* 10 (2003): 175–83.

2. Heidi L. Maibom, "The Mad, the Bad, and the Psychopath," *Neuroethics* 1 (2008): 167–84, at 175. See also the question raised by Manuel Vargas and Shaun Nichols: "Given that we do think it is appropriate to blame and punish transgressors of conventional rules, why isn't this enough to blame and punish psychopaths?" ("Psychopaths and Moral Knowledge," *Philosophy, Psychiatry, and Psychology* 14 [2007]: 157–62, at 159).

3. Maibom, "The Mad, the Bad, and the Psychopath," 182.

4. I have found only one other similar hybrid view in the literature, but it is presented only hypothetically: *if* a defender of an expressivist view of criminal responsibility wanted to maintain the criminal responsibility of the psychopath independently of a view of moral desert, it would look like such and such. This view is discussed by Peter Arenella in "Convicting the Morally Blameless: Reassessing the Relationship between Legal and Moral Accountability," *UCLA Law Review* 39 (1992): 1511–1622, esp. 1619–22. There *might* be a hybrid view compatible with the line Ishtiyaque Haji takes in "On Psychopaths and Culpability" (*Law and Philosophy* 17 [1998]: 117–40), but that is not entirely clear; at any rate, the view he could be suggesting would be quite different from the one toward which I am inclined.

5. R. J. R. Blair, "A Cognitive Developmental Approach to Morality: Investigating the Psychopath," *Cognition* 57 (1995): 1–29; and R. J. R. Blair, L. Jones, F. Clark, and M. Smith, "Is the Psychopath 'Morally Insane'?" *Personality and Individual Differences* 19 (1995): 741–52.

6. Larry P. Nucci and Elliot Turiel, "Social Interactions and the Development of Social Concepts in Preschool Children," *Child Development* 49 (1978): 400–07. See also Larry P. Nucci and Susan Herman, "Behavioral Disordered Children's Conceptions of Moral, Conventional, and Personal Issues," *Journal of Abnormal Child Psychology* 10 (1982): 411–26; Larry P. Nucci and Maria Santiago Nucci, "Children's Social Interactions in the Context of Moral and Conventional Transgressions," *Child Development* 53 (1982): 403–12; and Larry P. Nucci and Maria Santiago Nucci, "Children's Responses to Moral and Social Conventional Transgressions in Free-Play Settings," *Child Development* 53 (1982): 1337–42.

7. Nucci and Turiel, "Social Interactions and the Development of Social Concepts in Preschool Children," 400.

8. Ibid., 401.

9. Ibid., 402.

10. Drawn from Blair, "A Cognitive Developmental Approach to Morality," 15.

11. Ibid., 6; emphasis in original. See also Judith Smetana, "Preschool Children's Conceptions of Transgressions: Effects of Varying Moral and Conventional Domain-Related Attributes," *Developmental Psychology* 21 (1985): 18–29.

12. R. J. R. Blair, "Moral Reasoning and the Child with Psychopathic Tendencies," *Personality and Individual Differences* 22 (1997): 731–39, at 734.

13. See, e.g., Blair, "A Cognitive Developmental Approach to Morality," 6.

14. See Judith G. Smetana, "Preschool Children's Conceptions of Moral and Social Rules," *Child Development* 52 (1981): 1333–36, and Marida Hollos, Philip E. Leis, and Elliot Turiel, "Social Reasoning in IJO Children and Adolescents in Nigerian Communities," *Journal of Cross Cultural Psychology* 17 (1986): 352–74.

15. Blair, "A Cognitive Developmental Approach to Morality," 13–14.

16. The mean of respondents who said the transgression in question would not be OK.

17. Mean responses, on a scale of 1 to 10 (10 being worst).

18. The mean of respondents who continued to say the transgression would not be OK even if the teacher said it was OK.

19. These represent the general categories under which subjects' justifications of their judgments of wrongness were placed. If responses appealed to the welfare of the victim, they were categorized under "Other's welfare." If they appealed to rules, they were categorized as "Normative." If they appealed to disruption, they were categorized under "Disorder." If they appealed to long-term implications of the wrongdoing, they were categorized under "Lack of change." "Rudeness" and "Other" should then be self-explanatory. See Blair, "A Cognitive Developmental Approach to Morality," 16.

20. Ibid., 18.

21. Ibid., 20.

22. Ibid., 17. In his statement of this finding, Blair writes that psychopaths judged "conventional transgressions as moral on this criterion judgment; i.e., not *authority independent*" (ibid.; emphasis in original). This is a typographical error, however, confirmed by Blair in private correspondence. What he obviously meant given the surrounding context is that they viewed these as "authority independent."

23. See Blair, "Is the Psychopath 'Morally Insane'?"

24. See Blair, "Moral Reasoning and the Child with Psychopathic Tendencies." These were children labeled as merely having psychopathic *tendencies*, but this may be only because it is clinically forbidden (prior to age 18) to label them as "psychopaths." If they are indeed psychopaths (albeit child psychopaths), the difference between their and the adult psychopaths' answers on the modifiability portion of the task could be relevant to my later diagnosis, although so too could their simply being children. Thanks to Shaun Nichols for raising this issue with me. Blair ("A Cognitive Developmental Approach to Morality," 16–17) suggests that psychopaths

seem to fail the moral/conventional distinction in all its respects, but this is not at all clear to me. The numbers do reveal that psychopaths think that conventional transgressions are more closely related to moral transgressions in terms of being impermissible than nonpsychopaths, and they think that conventional transgressions are a bit more serious than do nonpsychopaths. But while these results are interesting, I do not see that the term 'failure' applies to psychopaths' performances here (and in children with psychopathic tendencies, there were no significant differences on these distinctions). While Blair maintains the two groups "can be differentiated" (ibid., 17) on all the criterion judgments, he also says explicitly that "[s]ignificant group differences were only shown in the results of the ANOVA on the *authority jurisdiction* (modifiability) criterion judgment" (ibid., 16; emphasis in original).

25. See, e.g., Shaun Nichols, *Sentimental Rules* (Oxford: Oxford University Press, 2004). See also Jeanette Kennett and Cordelia Fine, "Internalism and the Evidence from Psychopaths and 'Acquired Sociopaths' "; Adina L. Roskies, "Internalism and the Evidence from Pathology"; Michael Smith, "The Truth about Internalism"; and Jeanette Kennett and Cordelia Fine, "Could There Be an Empirical Test for Internalism"? all in *Moral Psychology, Volume 3: The Neuroscience of Morality: Emotion, Brain Disorders, and Development,* ed. Walter Sinnott-Armstrong (Cambridge, MA: MIT Press, 2008).

26. Levy, "The Responsibility of the Psychopath Revisited," 132.

27. Fine and Kennett, "Mental Impairment, Moral Understanding and Criminal Responsibility," 432; emphasis in original.

28. See Levy, "The Responsibility of the Psychopath Revisited," 136.

29. Maibom, "The Mad, the Bad, and the Psychopath," 169.

30. Ibid.

31. Ibid., 174–75. Jeanette Kennett presents a similar sort of argument for why a lack of empathy does not undermine some autistic agents' ability to arrive at moral understanding in "Autism, Empathy, and Moral Agency," *Philosophical Quarterly* 52 (2002): 340–57. I respond to Kennett's argument in "Moral Address, Moral Responsibility, and the Boundaries of the Moral Community," *Ethics* 118 (2007): 70–108, esp. 92–101.

32. Maibom, "The Mad, the Bad, and the Psychopath," 182.

33. See Daniel Kelly, Stephen Stich, Kevin J. Haley, Serena J. Eng, and Daniel M. T. Fessler, "Harm, Affect, and the Moral/Conventional Distinction," *Mind and Language* 22 (2007): 117–31.

34. Mordecai Nisan, "Moral Norms and Social Conventions: A Cross-Cultural Comparison," *Developmental Psychology* 23 (1987): 719–25.

35. Jonathan Haidt, Silvia Helena Koller, and Maria G. Dias, "Affect, Culture, and Morality, or Is It Wrong to Eat Your Dog?" *Journal of Personality and Social Psychology* 65 (1993): 613–28.

36. Larry Nucci and Elliot Turiel, "God's Word, Religious Rules, and Their Relation to Christian and Jewish Children's Concepts of Morality," *Child Development* 64 (1993): 1475–91.

37. Shaun Nichols, "Norms with Feeling: Towards a Psychological Account of Moral Judgment," *Cognition* 84 (2002): 221–36. All of the previous four examples are also discussed in Kelly et al., "Harm, Affect, and the Moral/Conventional Distinction," 120–21.

38. Kelly et al., "Harm, Affect, and the Moral/Conventional Distinction," 122–28.

39. Ibid., 129. Paulo Sousa, both singly and with co-authors, has recently argued that Kelly et al.'s conclusions are not quite as robust as they claim, but the worries Sousa advances about their methodology carry over to a kind of general (albeit guarded) skepticism about the moral/conventional distinction as well, so his conclusions are ultimately in line with the sort of view I will be presenting here. See Paolo Sousa, "On Testing the 'Moral Law'," *Mind and Language* 24 (2009): 209–34, and Paolo Sousa, Colin Holbrook, and Jared Piazza, "The Morality of Harm," *Cognition* 113 (2009): 80–92. Thanks to Shaun Nichols for the reference.

40. Elizabeth Fitton and Ann Dowker, "Qualitative and Quantitative Dimensions of Domain Differentiation," paper presented at the MOSAIC Conference in Liverpool in 2002.

41. For the most sustained defense of a moral contractualism of this sort, see T. M. Scanlon, *What We Owe to Each Other* (Cambridge, MA: Belknap Press, 1998).

42. Kelly et al., "Harm, Affect, and the Moral/Conventional Distinction," 129; emphasis in original.

43. Indeed, I think it is obvious that the "OK–not OK" distinction is far broader than the moral rightness–wrongness distinction, given that the former may well apply in nonmoral contexts such as the aesthetic or the prudential. Surely it is quite possible that if I judge that it is 'not OK' for Karen Finley to smear excrement on her body during a performance all I mean is that it makes her performance aesthetically worse than it otherwise might have been (without at all believing that it is *immoral* for her to do so). However, what seems obvious to me is apparently quite tendentious to some, insofar as they think we should not be so proprietary on what counts as "moral," that what so counts is a matter of what sorts of events to which people have certain sorts of emotional reactions. (I have only anecdotal evidence for this claim, but I am not going to call out adherents of this view by name; they know who they are.) I think this way of viewing the matter is seriously problematic for a host of reasons, not the least of which is that it conflates what are perfectly well-

understood and valuable conceptual categories, and it would also have us begging serious questions about the nature of moral judgment in metaethics.

44. In addition to Fitton and Dowker, see Elliot Turiel, Melanie Killen, and Charles C. Helwig, "Morality: Its Structure, Functions, and Vagaries," in *The Emergence of Morality in Young Children*, ed. Jerome Kagan and Sharon Lamb (Chicago: University of Chicago Press, 1987), 155–243, esp. 174–75.

45. See Turiel, Killen, and Helwig, "Morality," 170, and Blair, "Moral Reasoning and the Child with Psychopathic Tendencies," 734.

46. Turiel, Killen, and Helwig, "Morality," 169; they cite John Searle, *Speech Acts* (London: Cambridge University Press, 1969).

47. See Vargas and Nichols, "Psychopaths and Moral Knowledge," 158.

48. This is likely why incarcerated nonpsychopaths would not make the same inductive inference, then.

49. Blair, "A Cognitive Developmental Approach to Morality," 15.

50. Ibid., 18; emphasis in original.

51. Ibid., 14.

52. These conditions would also be relevant to blocking potential counterexamples to the view I am developing, such as the German man who volunteered to be cannibalized. Many people would likely continue to believe cannibalizing him to be impermissible, despite his granting permission for it. But his derangement might well be what prevents him from having the sort of authority necessary for rendering the action permissible. Thanks to Shaun Nichols for discussion on this point.

53. For anyone familiar with it, Stephen Darwall's work in *The Second-Person Standpoint* (Cambridge, MA: Harvard University Press, 2006) looms obviously and heavily over this paragraph and over much of what I say below.

54. Ibid., 8.

55. Ibid., see ch. 4.

56. Contrast what our reactions would be in this case to one in which the *principal* said it was OK for students to turn their backs on teachers. I suspect we would be far less quick to think that such behavior would then be rendered OK, and if so, it would make perfect sense to explain this phenomenon by referencing the fact that the principal just is not the relevant authority here; that is, he has no standing to relax the *teacher's* demand not to treat her rudely.

57. We may also think of implicit voicing as subjunctive: it is what would be voiced were the potential victim asked about it.

58. See my "Moral Address, Moral Responsibility, and the Boundaries of the Moral Community," 77–85.

59. See, e.g., R. J. R. Blair, "The Amygdala and Ventromedial Prefrontal Cortex in Morality and Psychopathy," *Trends in Cognitive Science* 11 (2007): 387–92, at 387. The next three paragraphs borrow from my previous remarks on this topic in "Moral Address, Moral Responsibility, and the Boundaries of the Moral Community," 97–101.

60. See my "Caring, Identification, and Agency," *Ethics* 114 (2003): 88–118.

61. See my "Moral Address, Moral Responsibility, and the Boundaries of the Moral Community," 97.

62. In the incredibly fascinating documentary *I, Psychopath*, a seemingly self-aware (and successful) psychopath, Sam Vaknin, relentlessly bullies the filmmaker and then follows this up by a clinical analysis of what he just did and what he imagined the filmmaker was feeling at the time (which was quite accurate). *I, Psychopath*, directed by Ian Walker (Liberty Productions, 2009).

63. Blair, "A Cognitive Developmental Approach to Morality," 24.

64. Victoria McGeer suggests a picture like this may be in place for those with autism as well. See her rich and fascinating essay "Varieties of Moral Agency: Lessons from Autism (and Psychopathy)," in *Moral Psychology*, 227–57.

65. Victor Tadros, *Criminal Responsibility* (Oxford: Oxford University Press, 2005), 55–56.

66. Ibid., see ch. 1, "The Nature of Responsibility."

67. Ibid., 71.

68. R. D. Hare, "Psychopaths and Their Nature," in *Psychopathy: Antisocial, Criminal and Violent Behavior*, ed. Theodore Millon, Erik Simonsen, Morten Birket-Smith, and Roger D. Davis (New York: Guilford Press, 1998), 205.

69. Cf. Maibom, "The Mad, the Bad, and the Psychopath," 173–75.

70. An abstraction capacity distinguishing him from a child, for instance.

71. I think this is exactly what Gary Watson has in mind by what he calls "attributability responsibility," or "aretaic responsibility" in his "Two Faces of Responsibility" (*Agency and Answerability* [Oxford: Oxford University Press, 2004]). While he is talking about a face of *moral* responsibility, however, I think this is the essential (and only) face of criminal responsibility. For discussion of the psychopath's ability to judge that my interests are not reason-giving for him, see Matt Talbert, "Blame and Responsiveness to Moral Reasons: Are Psychopaths Blameworthy?" *Pacific Philosophical Quarterly* 89 (2008): 516–35.

72. The originator of the view is Peter Strawson, "Freedom and Resentment," in *Free Will*, ed. Gary Watson, 2nd ed. (Oxford: Oxford University Press, 2003), 72–93. Many other theorists, including Michael McKenna, R. Jay Wallace, and Gary Watson, are Strawsonians to some degree or other, at least in this regard.

73. I take no stand here on whether these "reactive attitudes" are responses to a judgment of responsibility or are more immediate and *constitutive* of responsibility.

74. Darwall, *The Second-Person Standpoint*, 79.

75. Suppose we are the elected representatives with the task of determining whether or not murder is to be rendered illegal. It will simply be insufficient for those of us who believe it should be illegal to appeal to the fact that murder is immoral; how could we therefore justify why we should render murder but not adultery, say, illegal? We need some additional reason for why *this particular immorality* ought to be rendered a public wrong—a crime—as well. This is the sort of reason I am calling "political."

76. A somewhat similar formulation may be found in Larry Alexander and Kimberly Kessler Ferzan (with Stephen Morse), *Crime and Culpability* (Cambridge: Cambridge University Press, 2009), 265.

77. Again, I think this distinction essentially corresponds to the distinction Watson makes between the two faces of responsibility. What I am suggesting is that the mere expression of ends (what Watson calls "aretaic" or "attributability" responsibility) is sufficient for eligibility for criminal responsibility, whereas moral accountability-responsibility requires (perhaps in addition to aretaic responsibility, although I do not take a stand on that here) a facility with second-personal reasons.

78. I am grateful to Sander Voerman for raising this issue.

79. This more or less reflects the *malum prohibitum/mala in se* distinction.

80. Except the death penalty, perhaps!

81. I am grateful to many people for their contributions to this paper. First, thanks to Eileen Baker, Alison Denham, Daniel Jacobson, Daniel Kelly, Neil Levy, Shaun Nichols, Nicholas Sars, and Elijah Weber for their helpful remarks on earlier drafts of this paper. Thanks also to audiences at the 2010 Conference on Psychopathy in Swansea, the first New Orleans Invitational Seminar in Ethics (NOISE), the 2010 Society for Philosophy and Psychology, a Tilburg philosophy colloquium, and the 2010 Spindel Conference for their insights and suggestions. In particular, thanks to Eric Cave, Stephen Darwall, Janice Dowell, Heidi Maibom, Thomas Nadelhoffer, Douglas Portmore, Jesse Prinz, Michael Slote, David Sobel, Thomas Schramme, Walter Sinnott-Armstrong, Alan Thomas, Sander Voerman, and Steven Wall for their challenges, friendly (and not-so-friendly) suggestions, and overall discussion. In addition, thanks to the students in my spring 2010 political economy senior seminar at Tulane and my summer 2010 seminar on criminal and moral responsibility at Bowling Green State University for their insights and discussion on these topics. Last but not least, thanks to Stephen Finlay for his very thoughtful comments on the final version.

12 The Significance of Psychopathic Wrongdoing[1]

Matthew Talbert

12.1 Introduction

I argue below that psychopaths are sometimes open to moral blame on account of their wrongdoing. Thus, on my view, psychopaths are sometimes appropriate targets for negative reactive attitudes like resentment that characterize moral blame.

On the approach to moral responsibility that I pursue, blame is fundamentally a response to a certain characteristic significance that other agents' actions can have for us. The argument of this chapter depends, therefore, on the claim that despite their impairments, psychopaths possess rational and agential capacities that endow their behavior with a significance that makes blaming responses appropriate. As a kind of shorthand, I will often simply say that psychopaths are capable of acting in ways that express disregard, contempt, or ill will of a sort that reasonably grounds emotional responses like resentment.[2]

My defense of this proposal begins with a brief account of the approach to moral responsibility that I favor and a discussion of how psychopaths, with their various capacities and incapacities, fit into this approach. Next, I consider recent arguments by Neil Levy and David Shoemaker that psychopaths' incapacities entail that their actions cannot convey the type of malicious ill will to which blame responds. Finally, I consider Gary Watson's recent discussion of psychopathy. Watson grants that psychopaths express morally significant malice through their behavior, but he argues that their moral impairments still render them unfit for an important range of reactions involved in holding agents morally accountable for their behavior.

12.2 Attributionism and Psychopathy

The approach to moral responsibility that I favor is sometimes called "attributionism," though critics of the view most often use this term. The following account of attributionism from Neil Levy, who is one such critic, brings out some important features of the view:

On *attributionist* accounts, an agent is responsible for an action just in case that action is appropriately *reflective* of who she most deeply is. If it is appropriately reflective of who she is, it is attributable to her, and that is sufficient for us to hold her responsible.... It simply does not matter, on this account, whether the agent knows that her action is wrong. All that matters is that the action *expresses the agent's attitudes toward others*. The agent who intentionally harms another thereby expresses her contempt of that person, whether or not she is capable of appreciating the moral reasons that condemn such actions.[3]

David Shoemaker, another critic of attributionism, offers a related assessment of T. M. Scanlon's and Angela Smith's accounts of moral responsibility.[4] According to Shoemaker, "[b]oth Smith and Scanlon believe responsibility is fundamentally about *attributability*, that is, about actions or attitudes being properly attributable to—reflective of—the agent's self."[5] Thus, "[w]hat it means for A to be *morally responsible* for Φ is just that Φ is properly attributable to A in a way that renders A open to moral appraisal for Φ," and "[w]hat it means for A to be *blameworthy* for Φ is just that (1) A is morally responsible for Φ and (2) A has violated some normative standard(s) via Φ."[6] And when is Φ attributable to an agent in such a way that it is relevant to our moral appraisal of the agent? As Shoemaker notes, what is required on the views in question is that "Φ must bear a rational connection to the agent's evaluative judgments."[7]

Shoemaker's mention of evaluative judgments relates to Levy's point about the importance (for the views under discussion) of the way wrongdoers' behavior can express objectionable, blame-grounding attitudes toward the people they wrong. Whether wrongdoers' behavior expresses such attitudes depends on whether they guide their behavior by judgments about reasons. For example, if I know that my action will injure you and I still judge that I have reason to perform the action in order to achieve some trivial aim, then my action plausibly reflects a judgment that is contemptuous of your welfare: The judgment that your welfare is less important than whether I achieve my trivial aim. This offensive judgment is a reason to regard my action as wrong and unjustifiable, rather than merely injurious, and it makes it natural (though not obligatory) for you to target me with blaming attitudes like resentment.

As the quotation from Levy also suggests, a signal feature of attributionist accounts of moral responsibility is that wrongdoers' blameworthiness, and their openness to negative reactive attitudes, does not depend on whether they are able to recognize and respond to moral considerations. This is because even wrongdoers who lack this ability—who lack, as I will say, *moral competence*—may still guide their behavior by judgments that manifest contempt or ill will for those they mistreat, at least if they possess general powers of rationality and self-government. As Scanlon notes, a generally

rational creature who fails to see the force of moral reasons—who fails, for example, to see any reason for being concerned with moral requirements at all ... can nonetheless understand that a given action will injure others and can judge that this constitutes no reason against so acting.[8]

The point here is that—just as with a morally competent wrongdoer—a morally blind (but otherwise rational) agent may willingly and (by our lights) unjustifiably do something that he or she knows will injure you. Like a morally competent agent, such an individual thereby expresses the offensive judgment that your welfare matters little in comparison with whether his or her ends are achieved. This account of an agent's behavior will make sense if the agent is aware of the consequences of his or her behavior and if the agent has the ability to judge (by his or her own lights) whether these consequences count in favor of acting or refraining from action.[9] Insensitivity to specifically moral reasons is compatible with fulfillment of these conditions.

This discussion of moral blindness brings us to psychopathy. Psychopaths are persistent wrongdoers who have a variety of negative personality characteristics such as egocentricity, aggression, callousness, lack of empathy or remorse, and impulsivity. From the standpoint of assessing moral responsibility, the interesting thing about psychopaths is that their persistent wrongdoing appears to stem from a deeply rooted difficulty apprehending and responding to moral considerations. The etiology of this difficulty is not entirely clear, but James Blair, Derek Mitchell, and Karina Blair have recently advanced a compelling "neurocognitive" account of psychopathy and its development. According to this account, partial dysfunction of the amygdala is at the heart of the disorder. The amygdala dysfunction itself likely results from genetic anomalies and gives rise, in turn,

to impairments in aversive conditioning, instrumental learning, and the processing of fearful and sad experiences. These impairments interfere with socialization such that the individual does not learn to avoid actions that cause harm to other individuals. If such an individual has a reason to offend, because their other opportunities for financial resources or respect are limited, they will be more likely to offend than healthy developing individuals.[10]

While the psychopath's moral impairments are profound, they should not be overstated. As Walter Glannon notes, psychopaths appear to have "at least a shallow understanding of right and wrong" since they correctly answer questions about whether proposed actions are conventionally regarded as "right" or "wrong."[11] On Glannon's view, this is sufficient for attributing a limited form of moral responsibility to psychopaths. However, many theorists are unimpressed by the psychopath's ability to, as R. Jay Wallace puts it, "parrot moral discourse" since this is compatible with the absence of a "participant understanding" of that discourse.[12] Evidence that psychopaths lack a participant understanding of moral discourse is found, among other places, in their limited ability (as compared to nonpsychopaths) to distinguish authority-dependent conventional norms and non-authority-dependent moral norms.[13]

What is important for my purposes is that, despite their moral impairments and as the quotation from Blair and his coauthors suggests, psychopaths are capable of evaluating reasons and guiding their behavior on this basis. Psychopaths often do wrong because they judge something to count in favor of acting that way: Their use of violence, for example, is often instrumental rather than merely reactive.[14] According to the account I pursue here, psychopaths may thus be open to moral blame because it is possible for their wrongdoing to reflect the judgment that the consequences of their behavior do not give them reason to refrain from that behavior. Indeed, as Gary Watson notes, psychopaths are capable of seeing the prospect of another's harm and suffering as a *reason* to act: "They frequently enjoy forcing others into painful submission"; "they often intentionally or willingly oppose what matters most to us."[15]

However, there is evidence that the psychopath's rational impairments extend beyond their impaired moral understanding. This raises the possibility that psychopaths are too rationally impaired for the attributionist approach to moral responsibility to be applied to them. For one thing, psychopaths have deficits in fear and empathy. Not only do they not have the same fear responses as nonpsychopaths, they are also deficient with respect to recognizing fear or sadness in others.[16] Cordelia Fine and Jeanette Kennett appeal to this feature of psychopathy to argue that psychopaths lack deep moral understanding; it may also mean that psychopaths are sometimes nonculpably unaware of the consequences of their behavior.[17] As Paul Litton points out, "If psychopaths' experience of fear is limited compared to ours, then we can reasonably conclude that they do not fully comprehend the unpleasant nature of our experience with fear."[18] This suggests that it may not be plausible to attribute to psychopaths the judgment that others' fear or sadness is not a reason to refrain from a certain bit of behavior.

Furthermore, psychopaths are famously imprudent. Their response to threatening stimuli is reduced as compared to nonpsychopathic individuals, and they have difficulty changing behavior that has proven contrary to their interests.[19] We might think, then, that psychopaths are impaired not just for moral reasoning, but for practical reasoning more generally.[20]

On the other hand, there may be psychopaths who are not so seriously impaired for keeping track of their own interests. Perhaps so-called successful psychopaths are like this. A recent study defines members of this group as "individuals who fit the criteria of a psychopath, having certain fundamental traits (e.g., callousness), but [who] largely succeed in their exploitation."[21] The authors of this study found that "successful psychopaths were rated high in assertiveness, excitement-seeking, and activity, and especially low in agreeableness traits like straightforwardness, altruism, compliance, and modesty."[22] Additionally, the "successful psychopaths were high in competence, order, achievement-striving, and self-discipline" and thus were better able to act in their own interests than unsuccessful psychopaths.[23] In a related study, Babiak, Neumann, and Hare administered Hare's Revised Psychopathy Checklist (PCL–R) to 203 managers from seven U.S. and international companies.[24] Nine of the participants scored above 25 on the PCL–R and eight had a score above 30, which is "the common research threshold for psychopathy."[25] (Of the nine, seven held management positions, two were vice-presidents, and two were directors.[26]) These results not only "provide evidence that a high level of psychopathic traits does not necessarily impede progress and advancement in corporate organizations,"[27] they also suggest that at least some psychopaths are not grossly impaired for prudential reasoning.

However, despite the example of successful psychopaths, I admit that there is reason to worry that psychopaths do not possess the general rational capacities that are important for attributionist approaches to moral responsibility.[28] However, I set this concern aside below and assume that psychopaths possess sufficient general powers of rational agency that it makes sense to describe them as conducting themselves on the basis of judgments about the weight of reasons. This is a licit assumption because the critics I engage below are largely willing to allow it—they are mainly concerned with psychopaths' specifically moral impairments, with their inability to see moral norms as anything more than external conventions with no independent, overriding normative authority. Gary Watson nicely sums up the deficiencies these critics take to undermine the psychopath's blameworthiness:

Psychopaths appear to know what morality "requires" of them in the same way that they know that one must pay income taxes and that smoking in commercial airplanes is against the rules. What they cannot understand is that those requirements

have any kind of nonstrategic normative force for anyone; that is, they cannot regard moral demands as anything more than coercive pressures. They can know that
what they aim to do might hurt someone, but not that there is any sort of (noninstrumental) reason against doing or having done it.[29]

I assume below that psychopaths are impaired in the way Watson
describes.

12.3   Are Psychopaths Capable of Contempt?

In "The Responsibility of the Psychopath Revisited," Neil Levy takes on
the attributionist perspective directly and offers several considerations in
favor of the claim that psychopaths are not open to moral blame for their
bad behavior. Levy's approach to moral responsibility emphasizes agents'
histories, particularly the factors that explain how they came to be the way
they are. For example, Levy believes that "[a]gents are morally responsible
for an action if (roughly) they are capable of appreciating and responding
to moral reasons," and when they lack these capacities, "their responsibility
hinges on whether they are responsible *for* this fact."[30] Since "psychopathy
is a developmental disorder, for which there is no known cure, psychopaths
lacks [sic] control over their coming to be bad."[31] "Hence," concludes Levy,
"they ought to be excused from moral responsibility."[32] This means that
we should refrain from blaming psychopaths, exempting them both from
reactive attitudes like resentment and from "those aspects of the criminal
justice system which are expressive of blame."[33]

However, for the attributionist, whether psychopaths are morally responsible and blameworthy is not settled by noting that they cannot respond
to moral considerations or that they are not responsible for this fact about
themselves. This is because these considerations don't necessarily bear on
whether psychopaths are capable of contempt and ill will.

Levy addresses this rejoinder by arguing that psychopaths' moral impairments do, in fact, mean that they cannot express contempt or ill will
through their behavior. According to Levy,

it is simply false that expressing contempt, ill-will, or moral indifference is independent of moral knowledge. For an action to express contempt for others or for morality, the agent must be capable of appreciating moral facts. Contempt is a thoroughly
moralized attitude; only a moral agent is capable of it.[34]

I agree with Levy that contempt is a moralized attitude, but we disagree
about what this point comes to. I take Levy's view to be that contempt is a
moralized attitude in the sense that only *moral agents*—those who can make

use of moral concepts—can express contempt through their actions. But why should we believe this? One possibility—which would explain why psychopaths are not capable of contempt—is that expressing contempt requires an agent to make judgments with explicit moral content. If psychopaths cannot deploy moral concepts in the way required for their judgments to have explicit moral content, then, according to this view, their actions cannot express moralized attitudes like contempt.

I propose, however, that in order for an agent's actions to express contempt or ill will, the agent does not need to be able to form judgments with moral content. Contempt is certainly a moralized attitude, but this just means that contempt is an attitude with a certain sort of moral significance—something in which we take a certain sort of moral interest. When we speak of "contempt," then, we are squarely within the moral domain, but, as I shall argue, this need not entail that for an agent to be capable of contempt he or she must be able to use moral concepts.

Suppose, for example, that psychopaths cannot deploy concepts like "moral standing" (at least not in the way that nonpsychopaths do), and that their behavior is therefore not informed by judgments like, "You don't have moral standing, so I can disregard your objections to my treatment of you." What is important for my account is that this is still compatible with psychopaths guiding their behavior by judgments like, "The fact that this action will injure you is no reason to refrain from it." I suggested in the last section that insofar as psychopaths have the ability to make, and to guide their actions by, judgments about reasons, it will sometimes be reasonable to attribute this sort of judgment to psychopaths.

A judgment like "The fact that this action of mine will injure you is no reason to refrain from it" can reasonably have moral significance for us even though it does not have explicit moral content. For one thing, this judgment is in stark contrast with the judgment by which a good-willed agent would be moved. The judgment in question also conflicts with the injured party's view about the importance of his or her welfare; it is, therefore, a judgment to which the injured party has reason to object. This judgment has moral significance for the injured party, then, not because it involves moral concepts, but because it involves denying the significance of factors that are morally salient for the injured party.[35] Thus, psychopaths may be capable of behavior that has moral significance (for us) despite their impaired ability to recognize and find motivation in moral considerations.

In a way, of course, it is beside the point whether psychopathic behavior is properly described as expressing "contempt" or "ill will." What really matters is whether the expressive content of a psychopath's action is such that it is appropriate to respond to his or her behavior with characteristic blaming attitudes like resentment. Even if psychopaths are not capable of contempt because, as a matter of terminology, contempt involves an ability to use moral concepts, I would argue that blaming attitudes are still an appropriate response to psychopaths because of the type of disregard for others' interests of which they *are* capable. Suppose that a psychopath judges that my welfare doesn't have any significance as a reason to refrain from an action. Such a psychopath dismisses a consideration that by my lights ought not to be dismissed by someone who is—unlike a machine or a nonhuman animal—in the business of guiding his or her behavior by judgments about reasons. From my point of view, the psychopath's judgment involves a serious error about my standing, and this error is a proper basis for resentment regardless of whether the psychopath's attitude toward me is properly described as contempt.

12.4   Psychopaths as Unwitting Wrongdoers

To conclude his discussion of contempt, Levy introduces an example that is supposed to help us see that psychopaths' moral incapacity means that they do not express blame-grounding attitudes and qualities of will through their behavior. Levy asks us to imagine that

there is a kind of harm that is objectively morally relevant, but of which we are ignorant. Suppose, for instance, that plants can be harmed, and that this harm is a moral reason against killing or treading on them. In that case, many of us are (causally) responsible for a great many moral harms. But it is false that we express contempt, ill-will, or even *moral* indifference to these plants. Nor do we *flout* their standing as objects to whom moral consideration is owed. These attitudes all require a background of normative beliefs for their expression, in the relevant sense. Absence of moral regard does not entail, indeed it is incompatible with, presence of moral disregard. But just as we fail to express any moral attitudes toward plants, so psychopaths fail to express the relevant attitudes toward their victims.[36]

David Shoemaker offers a similar example to make the same point. "Suppose," says Shoemaker, that

a race of alien beings comes to live amongst us, and while in general they share our moral sensibilities, they find additional sources of moral reasons around them. In particular, they think it immoral to walk on the grass, precisely because of what it does to the grass: it bends and breaks it. It is intrinsically bad, they claim, for this sort of organism to be bent or broken, and they purport to ground this claim on their understanding of what it is like to be a blade of broken or bent grass. When it is pointed out to them that blades of grass do not feel or have consciousness, that there is nothing it is like to be a blade of grass, they reply that understanding what it is like to be something need not have anything to do with consciousness; sometimes, it can simply consist in projectively entering into the entity's being-space. Indeed, claim the aliens, they have the special capacity for doing just that, and they have come to recognize the grass's moral status thereby. We, of course, simply do not get what they are talking about.[37]

Now what should we say if a human fails to respect the moral status of grass?

Suppose, for instance, that as I am walking through the park, I see an interesting rock formation I would like to see up close but to do so involves tramping on some grass. I cannot "empathize" with the grass, and what the aliens deem immoral about grass-tramping I merely see as stupid: I am just incapable of viewing the grass's bending and breaking as giving me reasons of any kind. So as I chortle about the aliens' ridiculous moral beliefs, I tramp across the grass. I am spotted by an alien, however, who rails at me with indignation, hell-bent on publicly shaming me. Is this an appropriate reaction?[38]

Shoemaker says that these blaming responses would not be appropriate because when he walks on grass, he is not disrespecting the grass in a way that justifies moral indignation. As Shoemaker sees it, "while it is true that I fail to express respect for the grass, I am incapable of disrespecting it."[39] This inability to disrespect grass is supposed to stem from an inability to see any reason in favor of refraining from walking on grass: Such "an incapacity undermines the possibility of my expressing ill will in the sense warranting accountability-blame, namely, active disregard."[40]

I agree that the people in the above examples are not blameworthy for walking on plants because they do not express blame-grounding disrespect for plants. However, neither Shoemaker's nor Levy's example supports the conclusion that psychopaths are not fit targets for negative reactive attitudes. This is because psychopaths are importantly different from the people who harm plants in their examples.

The reason the people in these examples do not express disrespect is that they are unaware of the consequences of their actions. In Shoemaker's example, the humans know that walking on grass causes it to bend and break, and they know that the aliens say that this has a morally significant effect on grass's "being-space." However, in the context of the example, the aliens' claims are supposed to be bizarre; they are claims that it would be reasonable for the humans to reject.[41] Since the humans reasonably do not believe that there is any sense to talk of grass's being-space, they reasonably fail to be aware that walking on grass harms it. Similarly, in Levy's example, people may know that uprooting a plant harms it insofar as this disrupts its normal plant-like functioning, but they reasonably do not know that plants can be harmed in a way that turns out to be morally relevant—for example, that uprooting a plant causes it pain.

If the humans in these examples are wrongdoers, then they are unwitting wrongdoers, and they are unwitting in a way that is often *not* compatible with blame: Through no fault of their own, they don't know that their actions have certain consequences.[42] The psychopath, on the other hand, is an unwitting wrongdoer in a way that *is* compatible with blame: Psychopaths may not know that they do something wrong when they harm you, but they may well know that an action of theirs harms you. This is compatible with blame because someone who does not believe that it is wrong to harm you (but who knows that he or she harms you) treats you with contempt. As I have argued, the judgment that the possibility of harming you doesn't matter, or that your objections to being harmed can be overlooked, is a contemptuous judgment.

Levy's and Shoemaker's examples can be altered so that they have a better chance of supporting their claims about psychopaths. What is required is for the wrongdoing in the examples to more closely resemble psychopathic wrongdoing. We could imagine, for instance, that plants are caused great pain by being walked on *and that humans know this*, but that some humans are incapable of caring about this fact. If we think that these impaired humans do not express contempt for plants when they knowingly harm them, then we would have an example that supports Levy's and Shoemaker's conclusion. However, I would say that if an impaired human knows that walking on a plant seriously harms it, then walking on the plant expresses the contemptuous judgment that the harm doesn't matter. This would, I suggest, be a suitable basis for blame on the part of someone who takes the welfare of plants seriously.[43]

12.5   Can the Mere Possibility of Moral Understanding Contribute to Ill Will?

Another way to approach the issue of the psychopath's capacity for ill will is to ask whether, when we stipulate that a normal (i.e., nonpsychopathic) wrongdoer is capable of appreciating moral facts, we have added anything to the account of his or her wrongdoing that is necessary for the expression of ill will. What, in other words, do we learn about an instance of wrongdoing when we learn that the wrongdoer is morally competent? One thing we learn is that it was possible (at least at a suitably general level of psychological description) for the wrongdoer to have responded appropriately to moral considerations to which the wrongdoer in fact did not respond appropriately. But what does the presence of this unexercised ability have to do with whether the wrongdoer's behavior expresses ill will?

Consider a recent example of hypothetical psychopathic wrongdoing from David Shoemaker. Shoemaker argues that psychopaths are not open to blame in a way that licenses attitudes like resentment—they are not, in his words, "accountability-responsible."[44] However, psychopaths can be morally responsible for their behavior in more limited ways. For example, psychopaths can be "answerability-responsible" because it makes sense to ask them what considerations motivated their behavior. As Shoemaker suggests, we can reasonably ask a psychopath, "'Why did you cheat that old lady out of her life savings?,'" and the psychopath may truthfully "cite *various judgments of worth*: 'It's funny to see the look of panic on an old lady's face,' or 'Old people don't deserve to have any money.'"[45]

According to Shoemaker's and Levy's positions, a psychopath is not an apt target for resentment even if he or she acts on the judgments just mentioned, and this is because of the psychopath's inability to form appropriate moral judgments. However, suppose that we have two wrongdoers (*A* and *B*) who both cheat an old woman out of money and who both truthfully report that they did so because they wanted to see "the look of panic on an old lady's face." Next, suppose we find out that wrongdoer *A*, but not *B*, could have formed a morally preferable judgment about the normative status of the consequences of her action. *A* could have judged—though she did not— that the prospect of the old lady's suffering was a sufficient reason to not cheat her. While both wrongdoers failed to respond appropriately to moral considerations, the general facts about *A*'s psychology, but not *B*'s, were such that *A* could have responded appropriately to the moral considerations relevant to the situation. But as things actually transpired, neither *A* nor *B* responded appropriately to moral considerations. They both intentionally cheated the old lady for the reason mentioned above, so why should we think that only wrongdoer *A* expresses a quality of will that makes negative reactive attitudes appropriate? How does the fact that *A* had psychological access to a morally preferable, but entirely counterfactual, instance of moral awareness make the quality of her action, or the quality of her will, more malicious, or more morally significant than *B*'s?[46] Why, to put it differently, shouldn't we focus on the *actual features* of *A*'s and *B*'s behavior—which happen to be quite similar—when we come to assess their blameworthiness?

There may well be satisfactory answers to these questions, and if there are, then perhaps psychopaths are not open to blame.[47] My point is that before we accept the conclusion that the actions of psychopaths do not express attitudes to which blame properly responds, we need an account of how a normal wrongdoer's *possession* of the capacities that the psychopath lacks makes him or her capable of such attitudes. Without such an account, I suggest that if a psychopath unjustifiably, intentionally, and knowingly injures someone, then (prima facie and other things being equal) the psychopath's action expresses an attitude toward the injured party that makes the psychopath an apt target for the attitudes that characterize moral blame.

I don't mean to claim that there can never be a difference in the moral quality of a wrong committed by a psychopath and one committed by a nonpsychopathic wrongdoer. Morally competent wrongdoers can have a moral participant's understanding of the fact that they do wrong. Indeed, they can take a general stand *against* morality. Like Milton's Satan, the morally competent wrongdoer can say, "Evil, be thou my good." This is something the psychopath cannot do (at least not in the way a nonpsychopath can). There are, then, certain forms of moral badness of which the psychopath is not capable. However, this does not mean that the forms of badness of which the psychopath *is* capable are not sufficient for blameworthiness.

We might think that only knowing wrongdoing of the sort mentioned above can express blame-grounding ill will because only this sort of wrongdoing involves an explicit choice *against* some moral value. However, we should keep in mind that many normal wrongdoers are not knowing wrongdoers in this sense. Many people motivated by bias against a race, gender, or sexual orientation know that others regard their behavior as wrong, but they do not see their behavior as conflicting with values that they themselves take to be morally decisive. If we think that these bad actors are open to blame even though their actions don't involve a knowing choice against morality, then the fact that psychopaths are not capable of this sort of wrongdoing does not mean that they are not open to blame.

12.6   Gary Watson's View

In "The Trouble with Psychopaths," Gary Watson takes an approach to assessing the moral responsibility of psychopaths that is importantly different from Levy's and Shoemaker's. For one thing, Watson allows the plausibility of attributing morally significant, malicious behavior and ill will to psychopaths.[48] Psychopaths pass what Watson calls *the malice test*: They "are often not just dangerous but cruel. They frequently enjoy forcing others into painful submission.... That psychopaths are in this way 'into' or 'behind' the mischief and pain is what constitutes their malice."[49] This interpretation of psychopathic behavior is plausible because psychopaths possess the rational capacities I discussed in section 12.2. In virtue of these capacities, Watson says, "[p]sychopaths are capable of a complex mode of reflective agency that is ethically significant in ways that the activities of less complex creatures cannot be."[50]

The "trouble" with psychopaths is that while they pass *the malice test*, they do not meet *the moral competence requirement*.[51] On the one hand (and insofar as they pass the malice test), Watson says that we "rightly predicate viciousness of the attitudes and conduct of psychopaths" and that these attributions constitute a form of moral responsibility.[52] However, since psychopaths lack moral competence, they are not morally responsible in the crucial sense of being morally *accountable* for their behavior.[53] Because of their inability to recognize the normative significance of others' interests, Watson says, psychopaths "lack the capacity for moral reciprocity or mutual recognition that is necessary for intelligibly holding someone accountable to basic moral demands and expectations."[54]

For Watson, what makes it inappropriate to impose the moral demands and expectations associated with accountability on psychopaths is that they cannot enter into the context of mutual recognition in which these demands are at home. Thus, there is an important sense in which psychopaths' disorder "disqualifies them as members of the moral community."[55] We are, and must be, morally alienated from the psychopath because "[m]oral objections and other forms of moral address [e.g., our demands for moral recognition] presume or appeal to an authority that psychopaths cannot recognize."[56]

Unsurprisingly, Watson is critical of approaches that deny that moral competence is a requirement for moral responsibility. For example, Watson objects to T. M. Scanlon's claim that even in the absence of moral understanding, a generally rational wrongdoer is open to moral criticism that "'supports *demands* for acknowledgment'" of wrongdoing, as well as demands "'for apology, or for justification or explanation.'"[57] These demands for acknowledgment and apology look, says Watson, "like instances of holding accountable, like calls for avowal of responsibility."[58] However, this is "plainly not warranted by [Scanlon's] general rational competence view" because *general* (but nonmoral) rational competence is not sufficient for an agent to stand with us in a moral relationship characterized by reciprocity.[59] For Watson, because psychopaths are "incapable of the reciprocity that demanding and owing justification presumes, moral criticism [of the sort conveyed by the demands Scanlon mentions] is not only futile but senseless," for "[n]othing they could do could be intelligibly construed as an apology or acknowledgment."[60]

As the preceding hopefully makes clear, Watson's central reservation about the moral responsibility of psychopaths has to do with "the conceptual aptness of making a 'demand' of a creature that is incapable of recognizing one's standing to make demands."[61] Now it is certainly plausible to say with Watson that a condition on reasonably imposing a demand for apology or moral recognition on another agent is that the agent can recognize the legitimacy of the demand and the authority of the one who issues it. I admit, then, that Watson identifies an important sense in which psychopaths are not morally responsible for their behavior. Psychopaths are not morally responsible in the sense of being members of our moral community with whom we can engage in genuine moral dialogue or from whom we can reasonably demand an apology in the hope of restoring (or creating) a moral relationship.

It's important to note, however, that the sort of moral responsibility just identified is largely prospective. In his conclusion, Watson says,

Holding one another morally accountable honors the value of mutual recognition and expresses a basic form of respect. The *telos* of this practice is the prospect of code-liberation and reconciliation. In the case of psychopathy, I have argued, this hope is forlorn. Psychopaths are, in this sense, irredeemably alien.[62]

If holding another accountable involves the prospect of reconciliation, then psychopaths are not properly held accountable for their behavior. But holding accountable, so understood, is a relatively narrow slice of what is involved in judgments of moral responsibility and in holding others responsible for their behavior. Even if psychopaths are not reasonably open to demands for sincere apology or for moral reform, perhaps they are open to the emotional responses that are plausibly at the center of our blaming practices: the negative reactive attitudes.

However, Watson, like Shoemaker and Levy, does not mean to leave this option open. While there is little explicit discussion of the negative reactive attitudes in "The Trouble with Psychopaths," it is clear both that Watson means to include them in the range of responses that are involved in *holding accountable* and that he views these responses as inappropriate if a wrongdoer does not meet the moral competence requirement.[63] While Watson believes that psychopaths are "capable of acting in morally horrible ways, of exhibiting a kind of evil to which we respond accordingly," and that "[t]heir conduct *is* morally significant in this way," he does not see this as justifying our resentment:

what is a proper object of moral horror and hard feelings does not necessarily warrant resentment and indignation proper. These latter responses must fall short of their erstwhile targets [in the case of psychopaths]. Some agents of evil, therefore, are beyond moral accountability.[64]

In another brief reflection on the reactive attitudes, Watson clarifies his claim in earlier work that these "attitudes are 'incipiently forms of communication.'"[65] He says now that resentment is "'incipiently communicative' in that it involves a commitment, not to the communication of moral demands, but to the appropriateness of an inherently communicative stance."[66] And, of course, one must have some capacity for genuine moral conversation before it is appropriate to take up this communicative stance.

I take Watson's view to be, then, that psychopaths are not appropriate targets for resentment because it is part of the logic of resentment that it is apt only in the case of wrongdoers who possess moral competence. This is because resentment presumes that its target is, at least in a general way, a candidate for moral dialogue—one to whom we can reasonably express a demand for apology or a wish for moral reconciliation, and these demands and wishes are reasonable only in the case of morally competent, non-psychopathic agents. To my mind, however, characterizing resentment in this largely prospective way obscures an important aspect of resentment: namely, the way in which it is a manifestation of moral offense at past acts, and the way it marks certain actions as offensive because of their moral character and the quality of will that informs them.

Consider, as an alternative, Justin D'Arms and Daniel Jacobson's account of resentment. D'Arms and Jacobson propose that certain emotions are "cognitive sharpenings" of more basic "natural emotion kinds."[67] Cognitive sharpenings are "constructed by specifying a subclass of instances of an emotion, or other affective state, in terms of some thought that they happen to share."[68] For example, we "could take all the episodes of anger-that-one-was-denied-tenure together and treat them as a type of anger."[69] This "tenure rage" would be a cognitive sharpening of anger insofar as it is a form of anger that involves the belief that one was denied tenure. Similarly, resentment is a sort of moralized anger, a cognitive sharpening of a more basic natural emotion kind, the "constitutive thought" of which "is that one has not merely been slighted but wronged."[70] Thus, as D'Arms and Jacobson have it, if "you believe that because you deserve tenure, you were wronged by not getting it," then "[i]t is resentment, not merely anger, you feel."[71] On the other hand, if you come to think that you in fact did not deserve tenure, then while "[y]ou may still be disposed to *anger*," it would not be appropriate to describe this as resentment: "the more you judge that you have not been wronged, the more difficult it will be to understand yourself as resenting those who made the decision."[72]

Presumably, Watson regards resentment as having to do with more than just the belief that one was wronged. If we were to put his view in D'Arms and Jacobson's terms, perhaps we would say that resentment is a cognitive sharpening of anger characterized by the thought that another wronged me *and* that other is a potential moral interlocutor. Alternatively, or in addition, the constitutive thought might be that the person who wronged me could have responded appropriately to moral considerations and refrained from wronging me on that basis. Characterized in either way, resentment would be off target if it were aimed at a psychopath—or at least the emotional responses we might feel toward psychopaths would not be resentment, properly so called.

However, I don't think we have much reason to regard resentment as quintessentially involving the thoughts just mentioned. Certainly, it often does occur to us either that the one who wronged us could have been appropriately responsive to our moral standing, or that he or she might be inspired by our moral criticism to offer an apology. But it is also possible for emotional responses to wrongdoing to involve just the thought that others have treated us in a way that we did not deserve to be treated, that they did so on purpose and for reasons of their own that we do not view as justifying their behavior. A psychopath is capable of committing actions that have all these properties, so if judging that an action has these properties is the "constitutive thought" involved in resentment, then psychopaths are open to resentment, so defined.

As D'Arms and Jacobson suggest, emotions can be "sharpened out" in different ways by different constitutive thoughts. The point of the last paragraph is that there are at least two different, but related, ways of sharpening the emotion of anger that might plausibly be called "resentment" (or perhaps one of these forms of resentment is primary, and the other is a further refinement, or sharpening, of this primary sort). If this is so, then there may be a kind of resentment that is not appropriate in the case of the psychopath: the sort of resentment that involves the thought that the one who wronged us is a potential moral interlocutor. However, there will also be another sort of resentment, which is plausibly the more basic form, that involves a thought that *can* reasonably be had of a psychopath: the thought that, for no good reason, another has knowingly and intentionally treated us in a way that, by our lights, we did not deserve to be treated. Therefore, even if Watson is right about the importance of moral competence for (one kind of) resentment, psychopaths may still be open to a form of blame that involves negative reactive attitudes and that goes beyond the relatively shallow sort of blame that Watson (and Shoemaker) are willing to allow in the psychopath's case.

I grant the following to Watson (and Shoemaker). Psychopaths are not morally responsible for their behavior in the sense of being properly subject to certain demands, such as the demand for apology, or to the form of resentment that involves the thought that the one who is resented could have responded appropriately to moral reasons. I am comfortable with this concession because it leaves it open that psychopathic wrongdoing is expressive of ill will and that psychopaths can be morally responsible for their wrongdoing in the sense of being properly targeted with a form of resentment that involves the thought that one has been wronged rather than merely harmed.

As Watson shows, psychopaths are not members of our moral community in the sense of being moral interlocutors. Since moral accountability (in Watson's sense) involves demands that are reasonably imposed only on moral interlocutors, it addresses agents insofar as they are members of our moral community in this sense. However, psychopaths *are* members of our moral community in the sense of being capable of wronging us (rather than merely injuring us) and of treating us with contempt and disregard. An important role that (one form of) resentment plays is to respond to agents insofar as they are members of our moral community in this limited sense.

12.7   Psychopaths and Other Incorrigibles

Several points from the preceding sections can be brought into sharper focus by considering Watson's response to an earlier discussion of mine about the relation between psychopaths and other wrongdoers. Watson believes that the sort of view defended here is too inclusive because "[i]t accepts too many into the circle of moral accountability," but he notes that his own view faces the converse objection that it shrinks the circle of moral accountability too much because it can provide "no principled way to distinguish the psychopath's unreachability from that of the incorrigibly hardened and vicious nonpsychopathic criminal."[73]

In an earlier paper, I expressed something like this worry in the following way, as Watson quotes it,

Imagine the way prisoners in a Nazi concentration camp surely blamed and condemned their murderers.... I do not think that these demands and claims lost their point when they failed to move hardened concentration camp executioners. Of course, it may be true that the executioners in question could have been brought to recognize their crimes for what they are, but it is strange to suppose that it is only the psychologically improbable possibility of radical conversion at the last moment that makes blame appropriate here.[74]

In response, Watson distinguishes between the incorrigibility of psychopaths and the incorrigibility of nonpsychopathic wrongdoers who are committed to their wrongdoing but for whom responsiveness to moral considerations remains at least a dim possibility. For example, as Watson notes, "[o]ccasionally a Nazi or a Mafioso or white supremacist makes a genuine return to the moral point of view."[75] Watson says "return" because moral recognition depends here "upon suppressed or partial or partitioned moral sensibilities that are somehow reengaged or extended."[76] For the psychopath, there is no similar possibility of a return to morality; this means "not just that there is no chance that [psychopaths] will change but (again) that it makes no sense to address moral demands to them as though these could be intelligible to them."[77]

All this seems right, but Watson's observation is somewhat orthogonal to the point I was trying to make by invoking concentration camp guards. My point was not that we can't differentiate between hardened Nazis and psychopaths, but rather that the admitted differences between these two groups does not give us reason to think that only members of the former group are open to moral blame. For one thing—along the lines I sketched in section 12.5—even if the capacity for responding to moral reasons is not entirely extinguished in hardened Nazis, it is not clear that this is what makes their actions expressive of ill will toward their victims.

Now if the entire point of blaming attitudes like resentment were to provoke a return to morality on the part of a wrongdoer, then we would have reason to think that resentment is not appropriate in the case of psychopaths. However, the concentration camp example gives us reason to think that this is not so. I take it that many people find it reasonable—as opposed to being merely understandable—for concentration camp victims to resent even the most thoroughly hardened and unrepentant Nazis. If we assume that, though it remains a possibility, hardened Nazis are not going to reform themselves on the basis of being targeted by their victim's resentment, this suggests that we take resentment to be doing work besides aiming at eliciting apologies and moral reform. Thus, resentment seems apt even in cases where moral reform is so unlikely that any expectation of it would be unreasonable.[78]

Another thing I had in mind in the passage Watson quotes is that prisoners in a concentration camp, facing an evil that they cannot reasonably hope to reform or dissuade, might issue "demands and claims" (as I put it) without necessarily attempting to engage their captors in moral dialogue.[79] Rather, I imagine the demands and claims as ways the prisoners have of expressing their resentment by insisting on their own moral standing. One can reasonably insist on such a thing even in the face of implacable evil because the point of this insistence need not be to convince the wrongdoer of his or her error. The point may be, rather, to defiantly express moral values as one sees them, to stand up for oneself, and to commit oneself to the claim that one has standing to object to the treatment in question, even if one cannot convince others of this fact.[80] These are expressions of one's moral commitments, but these expressions do not depend for their sense on the possibility that they will be affirmed by a wrongdoer.

As I noted in the last section, Watson views resentment as in some way tied to demands that make sense only when they are posed to morally competent wrongdoers. Watson adds that "[i]n some elusive sense, resentment is 'meant to be expressed.'"[81] Presumably, Watson believes that resentment is meant to be expressed in such a way that its expression would be infelicitous if it were directed at someone who could not respond appropriately. I agree that resentment is meant to be expressed: It seeks an outlet. Part of what it is to feel resentment is to have an urge to express it. However, as the last paragraph indicates, I don't believe that expressions of resentment must aim at eliciting a certain response from a wrongdoer.

12.8   Conclusion

We hold wrongdoers morally responsible because of the significance of their actions for us, and the negative attitudes that characterize blame are responses to this significance. Therefore, one argument against blaming psychopaths is that it is inappropriate to find the sort of meaning in their actions that is involved in judging that someone is blameworthy. Perhaps psychopathic behavior lacks the relevant sort of significance. In this case, we might be obliged to view psychopaths with what P. F. Strawson called an "objective attitude" and to see them merely as things "to be managed or handled or cured or trained" and not as candidates for interpersonally engaged attitudes like resentment.[82]

There certainly are engaged responses that are out of place in the case of psychopaths. It does not make sense to expect moral acknowledgment or sincere apology from them, and if there is a form of resentment that essentially involves an attempt to elicit these responses, then it is not reasonably directed at psychopaths. There might also be a kind of moral sadness or disappointment that is not a reasonable response to psychopaths and their bad behavior. We can reasonably be disappointed that we have crossed paths with a psychopath, but it makes little sense to be disappointed *in the psychopath* for disregarding our moral standing instead of respecting it.[83]

The fact that the responses just mentioned are out of place gives us reason to view psychopaths as outside the bounds of the moral community. But there is at least one way in which psychopaths *are* part of the moral community: They can wrong us. Psychopaths can wrong us rather than merely injure us, and they can wrong us in ways that are deliberately contrary to our interests and that express commitments to which we are opposed and to which we have reason to object. This, I have argued, makes psychopathic wrongdoing significant for us in a way that makes it reasonable to respond to psychopaths with moral blame.

Notes

1. I am grateful to Thomas Schramme, Zac Cogley, David Shoemaker, Gary Watson, and Kyle Adams for their thoughtful comments on drafts of this chapter. A West Virginia University Faculty Senate Research Grant made part of this research possible.

2. My view is, of course, indebted to P. F. Strawson's "Freedom and Resentment," reprinted in Gary Watson (ed.), *Free Will*, 2nd edition (New York: Oxford University Press, 2003), 72–93. For Strawson, to regard individuals as morally responsible is to see them as open to positive and negative reactive attitudes. I find Strawson's approach instructive, particularly his account of blaming attitudes like resentment as "essentially reactions to the quality of others' wills towards us, as manifested in their behaviour: to their good or ill will or indifference or lack of concern" (83). However, in the next section, instead of characterizing moral responsibility simply in terms of openness to reactive attitudes, I characterize it in terms of attributability. I claim that agents are morally responsible for behavior that is attributable to them (in the right way), and that agents are blameworthy for *morally objectionable* behavior that is attributable to them (in the right way). At this point, I return to Strawson insofar as the objectionable behavior that I attribute to psychopaths is behavior that expresses ill will and thus grounds resentment. I should note that Strawson himself apparently did not view agents like psychopaths as open to resentment; I will say something about the "objective attitude" that Strawson encouraged toward the "morally undeveloped" in my conclusion (79).

3. Neil Levy, "The Responsibility of the Psychopath Revisited," *Philosophy, Psychiatry, and Psychology* 14 (2007): 129–138, 132 (the third italics is mine). In his recent book, *Hard Luck: How Luck Undermines Free Will and Moral Responsibility* (New York: Oxford University Press, 2011), Levy substitutes the label "quality of will theories" for "attributionism" (158, note 2). Angela Smith discusses problems with the label "attributionism" in "The Myth of Attributionism" (unpublished manuscript); I retain the usage here because it appears in work to which I refer.

4. See T. M. Scanlon, *What We Owe to Each Other* (Cambridge, MA: Harvard University Press, 1998), chapter 6, and *Moral Dimensions: Permissibility, Meaning, Blame*

(Cambridge, MA: Harvard University Press, 2008), chapter 4.; and Angela Smith, "Responsibility for Attitudes: Activity and Passivity in Mental Life," *Ethics* 115 (2005): 236–271, and "Control, Responsibility, and Moral Assessment," *Philosophical Studies* 138 (2008): 367–392. I defend a perspective related to Scanlon's and Smith's in "Blame and Responsiveness to Moral Reasons: Are Psychopaths Blameworthy?," *Pacific Philosophical Quarterly* 89 (2008): 516–535, and in "Moral Competence, Moral Blame, and Protest," *The Journal of Ethics* 16 (2012): 89–109.

5. David Shoemaker, "Attributability, Answerability, and Accountability: Toward a Wider Theory of Moral Responsibility," *Ethics* 121 (2011): 602–632, 604.

6. Ibid.

7. Ibid., 605.

8. Scanlon, *What We Owe to Each Other*, 288. Scanlon speaks of a mere failure to see the force of moral considerations, but it is clear from the context that he has in mind an agent who *cannot* see the force of these considerations. It is important to note that Scanlon is thinking here of an agent who judges that there is no reason to refrain from action rather than an agent who makes no judgment about reasons. Thanks to Thomas Schramme for encouraging greater clarity here.

9. In "Expressing Who We Are: Moral Responsibility and Awareness of Our Reasons for Action," *Analytic Philosophy* 52 (2011): 243–261, Levy argues that the conditions under which actions express attitudes is more demanding than many suspect. I agree with parts of Levy's argument even though his conclusion would restrict moral responsibility on an account like mine. This concession is compatible with the claim that moral blindness is not a bar to moral responsibility and that *some* actions of morally blind agents express blame-grounding attitudes.

10. James Blair et al., *The Psychopath: Emotion and the Brain* (Malden, MA: Blackwell Publishing, 2005), 139.

11. Walter Glannon, "Psychopathy and Responsibility," *Journal of Applied Ethics* 14 (1997): 263–275, 268.

12. R. Jay Wallace, *Responsibility and the Moral Sentiments* (Cambridge, Mass.: Harvard University Press, 1996), 178.

13. For philosophical discussions of some of the relevant evidence here, see Levy, "The Responsibility of the Psychopath Revisited," and Cordelia Fine and Jeanette Kennett, "Mental Impairment, Moral Understanding and Criminal Responsibility: Psychopathy and the Purposes of Punishment," *International Journal of Law and Psychiatry* 27 (2004): 425–443. Recently, David Shoemaker has questioned the use to which the conventional/moral distinction has been put in philosophical discussions of psychopathy, "Psychopathy, Responsibility, and the Moral/Conventional Distinction," *The Southern Journal of Philosophy* 49, Spindel Supplement (2011): 99–124 ; reprinted in chapter 11, this volume.

14. Blair et al., *The Psychopath*, 12–13 and 17.

15. Watson, "The Trouble with Psychopaths," in R. Jay Wallace et al. (eds.), *Reasons and Recognition: Essays on the Philosophy of T. M. Scanlon* (New York: Oxford University Press, 2011), 307–331, 316, 317.

16. Blair et al., 54–56 and 126.

17. Fine and Kennett, "Mental Impairment, Moral Understanding, and Criminal Responsibility," 428–429.

18. Paul Litton, "Psychopathy and Responsibility Theory," *Philosophy Compass* 5 (2010): 676–688, 686 note 17.

19. Blair et al., *The Psychopath*, 48–53 and 68–69.

20. See the following for helpful discussion of the psychopath's general rational deficiencies: Jeanette Kennett, "Do Psychopaths Threaten Moral Rationalism," *Philosophical Explorations* 9 (2006): 69–82; Heidi Maibom, "The Mad, the Bad, and the Psychopath," *Neuroethics* 1 (2008): 167–184.

21. Stephanie N. Mullins-Sweatt et al., "The Search for the Successful Psychopath," *Journal of Research in Personality* 44 (2010): 554–558, 554. For related conclusions based on reviews of a number of studies, see Yu Gao and Adrian Raine, "Successful and Unsuccessful Psychopaths: A Neurobiological Model," *Behavioral Sciences and the Law* 28 (2010): 194–210.

22. Sweatt et al., "The Search for the Successful Psychopath," 556.

23. Ibid.

24. Paul Babiak et al., "Corporate Psychopathy: Talking the Walk," *Behavioral Sciences and the Law* 28 (2010): 174–193.

25. Ibid., 183.

26. Ibid., 185.

27. Ibid., 192.

28. Paul Litton suggests a related problem for the account I gave in "Blame and Responsiveness to Moral Reasons." Perhaps psychopaths, "or an extreme subset of psychopaths," are "wantons" (agents who are unconcerned with which of their competing desires will ultimately move them in action), in which case "their antisocial conduct does not reflect normative commitments," "Psychopathy and Responsibility Theory," 681.

29. Watson, "The Trouble with Psychopaths," 309.

30. Levy, "The Responsibility of the Psychopath Revisited," 134–135.

31. Ibid., 135.

32. Ibid.

33. Ibid., 136.

34. Ibid., 135. Note that Levy says, "...express contempt for others or for morality." In this section, I am concerned with whether psychopaths can express contempt for others. Expressing contempt for morality is, I think, something very different; I discuss it briefly at the end of section 12.5. In *Hard Luck*, Levy raises the objection considered here against my argument in "Blame and Responsiveness to Moral Reasons." He says there that contempt is an "expression of the perceived worthlessness of another where the worth is measured against some evaluative standard.... The psychopath might judge himself superior to others, but does not have the evaluative resources for contempt" (208 note 18). I take this to mean that for an agent's behavior to express contempt, the agent must be able to assign less *moral* value to one person than another. As I explain in the text, I think that if a psychopath takes pleasure in injuring someone, and counts the injury in favor of acting a certain way, then he or she takes a morally significant, contemptuous stance toward the other even if he or she can't use a concept like moral value.

35. By contrast, when a wild animal injures us, this is not morally significant in the same way because it is much less plausible to interpret the animal as guiding its behavior by the judgment that our injuries don't count as reasons.

36. Levy, "The Responsibility of the Psychopath Revisited," 135.

37. Shoemaker, "Attributability, Answerability, and Accountability," 625.

38. Ibid., 626.

39. Ibid.

40. Ibid., 627.

41. I assume that Shoemaker would agree: If we thought it was *un*reasonable for the humans to reject the aliens' claims, then it would be more difficult to accept Shoemaker's conclusion that they are not blameworthy.

42. Paul Litton suggests a similar response to Levy's example, "Psychopathy and Responsibility Theory," 681.

43. I give a more detailed response to Shoemaker's example in "Aliens, Accountability, and Psychopaths: A Reply to Shoemaker," *Ethics*, 122 (2012): 562–574.

44. Shoemaker, "Attributability, Answerability, and Accountability," 623.

45. Ibid., 628. Emphasis added.

46. One might say that A's capacity for morally preferable judgments doesn't make *her action* worse than B's, but it does make her a more appropriate target for blame because it is fair to blame wrongdoers only if they could have avoided wrongdoing. R. Jay Wallace develops this sort of point in *Responsibility and the Moral Sentiments* (196–207), and I respond to it in "Moral Competence, Moral Blame, and Protest";

my response draws on Pamela Hieronymi, "The Force and Fairness of Blame," *Philosophical Perspectives* 18, (2004): 115–148. Here, I will just point out that concerns about the avoidability of blame are most intuitive in cases like that of a compulsive wrongdoer who cannot do otherwise *and* whose behavior is independent of his or her judgments about how to behave. The behavior of the psychopath, however, is often dependent on his or her judgments about how to behave. This means that psychopaths can avoid committing particular wrong acts if they judge themselves to have reason to do so (though they can't avoid these acts *for moral reasons*).

47. As we have seen, Levy has one proposal about why moral competence matters for blameworthiness, which I have rejected. In the next two sections, I'll consider Gary Watson's recent answer to these questions.

48. Watson, "The Trouble with Psychopaths," 308.

49. Ibid., 316.

50. Ibid.

51. Ibid., 308.

52. Ibid.

53. Watson is building here on his well-known distinction between the attributability and accountability "faces" of responsibility, "Two Faces of Responsibility," reprinted in Watson, *Agency and Answerability: Selected Essays* (New York: Oxford University Press, 2004), 260–288.

54. Watson, "The Trouble with Psychopaths," 308.

55. Ibid., 309.

56. Ibid.

57. Ibid., 313. Watson is quoting Scanlon, *What We Owe to Each Other*, 272; the emphasis is Watson's.

58. Ibid.

59. Ibid.

60. Ibid., 314.

61. Ibid.

62. Ibid., 322. In a note attached to this passage, Watson adds that "[t]he rationale of moral and legal accountability is therefore prospective, without being consequentialist" (331, note 71).

63. This aspect of Watson's view comes out more clearly in "Two Faces of Responsibility" and "Responsibility and the Limits of Evil: Variations on a Strawsonian Theme," in Watson, *Agency and Answerability*, 219–259.

64. Watson, "The Trouble with Psychopaths," 317.

65. Ibid., 328, note 35. The earlier characterization of resentment occurs in "Responsibility and the Limits of Evil," 230.

66. Ibid.

67. Justin D'Arms and Daniel Jacobson, "The Significance of Recalcitrant Emotion (or, Anti-quasijudgmentalism)," in A. Hatzimoysis (ed.), *Philosophy and the Emotions* (Cambridge: Cambridge University Press, 2003), 127–145.

68. Ibid., 137.

69. Ibid.

70. Ibid., 143. This sentence should not be read as implying that the natural emotion kind of anger has a constitutive thought along the lines of "I was slighted." For D'Arms and Jacobson, natural emotion kinds have no constitutive thoughts. Thanks to Zac Cogley for encouraging me to clarify this. It's also worth noting D'Arms and Jacobson's acknowledgment that "resentment" can refer to a sort of moralized envy, in which case it would not be associated with the constitutive thought mentioned in the text.

71. Ibid.

72. Ibid.

73. Watson, "The Trouble with Psychopaths," 317.

74. Ibid. Watson is quoting my "Blame and Responsiveness to Moral Reasons," 532; the ellipsis is Watson's.

75. Watson, "The Trouble with Psychopaths," 318.

76. Ibid.

77. Ibid. It may be possible to provide a psychopath with incentives to refrain from some of his or her wrongdoing, but Watson means that a psychopath can't be changed into a person who see others' interests as noninstrumental reasons.

78. Similarly, if ordinary conversation is a guide, many people make sense of the notion of resenting the dead and others who will never be in a position to know about our resentment or to reform themselves because of it.

79. I should have avoided the use of the word "demands" since I think Watson is right that demands are felicitous only when directed at those who can obey them.

80. I develop the claim that blame can sometimes be construed as a form of moral protest in "Moral Competence, Moral Blame, and Protest."

81. Watson, "The Trouble with Psychopaths," 328, note 35.

82. Strawson, "Freedom and Resentment," 79.

83. George Sher argues that a component of blame is the desire that a wrongdoer "not have performed his past bad act or not have his current bad character," *In Praise of Blame* (New York: Oxford University Press, 2006), 112. If this desire entails the wish that the wrongdoer had refrained from his bad act *for the right (moral) reason*, then psychopaths would not be open to blame on this interpretation.

13 Contesting Dangerousness, Risk, and Treatability: A Sociological View of Dangerous and Severe Personality Disorder (DSPD)

Susie Scott

13.1 Introduction

The sociology of mental health makes an important contribution to debates about psychopathology by shifting the focus of attention away from individual minds and behavior and toward the social and cultural context in which these are embedded (Rogers and Pilgrim 2010). Whereas colleagues in psychiatry and moral philosophy attempt to identify the distinguishing features of the sociopath, such as a lack of moral understanding, empathy, and responsibility and other presumed psychological deficits, sociology's concern is with the social processes through which such criteria are decided upon and used to categorize groups of people. Bracketing out (without dismissing) the question of whether or not those labeled sociopathic represent a distinct psychological type, or possess unique mental characteristics, the discipline looks instead to societal reactions to rule breaking, analyzing the extent to which presumed mental disorder can be viewed as mere social deviance (Busfield 2001; Kendell 2002) or the medicalization of "badness" (Conrad 2007). Disorder labels, categories, and criteria vary historically and cross-culturally, in line with changing social norms and values: Behavior is only defined as "mad" or abnormal in relation to presumptions about normality, reason, and rationality (Foucault 1965).

In this respect, some sociologists argue that notions of mental disorder are socially constructed rather than objectively "real" and empirically measurable. Critical psychiatry (Ingleby 2004) and antipsychiatry (Szasz 1961/1972; Laing 1965; Scheff 1966) have had a significant influence upon this perspective, pointing to the "myth" of mental illness as a misleading metaphor for mere norm violation (Szasz ibid.). Many conditions lie on the "contested boundaries" between mental disorder, physical illness, and social deviance (Busfield 1996) and so have an ambiguous status. Critics also point to the power of psychiatry as an institution, whose ultimate function is social control through the containment of those seen to pose a threat to social order (Scull 1979).

The reality or otherwise of mental illness remains highly disputed (Roth and Kroll 1986), but recent research argues for a less radical approach that encourages interdisciplinary dialogue. Social realism, for example, defends the idea of an underlying psychopathology but argues that this can only be conceptualized through cultural discourses (Rogers and Pilgrim 2010; Busfield 1996). Values-Based Medicine (VBM; Fulford et al. 2002), the approach taken in this chapter, recognizes that subjectivity, values, and bias inevitably shape understandings of mental disorder, at every stage of the clinical encounter, but that this does not discredit the good intentions of those working in psychiatric services. Rather than viewing mental health professionals cynically as agents of social control, we can look more sympathetically at the difficult positions they may be forced into by the prevailing political climate. Furthermore, VBM argues for a more open dialogue between practitioners and clients, who might share their concerns in a democratized process of service evaluation (Woodbridge and Fulford 2004, 32).

As an illustrative case study, I present a discussion of the contested concept dangerous and severe personality disorder (DSPD), which arose within a particular historical, political, and cultural context of mental health legislation in the United Kingdom (Morgan 2004; Corbett and Westwood 2005; Manning 2006). DSPD is closely related to notions of psychopathy and sociopathy, referring to people who are thought to be capable of extremely violent or aggressive behavior as a direct result of a personality disorder, typically antisocial personality disorder (Department of Health 2002). Crucially, however, it is not a clinical, diagnostic category in itself, and does not appear in either the *Diagnostic and Statistical Manual of Mental Disorders* (fourth edition, text revision) or the *International Classification of Diseases* (tenth revision) classification systems. Rather it is an administrative label that was produced by the UK government in the early twenty-first century in response to a media-fueled moral panic (Cohen 1972) about supposedly "dangerous" individuals. As detailed below, this construction of a pseudo-scientific category occurred through a traceable sequence of political events and was viewed with skepticism by those working in mental health services (Maden and Tyrer 2003; Manning 2006; Scott et al. 2011). Uncertain of whether the condition actually existed, and therefore the extent to which they had a duty of care toward those so labeled, these professional groups were left in a difficult position—ethically, socially, and personally—as they struggled to make risk assessments and treatment decisions about those presumed to have DSPD.

13.2 Background: The Social Creation of DSPD

The term DSPD first appeared in the UK government's Green Paper, "Managing Dangerous People with Severe Personality Disorders," where it was defined as "...people with severe personality disorder who because of their disorder, pose a risk of serious offending" (Home Office and the Department of Health 1999, 10). This occurred in the context of a media-fueled furor surrounding a high-profile criminal case against Michael Stone, who was convicted of murder shortly after being released from hospital on the grounds that his personality disorder was untreatable (for a more detailed discussion, see Maden 2007). This resulted in a review of UK mental health law and successive drafts of a new Mental Health Bill (Department of Health 2002, 2004). It provoked political debates about risk and dangerousness, as well as ethical debates about whether it was more important to protect individual freedom or public safety. The government's subsequent White Paper stated that "Concerns of risk will always take precedence, but care and treatment provided under formal powers should otherwise reflect the best interests of the patient" (Department of Health 2000, part I, paragraph 2 [16]).

The conceptualization of DSPD is problematic because it does not refer to any tangible symptoms or signs, but rather to perceptions of the individual's character which are highly subjective. The condition is constructed by a set of predictive indicators of dangerousness and risk; clinicians are expected to assess clients' *potential* for violent or intimidating behavior, rather than their actual history of it, and estimate the threat they might pose to public safety. This evokes wider arguments about the cultivation of a risk society (Beck 1992), based upon the anticipation, rational calculation, and attempted management of future hazards (Lupton 1999; Corbett and Westwood 2005). Risk assessment, risk appraisal, and the construction of risk profiles for potential offenders are powerful tools in the discursive armory of politicians and policy makers, serving the function of population governance (Rose 1989). Whereas Foucault (1976/1980) pointed to the expansion of judicial power–knowledge into extrajudicial spaces, such as forensic medicine (Morgan 2004), the case of DSPD demonstrates how this in turn drives the expansion of medical/psychiatric power–knowledge into erstwhile extraclinical spaces of social deviance.

In November 2006 a bill was introduced to Parliament to amend rather than replace the 1983 Mental Health Act (House of Lords 2006). A particularly controversial issue remained, however, in that the old "treatability test" (which required that patients suffering with psychopathic disorder could only be detained if a treatment was available that was "... likely to alleviate or prevent a deterioration" of a condition) was to be replaced by an "appropriate treatment test." The final version of this bill, passed in July 2007, included the following criterion for detention:

...appropriate treatment is available (that medical treatment is available which is appropriate in the patient's case, taking into account the nature or degree of his [sic] mental disorder and all other circumstances of his case). (Mental Health Act Commission 2007, clauses 4–6)

Furthermore, the term "medical treatment" here was defined as that which is intended "...to alleviate, or prevent a worsening of, the disorder or one or more of its symptoms or manifestations" (part 1, chapter 1, paragraph 7 [4]). That is, the condition itself need not be deemed treatable, merely its effects, which could include the risk of violence or harm to others. As in the original 1983 Act (Department of Health 1983), the term "medical treatment" includes "...nursing, psychological intervention and specialist mental health habilitation, rehabilitation and care" (section 145).

The view of psychiatrists throughout these debates was one of skepticism and uncertainty about whether DSPD exists, and if so, whether its potential treatability lies within their remit (Fallon Report 1999; Morgan 2004). A widespread criticism cited in psychiatric journals was that the UK government, a nonmedical institution, had imposed a quasi-diagnosis upon them and effectively asked them to act as agents of social control. For example, Mullen (2007), a forensic psychiatrist, spoke of the DSPD program having been "...born out of an ill-conceived attempt to hide the imposition of preventive detention and indefinite sentences behind the veneer of respectability provided by a mental health context." Tyrer (2007) similarly reviewed his colleagues' concerns about the ethical implications of detaining people for long periods (Moran 2001) and of giving doctors unlimited powers over their patients' freedom (Haddock et al. 2001). Nevertheless, Tyrer suggests that these concerns have faded somewhat in recent years, as psychiatrists have become resigned to the fact that they will have to deal with this client group eventually. Within forensic psychiatry, in particular, there is a cautious acceptance of DSPD as having some kind of reality, and a belief that some manifestations of such severe personality disorders may be treatable. Indeed, Mullen (2007) tempers his own criticism with an espousal of DSPD services as "... an exciting initiative for providing effective services to a group of offenders with mental illness who psychiatry, and the justice services, have so long ignored." Nevertheless, considerable disquiet remains about the nature of psychopathy in general and DSPD in particular: namely, whether we can assess risk or predict "dangerousness" (and if so, how), and the likelihood of any therapeutic services offered succeeding in reducing the number of offenses committed by these individuals (Mullen 2007).

13.3   Methods and Data

The data presented here come from a Wellcome Trust–funded study that I carried out with four colleagues in the United Kingdom (Scott et al. 2011). Semi-structured interviews were conducted with 46 mental health professionals in two community mental health teams (CMHTs), a medium secure unit and a personality disorder psychotherapy service in the south of England (for reasons of access and practicality). These included general adult psychiatrists (6), forensic psychiatrists (5), psychotherapists (1), generic psychologists (4), forensic psychologists (2), social workers (12), community psychiatric nurses (CPNs; 12), and occupational therapists (OTs; 4). The interviews began with a fictional vignette about a person (named "Stephen") who showed many of the characteristics of DSPD. This was designed to elicit discussion around how such a person might be categorized, the issues this case would raise, how such decisions had been made in the respondents' actual practice, the questionable treatability of DSPD, and how its features might differ from those of other conditions (e.g., psychosis or other types of personality disorder). The interviews were tape-recorded, transcribed, and analyzed using Atlas.ti software. In the "Results" section below, the reference number given in parenthesis following interview quotations refers to the interviewee.

Using the analytic approach of VBM, I show how these respondents cited many different models of sociopathy, not simply those that reflected their occupational training. Practitioners drew upon a repertoire of values, both implicit and explicit, which could be modified, combined, and discarded according to their clinical experience, collective decision-making processes, and practical constraints upon their work. In the discussion below, I refer to the different values held by our respondents, based upon Columbo et al.'s (2003) six models of mental disorder. The medical model focuses on physical symptoms and their treatment with drugs or surgery and assumes that mental illness has biochemical or genetic causes. The social model views mental disorder as a stress response to living in difficult social conditions, such as poverty, poor housing, and social exclusion. The cognitive–behavioral model refers to sets of learned behaviors or patterns of cognition that are abnormal and impaired, but which can be unlearned in therapy. The psychotherapeutic model interprets the meaning of symptoms using psychoanalytic theories, often referring to traumatic experiences in early childhood. The family model shifts the focus of attention away from individuals to their family unit, which is seen as needing therapeutic support to change its patterns of interaction. Finally, the conspiratorial model echoes theories of antipsychiatry by claiming that mental illness is merely a misnomer for the medicalization of social deviance.

13.4   Results

13.4.1   DSPD as a Contested Concept

The majority of the mental health professionals were skeptical of the existence and status of DSPD. Although they could identify features of other, recognized, personality disorders in the vignette, they remained wary of applying the DSPD label to clients as a diagnostic category. This may reflect the clinicians' awareness of the political context in which the term had emerged, which cast doubt on its status as a mental disorder. As one psychiatrist put it:

> I am a bit cynical about this whole thing. What I feel is that they are dragging psychiatrists to give a label to certain people so that they can lock them away. I think that that is not right; it is not our job. (2/044)

A forensic psychiatrist agreed that

> ...psychopathic disorder isn't a diagnosis. It is just a hotchpotch category and you can make just about anybody fit that if you really want to, if they have committed a grossly irresponsible act. (F 34)

The practitioners were reluctant to detain people who had committed violent offences and appeared to be suffering from a personality disorder on the basis that this behavior could be interpreted in different ways; their "dangerousness" could be attributed to "badness" rather than "madness." Another psychiatrist said:

> This is a new concept and everybody has got their own ideas about risk, really. More than in any other branch of medicine, in psychiatry there is so much inter-rater discrepancy that I don't think anybody is going to agree on which one would fit that [category]. It will be very, very subjective. (2/049)

Some respondents had similar reservations about the concept of "therapeutic benefit." This was suggested in the 2000 White Paper as a criterion for detention, replacing "treatability" and acting as a precursor to the notion of "appropriate treatment." For those detained because of a presumed risk to others rather than to themselves, a care plan was required to "...treat the underlying disorder and/or to manage the behaviors arising from the disorder" (section 3.4); in the latter case, this would not necessarily entail a direct therapeutic benefit to the patient. The White Paper also referred to a "therapeutic environment" in which such people would be held, and to "...the provision of interventions that are specifically designed to ameliorate the behaviors that cause them to be a risk to others" (section 3.6). This provided doctors with much greater powers of detention by widening the scope of cases to which the criteria could be applied: Therapeutic benefit could be interpreted as meaning mere *containment* of the individual to protect the public, without the need for treatment.

The possibility that treatability would be reduced from a necessary condition of detainment to just one option among many would mean that psychiatric care could become a matter of managing social problems as much as individual ones: safety would take precedence over clients' individual rights. This created ethical dilemmas for the clinicians, who felt uneasy about detaining people on these grounds, and so making the decisions collectively within a multidisciplinary team helped to share the burden of responsibility. As one psychologist reflected:

The danger is that it would be called a therapeutic environment but it would actually be a coercive environment... It is an ethical question, isn't it? Weighing up the benefits against the harm.... I think it is a terribly difficult ethical question when you are talking about long-term deprivation of liberty. I certainly wouldn't be wanting to make any of those decisions on my own. (2/043)

13.4.2 Values and Subjectivity

Given this uncertainty, many of the respondents said that they made decisions not only on the basis of "objective" medical evidence, risk assessment instruments, and occupational training, but also by attending to their subjective emotional reactions to clients. However useful their risk assessment inventories were, it was impossible to predict with certainty who would pose a serious risk of harm, and so, in addition to their professional training, the clinicians developed an additional repertoire of intuitive, case-based knowledge. Social workers and CPNs were particularly likely to admit this, as, for example, one CPN said:

There isn't a tick box answer with people... It has to go hand-in-hand with experience and skill and I still think gut feeling. Of course you can't run a service on a load of gut feeling but it certainly helps. (2/042)

These "gut feelings" about patients were generally negative and pertained not only to the assessment of risk to others but also to the difficulties these patients caused to services. Clinicians spoke of experiencing fear, suspicion, and general dislike toward the most aggressive and/or unrepentant individuals and found it particularly hard to deal with these clients' emotional indifference. Sometimes an individual would be able to say all of the "right" things to indicate that they were not a danger to themselves or others, but the clinician would be swayed by an instinctive fear: "...the hairs go up on the back of your neck" (CPN, 2/045). Another CPN spoke of a man whom she felt fitted into the DSPD category:

He actually scared me and if I come out feeling scared that is a good indication because I do not scare easily. (2/042)

This was a client group with whom practitioners were reluctant to work because they were often unpleasant to encounter and difficult to engage. They were described as "heart-sink patients" (psychiatrist, 2/056) who were "unrewarding and risky" to take on (social worker, 2/059), and essentially "not nice people... nobody wants them" (CPN, F027). Part of the reluctance to work with these clients was due to the disruptive effects that they were anticipated to have upon an inpatient unit; they were seen as egocentric, attention-seeking and manipulative, capable of "working the system" (cf. Goffman 1961). Consequently, there were feelings of resentment toward the clients, who were seen as undeserving of care: "I feel angry that he is taking advantage of us ... using our resources" (psychologist, F035). However, some participants expressed more sympathetic and paternal attitudes, particularly toward individuals who had clearly had troubled childhoods. They were seen as having "complex needs" or being "vulnerable" and "damaged," and thus as much in need of protection as the public they supposedly threatened.

13.4.3 Implicit and Explicit Values

When talking about DSPD, the practitioners' comments indicate that they drew upon the six aforementioned models of mental disorder described by Columbo et al. (2003): medical, social, cognitive–behavioral, psychotherapeutic, family, and conspiratorial. Additionally, these seemed to operate in relation to both "implicit" and "explicit" values, of which the respondents showed different levels of awareness. *Explicit* values were those that reflected each professional's occupational position and training whereas *implicit* values tended to reveal the respondents' personal values, moral judgments, and social attitudes and sometimes borrowed from the explicit models of other professions. For example, an explicit value for the psychiatrists was to "act in the patient's best interests," which often meant detaining them in hospital:

This group's professional training had taught them to identify diagnostic symptoms in whatever cases were presented and to recommend an appropriate form of treatment. By contrast, an explicit value for the social workers was to use the "least restrictive option," by allowing clients to remain in the community unless they posed a serious risk to others. They did suggest some forms of treatment, such as anger management classes, but felt that these should be offered on an outpatient basis. Furthermore, because each interviewee's explicit model reflected his or her occupational training, it was not the case that the medical model gained universal support. Social workers, for example, were more explicitly committed to the social, family, or conspiratorial models, drawing on the medical model only implicitly.

Implicit values often leaked out in the context of reflective afterthoughts and off-the-cuff remarks during the interviews. Respondents would give the answer that they thought they "ought" to give but then temper it with a personal opinion. For example, when asked whether she thought that DSPD was treatable, a social worker said, "It depends whether you would like my very personal opinion or what I have been told" (2/053).

Consequently, we found evidence of conflict between the values held, both *within* an individual's account and *between* the individuals in CMHTs. In the extracts below, I demonstrate how each of these types of conflict can result in a "slide to pragmatism": When uncertain or under pressure to make a decision, mental health professionals turn to whichever model is safest, most conventional, and least controversial to use within the context of their own occupational work role, and whichever is most pragmatic, given the legislation and services they have to work with.

13.4.4   Individual Practitioners' Ambivalence

Firstly, there may be a contradiction between the values people cite explicitly and those they privately endorse. Sometimes this clash of values was obvious and recognized by the respondents themselves. This was most apparent in the responses of psychiatrists, who wanted to express dissatisfaction with the system in which they had been trained. For example, one explained that this profession would regard DSPD as a "disorder" but that they personally did not equate this with the idea of "illness": "...it's just describing a kind of person ... [whose behavior is] outside of what is acceptable by society ... there is often little about them that distinguishes them from the rest of us" (1/020; medical + conspiratorial models).

At other times, the contradiction was more subtle, as the implicit models "leaked" out in throwaway remarks made after the respondent's self-conscious statement. For example, a psychiatrist responded to the vignette of

"Stephen" by pointing to indicators of "bipolar affective disorder," "substance abuse," and "drug-induced psychosis" but also referred to Stephen's
"psychosexual development" and "traumatic childhood" and more external factors such as "...social deprivation, violence in the family home ...
housing, education" (F/063; medical + psychotherapeutic + social + family
models). Moreover, while suggesting that he might be treated with antipsy-
chotic drugs, he acknowledged that it was difficult to determine Stephen's
treatability because "...these are concepts which are very ill defined." This
demonstrates an explicit adherence to the medical model, but an implicit
leaning toward the social, family, and conspiratorial models. This interviewee knew that he ought to cite conventional psychiatric wisdom but
felt uneasy about incorporating it into his own system of values. Similarly,
a psychologist admitted that she felt it was, "...wrong to take somebody in
just for detention. Wrong morally and wrong legally" (F/038). Psychiatrists
sometimes resolved the incongruity between their explicit and implicit values by rationalizing their decisions. For example, those who privately felt
that personality disordered individuals "...should not be locked up" (psychiatrist, 2/044), but whose professional training encouraged them to offer
inpatient treatment, justified their decision to themselves by reasoning that
it was "...in [a client's] best interests" to be detained, to prevent the client
from offending or from exacerbating a drug addiction.

A similar pattern was observed among the CPNs, who were aware of
many factors affecting a client's supposed dangerousness. This was reflected
in the comments of one CPN who spoke of "...medication management ...
to reduce the level of agitation or anger" but also said, in response to the
vignette, that he would want to "...look at his cognitive functioning" and
that "...social history is all-important" (1/016; medical + cognitive–behavioral + social models). The CPNs seemed to express the least dissatisfaction
with any particular model, perhaps because they had been trained to use a
more holistic approach, and were in any case ultimately answerable to the
hierarchical authority of psychiatrists.

Finally, several social workers used the medical model implicitly in contrast to their avowed commitment to the social model. For example, one
spoke in general terms about "...relationship problems and work issues"
and claimed that "...most self-harm is a reaction to life events rather than
mental health problems," but when discussing the vignette, suggested that
an appropriate treatment plan would involve "...a detox ... observe him
for behavior changes, mood swings etc. ... [and then] introduce one of the
new smart drugs such as Risperidone, Olanzepine or whatever" (2/051).
Some social workers, like the psychiatrists, tried to rationalize their willingness to detain clients by suggesting that they might benefit from "humane

containment" although in this case the contradiction was the reverse of that observed in the psychiatrists: social workers were caught between an explicit value of individual freedom and an implicit feeling that these clients should not be released. Nevertheless, as with the psychiatrists, this apparent contradiction might simply reflect a pragmatic realization of what *would* be done to treat such patients, in spite of any personal reservations about what *ought* (not) to be done.

13.4.5 Conflicting Values within Multidisciplinary Teams

We also found evidence of competing values and underlying pragmatic interests in the models held by the representatives of different professional groups within the multidisciplinary teams, even if each of these individuals' explicit and implicit values were congruent. This reflected the ethical debate about treatability versus risk, outlined above: Practitioners' views on the relative importance of these factors were shaped by a combination of the values they had been taught in their professional training and the practical implications of the decision for their own workloads. A typical example came from this psychiatrist:

It will be split right down the middle. I might be the big softy who will say, "let's give him a chance, let's see if there are areas we can help with, let's see if we can try and engage him or prepare him to engage with the psychotherapy service." Not to detain him because I don't think I will get past that barrier.... The other side will say that it is pointless, "we have had so many patients like this and what did they do? They cause mayhem and we had to get the police to remove them" this will often be a very senior nursing point of view.... The community nurses will also be asking, "what can we do? We don't have the expertise to deal with these people...." (2/056)

Similarly, a social worker observed that the members of the teams followed different approaches according to their explicit values:

ASWs [Approved Social Workers] definitely come at things from a different viewpoint. I am particularly concerned about nurses doing it [risk assessment] because their training is such that they are used to doing as they told by the doctors. I don't mean that in a derogatory sense but also they work from a systems approach whereas we work from a needs approach. So I think that we are better placed to look at the holistic needs of the whole family and the surrounding community. (2/062)

In other cases, there appeared to be a conflict between the implicit values held by the individuals within a professional group, as, for example, psychiatrists held different views. Although each group had been socialized into the same set of explicit, official values, they varied in the more subtle, personal views that they held and the way that they regarded their clients, and so case meetings about particular clients could result in different risk assessments. For example, one psychologist observed how doctors interpreted the "safety takes precedence" maxim differently:

My perception is that psychiatrists differ and that the psychologists hold the decision-making process. One of the psychiatrists is not so much concerned as to whether or not they are going to be treatable as, "is being detained going to reduce the symptoms or help them to manage better or do they pose such a risk to themselves?" The other is much more around the definition that we have got there and actually doing something to reduce the symptoms and the difficulties. For the one, risk is much higher up the list of issues. For the other, treatability is much more of an issue. (1/033)

Discussions about a client's potential treatability often evoked these conflicts of values because each profession had different ideas about what being "treatable" meant and what "treatment" might involve. Few of the respondents included mere detainment within this category, but in pointing to clinical interventions, different examples were cited, such as medication, drug and alcohol rehabilitation, and anger management classes. As one social worker explained:

This chap on the unit for example, I would say he is treatable.... Then you have got some doctors who will say that the tribunal [a review board that considers patients' appeals against detention and/or treatment decisions] has decided he is untreatable and there is nothing that we can do for this bloke. Even within psychiatry you have got people who will say he is treatable and others who will say he is not. From a social worker's point of view we are not usually in a position to say whether somebody is treatable or not. We would not necessarily have much say. Psychologists on the whole will say that people are treatable rather than not. Nurses in the community team will say he is untreatable because they are used in dealing with people on a short-term basis. "Untreatable" in this context will mean "untreatable in this setting." Most people will be looking at it within the remit of their resource and whether they are able to find resource that will meet that need. (F/037)

13.4.6   Reluctant Empowerment

The disputes within the CMHTs reflected each occupational group's interests in protecting their own professional reputation and in the possible consequences of making a "wrong" decision. These were more serious for some than for others, depending on their positions within the hierarchy of responsibility: even though the discussions were ostensibly democratic, there was an implicit recognition that the psychiatrists held the ultimate responsibility for the decisions that were made and so had most at stake. Nevertheless, each professional group was concerned with its own accountability and expressed values that were self-protective as well as altruistic.

In particular, we noted that many respondents wanted to "err on the side of caution" but that this meant different things to different occupational groups.

Psychiatrists were the most inclined to detain clients, interpreting the risk of harming oneself or others as being of greater significance than protecting the individual's right to freedom. On the one hand, this reflected their avowed commitment to "acting in the patient's best interests" (an explicit value), for they believed that the longer term therapeutic benefits of intervention would outweigh any immediate reservations clients had about being treated. On the other hand, the psychiatrists were more aware that making such decisions represented the "safe" option, serving strategically to protect themselves from criticism. If they had offered a client treatment, and even imposed it against his or her will, then they had "covered themselves" and could not so easily be blamed for any future "dangerousness": in the words of one psychiatrist, "...you have tried, you have done your natural best for that person" (F/034). Thus detaining high-risk clients served as an insurance policy of sorts, protecting the doctor as much as the client. For pragmatic reasons, they dismissed their colleagues' pleas (and indeed their own disquietude) that such individuals were "not treatable in our service" and found themselves complicit in the remedicalization of antisocial conduct. One CPN exemplified this view:

...at least then if that person is discharged, or you do the treatment and you don't get anywhere with them, then when they do offend—because they are a time bomb waiting to explode—you can get out your paper and say, "we tried." (2/050)

However, the psychiatrists often felt uneasy about this. For example, when discussing the case vignette, one psychiatrist said that she might have personal reservations about detaining people and regret the pressure this would put upon others in the CMHT. Nevertheless, she recognized that in practice, these would be overridden by concerns about risk—a slide to pragmatism:

I think that they [CPN and probation officer] would be wanting him to go on Section 3 [a legally enforceable order for compulsory treatment for up to six months, under Section 3 of the UK Mental Health Act 1983], but I would be thinking that on the ward they would not be very happy. They would be saying, "look, he hasn't got a psychiatric problem. He doesn't have to take an acute bed." So I'm sure that the colleagues will be divided as well. Inpatient setting will be saying, "we don't want him" and the community will be too worried to take him back. It is pulling in both directions.... In practice I think he would go on Section 3. He will go on Section 3 whether at that stage whether people think that he is completely treatable or not. It is that risk.... I think practically we would not discharge him. We would err on the

side of the risk … With his condition if he takes drugs it is likely that he will deteriorate further but otherwise I think he may just continue the way he is. Theoretically
you could justify it in this way. (2/044)

Social workers, meanwhile, were wary of sectioning clients because it
represented a possible infringement of their civil liberties. Their explicit
occupational value was to "use the least restrictive option"—that is, to let
the client remain in the community. However, alongside these altruistic
endeavors, they too cited concerns about being accused of professional
misconduct (they could be held legally responsible if a client was either
detained without evidence of their mental illness or released and then committed a violent offense) and held some grave personal reservations about
the power they wielded. For example, this social worker said:

I want to be sure that I'm making an application on solid legal grounds and following a thorough and appropriate assessment and good consultation with everybody
involved, and I will record that…. Being cynical, you have the ability as an ASW or
even as a recommended doctor to take some pieces of information and use them any
way you want to. You have that power. You have that professional independence.
There is information in this paper that I could use to support an application [to sec-
tion] if I had two medical recommendations. There is also information in here that I
could use to challenge an application so it is very much an "on the day" thing…. On
one level I am thinking, "discharge this guy. He is not ill," but this was not a detention issue. The other side of it was that he was a risk … what would I say if he set fire
to some papers in the B&B? I would be held accountable for that decision. (2/059)

By contrast, CPNs and OTs had the least to lose in this respect, because
their opinions would be subsumed beneath the ultimate decision-making
authority of the doctors: As one social worker put it, they were "used to
doing as they are told" (2/062). One CPN indicated that she was relieved
not to have to bear the responsibility for any "wrong" decisions and gladly
shared the burden with her team:

I can assess the risk but I wouldn't want the responsibility of saying, "yes, take them
away," unless I was part of a team. It is one of those things, don't you find, you want
it to be done but you don't want to do it yourself. I don't want to pull the string.
(2/042)

Thus it was recognized by all that, although they were working as a multidisciplinary team, the psychiatrists, as medical doctors, held the most power
in making treatment decisions. While some of the respondents were content with this (as the above comment shows), others expressed feelings of
resentment. For example, some social workers observed that the doctors
made only the most fleeting appearance at team meetings and would have

spent much less time with the clients than they had themselves, yet still had the power to determine the outcome. One social worker reflected bitterly,

Often in a case like this you will find that what happens is that the consultant saw the bloke in the ward round, made a Section 3 recommendation and has left the country. You have really got to fight in some cases to track the consultant down to get them to the meeting.... He makes his decision and signs a medical recommendation form and leaves it on the ward. Trying get him back or to even talk to him can be like a major difficulty.... You have only got to work with them for a while and you see that consultant psychiatrists have enormous power, even the ones that are quite approachable and continually refer to themselves as "team members" or "community focused." They are still extremely powerful people. You need only watch the way that patients defer to them and the way that CPNs will rush around at their bidding. If a consultant is to ask for a form, before he has finished asking three people will have rushed up to get it.... A consultant will turn up with his ivory, golden-nibbed pen and everything is brought to him. It is a structural thing. (2/059)

Another social worker expressed a similar view but was more diplomatic:

...logistics do sometimes mean that all the parties do not make it to be present at the ward round ... [but] I think that the views of nurses are usually given quite a lot of importance because often RMOs [Resident Medical Officers] are not seeing very much of somebody. They are flying in and out of the ward ... the hierarchicalism within the medical world puts much more weight on the word of the doctor than on a nurse. (2/052)

However, this distribution of power was also experienced as problematic by the doctors themselves insofar as they felt out of their depth in making treatment decisions about what they perceived to be a nebulous condition. As one psychiatrist put it, they were "...pinned like butterflies" (F/063) in a Catch-22 situation, because whichever decision they made could turn out retrospectively to have been "wrong." They were working with concepts that they felt were difficult to define, such as "therapeutic benefit" and "dangerousness" and were often unsure about who, what, and how to treat. A psychologist confessed that, "...we are only right half the time ... it is soft data in a soft science" (F/035), and a psychiatrist agreed that, "... we may miss important facts and facets of an individual" (F/063). One CPN observed that patients were "...caught up in a service which doesn't know what it is supposed to be doing" (2/046), and another agreed that "...we go on a wing and a prayer" (2/058).

13.4.7 Constraints and Pressures

Another factor influencing the decisions practitioners made was the limited resources available to them. They were aware that, even if they could identify features of DSPD that might be amenable to treatment (such as drug and alcohol addiction or difficulties with anger management), they had only limited amounts of funding, time, and facilities to offer clients. This reflects wider, ongoing debates about the rationing of health care resources within the UK's National Health Service and the pressure to deliver cost-efficient services (Busfield 2001). Thus we could detect an underlying conflict between the Hippocratic principle to which the staff adhered (to do good and to treat where possible) and the lived experience they had of working in a service in which demand for resources outstripped supply. One of the psychiatrists remarked that there was often a discrepancy between what they would like to provide in the "ideal" therapeutic service and the reality of what they could actually provide within the constraints of a general psychiatric ward (F/039). Although this psychiatrist had worked in a specialist personality disorder unit, there are not many of these in the UK, and he recognized that he was unusually lucky to have such resources:

In practice the general psychiatrist just might not make a recommendation because they don't think they can on their unit.... They are treatable in an ideal service ... with a stable therapeutic environment which includes group anger management and substance abuse therapy, etc., etc., but I think that the general psychiatrist will very often be justified in saying that they are not treatable in their service. (F/039)

Insofar as personality disordered clients were identified as being unrewarding or difficult to work with (unable to recognize that they had a "problem," disruptive of other patients, and unwilling to comply with treatment regimes), the staff were often reluctant to accept such people into their care. These clients were perceived to take up disproportionate amounts of staff time, bed space and places within therapy groups while seeming never to get "better" or to engage with the therapeutic interventions: They were a "waste" of time, energy, and money. To the staff, these resources were precious, and there were other clients who were deemed to be more "deserving" of care. As one psychiatrist said:

If they are unmanageable but if there is a genuine psychiatric illness then the ward would not say anything, but if it is due to a personality problem, disrupting the activities of the ward then they would think that they should not be wasting an acute bed because we have a dearth of beds. (2/044)

13.5   Conclusion

Mental health professionals express a complex set of attitudes to "risky" personality disordered individuals and to the concept of DSPD, combining different theoretical models to explain its origins and features. The use of these models reflects both explicit values (based on occupational training) and implicit values (based on personal, subjective beliefs and experiences of clients). Consequently, this study revealed conflicting values both within and between individual members of multidisciplinary teams. This supports the view that risk assessment, diagnosis, and management planning are not simply objective and rational procedures, but rather social processes of inter-action and negotiation involving struggles for power (Green et al. 2002).

These conflicts of values tend to be resolved by a "slide to pragmatism," whereby each practitioner decides to "err on the side of caution" in deci-sions about a client's treatability. This means making whichever choice will be least risky for their own professional reputation, and most pragmatic, given the resources available. The collective decisions of a CMHT therefore depend not only on the risk assessments that they make about a client's potential "dangerousness," but also on the risks that each occupational group perceives for itself, in terms of being held accountable for "wrong" decisions. As Abbott (1988, 33) argues, "Each profession is bound to a set of tasks by ties of jurisdiction, the strengths and weaknesses of these ties being established in the process of actual professional work." With con-tested conditions like DSPD, clinicians are themselves aware of the pro-visional, incomplete, and value-laden process of clinical decision making and so reflect on the threats this poses to their professional integrity. The approach of VBM is extremely useful in helping to understand the myriad ways in which explicit and implicit values interact, shaping every stage of the clinical encounter with "risky" personality disordered individuals.

However, there are some limitations in terms of whether and how the approach might be applied in practice. Firstly, within a multidisciplinary team, staff representing different occupations will have different levels of power and status, and so some models (and their incumbent values) will be listened to more than others. Secondly, even in the most democratic and egalitarian of teams, there will be structural constraints upon the kinds of treatments available to patients. Medicalized drug treatments are much cheaper than courses of psychotherapy, and so "the slide to pragmatism" in terms of a recourse to the medical model may be inevitable. Thirdly, where VBM suggests involving service users in the decisions made about their treatment, this may be practically and ethically challenging with "risky" personality disordered individuals. On a practical level, they may simply be unwilling to attend CMHT meetings because they do not see themselves as ill or in need of help. Additionally, given that manipulation and deceit are common features of antisocial personality disorders, it may be difficult to understand the values and needs of people classified as such. Meanwhile, on an ethical level, it may be questionable whether this client group *should* be involved in these decisions, insofar as they are deemed a danger to other people: If a client expresses an interest in being released from hospital even though the staff feel that the individual is dangerous, should his or her view be listened to? Should people whose expressed values endorse violence be considered equal partners in the decision-making process? Similar concerns might be raised about involving family members and carers in the decision-making process if there is evidence of childhood abuse within the client's history. This reflects the inevitable power relations inherent in any form of health care provision, especially psychiatry: To paraphrase Orwell (1945/2008), all values may be equal, but some are more equal than others. Despite such challenges, however, the VBM approach encourages a more balanced, holistic understanding of DSPD and its management.

Acknowledgments

An earlier version of this chapter appeared as an article in *Health Sociology Review* (Vol. 20, No. 2, pp. 157–171, June 2011). It was coauthored by my colleagues on the research team: Debbie Jones, Rachel Ballinger, Gillian Bendelow, and Bill Fulford. Some of the material presented here is reprinted with kind permission from *HSR*.

The study was made possible with funding from the Wellcome Trust. The grant was originally awarded to Dr. David Morgan, who tragically died before the study was completed. The vignette was developed by Dr. John Vile. I also gratefully acknowledge the help given by the interviewees in participating in the study and sharing their views with us.

References

Abbott, A. 1988. *The System of Professions: An Essay on the Division of Expert Labour.* Chicago: University of Chicago Press.

Beck, U. 1992. *Risk Society.* London: Sage.

Busfield, J. 1996. *Men, Women and Madness: Understanding Gender and Mental Disorder.* London: Macmillan.

Busfield, J. (ed.). 2001. *Rethinking the Sociology of Mental Health.* Oxford: Blackwell.

Cohen, S. 1972. *Folk Devils and Moral Panics: The Creation of the Mods and Rockers.* London: MacGibbon & Kee.

Columbo, A., G. Bendelow, B. Fulford, and S. Williams. 2003. Evaluating the Influence of Implicit Models of Mental Disorder on Processes of Shared Decision Making within Community-Based Multi-Disciplinary Teams. *Social Science & Medicine* 56:1557–1570.

Conrad, P. 2007. *The Medicalization of Society: On the Transformation of Human Conditions into Treatable Disorders*. Baltimore: Johns Hopkins University Press.

Corbett, K., and T. Westwood. 2005. Dangerous and Severe Personality Disorder: A Psychiatric Manifestation of Risk Society. *Critical Public Health* 15:121–133.

Department of Health. 1983. *Mental Health Act*. London: HMSO, The Stationery Office.

Department of Health. 2000. Reforming the Mental Health Act 1983: Proposals for Consultation. Cm 5016. White Paper. London: HMSO, The Stationery Office.

Department of Health. 2002. Draft Mental Health Bill (2002). London: HMSO, The Stationery Office.

Department of Health. 2004. Draft Mental Health Bill (2004). London: HMSO, The Stationery Office Fallon Report. 1999. *Report of the Committee of Inquiry into the Personality Disorder Unit, Ashworth Special Hospital*. London: The Stationery Office. Available: http://www.archive.official-documents.co.uk/document/cm41/4194/ash4194.htm.

Foucault, M. 1965. *Madness and Civilization*. New York: Random House.

Foucault, M. 1976/1980. *The History of Sexuality*, vol. 1. New York: Vintage.

Fulford, K. W. M., D. L. Dickenson, and T. H. Murray. 2002. *Healthcare Ethics and Human Values*. Oxford: Blackwell.

Goffman, E. 1961. *Asylums*. New York: Anchor Books, Doubleday.

Green, E. E., D. Thompson, and F. Griffiths. 2002. Narratives of Risk: Women at Midlife, Medical "Experts" and Health Technologies. *Health Risk & Society* 4:273–286.

Haddock, A. W., P. R. Snowden, M. Dolan, J. Parker, and H. Rees. 2001. Managing Dangerous People with Severe Personality Disorder: A Survey of Forensic Psychiatrists' Opinions. *Psychiatric Bulletin* 25:293–296.

Home Office and the Department of Health. 1999. *Managing Dangerous People with Severe Personality Disorder: Proposals for Development*. London: The Stationery Office.

House of Lords. 2006. *The Mental Health Bill [HL]*. Available: http://www.publications.parliament.uk/pa/ld200607/ldbills/001/07001.i-iv.html.

Ingleby, D. (ed.). 2004. *Critical Psychiatry*. 2nd ed. London: Free Association Books.

Kendell, R. E. 2002. The Distinction between Personality Disorder and Mental Illness: Review Essay. *British Journal of Psychiatry* 180:110–115.

Laing, R. D. 1965. *The Divided Self*. Harmondsworth: Penguin Books.

Lupton, D. 1999. *Risk*. London: Routledge.

Maden, A. 2007. Dangerous and Severe Personality Disorder: Antecedents and Origins. *British Journal of Psychiatry* 198 (suppl.49):s8–s11.

Maden, A., and P. Tyrer. 2003. Dangerous and Severe Personality Disorders: A New Personality Concept from the United Kingdom. *Journal of Personality Disorders* 17:489–496.

Manning, N. 2006. DSM–IV and Dangerous and Severe Personality Disorder—An Essay. *Social Science & Medicine* 63:1960–1971.

Mental Health Act Commission. 2007. Policy briefing for commissioners. Issue 17, July 2007. At: http://www.mhac.org.uk/?q=node/12 (accessed November 2010).

Moran, P. 2001. Dangerous Severe Personality Disorder—Bad Tidings from the UK. *International Journal of Social Psychiatry* 48:6–10.

Morgan, D. 2004. Mad or Bad? A Critique of Proposals for Managing Dangerously Disordered People. *Journal of Community & Applied Social Psychology* 14:104–114.

Mullen, P. E. 2007. Dangerous and Severe Personality Disorder and in Need of Treatment. *British Journal of Psychiatry* 190 (suppl. 49):s3–s7.

Orwell, G. 1945/2008. *Animal Farm: A Fairy Story*. London: Penguin Books.

Rogers, A., and D. Pilgrim. 2010. *A Sociology of Mental Health and Illness*. 4th ed. Milton Keynes: Open University Press.

Rose, N. 1989. *Governing the Soul: The Shaping of the Private Self*. London: Routledge.

Roth, M., and J. Kroll. 1986. *The Reality of Mental Illness*. Cambridge: Cambridge University Press.

Scheff, T. 1966. *Being Mentally Ill: A Sociological Theory*. Chicago: Aldine.

Scott, S., D. Jones, R. Balllinger, G. Bendelow, and B. Fulford. 2011. Managing Personality Disorders: The Slide to Pragmatism. *Health Sociology Review* 20:157–171.

Scull, A. T. 1979. *Museums of Madness*. Hampshire: Palgrave Macmillan.

Szasz, T. 1961/1972. *The Myth of Mental Illness*. St Albans, UK: Paladin.

Tyrer, P. 2007. An Agitation of Contrary Opinions. *British Journal of Psychiatry* 190 (suppl. 49):s1–s2.

Woodbridge, K., and K. W. M. Fulford. 2004. *Whose Values? A Workbook for Values-Based Practice in Mental Health Care*. London: Sainsbury Centre for Mental Health.

14 Conclusion: The Many Faces of Psychopathy

Thomas Schramme

The research on psychopathy is a good example of the chances, as well as the challenges, of interdisciplinary research. It is obvious that we will not make progress in philosophy when using a phenomenon like psychopathy in order to bear evidence for theoretical claims—for instance, regarding moral motivation or responsibility—unless we have a clear grasp of its empirical basis. This need of philosophical accounts to be empirically valid, however, does not yet lead to a real interdisciplinary approach since it does not require an interchange between different disciplines. It would still allow for philosophical theorists to simply draw on the empirical findings they find most suitable for their purposes. However, instead of merely taking these putatively nonphilosophical findings for granted, we need to consider that the notion of psychopathy and its various conceptualizations in different disciplines, subfields, or theories itself call for a genuinely philosophical perspective. This is because the scientific explanation of psychopathy is based on several concepts that require analysis. Examples of such terms have been discussed widely within this book, for instance "character," "personality," "emotion," "cognition," "rationality," "empathy," "moral knowledge," and "moral judgment." Again, these concepts have to be clarified with an eye to the empirical data—hence a need for interdisciplinarity.

The challenge encountered throughout this book and elsewhere, though, is that real interdisciplinarity is hard to come by; it is occasionally frustrating and possibly even detrimental to the purposes at hand. Although the contributions within this book have mostly pursued perspectives of the humanities, there is nevertheless no real consensus among the authors regarding the explanation of psychopathy. More generally speaking, the debate on psychopathy has not generated a conceptual congruence in referring to the phenomenon. There is hence a reasonable worry that we will always go on talking past each other and making claims that are based on restricted and sketchy knowledge. Still, one might not be so pessimistic.

After all, in comparison to other psychiatric entities, psychopathy has been researched for a relatively short period of time, so it might be a little early to ask for a universal explanation. Moreover, the philosophical interest in psychopathy has only recently gained momentum, so these viewpoints are hard to come by and scattered. Hopefully, this volume will succeed in one of its aims, namely, to enhance the ongoing interdisciplinary debate and to ignite further interest, also, in areas of study that have been less treated in the past.

It seems clear from the discussion about psychopathy we have had so far that there will probably never be a common overarching theme or conceptual unity of the different disciplines. This might even be a good thing since different research agendas and focuses allow and call for various disciplinary "languages." Yet, one potential common denominator that seems to me worth exploring in the future is the notion of moral agency (see, e.g., Kennett 2001). Psychopaths seem to be generally lacking in, or have impaired, moral agency, though this deficit might be due to different pathways—for instance, a lack or impairment of fellow feeling, of being responsive to normative reasons, of control, of motivation, or of other capacities. Although, again, "moral agency" is a concept mainly drawn from philosophy, it is nevertheless not uncommon in other disciplines as well. It applies to "an individual who can, to a significant extent, act effectively and competently in moral matters" (Watson 2013a, 3322). It seems to me that the notion of moral agency has the advantage of being able to account for different "levels" of deficits assumed in psychopathy (Rottschaefer 1998, 19f.), such as regarding moral understanding, judgment or knowledge, moral appreciation or care, moral motivation, moral intention, practical deliberation, moral control, and also moral development. In addition, it can be linked to more general, that is, not specifically moral, capacities, such as decision making or the formation of value judgments (cf. Prinz 2007, 270ff.). Finally, it allows the inclusion of self-regarding notions such as conscience, moral identity, self-evaluation, and self-concern, or, more generally, the moral self (Glover 1999, 26ff.; Noam and Wren 1993; Lapsley 2008; Glenn et al. 2010; Hitlin 2008; Watson 2013b).

Moral agency has a flip side, though not in the sense of being in opposition: The idea of moral patiency (Reader 2007). Regularly, human beings are not acting but "receiving" actions; they are moral patients as well as moral agents. Moral patiency involves an acknowledgment of our vulnerability, of our dependency on other people, and not least provides a normative reason to appreciate the necessity of morality as an instrument of coordinating behavior and providing mutual support. Now, if we see psychopathy as an impairment of moral agency, we also need to interpret it as an impairment of moral patiency. This seems to be in line with some of the findings in the relevant literature and also in this book. After all, psychopaths seem to be less aware, or even unaware, of their passive and vulnerable condition; they seem to be self-centered and occasionally feel invincible. They also do not seem to acknowledge the benefits of morality for pursuing even their very own interests.

Another aspect that has become clear throughout this book is that we need a positive as well as a negative approach in studying psychopathy, in the sense that we need to theorize about the positively required capacities for moral agency by studying the deficits of those who have impaired moral agency, that is, psychopaths, and, at the same time, need to also be aware of the fact that we will only get a good grasp of the deficits of psychopaths if we already assume certain normal capacities of human beings. In other words, we need to progress by combining psychological and psychiatric insights—where these disciplines should, of course, be informed by conceptual analyses of philosophy as well as relevant findings of other disciplines.

Finally, an outcome of this book is that the way we conceptualize the human psyche might be overhauled when discussing issues in moral agency (Wren 1991, x; Kennett and Fine 2009). We are prone to distinguishing between cognition or rationality, affect or emotion, and volition or conation. Although these divisions serve some analytic purposes, they also tend to emphasize just one aspect of a complex phenomenon. But emotions are not nonreflective, reasoning is not unemotional, motivation is not either based on reason or desire, and so on. For psychopathy, this means that it is not simply a rational, an emotional, or a volitional deficit, but that it can be all these in various ways.

Academic publications often end with the statement that more research is needed. This can become a rather trite and inauthentic declaration, which is not really backed by any actual beliefs of the authors. I hope it has become clear in this book, though, that there is indeed a genuine need for more concerted research on the topic of psychopathy and moral incapacity.

References

Glenn, A. L., S. Koleva, R. Iyer, J. Graham, and P. H. Ditto. 2010. Moral Identity in Psychopathy. *Judgment and Decision Making* 5:497–505.

Glover, J. 1999. *Humanity*. New Haven, Conn.: Yale University Press.

Hitlin, S. 2008. *Moral Selves, Evil Selves: The Social Psychology of Conscience*. 1st ed. New York: Palgrave Macmillan.

Kennett, J. 2001. *Agency and Responsibility: A Common-Sense Moral Psychology.* Oxford: Clarendon Press.

Kennett, J., and C. Fine. 2009. Will the Real Moral Judgment Please Stand Up? *Ethical Theory and Moral Practice* 12:77–96.

Lapsley, D. K. 2008. Moral Self-Identity as the Aim of Education. In *Handbook of Moral and Character Education,* ed. L. P. Nucci and D. Narvaez, 30–52. New York: Routledge.

Noam, G. G., and T. E. Wren. 1993. *The Moral Self.* Cambridge, Mass.: MIT Press.

Prinz, J. J. 2007. *The Emotional Construction of Morals.* Oxford: Oxford University Press.

Reader, S. 2007. The Other Side of Agency. *Philosophy (London, England)* 82:579–604.

Rottschaefer, W. A. 1998. *The Biology and Psychology of Moral Agency.* Cambridge: Cambridge University Press.

Watson, G. 2013a. Moral Agency. *The International Encyclopedia of Ethics,* ed. H. LaFollette, 3322–3333. London: Blackwell.

Watson, G. 2013b. Psychopathy and Prudential Deficits. *Proceedings of the Aristotelian Society.* 134th Session. Issue No. 3, Volume cxiii, 2012–2013.

Wren, T. E. 1991. *Caring about Morality: Philosophical Perspectives in Moral Psychology.* Cambridge, Mass.: MIT Press.

Contributors

Gwen Adshead, Southern Health NHS Foundation Trust, Ravenswood House, Fareham, United Kingdom

Piers Benn, Visiting Lecturer in Ethics, Department of Pastoral and Social Studies, Heythrop College, University of London, United Kingdom

John Deigh, School of Law and Department of Philosophy, University of Texas at Austin, USA

Alan R. Felthous, Department of Neurology & Psychiatry, Saint Louis University School of Medicine, St. Louis, Missouri, USA

Kerrin A. Jacobs, Institute of Cognitive Science, Osnabrück University, Osnabrück, Germany

Heidi L. Maibom, Department of Philosophy, Carleton University, Ottawa, Canada

Eric Matthews, The School of Divinity, History and Philosophy, University of Aberdeen, Aberdeen, United Kingdom

Henning Sass, Clinic for Psychiatry, Psychotherapy, and Psychosomatics, University Hospital Aachen, Aachen, Germany

Thomas Schramme, Department of Philosophy, Hamburg University, Germany

Susie Scott, Department of Sociology, School of Law, Politics and Sociology, University of Sussex, Brighton, United Kingdom

David W. Shoemaker, Department of Philosophy and the Murphy Institute, Tulane University, New Orleans, Louisiana, USA

Walter Sinnott-Armstrong, Department of Philosophy and Kenan Institute for Ethics, Duke University, Durham, North Carolina, USA

Matthew Talbert, Department of Philosophy, West Virginia University, Morgantown, West Virginia, USA

Name Index

Subject Index

accountability, 18, 26, 259, 264, 265, 267, 274, 275, 283, 285, 287–289, 291, 298, 312, 314, 317
affectivity, affective, 100, 116, 191
agency, 16, 80, 124, 155, 213, 224, 262, 279, 287, 322, 323. *See also* moral agency
agential capacities, 267, 275
rational agency, 190, 279
agent, 84, 87, 92, 141, 150, 157, 171, 190, 193, 195, 221, 225, 259, 262, 264, 276, 277, 280, 281, 287, 288, 295, 297. *See also* moral agent
aggression, aggressiveness, 7, 20, 46, 50, 71, 72, 76, 92, 98, 99, 105–107, 142, 147, 161, 235, 277
alexithymia, 21, 115, 122, 124, 129
altruism, 22, 92, 101–104, 106–108, 168, 279, 312, 314
amoralism, amorality, 3, 4, 11–13, 15, 17, 20, 24, 46, 53, 73, 75, 76, 78, 87, 91, 137–139, 144, 147, 148, 155, 162, 227
amoralist, 12, 13, 129, 144, 146, 170, 227, 228–230, 234, 241, 242
amygdala, 198, 277
anethopaths, 50, 52. *See also* Karpman, B.
anger, 94, 116, 161, 174, 180, 181, 210, 212–214, 289, 290, 299, 309, 310, 312, 316
apology, apologies, 217, 287–293

attributionism, 275, 276, 294
autonomy, autonomous agents, 81, 85, 141, 151, 157

badness, 78, 86, 87, 107, 286, 301, 306. *See also* madness
blame. *See* moral blame
blameworthiness, 182, 276, 280, 283, 293, 294, 297
brain, 8, 9, 27, 74, 76, 121, 130, 182, 183, 189, 190, 198, 225, 242

categorical, 6, 19, 58–61, 92. *See also* dimensional; Widiger, T. A.
character, 9, 10, 19, 42, 47, 49, 54, 56, 58, 63, 140, 170, 178, 230, 233, 263, 300, 303, 321
compassion, 22, 94, 97, 100, 102, 104, 169, 220
compatibilism, 181, 184
comportment, 21, 137, 138–145, 148, 149, 154, 156–159
conscience, 50, 171, 175–177, 209, 211, 223, 224, 232, 241, 322
contempt, 25, 117, 275–277, 280–282, 284, 291, 297
conventional rules, conventions, 14, 24, 77, 128, 193–195, 247–249, 251–259, 261, 265, 267–271, 278, 295, 309, 310. *See also* moral-conventional distinction
culpability, 3, 17, 262, 263

successful psychopaths, 7, 12, 279
sympathy, 14, 15, 19, 20, 22, 75, 91–
104, 106–110, 171, 172, 174, 179,
182, 183, 218, 220, 224, 237, 239,
240

Theory of mind, 15, 74, 75, 120,
121, 129, 239. *See also* empathy;
simulation
therapy, therapeutic, 63, 124, 147, 160,
161, 227, 305–307, 313, 315, 316
trauma, 125
treatability, 26, 27, 303–307, 310–313,
316, 317

untreatable, 303, 312

violence, 2, 3, 7, 72, 74, 76, 78, 84, 91,
93, 99, 101, 105–107, 109, 115–117,
120, 121, 126, 128, 129, 142, 161,
168, 170, 172–174, 183, 202, 278,
302–304, 306, 310, 314, 318
violence inhibition, 92, 99, 101,
105–107
virtue, 10, 19, 20, 24, 75, 87, 220, 233,
234

wanton, 148, 149, 151, 152, 296. *See
also* Frankfurt, H.
welfare, 92–94, 96, 98, 104, 248, 249,
251, 254, 258, 269, 276, 277, 281,
282, 284
wrongdoing, 25, 177, 178, 192, 229,
269, 275, 277, 278, 284–287, 290–
292, 294, 297, 299